League
of the
Iroquois

by

LEWIS HENRY MORGAN

Introduction by William N. Fenton

THE CITADEL PRESS
SECAUCUS, NEW JERSEY

William N. Fenton of Slingerlands, New York, is a long-time student of the Iroquois Indians and is Assistant Commissioner for the New York State Museum and Science Service, Albany. After attending Dartmouth College (A.B.), he studied anthropology at Yale (Ph.D.), and, save for brief forays into teaching, has spent his entire career in the public service: U.S. Indian Service, Bureau of American Ethnology at Smithsonian Institution, and the National Research Council. His monographs and books include: *The Iroquois Eagle Dance* (1954), *American Indian and White Relations to 1830* (1957); and he organized and edited: *Symposium on Local Diversity in Iroquois Culture* (1951) and *Symposium on Cherokee and Iroquois Culture* (1961).

Second Citadel printing, 1975
Copyright © 1962 by Corinth Books, Inc.
Citadel Press, Inc., Publishers
A subsidiary of Lyle Stuart, Inc.
120 Enterprise Avenue, Secaucus, New Jersey 07094
ISBN 0-8065-0293-2
Manufactured in the United States of America
Noble Offset Printers, Inc.
New York, N.Y. 10003

INTRODUCTION

LEWIS HENRY MORGAN

(1818-1881)

PIONEER ETHNOLOGIST

It is one hundred and ten years since Lewis Henry Morgan published his *League of the Ho-de-no-sau-nee, or Iroquois* (Rochester, 1851), and his is still the best general book on this classic people. Morgan gave the world, in the oft-quoted words of Major J. Wesley Powell, who founded the Bureau of American Ethnology, "its first scientific account of an Indian tribe." Since then so much has been written about the Iroquois that their combined ethnological and historical literature rivals that of any primitive people, being exceeded only in the bibliography of North America by the Eskimo and Navaho. And most Iroquoianists today would agree with the endorsement of Alexander Goldenweiser forty years ago, that "the best general treatise on the Iroquois" deserves another reprinting for the reading public.

This makes the fifth time in the century since its first appearance that the work is being reprinted— this time, the first edition. Each time it has been received by an enthusiastic public. Such enthusiasm is well-deserved, for Morgan wrote well and he was

v

an accurate and profound observer. The first edition appeared in two styles, one on tinted paper, with 22 colored plates and illustrations that had been prepared for his reports to the New York Board of Regents, full gilt edge, and bound in blue tooled leather boards, decorated with the *Gus-to-weh* or chief's feather head dress in gold; this deluxe edition was small, it was priced at thirty-five dollars, including a few presentation copies. A trade edition was for general sale at fifteen dollars, with map, plates, and cuts in black and white, bound in black cloth—a few in leather—with the same decoration. What Wilberforce Eames was to call "the best book ever written on the Indians of Central New York" was designed and manufactured with unusual care.

In 1901, Herbert M. Lloyd, at the suggestion of Francis Halsey, who was then editor of the *New York Times Saturday Review of Books and Art,* annotated a two volume edition which was published by Dodd, Mead & Company, New York. Lloyd included some text and a few illustrations, from Morgan's Regents' reports, that had been omitted from the first edition, presumably for mechanical reasons. The trade edition was evidently 300, and 30 copies were printed with color plates and bound in parchment. The two volumes bound as one to sell at five dollars followed in 1904, and again in 1922. Even the latter are scarce and expensive today.

Most recently, the Human Relations Area Files at Yale University, to satisfy the demand among anthropology students, amateur archeologists, and others for reading copies, produced a facsimile of the Lloyd 1901 edition in two paperbound volumes.

With Francis Parkman's *History of the Conspiracy of Pontiac*, launched in the same year, and Darwin's *The Origin of Species* (1859), that decade saw important firsts in ethnology, history and natural science.

II

Who would have guessed that out of the Greek revival in upstate New York at the mid-nineteenth century would have come the science of anthropology? Yet Lewis Henry Morgan who was born at Aurora on Cayuga Lake in 1818, when the smoke of the council fires of the People of the Great Pipe was barely perceptible, was as a lad to found a boys' club to read the classics before entering Union College, where he showed intellectual curiosity and an early talent for writing about man and nature. Then, as a man he made a fortune as a corporation lawyer in the milling town of Rochester, speculating in railroads and in mining in upper Michigan, and he represented Rochester's interest in the State Legislature, before turning his back on these evidences of conspicuous civic success and devoting his mind and fortune to the life of the intellect. This was really the resolution of a long-standing conflict in his personality and in the culture of nineteenth century America between material success and amateurism in science and the arts.

That the mind was to win out was foreseen in Morgan's role in the formation of societies. The Gordian Knot, the Grand Order of the Iroquois, with its chapters in the tribal territories of the League, the Pundits of Rochester which became simply "the club"—all were to follow the intellectual bent of Morgan's ethnological studies, maturing in his joining the American Association for the Advancement of Science at its 1856 meeting in Albany, where he "resolved to resume (ethnology) as soon as the state of my business would permit," and culminating in election to the National Academy of Sciences, in 1875.

To say that Morgan was the most important social scientist in nineteenth century America is an understatement. He belongs in that galaxy of brilliant New Yorkers which included DeWitt Clinton, Joseph Henry, and James Hall, who drew the attention of the whole world to New York State. Only recently has Resek placed Morgan in the scholarship of his century.[1] He has been claimed as the intellectual peer of Darwin, Herbert Spencer and Edward Tyler, and the Marxists who have played up his influence on Engels have played down his association with the Pundits of Rochester, Francis Parkman, and Henry Adams who were obviously capitalists and therefore, in their view, representatives of a misguided social system. But we now understand that he was less influenced by scholars of the day than by politicians, by his local church and pastor, the Rev. Joshua McIlvaine, and by the issues and pressures that beset the Rochester of his day. His voting record in the Legislature makes him out to be a man of his locality, for when he sanctioned Jay Gould's manipulation of Erie Rail-

[1] Carl Resek, *Lewis Henry Morgan: American Scholar* (The University of Chicago Press, 1960).

road stocks he was voting to break the monopoly of the New York Central and for lower freight rates on Rochester flour.

III

How Morgan came to write the *League* is, as we have intimated, a complex tale which recounts the birth of American ethnology. Underlying the transformation of the society of *The Gordian Knot* into *The Grand Order of the Iroquois* lay a certain boyish enthusiasm which was overburdened with a corresponding sense of guilt at the displacement of savages, if not the very idea of savagism. Morgan prefaces his book with a desire "To encourage a kinder feeling towards the Indian, founded upon a truer knowledge of his civil and domestic institutions . . . " This effort to recover the antiquities and customs of the Indians came at a time when the Ogden Land Company was most active in trying to extinguish the aboriginal title to the remaining Indian lands. What had started out as the preamble to the constitution of a new society and had been implemented by a program of active collecting to give coherence to and improve the ceremony of the lodge became the frame of reference for a new obsrvational science. Morgan effected the metamorphosis with the help of two personalities. He got Henry Rowe Schoolcraft of Albany, who that year was making a census for the State Legislature of the condition of the Six Nations, to come to Aurora in August of 1845 to lecture the society on giving up their juvenile pursuits for the more serious study of Indian lore. But the more important influence came from a chance meeting between Morgan and a young Seneca whom he found browsing in an Albany bookstore. That night, and for the next two days, through the young interpreter Ha-sa-no-an-da who was already on the path to sachemship, Morgan conducted the first ethnological interviews with the tribal delegates as informants on the structure of the Iroquois Confederacy, asking direct questions and eliciting the Seneca terms "as long as propriety would admit." Those who argue whether Albany is a cultural center are reminded how American ethnology was born in a hotel room.

Ely S. Parker was one of those rare individuals in acculturated societies who becomes at home in both cultures. As interpreter he had access to sources on tribal government, his family was a natural entree for Morgan into Seneca society, his parents and the Seneca leaders were eager that he have educational advantages, with Morgan he found common intellectual satisfaction in ethnology, and through the medium of the law which Morgan commanded he would learn to travel the whiteman's road. Ethnology then was a child of crisis, a meeting of minds, of two bibliophiles, each desirous of learning the other's institutions.

Morgan and Parker were destined for greater things. Parker as a newly elected honorary member came to Aurora to lecture the Grand Order on the harsh realities of Indian life. He enrolled at Aurora Academy, and his sister Caroline soon followed, but the next year found him in Washington "seeing the

Great White Father." This was the year that the Smithsonian Institution was founded; he met various great names of the day, and noted them in a diary. He admired the splendour of the Presidential Mansion; he felt the curious gaze of other tourists and sensed what it was to be a slave; he was entertained by the still charming Dolly Madison. He attended church, and was directed to sit in the gallery with the Negroes. The usher did not perceive a rising civil engineer, the future aide-de-camp of General U.S. Grant, or the sometime Commissioner of Indian Affairs.

Meanwhile Morgan was active in the "Longhouse." The assistance that Morgan gave as attorney to the unrelenting possessors of Tonawanda Reservation in defeating the Ogden Company's claim to their lands is easily overdone, as Resek contends, for his part was essentially that of a probing and recording scientist and sympathetic listener at a time when the Tonawanda leaders were trying to reestablish the power of the eight Federal Chiefs who traditionally represented the Seneca Nation in the League and who had been put out of office after the disastrous sale of Buffalo Creek Reservation. This fitted his interest in government[2]

Under the rules of Iroquois hospitality the Parker homestead on Tonawanda Creek became headquarters for visiting ethnologists. Here Morgan filled his

[2] I can validate this point on the essential role of the ethnologist in helping Indians to crystalize a point of view on their own culture out of my own field experience with the Seneca a century after Morgan, and I find Resek's point comforting considering the recent failure of the Senecas and Iroquoianists to forestall the building of the Kinzua Dam.

notebooks with placenames and notes on Indian geography. He was the principal recorder for the team, rewriting the observations of the others. The team visited Onondaga and Buffalo Creek; they learned to ask direct questions; and they soon discovered that ethnography is a systematic science which classifies cultural phenomena, establishes sequences, and is less concerned with events. From a classical education and legal training Morgan brought a comparative view of political institutions; he adopted a natural history approach to the description of cultural traits, and his systematic bent directed his enquiries into kinship and government. His earliest ethnological treatise, "Government and Institution of the Iroquois," shows a remarkable grasp of the essentials of Iroquois social structure that he was to develop later in the *League* (Bk. I, chs. iii-v). It was written for the "New Confederacy" in 1845, read before the New York Historical Society the following April, and afterwards used in the famous "Letters on the Iroquois" (I-XIV) by "Skenandoah," in *the American Review* (Feb., 1847, ff.). Earlier writers had failed to report fully the Roll Call of the Chiefs, the fifty sachems of the Iroquois Confederacy, which he lists by committee, title, and clan affiliation. He described their duties, how chosen, and he reported on matriliny—descent, inheritance, and succession. No one in the century since J. F. Lafitau, the Jesuit ethnologist, (*Moeurs des sauvages amériquains . . .* 2 vols., Paris, 1724), had understood the division into clans, or had described the classificatory system of kinship which Morgan was to build into his monumental *Systems*

of Consanguinity and Affinity of the Human Family
(1870).

Both Morgan and Parker were prolific letter
writers. Between field trips the ethnologist sent long
questionnaires and received lengthy answers describing events that Morgan did not always observe.
Parker was a superb informant, but he was not
always writing from home, and this is how, I am
convinced,[3] that he came to drop the Green Bean
Festival from the annual cycle (Bk. II, ch. ii, 198).
Ely's marked facility for putting Indian speeches on
paper was a direct outcome of interpreting, and
these reports on the recitation of Handsome Lake's
message, of the council for installing chiefs, and the
festivals of thanksgiving were used almost word for
word, as Morgan acknowledged, in the *League*.[4]

IV

Visitors to the New York State Museum in Albany
today may see exhibited in Morgan Hall specimens
of the material culture of the Iroquois that Morgan
and Parker furnished to the Indian Collection that
was annexed to the Cabinet of Natural History. Governments habitually ask experts to do what they are
performing well, and so in 1847, when Governor
John Young decided that Albany was not to be out-

[3] "Tonawanda Longhouse Ceremonies: ninety years after Lewis
Henry Morgan," Anthrop. Pap., No. 15, Bureau of American
Ethnology *Bulletin* 128, 140-166 (Washington, 1941).

[4] W. N. Fenton, "Iroquois studies at the mid-century," *Proceedings of the American Philosophical Society*, vol. 95, No. 3, 296-310
(Phila., 1951), 301-304.

done by Hartford, the Regents of the University made an appropriation and took up Morgan's response to supply the cabinet with "a momento of the red race . . . (which would be) . . . enabled to speak for itself through these silent memorials." These are now indeed "type specimens," for they are field-collected, documented, and published, and they may be studied again. It is in studies of material culture in the field and in the museum that anthropology most nearly approaches the other natural history disciplines. The trend was evident in Morgan's field notebooks of a visit to Tonawanda in November 1849, and in an "Expedition to Grand River, Canada, for Indian relics" (1850), which are preserved with his other manuscripts in the Library of the University of Rochester. We find detailed notes on the manufacture of moccasins, the fabrication of rope and burden straps from native fibres, the building of the bark longhouse with an explanation of the relationship of residence to kinship. Of Morgan's original deposit in the New York Indian Collection, which totalled some 269 catalogued specimens (478 items), the State Museum has currently identified 52 (71) specimens as extant and having survived the disastrous fire of 1911. But Morgan's three published Reports to the Regents, which document the provenience and use of each item, illustrating it with line drawings or colored plates, are "models of ethnographic reporting," as Resek states. They established a precedent for all scientific reporting in the State of New York.[5] These then were the

⁵ John M. Clarke, *James Hall of Albany: Geologist and Paleontologist,* 1911-1898 (Albany, 1923), 390, W. N. Fenton, "The

materials comprising Book III of the *League*, which was written in less than six months by repackaging the fourteen letters on the Iroquois and the three reports to the Regents.

V

The *League* occupies a unique place in Iroquois studies today. It gave a distinct flair to the field to take off from the classic attempt to describe Iroquois political structure, which is also a scientific first. Short on history, but long on social organization and the mechanics of a kinship state, the *League* grasped the concept of a whole culture. Its approach was functional and comparative and not historical.

Morgan has had rough treatment at the hands of revisionist historians, notably George Hunt in *The Wars of the Iroquois* (1940). Morgan's great prestige had given wide currency to the theory that Iroquois expansion rested on superior political organization conceived by superior intellects. Parkman, who greatly admired Morgan, had questioned this at the time; Hunt explained Iroquois success on their unique position in trade. Both the French Jesuit Joseph François Lafitau and Morgan were guilty of retrospective projection of the structure they found to an earlier century; but they both remain the most satisfactory of the early and recent writers; and

Museum and Anthropological Research," *Curator*, III (4), 1960: 327-355, 328. *Reports on the State Cabinet of Natural History* (Albany), II (1848), 84-91; III (1849) (Revised, 1950), 65-95; V (1851), 67-117.

what their critics fail to realize is the stability of
major social and political structures over long periods
of time. I believe, with Lafitau and Morgan, that the
political mechanisms of the League were ancient and
that they have remained its most conservative
aspects.

The colonial documents were just making their
appearance as Morgan wrote and he made an attempt to use them. He relied on Cadwallader Colden,
and of the French writers he knew only the Jesuit his-
torian Charlevoix, who had his bias, and the unreliable army officer and traveler Baron de Lahontan. It
is well that he concentrated on ethnology for he was
temperamentally unsuited to history, as he himself,
would later admit in a letter to Parkman. Parkman
had criticized Morgan for ascribing great wisdom to
the unknown founders of the League and for regarding as peculiarly Iroquois what is widespread.
Later in reading Parkman's *La Salle*, Morgan com-
mented that French sources, which he had found
unsatisfying, when studied in their full range by
Parkman, "can be made to yield satisfying results."[6]

It was only later that Morgan was to turn the
lens of ethnology to historical criticism. His first
paper suggested obtaining names of chiefs in six
languages and using these to identify signatures on
treaties, a project which he never carried out. It was
much later that he used ethnology to criticize Mexican chronicles (Resek, 132-133; Parkman Letters, II,
36). Here was a beginning of ethnohistory.

---

[6] *Letters of Francis Parkman*, W. R. Jacobs, ed., (Norman,
1960), II, 37.

The evolutionary and comparative view, which has always been a refuge for those impatient of history, began in "the species of government" (Bk. I, ch. vi), and culminated in *Ancient Society* (1877). Starting with Indian geography, the orientation was in space but not in time, and in abstract system.

An intense interest and prodigious contribution to kinship systems has all but obscured his affirmation of Maine on the relationship of kin to locality, which was sharply focussed in Morgan's thinking: that clans arise from clans by a process of local segmentation, that clans were formerly associated with villages, with residence, and burial of the dead.[7] *Ancient Society* demonstrated the evolution of kin societies to territorial states.

That Morgan's fieldwork would benefit by revision he would have first urged. On masks, medicines, ceremonialism, mythology, music, the dance, prehistory, personality studies, and language, enormous progress has been made in recent years.[8] By an extension of comparative data and analysis of the Roll Call of Iroquois Chiefs, we discover how localized to Tonawanda sources were Morgan's lists, and that no one is really wrong, there are just local differences and reinterpretations.[9] And the work of

---

[7] H. S. Maine, *Ancient Law* (1883); W. N. Fenton, "The concept of locality and the program of Iroquois Research" in *Symposium on local diversity in Iroquois Culture*, Bur. Amer. Ethnol. *Bulletin* 149 (Washington, 1951), 3-4.

[8] *Symposium on Cherokee and Iroquois Culture*, W. N. Fenton and John Gulick, eds., Bureau of American Ethnology *Bulletin* 180 (Washington, 1961). See the list of contributors, foreword, and bibliographies.

[9] Fenton, W. N., The Roll Call of the Iroquois Chiefs . . . *Smithsonian Misc. Coll.*, CXI (15), 1-73 (Washington, 1950), 57.

Lounsbury[10] and Chafe[11] has changed the writing of Iroquoian languages to a phonemic system, including all of the Seneca terms in Morgan's books.

Morgan was a functionalist who wrote felicitously, and his essential humanity emerges in his style. "The fabrics of a people unlock their social history. They speak a language which is silent, but yet more eloquent than the printed page." (p. 351). And what more graphic statement on the succession of weaponry is there than: "The tomahawk succeeded the war-club, as the rifle did the bow." (p. 363).

A final word on the book's place in the history of ideas. Though not entirely free of the ideas of savagism and primitivism, from which his predecessors never escaped, Morgan sought to describe the Iroquois in their own terms and fairly succeeded. Though they were partly horticulturists, he speaks of their bondage to the hunter state; and until he extended his field work to western tribes, after 1856, his descriptions had an ethnocentric ring.[12] Today these descriptions can be confirmed. Though he liked the Iroquois, it made him no less a scientist.

WILLIAM N. FENTON

Slingerlands, New York

---

[10] Floyd G. Lounsbury, "Iroquois-Cherokee Linguistic Relations," *Symposium on Cherokee and Iroquois Culture*, 9-17. (1961). "Oneida Verb Morphology," *Yale Univ. Pub. in Anthropology*, 48, 111 pp., 1953.

[11] Wallace L. Chafe, "Seneca Morphology," *International Journ. Amer. Linguistics*, vol. 26, et seq. (1960-61).

[12] Roy Harvey Pearce, *The Savages of America* (Baltimore, 1953), 133; Resek, *op. cit.*, 43-44.

LEAGUE

OF THE

HO-DE'-NO-SAU-NEE,

IROQUOIS.

BY LEWIS H. MORGAN,

CORRESPONDING MEMBER OF THE NEW YORK HISTORICAL SOCIETY; OF THE
AMERICAN ETHNOLOGICAL SOCIETY, ETC.

NESCIT VOX MISSA REVERTI.
Horace De Art. Poet., v. 390.

ROCHESTER:

SAGE & BROTHER, PUBLISHERS.
NEW YORK:—MARK H. NEWMAN & CO.
BOSTON:—GOULD & LINCOLN.

1851.

TO

H Ä·S A·N O·A N'·D A,

(ELY S. PARKER,)

A SENECA INDIAN,

𝕿𝔥𝔦𝔰 𝖂𝔬𝔯𝔨,

THE MATERIALS OF WHICH ARE THE

FRUIT OF OUR JOINT RESEARCHES,

IS INSCRIBED:

IN ACKNOWLEDGMENT OF THE OBLIGATIONS,

AND IN TESTIMONY OF THE FRIENDSHIP OF

THE AUTHOR.

HO·DE´·NO·SAU·NEE,

PEOPLE OF THE LONG HOUSE.

I. Gä-ne-ă´-ga-o-no´, or People Possessors of the Flint.
MOHAWK NATION.

II. O-nun´-dä-ga-o-no´, or People on the Hills.
ONONDAGA NATION.

III. Nun-da´-wä-o-no´, or Great Hill People.
SENECA NATION.

IV. O-na´-yote-kä-o-no´, or Granite People.
ONEIDA NATION.

V. Gwe-u´-gweh-o-no´, or People at the Mucky Land.
CAYUGA NATION.

VI. Dus-ga´-o-weh-o-no´, or Shirt Wearing People.
TUSCARORA NATION.

DÄ·AH·DE·A.

A SENECA. In the Costume of the Irequois.

PREFACE.

To encourage a kinder feeling towards the Indian, founded upon a truer knowledge of his civil and domestic institutions, and of his capabilities for future elevation, is the motive in which this work originated.

The present Iroquois, the descendants of that gifted race which formerly held under their jurisdiction the fairest portions of our Republic, now dwell within our limits as dependent nations, subject to the tutelage and supervision of the people who displaced their fathers. Their numbers, the circumstances of their past history and present condition, and more especially the relation in which they stand to the people of the State, suggest many important questions concerning their future destiny.

Born to an unpropitious fate, the inheritors of many wrongs, they have been unable, of themselves, to escape from the complicated difficulties which accelerate their decline. To aggravate these adverse influences, the public estimation of the Indian, resting, as it does, upon an imperfect knowledge of his character, and tinctured, as it ever has been, with the coloring of prejudice, is universally unjust.

The time has come in which it is befitting to cast

away all ancient antipathies, all inherited opinions; and
having taken a nearer view of their social life, condition
and wants, to study anew our duty concerning them.
Notwithstanding the embarrassments which have obstructed their progress, the obscurity in which they have
lived, and the prevailing indifference to their welfare,
they have gradually overcome many of the evils inherent
in their social system, and raised themselves to a considerable degree of prosperity. Their present condition,
when considered in connection with the ordeal through
which they have passed, testifies to the presence of an
element in their character which must eventually lead to
important results. It brings before us the question of
their ultimate reclamation, certainly a more interesting
subject, in itself, than any other connected with the
Indian. Can the residue of the Iroquois be reclaimed,
and finally raised to the position of citizens of the State?
To secure this end, at once so just and so beneficent, our
own people have an important part to perform.

As this work does not profess to be based upon authorities, a question may arise in the mind of the reader,
whence its materials were derived, or what reliance is to
be placed upon its statements. The credibility of a
witness is known to depend chiefly upon his means of
knowledge. For this reason, it may not be inappropriate
to state, that circumstances in early life, not necessary
to be related, brought the author in frequent intercourse
with the descendants of the Iroquois, and led to his
adoption as a Seneca. This gave him favorable opportunities for studying minutely into their social organization, and the structure and principles of the ancient

League. Copious notes were made from time to time, when leisure enabled him to prosecute his researches among them, until these had accumulated beyond the bounds of the present volume. As the materials increased in quantity and variety, the interest awakened in the subject finally induced the idea of its arrangement for publication.

The work properly commences with the second chapter. The first, being introductory, has no necessary connection with the residue, but was introduced to give to those unfamiliar with the civil history of the Iroquois, some preliminary information concerning the rise and decline of the League.

It remains for the author to acknowledge his obligations to Ely S. Parker, Hä-sa-no-an'-da, an educated Seneca Indian, to whom this volume is inscribed. He is indebted to him for invaluable assistance during the whole progress of the research, and for a share of the materials. His intelligence, and accurate knowledge of the institutions of his forefathers, have made his friendly services a peculiar privilege.

To Charles T. Porter Esq., of New York, who has made extensive inquiries into the civil and domestic institutions of the Iroquois, and prosecuted them, in many instances, in connection with the author, he is indebted for many valuable suggestions, and for some material.

Rochester, N. Y., January, 1851.

GENERAL CONTENTS.

BOOK I.
STRUCTURE OF THE LEAGUE.

BOOK II.
SPIRIT OF THE LEAGUE.

BOOK III.
INCIDENT TO THE LEAGUE.

APPENDIX.

VOWEL SOUNDS.

ä as in arm.

ă as in at.

a as in ale.

ĕ as in met.

ō as in tone.

TABLE OF CONTENTS.

BOOK I.

STRUCTURE OF THE LEAGUE.

CHAPTER I.

CHAPTER II.

CHAPTER III.

CHAPTER IV.

CHAPTER IV.

CHAPTER V.

CHAPTER VI.

BOOK III.

INCIDENT TO THE LEAGUE.

CHAPTER I.

CHAPTER II.

CHAPTER III.

CHAPTER IV.

APPENDIX.

No. 1.

No. 2.

BOOK FIRST.

STRUCTURE OF THE LEAGUE

GÄ-NO-SOTE
or
BARK HOUSE.

Interior View of
BARK HOUSE.

LEAGUE OF THE IROQUOIS.

BOOK I.

STRUCTURE OF THE LEAGUE.

CHAPTER I.

INTRODUCTORY OUTLINE. — ORIGIN OF THE IROQUOIS. — FORMATION OF THE LEAGUE. — INTERCOURSE WITH EUROPEANS. — WARS WITH INDIAN NATIONS. — WARS WITH THE FRENCH. — JESUIT MISSIONARIES. — NUMBER OF THE IROQUOIS. — FIDELITY TO THE ENGLISH. — DISPERSION OF THE NATIONS. — PRESENT CONDITION. — FUTURE PROSPECTS.

AMONG the Indian nations whose ancient seats were within the limits of our republic, the Iroquois have long continued to occupy the most conspicuous position. They achieved for themselves a more remarkable civil organization, and acquired a higher degree of influence, than any other race of Indian lineage, except those of Mexico and Peru. In the drama of European colonization, they stood, for nearly two centuries, with an unshaken front, against the devastations of war, the blighting influence of foreign intercourse and the still more fatal encroachments of a restless and advancing border population.

Under their federal system, the Iroquois flourished in independence, and capable of self-protection, long after the New England and Virginia races had surrendered their jurisdictions, and fallen into the condition of dependent nations; and they now stand forth upon the canvass of Indian history, prominent alike for the wisdom of their civil institutions, their sagacity in the administration of the League, and their courage in its defence. When their power and sovereignty finally passed away, it was through the events of peaceful intercourse, gradually progressing to this result, rather than from conquest or forcible subjugation. They fell under the giant embrace of civilization, victims of the successful warfare of intelligent social life upon the rugged obstacles of nature; and in a struggle which they were fated to witness as passive and silent spectators.

As there is no connected history of the rise, progress and decline of this Indian League, a brief general outline seems to be demanded, to refresh the mind of the reader, and to furnish a proper introduction to the following pages, which are devoted to an exposition of its structure, principles and spirit. The eventful history of this interesting portion of our indigenous population furnishes ample materials for a separate work, the execution of which, it is to be hoped, will ere long be accomplished by capable hands.

At the era of Dutch discovery (1609), the Iroquois were found in the possession of the same

territories between the Hudson and the Genesee
rivers, upon which they afterwards continued to reside until near the close of the eighteenth century.
At that time, the Five Nations, into which they had
become subdivided, were united in a League; but its
formation was subsequent to their establishment in
the territories out of which the state of New York
has since been erected.

Their remote origin, and their history anterior to
the discovery, are both enshrouded with obscurity.
Tradition interposes its feeble light to extricate,
from the confusion which time has wrought, some
of the leading events which preceded and marked
their political organization. It informs, us that prior
to their occupation of New York, they resided in
the vicinity of Montreal, upon the northern bank of
the St. Lawrence, where they lived in subjection
to the Adirondacks, a branch of the Algonquin
race, then in possession of the whole country north
of that river. At that time, the Iroquois were but
one nation, and few in number. From the Adirondacks they learned the art of husbandry, and while
associated with them, became inured to the hardships of the war-path and of the chase. After they
had multiplied in numbers and improved by experience, they made an attempt to secure the independent possession of the country they occupied;
but having been, in the struggle, overpowered and
vanquished by the Adirondacks, they were compelled to retire from the country, to escape extermination.

The period of their migration from the north cannot now be ascertained. Tradition informs us, that having ascended the St. Lawrence to lake Ontario, and coasted its eastern shore to the mouth of the Oswego river, they entered through this channel the central parts of New York. Their first settlements, they believe, were located upon the Seneca river, where for a time they dwelt together. At a subsequent day they divided into bands, and spread abroad to found new villages. One, crossing over to the Mohawk, established itself at *Gä-né-ga-hä'-gä*, below Utica, and afterwards became the Mohawk nation. This village, situated upon the south side of the Mohawk river, in Herkimer county, is supposed to have been the oldest settlement of that nation. For some years the Oneidas and Onondagas were one nation; but one part of it having become established at *Gä-no-a-lo'-häle*, east of the Oneida lake, in time became independent; while the other, planting themselves in the Onondaga valley and on the hills adjacent, became also a separate nation. In like manner, the Cayugas and Senecas were many years united, and resided upon the Seneca river; but one band of them having located themselves upon the east bank of the Cayuga lake, grew up in time into a distinct nation; while the residue, penetrating into the interior of western New York, finally settled at *Nun-da-wä'-o*, at the head of the Canandaigua lake, and there formed the nucleus of the Seneca nation.

The Onondagas have a legend that they sprang

out of the ground on the banks of the Oswego river; and the Senecas have a similar legend, that they sprang from the ground at *Nun-da-wä'-o.* By these legendary inventions, they designed to convey an impression of the remoteness of the period of their first occupation of New York.

These several bands were, at first, obliged to contend with the various tribes whom they found in possession of the country. After their expulsion, the interests and pursuits of the five nations not only became distinct, but the severance was followed by a gradual alienation, finally resulting in a state of open warfare, which continued for an unknown period. The project of a League originated with the Onondagas, among whom it was first suggested, as a means to enable them more effectually to resist the pressure of contiguous nations. The epoch of its establishment cannot now be decisively ascertained; although the circumstances attending its formation are still preserved by tradition with great minuteness. These traditions all refer to the northern shore of the Onondaga lake, as the place where the Iroquois chiefs assembled in general congress, to agree upon the terms and principles of the compact, by which their future destinies were to be linked together. It is evident from their traditionary history, which is entitled to considerable credit, that they had long occupied the country before their necessities or increase of numbers, made the League a feasible or desirable consummation. In relation to the period of its origin, there are some

circumstances connected with their first intercourse
with Europeans, tending to show that it had subsisted about a century at the era of Dutch discovery; on the other hand, their principal traditions
indicate a period far more remote.

After the formation of the League, the Iroquois
rose rapidly in power and influence. It gave them
additional strength by concentration of effort; a
constant increase of numbers by the unity of the
race; and a firmer establishment, through their
more ample means for self-protection and foreign
conquest. One of the first results of their federal
system was a universal spirit of aggression; a thirst
for military glory and political aggrandizement,
which made the old forests of America resound
with human conflicts from New England to the
Mississippi, and from the northern confines of the
great lakes to the Tennessee and the hills of Carolina.
Unrecorded, except by tradition, is the narrative of
the warlike achievements of this gifted and progressive race, who raised themselves, through the vicissitudes of incessant strife, to a general and acknowledged supremacy over these boundless territories.
Without considering the terrible and ferocious characteristics of Indian warfare, it must be admitted
that the empire which they reared over Indian nations, furnishes no slight evidence of their hardihood, courage and sagacity.

With the first consciousness of rising power, they
turned their long-cherished resentment upon the
Adirondacks, who had oppressed them in their in-

fancy as a nation, and had expelled them from their country, in the first struggle for the ascendency. This war raged for a long time with unceasing animosity, and was continued nearly fifty years after the commencement of French occupation, until the descendants of the ancient Adirondacks were almost totally extirpated. At the era of French discovery (1535), the latter nation appear to have been dispossessed of their original country, and driven down the St. Lawrence as far as Quebec. When Jaques Cartier first ascended this river in 1535, the country about Quebec was in the possession of a people speaking the Algonquin language, doubtless the Adirondacks, while the site of Montreal was occupied by a nation speaking the Huron tongue, of which the language of the Iroquois is a branch. After the permanent occupation of Canada by the French, in 1607, the Adirondacks became their allies; but the protection of the former was insufficient to shield them against the hostile visitations of their hereditary enemy.

A new era commenced with the Iroquois upon the establishment of the Dutch trading-post at Orange, now Albany, in 1615. The principal Indian nations upon the north were the Hurons and Adirondacks; upon the west, the Eries, Neuter Nation, Miamis, Ottawas, and Illinois; upon the south, the Shawnees, Cherokees, Catawbas, Susquehannocks, Nanticokes, Delawares, and some lesser tribes; and upon the east, the Minsi and New England Indians. Some of these nations had been subdued and made tributary. At this time, the Iroquois had grown up into a populous and powerful confederacy and were rapidly advancing to a general supremacy in the north-eastern section of the continent. No Indian race east of the Mississippi had reached such a position of authority and influence, or were bound together by such enduring institutions. Firmly established upon the territory of New York, and above the danger of displacement from adjacent nations, they had already entered upon that career of conquest, which they afterwards prosecuted with such signal success.

Friendly relations were established between the Iroquois and the Dutch, which continued without interruption until the latter surrendered their possessions upon the Hudson to the English, in 1664. During this period, a trade sprang up between them in furs, which the Iroquois exchanged for European fabrics, but more especially for firearms, in the use of which they were afterwards destined to become so expert. The English, in turn, cultivated the same relations of friendship which had been commenced with them by the Dutch. A "covenant chain" was established between them, which the Iroquois, with singular fidelity, preserved unbroken, until the independence of the American states terminated the jurisdiction of the English over the country.

It was otherwise, however, with the French. From the first to the last, they encountered the uncompromising and inveterate enmity of the League. As early as 1609, Champlain, having ascended through the lake which now bears his name into lake George, accompanied by the Adirondacks, fell in with a war-party of the Mohawks, numbering about two hundred, and an engagement ensued between them on the western shore of the lake. This was the first battle between the Iroquois and the Europeans, and the first time the former heard the sound of firearms, by the marvellous power of which they were then easily vanquished. The French having allied themselves with the Adirondacks and Hurons, given them arms and assistance, and incited them against the Iroquois, a spirit of hatred was aroused against them, which never ceased to burn until the final subjugation of Canada by the English, in 1760. Besides this alliance with their ancient enemies, the French were more inclined to resort to intimidation in their intercourse with the Iroquois, than to conciliation and forbearance. In addition to these errors of policy, was the deep and abiding interest taken by the latter in the country about Montreal, which in ancient times had been the home of their fathers, which had been the theatre of their first military success, and which they had long continued to hold by the slender tenure of Indian conquest. As the rival colonies of France and England were for many years nearly equally balanced, the enmity and power of the Hode'nosaunee were sufficient to turn the scale against the former. To this Indian League, France must chiefly ascribe the final overthrow of her magnificent schemes of colonization in the northern part of America.

With the possession of firearms commenced not only the rapid elevation, but absolute supremacy of the Iroquois over other Indian nations. In 1643, they expelled the Neuter Nation from the Niagara peninsula, and established a permanent settlement at the mouth of that river. They nearly exterminated, in 1653, the Eries, who occupied the south side of lake Erie and from thence east to the Genesee, and thus possessed themselves of the whole area of western New York, and the northern part of Ohio. About the year 1670, after they had finally completed the dispersion and subjugation of the Adirondacks and Hurons, they acquired possession of the whole country between lakes Huron, Erie and Ontario, and of the north bank of the St. Lawrence, to the mouth of the Ottawa river, near Montreal. On the north shore of lake Ontario they founded several villages, in the nature of colonial towns, to maintain possession of the conquered territory.

They also made constant inroads upon the New England Indians, who, after their partial subjugation by the English, were unable to cope with the formidable Iroquois. About the year 1670, they compelled them to break up many of their settlements, and flee for safety and protection to the borders of the English plantations. The name of the Iroquois had then become a terror among Indian nations. "I have been told," (says Colden) "by old men in New England, who remembered the time when the Mohawks made war on their Indians, that as soon as a single Mohawk was discovered in their country, their Indians raised a cry from hill to hill, a Mohawk! a Mohawk! upon which they fled like sheep before wolves, without attempting to make the least resistance."

In 1680, the Senecas with six hundred warriors invaded the country of the Illinois, upon the borders of the Mississippi, while La Salle was among the latter, preparing to descend that river to the sea. So great was the dread and consternation of the Illinois, that they were inclined to abandon their villages, and retire from the country, to escape the fury of the conquering foe. At various times, both before and after this period, the Iroquois turned their warfare against the Cherokees upon the Tennessee, and the Catawbas in South Carolina, frequently returning from their distant expeditions with numerous captives, to grace the narrative of their invasions. Of these inroads they still preserve many traditions. All the intermediate country between the Alleghany and the Tennessee acknowledged their authority, and the latter river became their southern boundary. War parties of the League also made irruptions into the country of the Miamis, others penetrated into the peninsula of Michigan, and still others were seen upon the distant shores of lake Superior. No distant solitude, or rugged fastness was too obscure or difficult to escape their visitation; no enterprise was too perilous, no fatigue too great for their courage and endurance. The fame of their achievements resounded over the continent.

On the south-east, also, they extended their conquests. As early as 1607, Captain John Smith, the founder of Virginia, encountered a band of the Iroquois, in several canoes, upon the upper part of the Chesapeak bay, then on their way to the territories of the Powhattan confederacy. The Shawnees, Susquehannocks, Nanticokes, Unamis, Delawares and Minsi, were vanquished one after another, and reduced to the condition of dependent nations. Even the Canarse Indians, in their sea-girt home upon Long Island, found no protection against their attacks. In fact, they traversed the whole country from the St. Lawrence to the Tennessee, and from the Atlantic to the Mississippi.

For about a century, from the year 1600 to the year 1700, the Iroquois were involved in an almost uninterrupted warfare. At the close of this period, they had subdued and held in nominal subjection all the principal Indian nations occupying the territories which are now embraced in the states of New York, Delaware, Maryland, New Jersey, Pennsylvania, the northern and western parts of Virginia, Ohio, Kentucky, Northern Tennessee, Illinois, Indiana, Michigan, a portion of the New England states, and the principal part of Upper Canada. Over these nations, the haughty and imperious Iroquois exercised a constant supervision. If any of them became involved in domestic difficulties, a delegation of chiefs went among them and restored tranquillity, prescribing at the same time their future conduct. Some of these nations, like the Delawares, they prohibited from going out to war, having denationalized them by taking from them all civil powers. According to the Indian notion, they were made women, and were henceforth to confine themselves to pursuits appropriate to the Indian female. Such was the general awe and fear inspired by their warlike achievements, that they dictated to Indian nations their own terms of intercourse, and insisted upon the fulfilment of their requirements. In the conquered territories they often established settlements or colonies of their own people, to exercise a species of superintendence over their acquired possessions.

The multitude of independent tribes into which the generic stocks of the continent had become subdivided, and their want of concert and unity, were extremely favorable to the career of conquest pursued by the Iroquois. In their disunited condition, they could but feebly resist the concentrated energies secured to the latter through the League.

About the year 1700, the Iroquois reached their culminating point. They had reared a colossal Indian empire, so far as its sway over the aborigines was concerned, and in comparison with any Indian power which had risen north of the Aztec monarchy. Having established their dominion securely against all races of Indian lineage, and strengthened the bonds of union among themselves beyond the power of civil dissensions, they would seem to have prepared themselves for a still higher progress, through the pursuits of peace; but a different and more deadly enemy than the Indian had already stretched out its arms to enfold them in its withering embrace.

During the same period, or rather from about the year 1640 to the year 1700, a constant warfare was maintained between the Iroquois and the French, interrupted occasionally by negotiations and brief intervals of peace. As the former possessed both banks of the St. Lawrence, and the circuits of lakes Erie and Ontario, they intercepted the fur trade, which the French were anxious to maintain with the western nations. Upon this trade much of the prosperity of the new colony depended, for it furnished the chief article of export, and yielded the most profitable returns. But the war parties of the League ranged through these territories so constantly, that it was impossible for the French to pass in safety through the lakes, or even up the St. Lawrence above Montreal. Their traders were captured, and the rich furs of the west not only became the spoil of the victors, but the traders themselves were often led into captivity, and perhaps to the stake. So great was the fear of these sudden attacks, that both the traders and the missionaries were obliged to ascend the Ottawa river to near its source, and from thence to cross over to the Sault St. Marie, and the shores of lake Superior. For these reasons the French were extremely anxious, either to detach the Iroquois from the English and gain their alliance, or to reduce them to subjection by conquest. They tried each successively, and in both were equally defeated. The untractable and politic Iroquois were averse to the former, and too powerful for the latter. On numerous occasions the ambassadors of the League were at Montreal and Quebec, to negotiate with them for the adjustment of difficulties, and the exchange of prisoners; in some of which negotiations, the terms of a peace, or at least of an armistice, were agreed upon; but these respites from warfare were of short duration. The ravages committed upon the settlements of the French were so frequent and so devastating, as to place the colony in imminent peril. But for the constant supplies from the mother country, the French power in Canada would inevitably have been overthrown at several different periods prior to 1700.

To retaliate for these frequent inroads, and to prevent their recurrence, the country of the Iroquois was often invaded by the French. On several occasions they drew out the whole force of the colony, to devastate the villages of the League; but after the most toilsome expeditions into the heart of the wilderness of New York, they returned without having accomplished sufficient to reward them for the fatigues and perils of the enterprise. The Iroquois invariably retired into the depths of the forest, leaving nothing but their deserted tenements and fields of corn to await the invader. In this manner the unwearied perseverance and indomitable courage of the French were rendered futile against such an evanescent adversary.

In 1665, M. Courcelles, governor of Canada, led a strong party into the country of the Mohawks; but the hardships they encountered rendered it necessary for them to return, without accomplishing their purpose. The next year, M. De Tracy, viceroy of New France, with 1200 French and 600 Indians, renewed the invasion with better success. He captured *Te-ä-ton-ta-lo'-ga*, one of the principal villages of the Mohawks, situated at the mouth of the Schoharie creek; but after destroying the town, and the stores of corn, which they found in caches, they were obliged to retire without meeting an opposing force. Again, in 1684, M. De La Barre, then governor of Canada, entered the country of the Onondagas with about 1800 men. Having reached Hungry bay, on the east shore of lake Ontario, a conference was had with a delegation of Iroquois chiefs, headed by Garangula, the celebrated Onondaga orator. After they had exchanged recriminations and mutual defiance, a species of armistice was finally agreed upon, and thus the expedition ended.

A more successful enterprise was projected and carried into execution, in 1687, by M. De Nonville, then governor of Canada. Having raised a force of 2000 French and 600 Indians, he embarked them in a fleet of 200 bateau, and as many birch bark canoes. After coasting lake Ontario from Kingston to Irondequoit bay, in the territory of the Senecas, he landed at the head of this bay, and found himself within a few miles of the principal villages of the Senecas, which were then in the counties of Ontario and Monroe. The nearest village was *Gä-o-sä-ga'-o*, near Victor, in the county of Ontario, and the next *Gä-nun-dä'-gwa*, at the foot of the Canandaigua lake. Taking the trail which led directly to these villages, De Nonville marched upon the first. After repulsing a body of 500 Senecas, with whom he had a sharp engagement, he took and destroyed the town, which had been deserted by its inhabitants. Meeting with no further opposition, as the Senecas had retired into the interior, he marched southward as far as *Da-yo-de-hok'-to*, a village situated at the bend of the Honeoye outlet, west of Mendon, in the county of Monroe. This was the largest village of the Senecas, according to the official statement of De Nonville, and was the place selected for the execution of the *acté*, by which they took formal possession of the country of the Seneca-Iroquois, in the name of France. Four villages, with their extensive fields of corn then growing, were burned and devastated, after which the French army retired.

To retaliate for this invasion, a formidable party of the Iroquois, in the fall of the same year, made a sudden descent upon fort Chambly, on the Sorel river, near Montreal. Unable to capture the fort, which was resolutely defended by the garrison, they ravaged the settlements adjacent, and returned with a number of captives. About the same time, a party of 800 attacked Frontenac, on the site of Kingston, and destroyed and laid waste the plantations and establishments of the French without the fortification. In July of the ensuing year, the French were made to feel still more sensibly the power of their revenge. A band of 1200 warriors, animated with the fiercest resentment, made a descent upon the island of Montreal. They had covered their plans with such secrecy, and advanced with such celerity, that the inhabitants had no admonition of their approach. Their first intimation of impending danger was the fearful onset of the Iroquois. Unprepared, and without the means of resistance, they were overpowered and slain in every direction. All that were without the fortifications fell under the rifle or the relentless tomahawk. Their houses were burned, their plantations ravaged, and the whole island covered with desolation. About a thousand of the French, according to some writers, perished in this invasion, or were carried into captivity. When the work of destruction was completed, the Iroquois retired, bearing with them the spoils of the island, and about 200 prisoners.

Overwhelmed by this sudden disaster, the French destroyed their forts at Niagara and Frontenac, and thus yielded the whole country west of Montreal to the possession of the Iroquois. At this critical period Count Frontenac again became governor of Canada, and during the short residue of his life, devoted himself, with untiring energy, to restore its declining prosperity. War had now commenced between the English and French, which drew his first attention to the defence of Quebec against the attack of the English; but after this had been successfully resisted, he again sought to chastise the fierce enemy, who had so long disputed with the French the possession of Canada. In the winter of 1692, he sent a detachment of 600 French and Indians against the Mohawks; which, after travelling through the dense forests upon snow-shoes, and encountering almost insurmountable obstacles, finally reached in safety the vicinity of the Mohawk villages. They surprised and captured three of these, took three hundred prisoners, and returned with the loss of thirty men. Again, in 1696, Count Frontenac conducted an expedition in person against the Onondagas and Oneidas, with a thousand French and as many Indians. Having ascended the St. Lawrence in bateau and bark canoes, he coasted the eastern shore of the lake, to the mouth of the Oswego river. From thence he marched to the salt springs, near the site of Syracuse, and up the Onondaga valley to the principal village of the Onondagas. He found it, as usual, deserted, although fortified with palisades, and supplied with stores of corn. The village was then burned, and the growing corn, which was found in great abundance in the fields adjacent, was cut down with the sabre. A detachment was then sent against the Oneidas, under M. De Vaudreuil, by whom their fields also were laid waste, after which the French army returned to Canada.

This was the last French invasion of the territories of the Iroquois. A general peace soon followed, and continued without interruption, until the war of 1755, which finally resulted in the conquest of Canada by the English, in 1760.

From the commencement of English intercourse with the Iroquois, down to the independence of the American states, the covenant of friendship between them remained unbroken. The importance of conciliating this powerful confederacy was fully appreciated by the colonial authorities, especially during the infancy of the English establishments. Unwearied pains were taken by them to secure and retain their favor and confidence. Each successive governor announced his arrival to the Sachems of the League, and invited them to meet him in council, at an early day, to renew the "covenant chain." Each new alliance was cemented by presents, by mutual professions of kindness, and by assurances of mutual assistance. An intercourse sprang up between them in matters of trade, and in public affairs, which continued to increase, until councils with the Iroquois became nearly as frequent as the sessions of the provincial legislature. Independent of the profitable trade in furs, with which they enriched their commerce, they felt the necessity of interposing the power of the Indian League, as a barrier to French progress, not only towards their own settlements, but also towards the west. The •French were constantly striving to open an extensive fur trade with the western nations, and for its necessary protection, to extend their possessions up the St. Lawrence, and upon the northern shores of lake Ontario. With the exclusive navigation of this river and lake, they would have obtained nearly the absolute control of this important trade ; under the powerful stimulus of which, the strength and prosperity of the French colony would have risen with such rapidity, as to threaten the security of the English possessions. Both the English and the French were fully aware of the important part the Iroquois were destined to bear in the drama of colonization; but the former, by their superior advantage of position, and from their greater dependence upon the forbearance of the League, were induced to pursue a course of policy which gained their unchangeable friendship. The French would inevitably, if unopposed by them, have possessed themselves of the greater part of New York, and, perhaps, have established their empire so firmly, that the united forces of the English colonies would have been unable to effect their displacement.   At one period, the French had pushed their settlements up lake Champlain, until both sides of the lake, as far up as the foot of lake George, were covered with French grants.

A reference, at least, to the missionary efforts of the French, while in the occupation of Canada, ought not to be omitted. While the English entirely neglected the spiritual welfare of the Indians, the French were unremitted in their efforts to spread Christianity among them. The privations, and hardships endured by the Jesuit missionaries, and the zeal, the fidelity and devotion, exhibited by them, in their efforts for the conversion of the Indian, are unsurpassed in the history of Christianity. They traversed the forests of America alone and unprotected; they dwelt in the depth of the wilderness, without shelter, and almost without raiment; they passed the ordeal of Indian captivity, and the fires of the torture; they suffered from hunger and violence; but in the midst of all, they never forgot the mission with which they were intrusted. The fruits of these labors of christian devotion are yet visible among the descendants of the ancient Iroquois; for the precepts spread abroad among them by the missionaries are still in the Indian mind, and many of them have been incorporated by them into their own religious system. The intercourse of the French Jesuits with the Iroquois furnishes, in some respects, the most pleasing portion of their history.

In 1715, the Tuscaroras, having been expelled from North Carolina, turned to the north, and sought a home among the Iroquois, on the ground of a common origin. That they were originally descended from the same stock is sufficiently evinced by their language. They were admitted into the League as a constituent member, and a portion of the Oneida territory assigned to them as their future home. After this event, the Iroquois, who had before been styled by the English the " Five Nations," were known by them under the name of the " Six Nations."

With this brief and barren outline of prominent

events, the civil history of the Iroquois, prior to 1760, is dismissed.

It is difficult to form a correct estimate of their number; the opinions of those having the best opportunities of judging have been so various. La Hontan placed them at 70,000. The estimate made by Col. Coursey, at Albany, in 1677, gave them about 15,000; but it is known that his means of judging were very imperfect. Bancroft estimates them, including the Tuscaroras, at 17,000. Calculations made at a later day, after they had greatly declined in number, allowed them 10,000. This was substantially the estimate of Sir William Johnson, in 1763. There is a tradition among the Senecas, that at the period of their highest prosperity and numbers, they took a census of their nation, by placing a kernel of white flint corn for each Seneca, in a corn husk basket, which, from the description of its size, would hold ten or twelve quarts. Taking the smallest size, and making the estimate accordingly, it will give us the number of Senecas alone at 17,760. At the present time there are about 7,000 Iroquois within the United States and Canada, who have continued to preserve their lineage and nationality through all their vicissitudes. This appears from the reports of the Indian Department, and from other sources of information.

It is well understood, that the decline of the Iroquois commenced with their first intercourse with Europeans. The possession of firearms, and their use in Indian warfare, the introduction of ardent spirits among them, with its train of frightful excesses, and their incessant conflicts with the French, and with Indian nations, were calculated to waste them away with great rapidity. In 1750, from these various causes, they had become diminished about one half. Another and a prominent cause of the decline of the Iroquois, was the large numbers induced, at various times, to emigrate to the banks of the St. Lawrence, under the influence of the Jesuit missionaries, and who, by placing themselves under French protection, became the enemies of their kindred, and of the League. The most successful colony of this description, was that established by the Abbé Picquet at *Swe-gă'-che*, on the site of Ogdensburg, in 1749. The first year, he constructed a fort of palisades, and commenced with six Iroquois families; in the second year, the number of families had increased to eighty-seven, and in the third, to 396. Such was the influx from the territories of the League to the new missionary establishment, that, in 1754, the number of inhabitants in their three villages, at and near *Swe-gă'-che* was estimated by the French at 3,000. This band were afterwards known as the "Praying Indians," from their conversion to Christianity. Their descendants now reside upon the St. Regis reservation, in the county of St. Lawrence.

The period of their greatest prosperity, and of their highest numbers, was evidently about the year 1650, shortly after the commencement of their intercourse with Europeans. At that time, their total population may be safely placed at 25,000. A higher estimate would be better supported by such data as the case affords, than a lesser one; although the impression of later writers seems to be the contrary. An approximation to the relative strength of the several nations of the League, upon this basis, may be made by the following apportionment: To the Senecas, 10,000; to the Cayugas, 3000; to the Onondagas, 4000; to the Oneidas, 3000; and to the Mohawks, 5000. A century later, their total population was probably about half this number, the Mohawks having wasted away the most rapidly.

A few brief observations upon the modern transactions of the Iroquois will close this outline. From the close of the French war until the commencement of the American Revolution, was a time of general peace. The Revolution placed them in a position of great difficulty, as the Continental congress negotiated to secure their neutrality, and the English to obtain their assistance. Their sympathies, as was anticipated, were strongly enlisted in favor of their ancient ally, with whom, for upward of a century, they had maintained an unbroken friendship. They were thoroughly English in sentiment. Having no motive of self-interest to engage them on either side, neutrality was the true policy of the League; more especially, as the final success of the American arms might lead to the forfeiture of their country, if they enlisted against them. In the end, the appeals and the appliances of the English were found irresistible; and, placing their country and the homes of their fathers in the event of the struggle, the people of the Long House went out for the last time in battle array, not to peril their lives for themselves, but to keep the " covenant chain" with a transatlantic ally.

When the question of declaring for the English came before the council of sachems and chiefs, the Oneidas alone resisted the measure, as unwise and inexpedient. Their opposition defeated the war measure, as an act of the League, unanimity being a fundamental law in the legislation of the Iroquois. But the course of events had, at this time, greatly impaired and weakened the confederacy. Their power and numbers had wasted away; their political existence, as an independent people, was drawing to its close; and it was found impossible, under the pressure of circumstances, to adhere to the ancient principles of the League. It was finally determined, that each nation might engage in the war upon its own responsibility; so that, ultimately, the Mohawks, Onondagas, Cayugas and Senecas took up the rifle for the English. The border wars of the Revolution, in which the Iroquois participated, and the devastations which they committed in the valleys of the Mohawk and Susquehanna, and their tributaries, are too familiar to require a recital. Their irruptions into the border settlements were so frequent, and the track of their invasions was marked with such desolation, that the American congress were obliged to send against them a pow-

erful detachment, to lay waste their villages, and
to overawe them with the fear of final extirpation.
General Sullivan, in 1779, led an army of four
thousand men into the Seneca territory, which he
penetrated as far as the Genesee, at that time the
centre of their population. After destroying their
principal towns, their fruit orchards, and stores of
grain, he returned to Pennsylvania; having first
sent a detachment into the Cayuga territory to
ravage their settlements.

The treaty of peace between Great Britain and
the United States, in 1783, made no provision for
the Iroquois, who were abandoned in adversity by
their ally, and left to make such terms as they could
with the successful republic. A few years afterwards a general peace was established with the
north-western Indian nations, including the Iroquois,
all of whom had, more or less, become involved in
the general controversy. With the restoration of
peace, the political transactions of the League were
substantially closed. This was, in effect, the ter-
mination of their political existence. The jurisdiction of the United States was extended over their
ancient territories, and from that time forth they
became dependent nations.

During the progress of the Revolution, the Mohawks abandoned their country and removed to Canada, finally establishing themselves partly upon Grand
River, in the Niagara peninsula, and partly near
Kingston, where they now reside upon two reservations secured to them by the British government.

The Oneidas, notwithstanding their friendly position during the war, in the end fared little better than their Mohawk brethren. A rapid influx of population, the tide of which set to the westward with the restoration of peace, soon rendered their possessions valueless. Negotiations were immediately commenced by the State for the purchase of their lands, which they yielded from time to time in large grants, until their original possessions were narrowed down to one small reservation. In these negotiations, as well with the other Iroquois nations as with the Oneidas, the policy of the State of New York was ever just and humane. Although their country, with the exception of that of the Oneidas, might have been considered as forfeited by the event of the Revolution, yet the government never enforced the rights of conquest, but extinguished the Indian title to the country by purchase, and treaty stipulations. A portion of the Oneida nation emigrated to a reservation on the river Thames, in Canada, where about 400 of them now reside. Another and a larger band removed to Green Bay, in Wisconsin, where they still make their homes to the number of seven hundred. But a small part of the nation have remained around the seat of their ancient council-fire. One hundred and twenty-six, according to the census of the last year, are now dwelling near Oneida castle, in the county of Oneida, and have become fully habituated to an agricultural life.

Perhaps, in the result, the Onondagas have been the most fortunate nation of the League. They still retain their beautiful and secluded valley of Onondaga, with sufficient territory for their comfortable maintenance, even with the limited production of Indian husbandry. After the Revolution, they granted their lands to the State by treaty, with the exception of the tract they now occupy, the proceeds, as in other cases, being invested by the government for their benefit. About a hundred and fifty Onondagas now reside with the Senecas; another party are established on Grand river, in Canada, and a few have removed to the west. The total number still remaining at Onondaga is about two hundred and fifty.

Over the fate of the Cayugas a feeling of regret and sympathy is awakened, as having been even less fortunate than their unfortunate kindred. This nation has become literally scattered abroad. Immediately after the Revolution, the tide of population began to press upon them, and hem them in on every side, to such a degree, that they were obliged wholly to surrender their domain. In the brief space of twelve years after the first house of the white man was erected in Cayuga county (1789) the whole nation was uprooted and gone. In 1795, they ceded, by treaty, all their lands to the State, with the exception of one reservation, which they finally abandoned about the year 1800. A portion of them removed to Green Bay, another to Grand river, and still another, and a much larger band, settled at Sandusky, in Ohio, from whence they were removed by government, a few years since, into the

Indian territory, west of the Mississippi. About one hundred and twenty-five still reside among the Senecas, in western New York, and yet retain their name and lineage, and have their separate chiefs. Those west of the Mississippi, and those residing with the Senecas, divide between them the State annuity of $2,300, which was secured to them upon the sale of their former possessions.

The Tuscaroras, after removing from the Oneida territory, finally located near the Niagara river, in the vicinity of Lewiston, on a tract given to them by the Senecas, where about three hundred of them now reside.

After the displacement of the Cayugas, the flow of population, still advancing westward with constantly augmenting force, next began to press upon the broad domains of the Senecas. They passed through the same ordeal to which the other nations had been subjected, by means of which they were speedily induced to grant away their lands, not by townships and counties, but from river to river, reserving here and there a small oasis, sufficient to rescue a favorite village with its burial-place. Their wide-spread territories were in a few years narrowed down, to gratify the demands of the white man, until the residue of the Senecas are now shut up within three small reservations, the Tonawanda, the Cattaraugus and the Allegany, which, united, would not cover the area of one of the lesser counties of the State. To embitter their sense of desolation as a nation, the "preëmptive right" to these last remnants of their ancient possessions is now held by a company of land speculators, the Ogden Land Company, who, to wrest away these few acres, have pursued and hunted them for the last fourteen years, with a degree of wickedness hardly to be paralleled in the history of human avarice. Not only have every principle of honesty, every dictate of humanity, every christian precept been violated by this company, in their eager artifices to despoil the Senecas; but the darkest frauds, the basest bribery, and the most execrable intrigues which soulless avarice could suggest, have been practiced, in open day, upon this defenceless and much-injured people. The natural feelings of man, and the sense of public justice are violated and appalled at the narration of their proceedings. It is no small crime against humanity to seize the firesides and the property of a whole community, without an equivalent, and against their will; and then to drive them, beggared and outraged, into a wild and inhospitable wilderness. And yet this is the exact scheme of the Ogden Land Company; the one in which they have long been engaged, and the one which they still continue to prosecute. The Georgia treaty with the Cherokees, so justly held up to execration, is a white page, compared with the treaties of 1838 and 1842, which were forced upon the Senecas. This project has already, however, in part, been defeated, by the load of iniquity which hung upon the skirts of these treaties; and it is to be hoped, for the credit of humanity, that the cause of the Indian will yet triumph, and that the residue of the Senecas will be permitted to dwell in peace in the land of their nativity.[1]

The census of last year fixes the number of Senecas upon their then reservations, in western New York, at two thousand seven hundred and twelve. A small band, after the Revolution, emigrated to Grand river, where they now have a miniature of the ancient League, and another removed to Sandusky, and from thence into the Indian territory. Those at present within the State are rapidly improving in their social and moral condition ; as also, it is believed, are those residing upon Grand river, in Canada, where there are now about 700 Mohawks, besides 500 near Kingston, 400 Onondagas, 700 Cayugas, 300 Tuscaroras, and 200 Senecas and Oneidas.

From the sales of the lands of the Iroquois, at various times, large sums of money have accrued, which have been invested by the State and national governments for their benefit; and the interest arising from the same is now paid over and distributed among them semi-annually. The Senecas alone have an annual income from these sources, amounting to $18,000.

There are still residing in the State of New York about four thousand Iroquois. The several frag-

---

[1] The Buffalo Reservation, which made the fourth reserved tract, and was the most valuable, has fallen into the hands of the Ogden Company, but not so much by virtue of the treaties, as by skilful management. It contains 49,000 acres of land bordering the corporate limits of the city of Buffalo, and was supposed to be worth over a million of dollars. For the land, and its farming improvements, the Company paid the Senecas about one hundred thousand dollars.

ments of the nations yet continue their relationships and intercourse with each other, and cling to
the shadow of the ancient League. At intervals
of one or two years, they assemble in general council to raise up, with their primitive forms and ceremonies, sachems to fill vacancies occasioned by death
or deposition. These councils are summoned and conducted, in all respects, as they were wont to be in
the days of Indian sovereignty. They still cherish
the remembrance of their fathers, and the institutions which they transmitted to them, with religious
affection In each nation, also, with the exception
of the Oneidas and Tuscaroras, the larger portion of
the people continue to adhere to their ancient faith
and worship; celebrating their religious festivals
after the original method, and preserving, in their
social intercourse, the habits and the customs of
their ancestors. It is another singular fact, in connection with their history, that since their adoption
of agricultural pursuits, as the exclusive source of
subsistence, their further decline has been arrested,
and they are now increasing in numbers. In many
respects they have become an interesting portion of
our population, yielding many hopes of their future
elevation. The policy of the State towards them has
ever been enlightened, humane and just, the government seizing upon every opportunity to promote
their welfare, to protect their interests, and to extend to them facilities for education. It is a pleasing and a proud reflection, that there is a universal
spirit of kindness, sympathy and benevolence tow-

ards the Iroquois, among the people of New York. They would shield them in their defenceless condition, stimulate their efforts for social improvement, encourage their aspirations for a higher life, and finally, when they have become sufficiently advanced in agricultural life, raise them to the condition of citizens of the State.

The materials for the preceding chapter were drawn from the following sources : Colden's Hist. Five Nations ; Charlevoix's Hist. New France ; Smith's Hist. N. Y.; Macauley's Hist. N. Y.; Doc. Hist. N. Y.; Morse's Hist. Am. Rev.; Bancroft's Hist. U. S.; Warburton's Conquest of Canada; Marshall's Nar. De Nonville's Exped.; Schoolcraft's Notes on the Iroquois ; Doc's of the Indian Department; MSS. Treaties with the Iroquois, State Dep. Alby.; Traditions of the Onondagas, Tuscaroras, Senecas and Cayugas.

CHAPTER II.

OUR Indian ｇ graphy, excluding lines of latitude, descriptions of soil and climate, and precise territorial limits, confines itself to the external features of the country, and to the period when the hemlock and the maple, the pine and the oak, interlocked their branches in endless alternation, spreading out from river to river, and from lake to lake, in one vast, continuous, interminable forest.

As the aboriginal, or poetic period of our territorial history recedes from us, each passing year both deepens the obscurity upon the Indian's footsteps, and diminishes the power of the imagination to recall the stupendous forest scenery by which he was surrounded. To obtain a glance at the face of nature during the era of Indian occupation, the wave of improvement must be rolled backward, not only displacing, in its recession, the city and the village which have sprung up in the wilderness; but restoring, also, by a simultaneous effort, the original drapery of nature, when clothed in her wild attire.[1]

Surrounded by all the grandeur of this forest scenery, the Indian constructed his *Gä-no'-sote*, or Bark House, upon the winding stream, or on the margin of the lake; and, one of the multitudinous inhabitants of the forest, he passed his days and years in sylvan pursuits, unless he went forth upon the warpath in quest of adventure or renown.

Between the Hudson and lake Erie, our broad territory was occupied by the *Ho-dé'-no-sau-nee*, or Iroquois, scattered far and wide, in small encampments, or in disconnected villages. Their councilfires, emblematical of civil jurisdiction, burned continuously from the Hudson to Niagara. At the era of Dutch discovery, (1609) they had pushed their permanent possession as far west as the Genesee; and shortly after, about 1650, they extended it to the Niagara. They then occupied the entire territory of our State west of the Hudson, with the exception of certain tracts upon that river below the junction of the Mohawk, in the possession of the River Indians, and the country of the Delawares, upon the Delaware river. But both these had been subdued by the conquering Iroquois, and had become tributary nations.

The villages of the Mohawks were chiefly located

---

[1] In those forest days, the graceful swan folded her wings in unmolested seclusion upon our inland lakes; but with the departure of the Indian, she spread them again, and followed him. They sat upon the water in pairs, and not in flocks. It is said they still frequent the small lakes in the wild regions of Northern New York. The American swan (Cygnus Americanus) was called by the Senecas *Ah-weh'-ah·ah*

in the valley of the Mohawk, upon the south side of the river. Around and near the Oneida lake were the principal villages of the Oneidas. The Onondagas were established in the valley of the river of that name, and upon the hills adjacent. On the east shore of the Cayuga lake, and upon the ridge to the eastward, were the settlements of the Cayugas. In the counties of Ontario and Monroe were found the principal villages of the Senecas, the most populous nation of the League. These were their chief localities at the era of their discovery. At a later period, in the progress of their intercourse and warfare with the whites, many of their ancient settlements were abandoned, and new ones established. This was especially the case with the Senecas, until their villages, at various periods, have been sprinkled over the whole area of western New York.

This territory, lying between the Hudson and lake Erie, and embracing the most valuable portions of our State, constituted the Home Country of the Iroquois, as distinguished from other territories upon the north, south, east and west, which they held in subjection by conquest, and occupied only in the season of the hunt. At the era of their highest military supremacy, about the year 1660, the Iroquois, in their warlike expeditions, ranged unresisted from New England to the Mississippi, and from the St. Lawrence to the Tennessee. They held under their dominion the greater part of these vast territories by the slender tenure of Indian conquest. But New

York was their hereditary country, the centre of
their power, and the seat of their council-fires.
Here were their villages, their fields of maize and
tobacco, their fishing and hunting grounds, and the
burial-places of their fathers. The Long House, to
which they likened their political edifice, opened its
eastern door upon the Hudson, while the western
looked out upon Niagara. At the epoch of their
discovery, this fair domain was the patrimony of
the Iroquois, the land of their nativity, if not of
their remote origin, and they had defended it
against hostile bands with a patriotism as glowing,
as such a fair possession could inspire in the heart
of man. They were not insensible to the political
advantages afforded by their geographical position.
It was their boast that they occupied the highest
part of the continent. Situated upon the head-waters of the Hudson, the Delaware, the Susquehanna,
the Ohio and the St. Lawrence flowing in every
direction to the sea, they held within their jurisdiction, as it were, the gates of the country, and could,
through them, descend at will upon any point. At
the same time, lake Ontario, and the mountains
upon the north, and the range of the Alleganies
upon the south gave to their country itself an iso-
lation, which protected them, in a great measure,
against the external pressure of migratory bands;
while the lakes and streams, which in so remarkable
a manner intersected every part of the Long House,
and whose head-waters were separated only by short
portages, and its continuous valleys, divided by no

mountain barriers, offered them every facility for the most rapid inter-communication. They themselves declared that "their country possessed many advantages superior to any other part of America."

A boundary line would seem at first to be a difficult problem in Indian geography. But a peculiar custom of our predecessors has divested this subject of much of its embarrassment, and enabled us to ascertain with considerable certainty the territorial limits of the nations of the League. The Iroquois rejected all natural boundaries, and substituted longitudinal lines. This appears to have resulted from the custom of establishing themselves upon both banks of the streams upon which they resided. Having no knowledge of the use of wells, they were accustomed to fix their habitations upon the banks of creeks, and easily forded rivers, or in the vicinity of copious springs. Inland lakes were never divided by a boundary line; but the line itself was deflected, that the entire circuit of each lake might be possessed by a single nation. The natural limits which rivers and lakes might furnish having thus been disregarded, and straight lines substituted, the inquiry is freed from some of its difficulties, and greater certainty is given to their boundaries, when certain points upon them are decisively ascertained.

After the expulsion of the Neuter Nation (*Je-go'-sä-sa*) from the borders of the Niagara river, in 1643,[1] and of the Eries (*Gä-quä'-ga-o-no*) from the

---

[1] Charlevoix, v. i. p. 377. The Neuter Nation were known to the Iroquois as the "Cat Nation;" the word itself (*Je-go'-sä-sa*) signifying "a wild

country between the Genesee and lake Erie in 1655,[1] the Senecas, who before these periods had resided east of the Genesee, extended their jurisdiction over the whole area between the Seneca lake and lake Erie.   On the east, their territory joined that of the Cayugas.   The line of boundary between them, which is well authenticated, commenced at the head of Sodus bay, on lake Ontario, and running south, nearly upon the longitude of Washington, crossed the Clyde river near the village of that name, and the Seneca river about four miles east of its outlet from the Seneca lake.   Continuing south, and inclining a little to the east, the line ran near the lake at its head, and having crossed the Chemung river east of Elmira, it passed into Pennsylvania.

The territory of the Cayugas lay upon both sides of the Cayuga lake, and extended to the eastward so as to include the Owasco.   As the Senecas were the hereditary " Door-keepers" of the Long House, in their figurative way of designating each other, they were styled the first fire ; and so on to the Mohawks, who were the fifth.   Between the Cayugas and Onondagas, who were the third fire, the limital line is not as well defined ; as the latter claimed farther to the westward than the boundary assigned. It commenced on lake Ontario, near the mouth of the Oswego river, and on its west side, and passing between the Cross and Otter lakes, continued south

cat." Charlevoix has assigned this name to the Eries, (v. ii. p. 62.)   [1] Ib. v. ii. p. 62.

into Pennsylvania, crossing the Susquehanna west of Owego.

On the boundary line between the Onondagas and Oneidas, the most prominent point was the Deep Spring (*De-o-song'-wa*) near Manlius, in the county of Onondaga. This spring not only marked the limital line between them, but it was a well known stopping-place on the great central trail or highway of the Iroquois, which passed through the heart of their territories from the Hudson to lake Erie. From the Deep Spring, the line ran due south into Pennsylvania, crossing the Susquehanna near its confluence with the Chenango. North of this spring the line was deflected to the west, leaving in the Oneida territory the whole circuit of that lake. Crossing the *She-u'-kä*, or Oneida outlet, a few miles below the lake, the line inclined again to the east, until it reached the meridian of the Deep Spring. From thence it ran due north, crossing the Black river at the site of Watertown, and the St. Lawrence to the eastward of the Thousand Islands.

The testimony of the Iroquois concerning this boundary line is confirmed by facts contained in existing treaties. At the treaty of Fort Schuyler, the Oneidas, after ceding "all their lands to the people of the state of New York forever," reserved, in addition to their principal reservation, "a convenient piece of ground at the fishing-place in the Oneida river, about three miles from where it issues from the Oneida lake, to remain as well to the Oneidas and their posterity, as for the inhabitants of the State to encamp upon."[1] In the same treaty it appears, that the Deep Spring was upon the west boundary of the Oneida reservation.[2]

The Tuscaroras, upon their expulsion from North Carolina, in 1712, turned to the north, and sought the protection of the *Ho-dé'-no-sau-nee*, on the ground of generic origin. They were admitted into the League as the Sixth nation, and were ever afterwards regarded as a constituent member of the confederacy, although never admitted to a full equality. A portion of the Oneida territory was assigned to them, lying upon the Unadilla river on the east, the Chenango on the west, and the Susquehanna on the south. Whether they occupied entirely across the southern skirt of the Oneida territory, as their boundary is run upon the accompanying map, is a matter of doubt, as the Oneidas might thereby have cut off their southern possessions in Pennsylvania and Virginia. To these southern lands the Tusca-

[1] Vide Treaty of Fort Schuyler, September 22, 1778. MSS. State Department, Albany.

[2] Judge Jones of Utica, in 1846, in a letter in the author's possession, speaks of this spring as follows: "Near the summit of what was formerly called the Canaseraga hill, near where now runs the road from Chittenango to Manlius, is a large, well-known, ever-living spring, familiarly known as the "Big Spring." The excavation, whether made by Omnipotence, or by human hands, may be fifteen feet in diameter, and several feet deep, with sloping sides, easy of descent, and in the bottom is a reservoir ever full. What is quite singular is, that the water runs in at the lower, and disappears at the upper side of the reservoir. This spring, while the old woods were its shade, and the wild deer descended to taste its limpid waters, was long the favorite meeting-place between the Oneidas and Onondagas. Here for ages had the old men of the two nations met to rehearse their deeds of war; here the young braves met in friendly conclave. * * This was the boundary between the nations."

roras had no title, and it is probable that their territorial rights, which were never absolute, were restricted between the Unadilla and the Chenango. The Oneidas, as the original owners of this tract, were made a party, with the Tuscaroras, to the treaty of Fort Herkimer, in 1785, by which it was ceded to the State.[1] The Tuscaroras were partially scattered among the other nations, although they continued to preserve their nationality. They had some settlements at a later day near the Oneida lake, a village at the inlet of the Cayuga, and one in the valley of the Genesee, below Avon. At a subsequent period, the Senecas gave them a tract upon the Niagara river, where they afterwards removed; and their descendants still occupy a reserved portion of this land, near Lewiston, in the county of Niagara.

There were two other small bands, or remnants of tribes, located within the territories of the Oneidas; the Mohekunnuks, situated a few miles south of Oneida castle, and the New England Indians, south of Clinton. For these lands they also were indebted to the generosity of the Oneidas, to whom, as refugees, they applied for " a place to spread their blankets;" and their possessions were subsequently secured to each band by treaty.

Of the several boundaries, that between the Oneidas and the Mohawks is the most difficult to establish; there being a disagreement between the

---

[1] Vide Treaty of Fort Herkimer, June 28, 1785. MSS. State Dep.

line of boundary as given by the Iroquois, and that indicated, although imperfectly, by existing treaties. According to their own evidence, and it is the safest authority, this line came down from the north near the west boundary of Herkimer county, and, crossing the Mohawk about five miles below Utica, continued south into Pennsylvania. On the other hand, it appears from various treaties with the Oneidas, that they sold lands to the State on both sides of the Mohawk, as low down as Herkimer and the German Flats, and also on the Mohawk branch of the Delaware, as far east as Delhi. After the departure of the Mohawks, the Oneidas might have asserted claims against the State, which they would not against their brethren; so also the State may have preferred to include these lands, to prevent all future disputation. The upper castle of the Mohawks, *Gä-ne-ga-hä'-gä*,[1] was situated in the town of Danube, Herkimer county, nearly opposite the junction of the West Canada creek with the Mohawk. From these facts, the boundary given may be regarded as the most reliable. The territory of the Mohawks extended to the Hudson and lake Champlain on the east, with the exceptions before mentioned, and northward to the St. Lawrence.

Such were the territorial divisions between the several nations of the League. In their hunting excursions they were accustomed to confine them-

---

[1] This was, doubtless, the oldest village of the Mohawks; as it is the one from which the nation takes its name. It is *Gä-ne-ä'-gä* in the Seneca dialect.

selves to their own domains: which, to a people who subsisted, in part, by the chase, was a matter of some moment. Upon their foreign hunting grounds, which were numerous and boundless, either nation was at liberty to encamp. By establishing these territorial limits between the nations of the League, the political individuality of each was continued in view.

In intimate connection with our Indian geography are the Trails, or forest highways of the Iroquois. A central trail passed through the State from east to west, intersected at numerous points by cross trails, which passed along the banks of the lakes and rivers. It commenced at the site of Albany on the Hudson, and having touched the Mohawk at Schenectady, it followed up this river to the carrying-place at Rome. From thence, proceeding westward, it crossed the Onondaga valley, the foot of the Cayuga and of the Seneca lakes, the Genesee valley at Avon, and finally came out upon the Buffalo creek, at the site of Buffalo. This route of travel was so judiciously selected, that after the country was surveyed, the turnpikes were laid out upon the Indian highway, with slight variations, through the whole length of the State. This trail not only connected the principal villages of the Iroquois, but established the route of travel into Canada on the west, and over the Hudson on the east. The pursuits of trade, and the development of the resources of the country in modern times have shown this to be one of the great natural highways of the continent. It appears now to be indicated by the geographical features of the territory; but as extensive intercourse was necessary to its discovery, the establishment of this great route of travel furnishes evidence of a more general intercourse of the Iroquois with the east and west, than has ever been ascribed to them.

Upon the banks of the Susquehanna and its branches, the sources of which are near the Mohawk, and upon the banks of the Chemung and its tributaries, which have their sources near the Genesee, were other trails, all of which converged upon Tioga, at the junction of these two principal rivers. They became thus gathered into one, which, descending the Susquehanna, formed the great southern trail into Pennsylvania and Virginia.

For centuries upon centuries, and by race after race, these old and deeply worn trails had been trod by the red man. From the Atlantic to the Mississippi, and from the northern lakes to the Mexican gulf, the main Indian routes through the country were as accurately and judiciously traced, and as familiar as our own. On many of these distant footpaths the Iroquois had conducted warlike expeditions, and had thus become practically versed in the geography of the country. Within their immediate territories, they were quite as familiar with the geographical features, the routes of travel, the lakes, and hills and streams, as we ourselves have since become.

In the accompanying map, an attempt has been made to restore the geographical names of the Iro-

quois, as they stood at the period of its date (1720.)
Many of our own names have their radices in the
dialects of the Iroquois; and as to such names, this
map is designed to furnish an index of their origin
and signification. Our geography is as yet incom-
plete in the christening of some of the features of
nature, while some of the names in actual use might
be profitably exchanged for the aboriginal; in both
of which cases such a map will at least offer a choice.
The date given to it introduces some anachronisms,
which will be obvious to the critical eye; but these
do not furnish a sufficient reason for an earlier, or a
later date. The descendants of the Iroquois have
preserved, with great fidelity, the names of their
ancient localities; and have bestowed them upon
our cities and villages as they have successively appeared. It is but a fit tribute to our Indian predecessors, to record the baptismal names of our rivers,
lakes and streams, and also of their ancient sites.

An effort has been made to furnish these names
in the particular dialect of the nation within whose
territories the places or objects named were situated; and, with a few exceptions, this has been accomplished. The nations spoke different dialects
of a common language; and although they could
understand each other with readiness, the distinctions between them were very decisive. These dialectical differences are more strongly marked in
their geographical names than in the body of the
several dialects themselves; furnishing, perhaps, the
principal reason why these names are written so

variously. Thus the Iroquois name of Buffalo, in the Seneca dialect is, *Do-sho'-weh*, in Cayuga *De-o-sho'-weh*, in Onondaga *De-o-sa'-weh*, in Oneida *De-ose'-lole*, in Mohawk *De-o-hose'-lole* and in Tuscarora *Ne-o-thro'-rä.* For the same purpose, and in the same order, the variations in the name of Utica may be cited : *Nun-da-dä'-sis, Nun-da-dä'-ses, None-da-dä'-sis, Ya-nun-da-dä'-sis, Yo-none-dä'-sis, Ya-nun-nä'-rats.* The resemblance in these examples are nearer than they are usually found. In the transition of these names from the unwritten dialects of the Iroquois into our language, they lose much of their euphony, and the force of their accent. It would therefore be difficult to judge of the language itself from these specimens. That entire accuracy has been attained in the spelling of these words is not expected. Indeed, many of their elementary sounds, in the manner, and in the combination in which they use them, it is impossible to express with our letters. But they are as nearly accurate, as the frequent repetition of each name by the native speaker, that the sound of each syllable might be obtained, together with a careful revision of the whole, would enable the author to make them. In the Appendix No. 1, will be found a table, containing a list of all the names upon the map, arranged by counties, with the signification of each. As the county lines are dotted on the map, it will be easy to refer to any locality.

The trails (*Wä-ä-gwen'-ne-yuh,*) or highways of travel pursued by our predecessors, are also traced upon the map. Among the number, will be found the great central trail from the site of Albany to that of Buffalo, which is traced minutely from point to point, throughout its whole extent.

It remains to notice the origin and signification of the names of the several nations. After the formation of the League, the Iroquois called themselves the *Ho-de'-no-sau-nee*, which signifies "the people of the long house." It grew out of the circumstance, that they likened their confederacy to a long house, having partitions and separate fires, after their ancient method of building houses, within which the several nations were sheltered under a common roof. Among themselves they never had any other name. The various names given to them at different periods were entirely accidental, none of them being designations by which they ever recognized themselves.

The Senecas called themselves the *Nun-da-wä'-o-no*, which signifies "the great hill people." *Nun-da-wä'-o*, the radix of the word, means "a great hill," and the terminal syllables, *o-no*, convey the idea of "people." This was the name of their oldest village, situated upon a hill at the head of the Canandaigua lake, near Naples, where, according to the Seneca fable, they sprang out of the ground.

Gue'-u-gweh-o-no, the name of the Cayugas, signifies "the people at the mucky land;" the root of the word literally meaning "the mucky land." It doubtless referred to the marsh at the foot of the Cayuga lake, near which their first settlement was, in all probability, established.

O-nun-dä'-ga, the origin of the name of the Onondagas, signifies " on the hills ;" hence the name they gave themselves, *O-nun-dä'-ga-o-no*, is rendered "the people on the hills." It appears from various authors, that their principal village, at the era of their discovery, was on one of the eminences overlooking the Onondaga valley.

The Oneidas have been so long distinguished as " the people of the stone," that it is perhaps venturesome to suggest a change. *O-na-yote'-kä*, however, the radix from which their name is derived, signifies not only " a stone," but one of the species known to us as granite. In the Seneca dialect, it means this particular rock ; hence the propriety of rendering literally their national name, *O-na-yote'-kä-o-no*, " the granite people." [1]

There is doubt about the signification of the name of the Mohawks, *Gä-ne-ä'-ga-o-no*, from the fact that the Oneidas, Onondagas and Senecas have lost its meaning. But the Mohawks render the root of the word, "the possessor of the flint," without being able to give any further explanation. It is to be observed, however, that the word as given by the latter, *Gä-ne-ga-hä'-gä*, has one syllable more than the corresponding word in Seneca, which may account for the loss of its signification. In a report enumerating our Indian nations, ascribed to M. De Joncaire, is the following passage bearing upon this subject : "The Mohawks have for

[1] The original Oneida Stone, now in the cemetery at Utica is said to be a boulder of granite.

a device of the village *a steel and a flint*." [1]   The
possession of such a novelty may have been, at an
early day, sufficient to change not only the name
of the village, but also of the nation.

The name of the Tuscaroras, *Dus-ga-o'-weh*, is rendered " the shirt-wearing people;" and was a name
adopted before their emigration from Carolina,
and after the commencement of their intercourse
with the whites.   All of the preceding names are
given in the Seneca dialect to preserve uniformity ;
as not only the terminations, but the radices themselves are different in the several dialects.

The geographical names, the courses of the trails,
and the locations of the villages of the Iroquois,
will be more particularly considered in a subsequent
chapter.

[1] Doc. Hist. N. Y. v. i. p. 22.

CHAPTER III.

INTEREST IN OUR PREDECESSORS. — THE HUNTER STATE. — ITS INSTI-
TUTIONS TRANSITORY. — ORIGIN OF THE LEAGUE. — SACHEMSHIPS. —
HEREDITARY TITLES. — COUNCIL OF THE LEAGUE. — EQUALITY OF
THE SACHEMS. — CHIEFS. — MILITARY CHIEFTAINS. — POPULAR IN-
FLUENCE. — UNITY OF THE RACE.

THE social history and political transactions of
the Indian are as easily enveloped in obscurity,
as his footsteps through the forest are obliterated
by the leaves of autumn. Nation upon nation, and
race after race have sprung up and hastened onward
to their fall; and neither the first nor the last
could explain its origin, or number the years of its
duration.

From this general uncertainty of knowledge
which surrounds our Indian races, we turn with
some degree of encouragement to the Iroquois, the
last in the order of succession which exercised dominion over the territories out of which New York
was erected. We stand with them in many interesting relations. Having flourished side by side
with our early population, the events of their decline became interwoven with our civil affairs; and
having finally yielded up their sovereignty, from
the rulers of the land, they became dependent na-

tions, dwelling under the protection of the government which displaced them.

To the Iroquois, by common consent, has been assigned the highest position among the Indian races of the continent living in the hunter state. In legislation, in eloquence, in fortitude and in military sagacity they had no equals. "No frightful solitude in the wilderness, no impenetrable recess in the frozen north" was proof against their courage and daring. Space offered no protection, distance no shelter from their war parties, which ranged equally the hills of New England, the declivities of the Alleganies the prairies of the Mississippi, and the forests of the Tennessee. In the establishment of a League for the double purpose of acquiring strength and securing peace, their capacity for civil organization, and their wisdom in legislation were favorably exhibited. During the expansion of the power of the Iroquois, from the commencement of the seventeenth to the middle of the eighteenth centuries, there sprang up among them a class of orators and chiefs, unrivalled among the red men for eloquence in council, and bravery upon the war-path. In a word, the League of the Iroquois exhibited the highest development of the Indian ever reached by him in the hunter state.

Many circumstances thus unite to invest its history with permanent interest. An analysis of its civil and domestic institutions will exhibit all the elements of Indian society, and of Indian life, throughout the republic. From the higher legislation of the Iroquois, and the increased weight and diversity of affairs under the League, there resulted a fuller manifestation of the Indian character than is to be found in any other race except the Aztec. Their institutions contain the sum and substance of those of the whole Indian family. While, however, their political events have been diligently collected and arranged, the government which they constructed, the social ties by which they were bound together, and the motives and restraints by which they were influenced have scarcely been made subjects of inquiry, and never of extended investigation. The League of the Iroquois, dismembered and in fragments, still clings together in the twilight of its existence, by the shreds of that moral faith, which no political misfortunes could loosen, and no lapse of years could rend asunder. There are reasons for this spectacle, which no mere alliance of nations can explain, and which history has hitherto failed to reach. It is not the purpose of this work to narrate their political events; but to inquire into the structure and spirit of the government, and the nature of the institutions, under and through which these historical results were produced.

In entering upon such a theme of inquiry as an Indian organization, there are some general considerations which press upon the attention, and which are worthy of previous thought. By the formation of societies and governments, mankind are brought largely under the influence of the so-

cial relations, and their progress has been found to
be in exact proportion to the wisdom of the institutions under which their minds were developed.
The passion of the red man for the hunter life has
proved to be a principle too deeply inwrought, to be
controlled by efforts of legislation.   His government, if one was sought to be established, must
have conformed to this irresistible tendency of his
mind, this inborn sentiment; otherwise it would
have been disregarded.   The effect of this powerful
principle has been to enchain the tribes of North
America to their primitive state.   Another effect
of this principle, and still more fatal to their political prosperity, is to be found in the repeated subdivisions of the generic stocks of the continent, by
which all large accumulations of numbers and
power, in any race or nation, have been prevented.
Whenever a hunting-ground became too thickly pop-
ulated for the easy subsistence of its occupants, a
band, under some favorite chief, put forth, like the
swarm from the parent hive, in quest of a new habitation; and in course of time became independent.
We have here the true reason, why the red race
has never risen, or can rise above its present level.
The fewness of the generic stocks, the unlimited
number of independent tribes, and their past history establish the correctness of this position.

It is obvious that the founders of the League
were aware of the enfeebling effects of these repeated subdivisions, and sought, by the counter
principle of federation, to arrest the evil.   They

aimed to knit the whole race together under such a system of relationships, that, by its natural expansion, an Indian empire would be developed, of sufficient magnitude to control surrounding nations, and thus secure an exemption from perpetual warfare. We must regard it, therefore, as no ordinary achievement, that the legislators of the Iroquois united the several tribes into independent nations, and between these nations established a perfect and harmonious union. And beyond this, that by a still higher effort of legislation, they succeeded in so adjusting the confederacy, that as a political fabric composed of independent parts, it was adapted to the hunter state, and yet contained the elements of an energetic government.

It is another singular feature in connection with Indian organizations, that their decline and fall are sudden, and usually simultaneous. A rude shock from without or within but too easily disturbs their inter-relations; and when once cast back upon the predominating sentiment of Indian life, the hunter inclination, a powerful nation rapidly dissolves into a multitude of fragments, and is lost and forgotten in the undistinguished mass of lesser tribes. But the League of the Iroquois was subjected to a severer test. It went down before the Saxon, and not the Indian race. If it had been left to resist the pressure of surrounding nations, living, like the Iroquois themselves, a hunter life, there is reason to believe that it would have subsisted for ages; and perhaps, having broken the hunter spell, would have introduced civilization by an original and spontaneous movement.

Of the Indian character it is an original peculiarity, that he has no desire to perpetuate himself in the remembrance of distant generations, by monumental inscriptions, or other erections fabricated by the art and industry of man. The Iroquois would have passed away, without leaving a vestige or memorial of their existence behind, if to them had been intrusted the preservation of their name and deeds. A verbal language, a people without a city, a government without a record, are as fleeting as the deer and the wild fowl, the Indian's co-tenants of the forest. With the departure of the individual, every vestige of Indian sovereignty vanishes. He leaves but the arrow-head upon the hillside, fit emblem of his pursuits; and the rude pipe, and ruder vessel entombed beside his bones—at once the record of his superstition, and the evidence of his existence. If the red man had any ambition for immortality, he would intrust his fame to the unwritten remembrance of his tribe and race, rather than to inscriptions on columns in his native land, or other monument more durable than brass, which neither wasting rain, nor raging wind, nor flight of time could overthrow.[1]

[1] Compare the sentiments of Pericles,— with those of Horace,—

Ἀνδρῶν γὰρ ἐπιφανῶν πᾶσα γῆ τάφος, καὶ οὐ στηλῶν μόνον ἐν τῇ οἰκείᾳ σημαίνει ἐπιγραφὴ, ἀλλὰ καὶ ἐν τῇ μὴ προσηκούσῃ ἄγραφος μνήμη παρ᾽ ἑκάστῳ τῆς γνώμης μᾶλλον ἢ τοῦ ἔργου ἐνδιαιτᾶται,

THUCYD., Lib. 2, c. 43.

Exegi monumentum ære perennius,
Regalique situ pyramidum altius;
Quod non imber edax, non Aquilo impotens
Possit diruere, aut innumerabiles
Annorum series, et fuga temporum.
            HOR., Lib. 3, Ode 30.

Since this race must ever figure upon the opening pages of our territorial history, and some judgment be passed upon them, it becomes our duty to search out their government and institutions, and to record with impartiality their political transactions; lest, in addition to the extinguishment of their Council Fires, we subject their memory, as a people, to an unjust and unmerited judgment.

Upon an extended examination of their institutions, it will become apparent, that the League was established upon the principles, and was designed to be but an elaboration, of the Family Relationships. These relations are older than the notions of society or government, and are consistent alike with the hunter, the pastoral and the civilized state. The several nations of the Iroquois, united, constituted one Family, dwelling together in one Long House; and these ties of family relationship were carried throughout their civil and social system, from individuals to tribes, from tribes to nations, and from the nations to the League itself, and bound them together in one common, indissoluble brotherhood.

In their own account of the origin of the League, the Iroquois invariably go back to a remote and uncertain period, when the compact between the Five Nations was formed, its details and provisions were settled, and those laws and institutions were established, under which, without essential change, they afterwards continued to flourish. If we may trust their testimony, the system under which they confederated was not of gradual construction, under the suggestions of necessity; but was the result of one protracted effort of legislation. The nations were, at the time, separate and hostile bands, although of generic origin, and were drawn together in council to deliberate upon the plan of a League, which a wise man of the Onondaga nation had projected, and under which, he undertook to assure them, the united nations could elevate themselves to a general supremacy. Tradition has preserved the name of *Da-gä-no-we'-dä* as the founder of the League, and the first lawgiver of the *Ho-de'-no-sau-nee*. It likewise points to the northern shore of the *Gä-nun'-ta-ah*, or Onondaga lake, as the place where the first council-fire was kindled, around which the chiefs and wise men of the several nations were gathered, and where, after a debate of many days, its establishment was effected.

Their traditions further inform us, that the confederacy, as framed by this council, with its laws, rules, inter-relationships of the people and mode of administration, has come down through many generations to the present age, with scarcely a change; except the addition of an inferior class of rulers, called chiefs, in contradistinction to the sachems, and a modification of the law in relation to marriage. Without entering here upon any inquiry to show the probable accuracy of their traditions, it will be sufficient to investigate the structure of the government, as it stood in its full vigor at the commencement of the last century, and to deduce the general principles upon which it was founded.

The central government was organized and administered upon the same principles which regulated that of each nation, in its separate capacity; the nations sustaining nearly the same relation to the League, that the American states bear to the Union. In the former, several oligarchies were contained within one, in the same manner as in the latter, several republics are embraced within one republic. To obtain a general conception of the character of a government, the ruler, or ruling body, or bodies, as the case may be, would be the first object of attention; and when their powers and tenure of office are discovered, the true index is obtained to the nature of the government. In the case of the *Ho-dé-no-sau-nee*, the organization was externally so obscure, as to induce a universal belief that the relations between ruler and people were simply those of chief and follower—the earliest and lowest political relation between man and man; while, in point of fact, the Iroquois had emerged from this primitive state of society, and had organized a systematic government.

At the institution of the League, fifty permanent sachemships were created, with appropriate names; and in the sachems who held these titles were vested the supreme powers of the confederacy. To secure order in the succession, and to determine the individuals entitled, the sachemships were made hereditary, under limited and peculiar laws of descent. The sachems themselves were equal in rank and authority, and instead of holding separate territorial jurisdictions, their powers were joint, and co-extensive with the League. As a safeguard against contention and fraud, each sachem was "raised up," and invested with his title by a council of all the sachems, with suitable forms and ceremonies. Until this ceremony of confirmation or investiture, no one could become a ruler. He received, when raised up, the name of the sachemship itself, as in the case of titles of nobility, and so also did his successors, from generation to generation. The sachemships were distributed unequally between the five nations, but without thereby giving to either a preponderance of political power. Nine of them were assigned to the Mohawk nation, nine to the Oneida, fourteen to the Onondaga, ten to the Cayuga and eight to the Seneca. The sachems, united, formed the Council of the League, the ruling body, in which resided the executive, legislative and judicial authority. It thus appears that the government of the Iroquois was an oligarchy, taking the term, at least, in the literal sense, "the rule of the few;" and, while more system is observable in this than in the oligarchies of antiquity, it seems, also, better calculated, in its framework, to resist political changes.

This specimen of Indian legislation is so remarkable, that a table of these sachemships, with their division into classes, indicating certain inter-relations, hereafter to be explained, is inserted in the Seneca dialect.

Titles or Sachemships of the Iroquois, founded at the institution of the League ; which have been borne by their Sachems in succession, from its formation to the present time.

GÄ-NE-Ä'-GA-O-NO, OR MOHAWK NATION.

I. 1. Da-gä-e'-o-gä.[1]   2. Hä-yo-went'-hä.[2]   3. Da-gä-no-we'-dä.[3]

II. 4. So-ä-e-wä'-ah.[4]   5. Da-yo'-ho-go.[5]   6. O-ä-ä'-go -wä.[6]

III. 7. Da-an-no-gä'-e-neh.[7]   8. Sä-da'-gä-e-wä-deh.[8]   9. Häs-dä-weh'-se-ont-hä.[9]

O-NA-YOTE'-KAH-O-NO, OR ONEIDA NATION.

I. 1. Ho-däs'-hä-teh.[10]   2. Ga-no-gweh'-yo-do.[11]   3. Da-yo-hä'-gwen-da.[12]

II. 4. So-no-sase'.[13]   5. To-no-ä-gä'-o.[14]   6. Hä-de-ä-dun-nent'-hä.[15]

III. 7. Da-wä-dä'-o-dä-yo.[16]   8. Gä-ne-ä-dus'-ha-yeh.[17]   9. Ho-wus'-hä-da-o.[18]

O-NUN-DAH'-GA-O-NO, OR ONONDAGA NATION.

I. 1. To-do-dä'-ho.[19]   2. To-nes'-sa-ah.   3. Da-ät-ga-dose.[20]

---

[1] This name signifies "Neutral, or the Shield."   [2] "Man who combs."   [3] "Endless."   [4] "Small speech."   [5] "At the forks."   [6] "At the great river."   [7] "Dragging his horns."   [8] "Even tempered."   [9] "Hanging up rattles." The Sachems of the first class belonged to the Turtle Tribe, of the second to the Wolf Tribe, and of the third to the Bear Tribe.

[10] "A man bearing a burden."   [11] "A man covered with cat tail down."   [12] "Opening through the woods."   [13] "A long string."   [14] "A man with a headache."   [15] "Swallowing himself."   [16] "Place of the echo."   [17] "War club on the ground."   [18] "A man steaming himself." The sachems of the first class in the Oneida nation belonged to the Wolf Tribe, of the second to the Turtle Tribe, and of the third to the Bear Tribe.

[19] "Tangled." This was the most dignified title in the list. It belonged to the Bear Tribe.   [20] "On the watch," Bear Tribe. This sachem and the one before him were hereditary counsellors of *To-do-dä'-ho.*

II. 4. Gä-neä-dä'-je-wake.[1] 5. Ah-wä'-ga-yat.[2] 6. Da-ä-yat'-gwä-e.

III. 7. Ho-no-we-nă'-to.[3]

IV. 8. Gä-wă-nă'-san-do.[4] 9. Hä-e'-ho.[5] 10. Ho-yo-ne-ä'-ne.[6] 11. Sa-dä'-quä-seh.[7]

V. 12. Sä-go-ga-hä'.[8] 13. Ho-sa-hä'-ho.[9] 14. Skä-no'-wun-de.[10]

GUE'-U-GWEH-O-NO, OR CAYUGA NATION.

I. 1. Da-gä'-ă-yo.[1] 2. Da-je-no'-dä-weh-o. 3. Gä-dä'-gwä'-sa. 4. So-yo-wase'. 5. Hä-de-äs'-yo-no.

II. 6. Da-yo-o-yo'-go. 7. Jote-ho-weh'-ko.[12] 8. De-ä-wate'-ho.

III. 9. To-dä-e-ho'. 10. Des-gä'-heh.

NUN-DA-WAH'-O-NO, OR SENECA NATION.

I. 1. Gä-ne-o-di'yo.[13] 2. Sä-dä-gä'-o-yase.[14]

II. 3. Ga-no-gi'-e.[15] 4. Sä-geh'-jo-wä.[16]

III. 5. Sä-de-a-no'-wus.[17] 6. Nis-hä-ne-a'-nent.[18]

IV. 7. Gä-no-go-e-dä'-we.[19] 8. Do-ne-ho-gä'-weh.[20]

These titles or names were hereditary in the several tribes of which each nation was composed. When an individual was made a sachem, upon the

---

[1] This word signifies "bitter body." The title belonged to the Snipe Tribe. [2] Turtle Tribe. [3] This sachem was the hereditary keeper of the Wampum, Wolf Tribe. [4] Deer Tribe. [5] Deer Tribe. [6] Turtle Tribe. [7] Bear Tribe. [8] Signifies "Having a glimpse," Deer Tribe. [9] "Large mouth," Turtle Tribe. [10] "Over the creek," Turtle Tribe.

[11] "Man frightened." [12] "Very cold." The tribes of the Cayuga sachems were as follows: 1 Deer, 2 Heron, 3 and 4 Bear, 5 and 7 Turtle, 8 Heron, 9 and 10 Snipe. [13] "Handsome lake," Turtle Tribe. [14] "Level heavens," Snipe Tribe. [15] Turtle Tribe. [16] "Great forehead," Hawk Tribe. [17] "Assistant," Bear Tribe. [18] "Falling day," Snipe Tribe. [19] "Hair burned off," Snipe Tribe. [20] "Open door," Wolf Tribe.

death or deposition of one of the fifty, his name was "taken away," and the name of the sachemship held by his predecessor was conferred upon him. Thus, upon the demise of the Seneca sachem, who held the title *Gä-ne-o-di'-yo*, a successor would be raised up from the Turtle tribe, in which the sachemship was hereditary, and after the ceremony of investiture, the person would be known among the Iroquois only under the name of *Gä-ne-o-di'-yo*. These fifty titles, excepting two, have been held by as many sachems, in succession, as generations have passed away since the formation of the League.

The Onondaga nation, being situated in a central position, were made the keepers both of the Council Brand, and of the Wampum, in which the structure and principles of their government, and their laws and treaties were recorded. At stated periods, usually in the autumn of each year, the sachems of the League assembled in council at Onondaga, which was in effect the seat of government, to legislate for the common welfare. Exigencies of a public or domestic character often led to the summoning of this council at extraordinary seasons, but the place was not confined to Onondaga. It could be appointed in the territory of either of the nations, under established usages. Originally the object of the general council was to raise up sachems to fill vacancies. In the course of time, as their intercourse with foreign nations became more important, it assumed the charge of all matters which concerned the League. It declared war and made peace,

sent and received embassies, entered into treaties
of alliance, regulated the affairs of subjugated nations, received new members into the League, extended its protection over feeble tribes, in a word,
took all needful measures to promote their prosperity, and enlarge their dominion.

Notwithstanding the equality of rights, privileges
and powers between the members of this body of
sachems, there were certain discriminations between
them, which rendered some more dignified than
others. The strongest illustration is found in the
Onondaga sachem, *To-do-dä'-ho*, who has always
been regarded as the most noble sachem of the
League. As an acknowledgment of his eminence,
two of the Onondaga sachems were assigned to him
as hereditary counsellors. The great respect and
deference paid by the Iroquois to this title, has led
to the vulgar error, that *To-do-dä'-ho* was the king
or civil head of the confederacy. He possessed, in
fact, no unusual or executive powers, no authority
which was not equally enjoyed by his compeers;
and when the light of tradition is introduced, to
clear up the apparent anomaly, it will be seen, that
the reverence of the people was rather for the title
itself, than for the person who held it, as it was one
of their illustrious names. At the establishment of
the League, an Onondaga by the name of *To-do-dä'-
ho* had rendered himself a potent ruler, by the force
of his military achievements. Tradition says that
he had conquered the Cayugas and the Senecas. It
represents his head as covered with tangled serpents,

and his look, when angry, as so terrible, that whoever looked upon him fell dead. It relates, that
when the League was formed, the snakes were
combed out of his hair by a Mohawk sachem, who
was hence named Hä-yo-went'-hä, "the man who
combs." *To-do-dä'-ho* was reluctant to consent to the
new order of things, as he would thereby be shorn
of his absolute power, and be placed among a number of equals. To remove these objections in some
measure, and to commemorate his magnanimity, the
first sachemship was named after him, and was dignified above the others by special marks of honor ;
but such, however, as were in perfect consistency
with an equal distribution of powers among all the
sachems as a body. Down to the present day,
among the Iroquois, this name is the personification
of heroism, of forecast, and of dignity of character;
and this title has ever been regarded as more illustrious than any other, in the catalogue of Iroquois
nobility.

To several other of these officers or names, particular duties were affixed at the institution of the
League. For example: the Senecas were made the
door-keepers of the Long House; and having im-
posed upon *Do-ne-ho-gä'-weh*, the eighth sachem, the
duty of watching the door, they gave to him a sub-
sachem, or assistant, to enable him to execute this
trust. This sub-sachem was raised up at the same
time with his superior, with the same forms and
ceremonies, and received the name or title which
was created simultaneously with that of the sachem-

ship. It was his duty to stand behind the sachem
on all public occasions, and to act as his runner or
attendant, as well as in the capacity of a counsellor.
Ho-no-wĕ-nă'-to, the Onondaga sachem who was
made the keeper of the wampum, had also a sub-
sachem, or assistant. Several other sachems, to
whom special responsibilities were confided, were
allowed sub-sachems, to enable them to fulfil their
duties, or perhaps as a mark of honor. All of these
special marks of distinction were consistent with
perfect equality among the sachems, as members of
one ruling body, in the administration of the affairs
of the League. When their method of legislating
is considered, this fact will appear with greater distinctness.

The several sachems, in whom, when united in
general council, resided the supreme powers of the
League, formed, when apart in their own territories,
the ruling bodies of their respective nations. When
assembled as the Council of the League, the power
of each sachem became co-extensive with the government, and direct relations were created between
all the people and each individual ruler; but when
the sachems of a nation were convened in council, all
its internal affairs fell under their immediate cognizance. For all purposes of a local and domestic,
and many of a political character, the nations were
entirely independent of each other. The nine Mohawk sachems administered the affairs of that nation with joint authority, precisely in the same
manner as they did, in connection with their col-

leagues, the affairs of the League at large. With similar powers, the ten Cayuga sachems regulated the domestic affairs of their nation.

As the sachems of each nation stood upon a perfect equality, in authority and privileges, the measure of influence was determined entirely by the talents and address of the individual. In the councils of the nation, which were of frequent occurrence, all business of national concernment was transacted; and, although the questions moved on such occasions would be finally settled by the opinions of the sachems, yet such was the spirit of the Iroquois system of government, that the influence of the inferior chiefs, the warriors, and even of the women would make itself felt, whenever the subject itself aroused a general public interest.

If we seek their warrant for the exercise of power in the etymology of the word *Ho-yar-na-go'-war*, by which the sachems were known as a class, it will be found to intimate a check upon, rather than an enlargement of their authority; for it signifies, simply, "counsellor of the people," a beautiful as well as appropriate designation of a ruler. But within their sphere of action, their powers were highly arbitrary in ancient times.

Next to the sachems, in position, stood the Chiefs, an inferior class of rulers, the very existence of whose office was an anomaly in the oligarchy of the Iroquois. Many years after the establishment of the League, even subsequent to the commencement of their intercourse with the whites, there arose a

necessity for raising up this class. It was an innovation upon the original frame-work of the confederacy, but it was demanded by circumstances which
could not be resisted. The office of chief *Hä-seh-
no-wä'-neh*, which is rendered "an elevated name,"
was made elective, and the reward of merit; but
without any power of descent, the title terminating
with the individual. No limit to the number was
established. The Senecas, still residing in New
York, number about 2,500, and exclusive of the
eight sachems, they have about seventy chiefs. At
first their powers were extremely limited, and confined to a participation in the local affairs of their
own nation, in the management of which they acted
as the counsellors and assistants of the sachems,
rather than in the capacity of rulers. But they
continued to increase in influence, with their multi-
plication in numbers, and to encroach upon the
powers of the sachems, until at the present time,
when the League is mostly dismembered, and their
internal organization has undergone some essential
changes, they have raised themselves to an equality,
in many respects, with the sachems themselves.
After their election, they were raised up by a council of the nation; but a ratification, by the general
council of the sachems, was necessary to complete
the investiture. The tenure of this office still continues the same.

The powers and duties of the sachems and chiefs
were entirely of a civil character, and confined, by
their organic laws, to the affairs of peace. No

sachem could go out to war in his official capacity, as a civil ruler. If disposed to take the war-path, he laid aside his civil office, for the time being, and became a common warrior. It becomes an important inquiry, therefore, to ascertain in whom the military power was vested. The Iroquois had no distinct class of war-chiefs, raised up and set apart to command in time of war; neither do the sachems or chiefs appear to have possessed the power of appointing such persons as they considered suitable to the post of command. All military operations were left entirely to private enterprise, and to the system of voluntary service, the sachems seeking rather to repress and restrain, than to encourage the martial ardor of the people. Their principal war-captains were to be found among the class called chiefs, many of whom were elected to this office in reward for their military achievements. The singular method of warfare among the Iroquois renders it extremely difficult to obtain a complete and satisfactory explanation of the manner in which their warlike operations were conducted. Their whole civil policy was averse to the concentration of power in the hands of any single individual, but inclined to the opposite principle of division among a number of equals; and this policy they carried into their military as well as through their civil organization. Small bands were, in the first instance, organized by individual leaders, each of which, if they were afterwards united upon the same enterprise, continued under its own captain, and the whole force, as well as the conduct of the expedition, was under their joint management. They appointed no one of their number to absolute command, but the general direction was left open to the strongest will, or the most persuasive voice.

As they were at war with all nations not in their actual alliance, it was lawful for any warrior to organize a party, and seek adventures wherever he pleased to direct his steps. Perhaps some chief, filled with martial ardor, planned an inroad upon the Cherokees of the south; and, having given a war-dance, and thus enlisted all who wished to share the glory of the adventure, took the war-path at once, upon his distant and perilous enterprise. In such ways as this, many expeditions originated; and it is believed that a great part of the warlike transactions of the Iroquois were nothing more than personal adventures, or the daring deeds of inconsiderable war-parties. Under such a state of things, a favorite leader, possessed of the confidence of the people from his warlike achievements, would be in no want of followers, in the midst of a general war; nor would the League be in any danger of losing the services of its most capable military commanders. To obviate the dangerous consequences of disagreement, when the several nations were prosecuting a common war, and their forces were united into one body, an expedient was resorted to for securing unanimity in their plans, in the establishment of two supreme military chieftaincies. The two chieftains who held these offices were designed rather to take the general supervision of the affairs of war, than the actual command in the field, although they were not debarred from assuming it, if they were disposed to do so. These war-chiefships were made hereditary, like the sachemships, and vacancies were filled in the same manner. When the Senecas, at the institution of the League, were made the door-keepers, these chieftaincies were assigned to them, for the reason, that being at the door, they would first take the war-path to drive back the invader. The first of these was named *Ta-wan'-ne-ars*,[1] "needle breaker," and the title made hereditary in the Wolf tribe; the second was named *So-no'-so-wä*, "great oyster shell," and the office assigned to the Turtle tribe. To these high chieftains, as the Iroquois now affirm, was intrusted the supreme command of the forces of the League, and the general management of its military affairs.

During the Revolution, Tä-yen-dä-na-ga, Joseph Brant, commanded the war-parties of the Mohawks; and, from his conspicuous position and the high confidence reposed in him, rather than from any claim advanced by himself, the title of military chieftain of the League has been conceded to him by some writers. But this is entirely a mistake, or rather, a false assertion, which is expressly contradicted by all of the Iroquois nations, including the Mohawks themselves.

It is, perhaps, in itself singular, that no religious

---

[1] Governor Blacksnake, who now resides upon the Allegany reserva- tion, and is upwards of a hundred years of age, now holds this title.

functionaries were recognized in the League. This is shown by the fact, that none were ever raised up by the general council of sachems, to fill a sacerdotal office. There was, however, a class in each nation, styled *Ho-nun-de'-unt*, "keepers of the faith," who were regularly appointed to officiate at their festivals, and to take the general supervision of their religious affairs.

With the officers above enumerated, the administration of the League was intrusted. The congress of sachems took the charge of all those matters which pertained to the public welfare. With them resided the executive, legislative and judicial authority, so far as they were not possessed by the people; although their powers in many things appear to have been rather advisory than executive. The chiefs, from counsellors and intermediaries between the sachems and the people, increased in influence, until they became rulers with the sachems themselves, thus widening and liberalizing the oligarchy. In all matters of war, the power appears to have resided chiefly with the people, and its prosecution to have been left to private adventure. If several bands united, they had as many generals as bands, who governed their proceedings by a council, in which, as in civil affairs, unanimity was a fundamental law. The two high military chieftains had rather the planning and general management of the campaign, than the actual conduct of the forces. Running through their whole system of administration, was a public sentiment, which gave its own tendency to affairs, and illustrated to a remarkable degree, that the government rested upon the popular will, and not upon the arbitrary sway of chiefs.

From whatever point the general features of the League are scrutinized, it must be regarded as a beautiful, as well as a remarkable structure—the triumph of Indian legislation. When the possessions of the Iroquois were enlarged by conquest followed by occupation, it was an expansion, and not a dismemberment of the confederacy, one of its leading objects being the absorption of contiguous nations. To the Eries and to the Neuter nation, according to tradition, the Iroquois offered the alternative of admission into the League, or extermination; and the strangeness of this proposition will disappear, when it is remembered, than an Indian nation regards itself as at war with all others not in actual alliance. Peace itself was one of the ultimate objects aimed at by the founders of this Indian oligarchy, to be secured by the admission, or subjugation of surrounding nations. In their progressive course, their empire enlarged, until they had stretched their chain around the half of our republic, and rendered their names a terror from the hills of New England to the deepest seclusions upon the Mississippi; when the advent of another race arrested their career, and prepared the way for the gradual extinguishment of their councilfires, and the desolation of the Long House.

With a mere confederacy of Indian nations, the constant tendency would be to a rupture, from remoteness of position and interest, and from the inherent weakness of such a compact. In the case under consideration, something more lasting was aimed at, than a simple union of the five nations, in the nature of an alliance. A blending of the national sovereignties into one government, was sought for and achieved by these forest statesmen. The League made the *Ho-dé-no-sau-nee* one people, with one government, one system of institutions, one executive will. Yet the powers of the government were not so entirely centralized, that the national independencies disappeared. This was very far from the fact. The crowning feature of the League, as a political structure, was the perfect independence and individuality of the national sovereignties, in the midst of a central and embracing government, which presented such a cemented exterior, that its subdivisions would scarcely have been discovered in the general transactions of the League.

How these ends were attained we have yet to examine.

The government sat lightly upon the people, who, in effect, were governed but little. It secured to each that individual independence, which the *Ho-dé-no-sau-nee* knew how to prize as well as the Saxon race; and which, amid all their political changes, they have continued to preserve.

Social

CHAPTER IV.

Division into Tribes. — Family Relationships. — Descent in the Female Line. — Degrees of Consanguinity. — Succession of Sachems. — Names. — Nature of a Tribe. — Equality of the Nations. — National Epithets. — Office of Chief Elective. — Distinguished Men were Chiefs. — Stability of the Oligarchy.

The division of a people into tribes is the most simple organization of society. Each tribe being in the nature of a family, the ties of relationship which bind its individual members together are indispensable, until they are rendered unnecessary by the adoption of a form of government, and the substitution of other ties, which answer the same ends of protection and security.

When a people have long remained in the tribal state, it becomes extremely difficult to remove all traces of such organic divisions by the substitution of new institutions. In the tribes of the Jews, this position is illustrated. Among the Greeks also, especially the Athenians, the traces of their original divisions never entirely disappeared. Solon substituted classes for tribes, but subsequently Cleisthenes restored the tribes, retaining however the classes, and increased the number; thus perpetuating this early social organization of the Athenians among their civil institutions. The Athenian tribe was a group of families, with subdivisions; the Roman tribes, established by Romulus, the same. On the other hand, the Jewish tribes embraced only the lineal descendants of a common father; and its individual members being of consanguinity, the tribe itself was essentially different from the Grecian. The Iroquois tribe was unlike them all. It was not a group of families; neither was it made up of the descendants of a common father, as the father and his child were never of the same tribe. In the sequel, however, it will be discovered to be nearest the Jewish; differing from it, as from all other similar institutions of the old world, chiefly in this, that descent followed, in all cases, the female line.

The founders of the Iroquois Confederacy did not seek to suspend the tribal divisions of the people, to introduce a different social organization; but on the contrary, they rested the League itself upon the tribes, and through them, sought to interweave the race into one political family. A careful exploration of those tribal relationships which characterize the political system of the Iroquois, becomes, therefore, of importance. Without such knowledge as this will afford, their government itself is wholly unmeaning and inexplicable.

In each nation there were eight tribes, which were arranged in two divisions, and named as follows:

| Wolf, | Bear, | Beaver, | Turtle. |
| Deer, | Snipe, | Heron, | Hawk. |

These are common to all latitudes between Louisiana and Montreal, and hence in themselves are incapable of throwing any light upon the land, or locality in which the race originated.[1] These names had doubtless an emblematical signification, which reached beyond the object itself. Of the origin of their tribal divisions but little is known, and to it, perhaps, but little importance attaches. Tradition declares that the Bear and the Deer were the original tribes, and that the residue were subdivisions. Evidence of the existence of seven of the tribes at the establishment of the Oligarchy, is furnished in the distribution of the Onondaga and Seneca sachemships. The fourteen assigned to the former nation were divided between the Wolf, Bear, Beaver, Turtle, Snipe and Deer tribes; while the eight belonging to the latter, were given to the Wolf, Bear, Turtle, Snipe and Hawk, to the exclusion of the others, if they then existed; and in these several tribes they were made perpetually hereditary.

[1] Table exhibiting the scientific names of the animals adopted by the Iroquois as the emblems of their respective tribes. It follows the classification employed in the Nat. History of New York. The species have been determined from careful descriptions obtained of the Senecas.

Animal.	Seneca Name.	Order.	Family.	Genus.	Species.
Wolf.	Tor-yoh'-ne.	Carnivora.	Canidæ.	Lupus.	Occidentalis.
Bear.	Ne-o-ar'-gu-ye.	Carnivora.	Ursidæ.	Ursus.	Americanus.
Beaver.	Non-gar-ne'-e-ar-goh.	Rodentia.	Castoridæ.	Castor.	Fiber.
Turtle.	Gä-ne-e-ar-teh-go'-wä.	Chelonia.	Chelonidæ.	Chelonura.	Serpentina.
Deer.	Nä-o'-geh.	Ungulata.	Cervidæ.	Cervus.	Virginianus.
Snipe.	Doo-ese-doo-we'.	Grallæ.	Scolopacidæ.	Totanus.	Semipalmatus.
Heron.	Jo-äs'-seh.	Grallæ.	Ardeidæ.	Ardea.	Candidissima.
Hawk.	Os-sweh-gä-dä-gä'-ah.	Accipitres.	Falconidæ.	Falco.	Columbarius.

NOTE. Some doubt rests upon the Heron and the Snipe concerning the species. In the former case the choice lies between the Ardea Candidissima, and the Ardea Leuce. In the latter, the large number of the species introduces a difficulty. The Semipalmatus corresponds most nearly with the description of the bird.

The division of the people of each nation into eight tribes, whether pre-existing, or perfected at the establishment of the Confederacy, did not terminate in its objects with the nation itself.[1] It became the means of effecting the most perfect union of separate nations " ever devised by the wit of man." In effect, the Wolf tribe was divided into five parts, and one fifth of it placed in each of the five nations. The remaining tribes were subjected to the same division and distribution. Between those of the same name—or in other words, between the separated parts of each tribe—there existed a tie of brotherhood, which linked the nations together with indissoluble bonds. The Mohawk of the Wolf tribe recognized the Seneca of the Wolf tribe as his brother, and they were bound to each other by the ties of consanguinity. In like manner the Oneida of the Turtle or other tribe received the Cayuga or Onondaga of the same tribe, as a brother, and with a fraternal welcome. This relationship was not ideal, but was founded upon actual consanguinity. In the eyes of an Iroquois, every member of his own tribe, in whatever nation, was as much his brother or his sister as if children

[1] The Senecas had eight tribes, the Cayugas eight, the Tuscaroras seven, the Onondagas eight, the Oneidas three, and the Mohawks three. The descendants of the ancient Oneidas and Mohawks affirm that their ancestors never had but three tribes, the Wolf, Bear and Turtle. On old treaties with these nations now in the State Department, these titles appear as their only social divisions. But by the original laws of the League, neither of these tribes could intermarry. Hence there appears to have been a necessity for the existence originally of the remaining tribes, or some of them, to admit of the verity of this law in relation to marriage.

of the same mother. This cross-relationship between
the tribes of the same name, and which was stronger,
if possible, than the chain of brotherhood between the
several tribes of the same nation, is still preserved in
all its original strength. It doubtless furnishes the
chief reason of the tenacity with which the fragments
of the League still cling together. If either of the five
nations had wished to cast off the alliance, it must
also have broken this bond of brotherhood. Had
the nations fallen into collision, it would have turned Hawk tribe against Hawk tribe, Heron against
Heron, brother against brother. The history of the
Ho-dé'-no-sau-nee exhibits the wisdom of these organic provisions; for, during the long period through
which the League subsisted, they never fell into anarchy, nor even approximated to dissolution from
internal disorders.

With the progress of the inquiry, it becomes
more apparent that the Confederacy was in effect a
League of Tribes. With the ties of kindred as its
principle of union, the whole race was interwoven
into one great family, composed of tribes in its first
subdivision, (for the nations were counterparts of
each other;) and the tribes themselves, in their
subdivisions, composed of parts of many households.
Without these close inter-relations, resting, as many
of them do, upon the strong impulses of nature, a
mere alliance between the Iroquois nations would
have been feeble and transitory.

In this manner was constructed the *League* of the
Ho-dé'-no-sau-nee, in itself an extraordinary speci-

men of Indian legislation. Simple in its foundation upon the family relationships, effective in the lasting vigor inherent in the ties of kindred, and perfect in its success, in achieving a permanent and harmonious union of the nations, it forms an enduring monument to that proud and progressive race, who reared under its protection a wide-spread Indian sovereignty.

All the institutions of the Iroquois have regard to the division of the people into tribes. Originally with reference to marriage, the Wolf, Bear, Beaver, and Turtle tribes, being brothers to each other, were not allowed to intermarry. The four opposite tribes, being also brothers to each other, were likewise prohibited from intermarrying. Either of the first four tribes, however, could intermarry with either of the last four, the relation between them being that of cousins. Thus Hawk could intermarry with Bear or Beaver, Heron with Turtle; but not Beaver and Turtle, nor Deer and Deer. Whoever violated these laws of marriage incurred the deepest detestation and disgrace. In process of time, however, the rigor of the system was relaxed, until finally the prohibition was confined to the tribe of the individual, which, among the residue of the Iroquois, is still religiously observed. They can now marry into any tribe but their own. Under the original as well as modern regulation, the husband and wife were of different tribes. The children always followed the tribe of the mother.

As the whole Iroquois system rested upon the

tribes as an organic division of the people, it was very natural that the separate rights of each should be jealously guarded. Not the least remarkable among their institutions, was that which confined the transmission of all titles, rights and property in the female line to the exclusion of the male. It is strangely unlike the canons of descent adopted by civilized nations, but it secured several important objects. If the Deer tribe of the Cayugas, for example, received a sachemship at the original distribution of these offices, the descent of such title being limited to the female line, it could never pass out of the tribe. It thus became instrumental in giving to the tribe individuality. A still more marked result, and perhaps a leading object of this enactment was the perpetual disinheritance of the son. Being of the tribe of his mother formed an impassable barrier against him; and he could neither succeed his father as a sachem, nor inherit from him even his medal, or his tomahawk. The inheritance, for the protection of tribal rights, was thus directed from the lineal descendants of the sachem, to his brothers, or his sisters' children, or, under certain circumstances, to some individual of the tribe at large; each and all of whom were in his tribe, while his children, being in another tribe, as before remarked, were placed out of the line of succession.

By the operation of this principle, also, the certainty of descent in the tribe, of their principal chiefs, was secured by a rule infallible; for the child must be the son of its mother, although not necessarily of its mother's husband. If the purity of blood be of any moment, the lawgivers of the Iroquois established the only certain rule the case admits of, whereby the assurance might be enjoyed that the ruling sachem was of the same family or tribe with the first taker of the title.

The Iroquois mode of computing degrees of consanguinity was unlike that of the civil or canon law; but was yet a clear and definite system. No distinction was made between the lineal and collateral lines, either in the ascending or descending series. To understand this subject, it must be borne in mind, that of the grandparents one only, the maternal grandmother, necessarily was, and of the parents only the mother, and, in the descending line, only the sisters' children could be of the same tribe with the propositus, or individual from whom the degrees of relationship were reckoned. By careful attention to this rule, the reasons of the following relationships will be readily perceived. The maternal grandmother and her sisters were equally grandmothers; the mother and her sisters were equally mothers; the children of a mother's sisters were brothers and sisters; the children of a sister were nephews and nieces; and the grandchildren of a sister were his grandchildren. These were the chief relatives within the tribe, though not fully extended as to number. Out of the tribe, the paternal grandfather and his brothers were equally grandfathers; the father and his brothers equally fathers; the father's sisters were aunts, while, in the tribe, the mother's brothers were uncles; 'the father's sister's children were cousins as in the civil law; the children of these cousins were nephews and nieces, and the children of these nephews and nieces were his grandchildren, or the grandchildren of the propositus. Again: the children of a brother were his children, and the grandchildren of a brother were his grandchildren; also, the children of a father's brother were his brothers and sisters, instead of cousins, as under the civil law; and lastly, their children were his grandchildren.

It was the leading object of the Iroquois law of descent, to merge the collateral in the lineal line, as sufficiently appears in the above outline. By the civil law, every departure from the common ancestor in the descending series, removed the collateral from the lineal; while, by the law under consideration, the two lines were finally brought into one.[1] Under the civil law mode of computation, the degrees of relationship become too remote to be traced among collaterals; while, by the mode of the Iroquois, none of the collaterals were lost by remoteness of degree. The number of those linked together by the nearer family ties was largely multi-

---

[1] The following are the names of the several degrees of relationship recognized among the *Ho-de'-no-sau-nee*, in the language of the Senecas:—

Hoc-sote',	Grandfather.
Uc-sote',	Grandmother.
Hä'-nih,	Father.
Noh-yeh',	Mother.
Ho-ah'-wuk,	Son.
Go-ah'-wuk,	Daughter.
Kä-yä'-dä,	Grandchildren.

Hoc-no'-seh,	Uncle.
Ah-geh'-huc,	Aunt.
Hä-yan-wän-deh',	Nephew.
Kä-yan-wän-deh',	Niece.
Dä-ya-gwä -dan-no-dä,	Brothers and Sisters.
Ah-gare'-seh,	Cousin.

plied by preventing, in this manner, the subdivision of a family into collateral branches. These relationships, so novel and original, did not exist simply in theory, but were actual, and of constant recognition, and lay at the foundation of their political, as well as social organization.

The succession of the rulers of the League is one of the most intricate subjects to be met with in the political system of the Iroquois. It has been so difficult to procure a satisfactory exposition of the enactments by which the mode of succession was regulated, that the sachemships have sometimes been considered elective, at others as hereditary. Many of the obstacles which beset the inquiry are removed by the single fact, that the title of sachem was absolutely hereditary in the tribe to which it was originally assigned, and could never pass out of it, but with its extinction. How far these titles were hereditary in that part of the family of the sachem who were of the same tribe with himself, becomes the true question to consider. The sachem's brothers, and the sons of his sisters were of his tribe, and, consequently, in the line of succession. Between a brother and a nephew of the deceased, there was no law which established a preference; neither between several brothers, on the one hand, and sons of several sisters on the other, was there any law of primogeniture; nor, finally, was there any positive law, that the choice should be confined to the brothers of the deceased ruler, and the descendants of his sisters in the female line, until all these should fail, before a selection could be made from the tribe at large.   Hence, it appears, so far as positive enactments were concerned, that the office of sachem was hereditary in the particular tribe in which it ran; while it was elective, as between the male members of the tribe itself.[1]

In the absence of laws, designating with certainty the individual upon whom the inheritance should fall, custom would come in and assume the force of law, in directing the manner of choice, from among a number equally eligible.   Upon the decease of a sachem, a tribal council assembled to determine upon his successor.   The choice usually fell upon a son of one of the deceased ruler's sisters, or upon one of his brothers—in the absence of physical and moral objections; and this preference of one of his near relatives would be suggested by feelings of respect for his memory.   Infancy was no obstacle, it involving only the necessity of setting over the infant a guardian, to discharge the duties of a sachem until he attained a suitable age.   It sometimes occurred that all the relatives of the deceased were set aside, and a selection was made from the tribe generally; but it seldom thus happened, unless from the great unfitness of the near relatives of the deceased.

[1] Laws of succession somewhat similar existed among the Aztecs. "The sovereign was selected from the brothers of the deceased prince, or, in default of them, from his nephews, thus the election was always restricted to the same family.   *   *   *   The scheme of election, however defective, argues a more refined and calculating policy than was to have been expected from a barbarous nation."— Prescott's Conquest of Mexico, vol. i. p. 23.

When the individual was finally determined, the nation summoned a council, in the name of the deceased, of all the sachems of the League; and the new sachem was raised up by such council, and invested with his office.

In connection with the power of the tribes to designate the sachems, should be noticed the equal power of deposition. If, by misconduct, a sachem lost the confidence and respect of his tribe, and became unworthy of authority, a tribal council at once deposed him; and, having selected a successor, summoned a council of the League to perform the ceremony of his investiture.

Still further to illustrate the characteristics of the tribes of the Iroquois, some reference to their mode of bestowing names would not be inapt.[1] Soon after the birth of an infant, the near relatives of the same tribe selected a name. At the first subsequent council of the nation, the birth and name were publicly announced, together with the name and tribe of the father, and the name and tribe of the mother. In each nation the proper names were so strongly marked by a tribal peculiarity, that the tribe of the individual could usually be determined from the name alone. Making, as they did, a part of their language, they were all significant. When an individual was raised up as a sachem, his original name was laid aside, and that of the sachemship

[1] Like the ancient Saxons, the Iroquois had neither a prenomen, nor a cognomen; but contented themselves with a single name. The name of an individual was often changed at different periods of life, as when the youth became a warrior; and again, at the approach of age.

itself assumed.   In like manner, at the raising
up of a chief, the council of the nation which performed the ceremony, took away the former name
of the incipient chief and assigned him a new one,
perhaps, like Napoleon's titles, commemorative of
the event which led to its bestowment.   Thus, when
the celebrated Red-Jacket was elevated by election
to the dignity of a chief, his original name, *O-te-ti-*
än'-i, "always ready," was taken from him, and in
its place was bestowed *Sä-go-ye-wät'-hä*, "keeper
awake," in allusion to the powers of his eloquence.

Each tribe in the nation thus formed a species of
separate community.   The members were all of
consanguinity, and their relationships easily traced.
In like manner those of the same tribe in each of
the other nations were their consanguinii, and their
relationships, near and remote, were also traceable.
As two tribes were necessarily joined in each
family, there was a perfect diffusion of tribes
throughout the nation, and throughout the League.
In this manner the race of the Iroquois, although
consisting of different nations, was blended into
one people.   The League was in effect established,
and rested for its stability, upon the natural faith
of kindred.

It now remains to define a tribe of the *Ho-de'-no-*
sau-nee.   From the preceding considerations it sufficiently appears, that it was not, like the Grecian
and Roman, a circle or group of families ; for two
tribes were necessarily represented in every family ;
neither, like the Jewish, was it constituted of the

lineal descendants of a common father; on the contrary, it distinctly involved the idea of descent from a common mother; nor has it any resemblance to the Scottish clan, or the Canton of the Switzer. In the formation of an Iroquois tribe, a portion was taken from many households, and bound together by a tribal bond.

The wife, her children, and her descendants in the female line, would, in perpetuity, be linked with the destinies of her own tribe; while the husband, his brothers and sisters, and the descendants of the latter, in the female line, would, in like manner, be united to another tribe, and held by its affinities. Herein was a bond of union between the several tribes of the same nation, corresponding, in some degree, with the cross-relationship founded upon consanguinity, which bound together the tribes of the same emblem in the different nations.

The Iroquois claim to have originated the idea of a division of the people into tribes, as a means of creating new relationships by which to bind the people more firmly together. It is further asserted by them, that they forced, or introduced this social organization among the Cherokees, the Chippeways, (Massasaugas) and several other Indian nations, with whom, in ancient times, they were in constant intercourse. The fact that this division of the people of the same nation into tribes does not prevail generally among our Indian races, favors the assertion of the Iroquois. On the other hand, the laws of descent, at least of the crown, among the Aztecs,

dimly shadows forth the existence of a similar social organization, which may have been reproduced
among the Iroquois, or preserved through a remote
affinity of blood.   At all events, it was the life and
strength of the League.

Of the comparative value of these institutions,
when contrasted with those of civilized countries,
and of their capability of elevating the race, it is
not necessary here to inquire.   It was the boast of
the Iroquois that the great object of their confederacy was peace—to break up the spirit of perpetual warfare, which had wasted the red race from
age to age.   Such an insight into the true end of all
legitimate government, by those who constructed this
tribal league, excites as great surprise as admiration.
It is the highest and the noblest aspect in which
human institutions can be viewed; and the thought
itself—universal peace among Indian races possible
of attainment—was a ray of intellect from no ordinary mind.   To consummate such a purpose, the
Iroquois nations were to be concentrated into one
political fraternity; and in a manner effectively to
prevent offshoots and secessions.   By its natural
growth, this fraternity would accumulate sufficient
power to absorb adjacent nations, moulding them,
successively, by affiliation, into one common family.
Thus, in its nature, it was designed to be a progressive confederacy.   What means could have been
employed with greater promise of success than the
stupendous system of relationships, which was
fabricated through the division of the *Ho-dé'-no-*

sau-nee into tribes? It was a system sufficiently
ample to enfold the whole Indian race. Unlimited
in their capacity for extension, inflexible in their
relationships, the tribes thus interleagued would
have suffered no loss of unity by their enlargement,
nor loss of strength by the increasing distance between their council-fires. The destiny of this
League, if it had been left to work out its own results among the red races exclusively, it is impossible to conjecture. With vast capacities for enlargement, and remarkable durability of structure,
it must have attained a great elevation, and a
general supremacy.

It is apparent from the examination of such evidences as can be discovered, that the several Iroquois nations occupied positions of entire equality
in the League, in rights, privileges and obligations.
Such special immunities as were granted to either,
must be put down to the chances of location, and
to the numerical differences at the institution of the
Confederacy; since they neither indicate an intention to establish an unequal alliance, nor exhibit the
exercise of privileges by either nation, inconsistent
with the principle of political equality, on which
the League was founded.

The sources of information, from which this conclusion is drawn, are to be found in the mass of Iroquois traditions, and in the structure of the Confederacy itself. Those traditions which reach beyond the formation of the League, are vague and
unreliable, while all such as refer to its establish-

ment assume a connected and distinctive form. It
follows that confidence may be reposed in such in-
ferences as are derived from these traditions, and
corroborated by the internal structure of the government, and by the institutions of the League.

There were provisions apparently vesting in certain nations superior authority, which it is desirable
to introduce and explain. The most prominent was
the unequal distribution of sachemships, indicating
an unequal distribution of power: the Onondagas,
for example, having fourteen sachems, while the
Senecas, by far the most powerful nation in the Confederacy, were entitled to but eight. It is true,
ceteris paribus, that a larger body of sachems would
exercise a greater influence in general council; but
it will appear, when the mode of deciding questions
is considered, that it gave no increase of power, for
each nation had an equal voice, and a negative upon
the others.

By another organic provision, the custody of the
" Council Brand," and also of the " Wampum," into
which the laws of the League "had been talked,"
was given by hereditary grant to the Onondagas.
This is sufficiently explained by their central position, which made the council-fire in the Onondaga
valley, in effect, the seat of government of the
League. It was equally a convenience to all, and
does not necessarily involve a preference enforced
by superior power.

The *To-do-dä'-ho* was likewise among the Onondaga sachems. Upon this point, it has heretofore

been stated, that the higher degree of consideration attached to this title resulted exclusively from the exalted estimation in which the original *To-do-dä'-ho* was held, on account of his martial prowess and achievements.

An apparent inequality between the nations of the League is also observable in the award of the two highest military chieftains to the Senecas. It will be sufficient, on this difficult feature in the system of the Iroquois, to note, that when they constructed their political edifice, the Long House, with its door opening upon the west, they admitted the supposition that all hostile onsets were to be expected from that direction; and on placing the Senecas as a perpetual shield before its western portal, these war-captains were granted, as among the means needful for its protection.

The Mohawks were receivers of tribute from subjugated nations. This hereditary privilege must be placed upon the same footing with the preceding. It may, perhaps, indicate that the nations upon their borders were in subjection.

Unequal terms in a Confederacy of independent nations would not be expected. True wisdom would dictate the principle of equality, as the only certain foundation on which a durable structure could be erected. That such was the principle adopted by the legislators of the Iroquois, is evinced by the equality of rights and immunities subsisting between the sachems of the League. Their authority was not limited to their own nation, but was co-extensive with the Confederacy.   The Cayuga sachem, while in the midst of the Oneidas, could enforce from them the same obedience that was due to him from his own people; and when in general council with his compeers, he had an equal voice in the disposal of all business which came before it.   The special privileges enumerated, and some others which existed, were of but little moment, when compared with the fact that the nations were independent, and that each had an equal participation in the administration of the government.

At the epoch of the League, the several nations occupied the territory between the Hudson and the Genesee, and were separated by much the same internal boundaries, as at the period when they yielded up their sovereignty.   From geographical position, or from relative importance, or yet, for the mere purpose of establishing between the nations relationships similar to those existing between the tribes, certain rules of precedence, and national ties, were constituted between them.   The nations were divided into two classes, or divisions; and when assembled in general council were arranged upon opposite sides of the " council-fire."   On the one side stood the Mohawks, Onondagas and Senecas, who, as nations, were regarded as brothers to each other, but as fathers to the other nations.   Upon the other side were the Oneidas and Cayugas, and at a subsequent day, the Tuscaroras, who, in like manner, were brother nations to each other, but children to the first three.   These divisions were in harmony

with their system of relationships, or more properly
formed a part of it. They may have secured for the
senior nations increased respect, but they involved
no idea of dependence in the junior, or inequality
in civil rights.

When the nations were enumerated, the Mohawks
were placed first, but for what reason is not precisely understood. In the councils of the Confederacy they were styled *Da-gä-e-o'-gä*, which became
their national epithet. It was a term of respect,
and signifies " neutral," or, as it may be rendered,
" the shield." Its origin is lost in obscurity.

The Onondagas were placed next in the order
of precedence, and were addressed in council by the
appellation *Ho-de'-san-no-ge-tä*. This term signifies
" name-bearer," and was conferred in commemora-
tion of the circumstance, that the Onondagas bestowed the names upon the fifty original sachems.
This was a privilege of some moment, as these
" names" were to descend from generation to generation, upon the successive rulers of the *Ho-de'-no-
sau-nee.*

Next in order stood the Senecas, justly proud of
their national designation, *Ho-nan-ne-ho'-ont*, or
" the door-keeper." To them, as elsewhere remarked, belonged the hereditary guardianship of the
door of the Long House.

The Oneidas occupied the fourth place in the Iroquois order of precedence, and originally had no
appellation by which they were distinguished. At
a subsequent and quite modern period, the epithet

Ne-ar-de-on-dar-go'-war, or " Great Tree," was conferred upon them by their confederates. This name was
seized upon from some occurrence at a treaty with
the people of *Wastow*, or Boston.

Of the five original nations, the Cayugas were
placed last in the enumeration. They were designated in council by the appellation, *So-nus'-ho-gwä-
to-war*, signifying " Great Pipe." Tradition refers
this epithet to the incident, that the leading Cayuga
chief in attendance at the council which established
the League smoked a pipe of unusual dimensions
and workmanship.

The admission of the Tuscaroras having been
long subsequent to the formation of the League,
they were never received into an equal alliance with
the other nations. After their disastrous overthrow,
and expulsion from North Carolina, they turned towards the country of the Iroquois, and were admitted about the year 1715, as the sixth nation, into
the Confederacy. But they were never allowed to
have a sachem, who could sit as an equal in the
council of sachems. The five nations were unwilling to enlarge the number of sachemships founded
at the institution of the League. For purposes of
national government, however, they were organized
like the other nations, with similar tribes, relationships, laws and institutions. They also enjoyed a
nominal equality in the councils of the League, by
the courtesy of the other five, and their sachems
were " raised up" with the same ceremonies. They
were not dependent, but were admitted to as full

equality as could be granted them, without enlarging the frame-work of the Confederacy. In the councils of the League, they had no national designation.

At the establishment of the Confederacy, the office of chief, *Hä-seh-no-wä'-neh*, " an elevated name," was entirely unknown among the Iroquois. Their traditions, as elsewhere stated, affirm that this title was instituted long subsequent to the foundation of the fifty sachemships, and the full adjustment of the League. The necessity in which this office had its origin, and the illustration which it furnishes of a position elsewhere advanced, that all political institutions, as they unfold, progress from monarchy towards democracy, leads to the presentation of this subject in this place.

When the power of the *Ho-de'-no-sau-nee* began to develop, under the new system of oligarchies within an oligarchy, there sprang up around the sachems a class of warriors, distinguished for enterprise upon the war-path, and eloquence in council, who demanded some participation in the administration of public affairs. The serious objections to the enlargement of the number of rulers, involving, as it did, changes in the frame-work of the government, for a long period enabled the sachems to resist the encroachment. In the progress of events, this class became too powerful to be withstood, and the sachems were compelled to raise them up in the subordinate station of chiefs. The title was purely elective, and the reward of merit. Unlike the sachemships, the name was not hereditary in the tribe or family of the individual, but terminated with the chief himself; unless subsequently bestowed by the tribe upon some other person, to preserve it as one of their illustrious names. These chiefs were originally invested with very limited powers; their principal office being that of advisers and counsellors of the sachems. Having thus obtained a foothold in the government, this class, to the number of which there was no limit, gradually enlarged their influence, and from generation to generation drew nearer to an equality with the sachems themselves.[1] By this innovation the government was liberalized, to the sensible diminution of the power of the sachems, which, at the institution of the League, was extremely arbitrary.

It is a singular fact, that none of the sachems of the Iroquois, save Logan,[2] have ever become distinguished in history; although each of the fifty titles or sachemships have been held by as many individuals, as generations have passed away since the foundation of the Confederacy. If the immortality of men, " worthy of praise," is committed to the guardianship of the Muse—

" Dignum laude virum Musa vetat mori,"

[1] At the present time among the dismembered fragments of the Iroquois nations, the chiefs are found to be nearly, if not in all respects, upon an equality with the sachems, although the offices are still held by different tenures.

[2] Logan was one of the ten Cayuga sachems, but which of the ten names or sachemships he held, is not at present ascertained. His father, Shikellimus or *Shikalimo*, who is usually mentioned as a Cayuga sachem, was but a chief.

—the muse of tradition, if such a conception may be indulged, has been enabled, out of this long line of sachems, to record the deeds of none, save the military achievements of the first *To-do-dä'-ho*, the wisdom in legislation of the first *Da-gä-no-we'-dä*,[1] and the sacred mission of *Gä-ne-o-di'-yo*, who pretended to have received a revelation from the Great Spirit. The residue have left behind them no remembrances conferring special dignity upon the sachemships entrusted to their keeping.

The celebrated orators, wise men, and military leaders of the *Ho-de'-no-sau-nee*, are all to be found in the class of chiefs. One reason for this may exist in the organic provision which confined the duties of the sachems exclusively to the affairs of peace; and another may be, that the office of chief was bestowed in reward of public services, thus casting it by necessity upon the men highest in capacity among them. In the list of those chiefs who have earned a place upon the historic page, as well as in the "unwritten remembrance" of their tribe and race, might be enumerated many who have left behind them a reputation, which will not soon fade from the minds of men.

[1] *Da-gä-no-we'-dä*, the founder of the confederacy, and *Hä-yo-went'-hä*, his speaker, through whom he laid his plans of government before the council which framed the League, were both "raised up" among the fifty original sachems, and in the Mohawk nation; but after their decease these two sachemships were left vacant, and have since continued so.

Da-gä-no-we'-dä was an Onondaga, but was adopted by the Mohawks, and raised up as one of their sachems. Having an impediment in his speech, he chose *Hä-yo-went'-hä* for his speaker. They were both unwilling to accept office, except upon the express condition, that their sachemships should ever remain vacant after their decease. These are the two most illustrious names among the Iroquois.

By the institution of this office, the stability of the government was increased rather than diminished. In their own figurative enunciation of the idea, the chiefs served as braces in the Long House—an apt expression of the place they occupied in their political structure. It furnished a position and a reward for the ambitious, and the means of allaying discontent, without changing the ruling body. In this particular, the oligarchy of the Iroquois appears to have enjoyed some superiority over those of antiquity.

"In aristocratical governments," says Montesquieu, "there are two principal sources of disorder: excessive inequality between the governors and the governed, and the same inequality between the different members of the body that governs."[1] The government of the *Ho-de'-no-sau-nee* was exposed to neither of these difficulties. Between the people and the sachems, the chiefs formed a connecting link; while the sachems themselves were perfectly equal in political privileges.

The unchangeable number of the rulers, and the stability of the tenure by which the office itself is held, are both sources of security in an oligarchy. To the former safeguard the Iroquois adhered so firmly, that upon the admission of the Tuscaroras, as the sixth nation of the League, they were unwilling to increase the original number of sachemships; and the Tuscaroras have not to this day a sachem who is admitted to all the privileges of a sachem of

---

[1] Montesquieu, Spirit of Laws, lib. v. cap. 8.

the Confederacy. The latter is established by the career of *Sä-go-ye-wät'-hä*, the most gifted and intellectual of the race of the Iroquois, and, perhaps, of the whole Indian family. With all the influence which he exercised over the people by the power of his eloquence, and with all the art and intrigue which his capacity could suggest, he was never able to elevate himself higher than to the title of Chief. To attain even this dignity, it is said that he practiced upon the superstitious fears of the people. The Senecas themselves aver, that it would have been unwise to raise up a man of his intellectual power and extended influence to the office of sachem; as it would have concentrated in his hands too much authority. Nearly the same observations apply to the celebrated Joseph Brant, *Tä-yen-dä-na'-ga*, whose abilities as a military leader secured to him the command of the war parties of the Mohawks during the Revolution. He was also but a chief, and held no other office or title in the nation, or in the Confederacy. By the force of his character, he acquired the same influence over the Mohawks which *Sä-go-ye-wät'-hä* maintained over the Senecas by his eloquence. The lives of these distinguished chiefs, both equally ambitious, but who pursued very different pathways to distinction, sufficiently prove, that the office of sachem was surrounded by impassable barriers against those who were without the immediate family of the sachem, and the tribe in which the title was hereditary.

CHAPTER V.

In an oligarchy, where the administrative power is vested in the members of the Ruling Body jointly, a Council of the Oligarchs becomes the instrumentality through which the will of this body is ascertained and enforced. For this reason the Councils of the Iroquois are important subjects of investigation. By them were exercised all the legislative and executive authority incident to the League, and necessary for its security against outward attack and internal dissensions. When the sachems were not assembled around the general council-fire, the government itself had no visible existence. Upon no point, therefore, can an examination be better directed, to ascertain the degree of power vested in the Ruling Body, and the manner in which their domestic administration, and political relations were conducted. When the sachems were scattered, like the people, over a large territory, they exercised a local and individual authority in the matters of every-day life, or in national council jointly adjusted the affairs of their respective nations. Those higher

washed
power.

AH-SO-QUA-TA.

PIPES

and more important concernments, which involved the interests of the League, were reserved to the sachems in general council. In this council resided the animating principle, by which their political machinery was moved. It was, in effect, the government.

The oligarchical form of government is not without its advantages, although indicative of a low state of civilization. A comparison of views, by the agency of a council, would at any time be favorable to the development of talent. It was especially the case among the Iroquois, in consequence of the greater diversity of interests, and the more extended reach of affairs incident to several nations in close alliance. Events of greater magnitude would spring up in the midst of a flourishing confederacy, than in a nation of inconsiderable importance; and it is demonstrated by the political history of all governments, that men develop intellect in exact proportion to the magnitude of the events with which they become identified. For these reasons, the League was favorable to the production of men higher in capacity than would arise among nations whose institutions and systems of government were inferior.

The extremely liberal character of their oligarchy is manifested by the *modus procedendi* of these councils. It is obvious that the sachems were not set over the people as arbitrary rulers, to legislate as their own will might dictate, irrespective of the popular voice; on the contrary, there is reason to believe that a public sentiment sprang up on

questions of general interest, which no council felt
at liberty to disregard. By deferring all action
upon such questions until a council brought together
the sachems of the League, attended by a concourse
of inferior chiefs and warriors, an opportunity was
given to the people to judge for themselves, and to
take such measures as were necessary to give expression and force to their opinions. If the band of
warriors became interested in the passing question,
they held a council apart, and having given it a full
consideration, appointed an orator to communicate
their views to the sachems, their *Patres Conscripti.*
In like manner would the chiefs, and even the women proceed, if they entertained opinions which
they wished to urge upon the consideration of the
council. From the publicity with which the affairs
of the League were conducted, and the indirect participation in their adjustment thus allowed the people, a favorable indication is afforded of the democratic spirit of the government.

Oratory, from the constitutional organization of
the council, was necessarily brought into high repute. Questions involving the safety of the race,
and the preservation of the League, were frequently
before it. In those warlike periods, when the Confederacy was moving onward amid incessant conflicts with contiguous nations, or, perchance, resist-
ing sudden tides of migratory population, there was
no dearth of those exciting causes, of those emer-
gencies of peril, which rouse the spirit of the people, and summon into activity their highest energies.

Whenever events converged to such a crisis, the council was the first resort; and there, under the pressure of dangers, and in the glow of patriotism, the eloquence of the Iroquois flowed as pure and spontaneous as the fountains of their thousand streamlets.

The Indian has a quick and enthusiastic appreciation of eloquence. Highly impulsive in his nature, and with passions untaught of restraint, he is strongly susceptible of its influence. By the cultivation and exercise of this capacity, was opened the pathway to distinction; and the chief or warrior gifted with its magical power could elevate himself as rapidly, as he who gained renown upon the warpath. With the Iroquois, as with the Romans, the two professions, oratory and arms,[1] could establish men in the highest degree of personal consideration. To the ambitious Roman in the majestic days of the Republic, and to the proud Indian in his sylvan house, the two pursuits equally commended themselves; and in one or the other alone, could either expect success.

It is a singular fact, resulting from the structure of Indian institutions, that nearly every transaction, whether social or political, orginated or terminated in a council. This universal and favorite mode of doing business became interwoven with all the af-

[1] Duæ sunt artes quæ possunt locare homines in amplissimo gradu dignitatis; una imperatoris, altera orationis boni: ab hoc enim pacis ornamenta retinentur; ab illo belli pericula repelluntur.—Cicero Pro Muraena, § 14.

fairs of public and private life. In council, public transactions of every name and character were planned, scrutinized and adopted. The succession of their rulers, their athletic games, dances, and religious festivals, and their social intercourse, were all alike identified with councils. It may be said that the life of the Iroquois was either spent in the chase, on the war-path, or at the council-fire. They formed the three leading objects of his existence; and it would be difficult to determine for which he possessed the strongest predilection. Regarding them in this light, and it is believed they are not over-estimated, a narrative of these councils would furnish an accurate and copious history of the Iroquois, both political and social. The absence of these records, now irreparable, has greatly abridged the fulness, and diminished the accuracy of our aboriginal history.

The councils of the League were of three distinct kinds; and they may be distinguished under the heads of civil, mourning and religious. Their civil councils, *Ho-de-os'-seh*, were such as convened to transact business with foreign nations, and to regulate the internal administration of the Confederacy. The mourning councils, *Hen-nun-do-nuh'-seh*, were those summoned to "raise up" sachems to fill such vacancies as had been occasioned by death or deposition, and also to ratify the investiture of such chiefs as the nations had raised up in reward of public services. Their religious councils, *Gä-e-wé'-yo-do Ho-*

de-os-hen'-dä-ko, were, as the name imports, devoted to religious observances.

No event of any importance ever transpired without passing under the cognizance of one or another of these species of councils; for all affairs seem to have converged towards them by a natural and inevitable tendency. An exposition of the mode of summoning each, of their respective powers and jurisdictions, and of the manner of transacting business, may serve to unfold the workings of their political system, their social relations, and the range of their intellectual capacities.

The name *Ho-de-os'-seh*, by which the Iroquois designated a civil council, signifies "advising together." It was bestowed upon any council of sachems, which convened to take charge of the public relations of the League, or to provide for its internal administration. Each nation had power, under established regulations, to convene such a council, and prescribe the time and place of convocation.

If the envoy of a foreign people desired to submit a proposition to the sachems of the League, and applied to the Senecas for that purpose, the sachems of that nation would first determine whether the question was of sufficient importance to authorize a council. If they arrived at an affirmative conclusion, they immediately sent out runners to the Cayugas, the nation nearest in position, with a belt of wampum. This belt announced, that, on a certain day thereafter, at such a place, and for such and such purposes, mentioning them, a council of the

League would assemble. The Cayugas then notified the Onondagas, they the Oneidas, and these the Mohawks. Each nation, within its own confines, spread the information far and wide; and thus, in a space of time astonishingly brief, intelligence of the council was heralded from one extremity of their country to the other. It produced a stir among the people in proportion to the magnitude and importance of the business to be transacted. If the subject was calculated to arouse a deep feeling of interest, one common impulse from the Hudson to the Niagara, and from the St. Lawrence to the Susquehanna, drew them towards the council-fire. Sachems, chiefs and warriors, women, and even children, deserted their hunting grounds and woodland seclusions, and taking the trail, literally flocked to the place of council. When the day arrived, a multitude had gathered together, from the most remote and toilsome distances, but yet animated by an unyielding spirit of hardihood and endurance.

Their mode of opening a council, and proceeding with the business before it, was extremely simple, yet dilatory, when contrasted with the modes of civilized life. Questions were usually reduced to single propositions, calling for an affirmative or negative response, and were thus either adopted or rejected. When the sachems were assembled in the midst of their people, and all were in readiness to proceed, the envoy was introduced before them. One of the sachems, by previous appointment, then arose, and having thanked the Great Spirit for his continued beneficence in permitting them to meet together, he informed the envoy that the council was prepared to hear him upon the business for which it had convened. The council being thus opened, the representative proceeded to unfold the objects of his mission. He submitted his propositions in regular form, and sustained them by such arguments as the case required. The sachems listened with earnest and respectful attention to the end of his address, that they might clearly understand the questions to be decided and answered. After the envoy had concluded his speech, he withdrew from the council, as was customary, to await at a distance the result of its deliberations. It then became the duty of the sachems to agree upon an answer; in doing which, as would be expected, they passed through the ordinary routine of speeches, consultations, and animated discussions. Such was the usual course of proceeding in the Iroquois council. Variations might be introduced by circumstances.

At this place another peculiar institution of the *Ho-dé'-no-sau-nee* is presented. All the sachems of the League, in whom originally was vested the entire civil power, were required to be of " one mind," to give efficacy to their legislation. Unanimity was a fundamental law. The idea of majorities and minorities were entirely unknown to our Indian predecessors.

To hasten their deliberations to a conclusion, and

ascertain the result, they adopted an expedient which dispensed entirely with the necessity of casting votes. The founders of the Confederacy, seeking to obviate as far as possible altercation in council, and to facilitate their progress to unanimity, divided the sachems of each nation into classes, usually of two and three each, as will be seen by referring to the table of sachemships. No sachem was permitted to express an opinion in council, until he had agreed with the other sachem or sachems of his class, upon the opinion to be expressed, and had received an appointment to act as speaker for the class. Thus the eight Seneca sachems, being in four classes, could have but four opinions; the ten Cayuga sachems but four. In this manner each class was brought to unanimity within itself. A cross-consultation was then held between the four sachems who represented the four classes; and when they had agreed, they appointed one of their number to express their resulting opinion, which was the answer of their nation. The several nations having, by this ingenious method, become of "one mind" separately, it only remained to compare their several opinions, to arrive at the final sentiment of all the sachems of the League. This was effected by a conference between the individual representatives of the several nations; and when they had arrived at unanimity, the answer of the League was determined.

The sovereignty of the nations, by this mode of giving assent, was not only preserved, but made subservient to the effort itself to secure unanimity. If any sachem was obdurate or unreasonable, influences were brought to bear upon him which he could not well resist; and it was seldom that inconvenience resulted from their inflexible adherence to the rule. When, however, all efforts to produce unanimity failed of success, the whole matter was laid aside. Farther action became at once impossible. A result, either favorable or adverse, having, in this way, been reached, it was communicated to the envoy by a speaker selected for the purpose. This orator was always chosen from the nation with whom the council originated, and it was usual with him to review the whole subject presented to the council in a formal speech, and at the same time to announce the conclusions to which the sachems of the Confederacy had arrived. This concluding speech terminated the business of the council, and the Indian diplomatist took his departure.

The war against the Eries, which resulted in the extermination or expulsion of that nation from the western part of this State, about the year 1653, was declared by the sachems of the Iroquois in general council. The French war, also, which they waged with such indomitable courage and perseverance for so many years, was resolved upon in the same manner. Their traditions record other struggles with Indian nations, some of which were engaged in by the League, and others either commenced or assumed by a nation separately. At the beginning of the American Revolution, the Iroquois could not agree in council to make war as a confederacy upon our confederacy. A number of the Oneida sachems firmly resisted the assumption of hostilities, and thus defeated the measure as an act of the League, for the want of unanimity. Some of the nations, however, especially the Mohawks, were so interlinked with the British, that neutrality was impossible. Under this pressure of circumstances, it was resolved in council to suspend the rule, and leave each nation to engage in the war upon its own responsibility.

In the councils of the Iroquois, the dignity and order ever preserved have become proverbial. The gravity of Nestor was exemplified by their sages, and more than the harmony of the Grecian chiefs existed among their sachems. In their elevation to the highest degree of political distinction ever reached by any Indian race, except the Aztec, the clearest evidence is presented of the wisdom and prudence with which these councils watched over the public welfare.

The succession of the Ruling Body, whether secured by election, or by laws of inheritance, is an event of deep importance to the people, whose personal security and welfare are to a large extent under the guardianship of their rulers. It seems to have been the aim of the *Ho-de'-no-sau-nee* to avoid the dangers of an hereditary transmission of power, without fully adopting the opposite principle of a free election, founded upon merit and capacity. Their system was a modification of the two opposite rules, and claims the merit of originality, as well as of adaptation to their social and political condition.

It is in accordance with the principles, and necessary to the existence of an oligarchy, that the ruling body should possess a general, if not an absolute authority over the admission of its members, and over the succession to its dignities, where the vacancies are occasioned by death. In some respects the oligarchy of the Iroquois was wider than those of antiquity. The tribes retained the power of designating successors, independent of the oligarchs; while, for the security of the latter, the number was limited by the fundamental law. It was the province of the ruling body to "raise up" the sachems selected by the tribes, and to invest them with office. In the ancient oligarchies, which were less liberal and much less systematic in their construction, the whole power of making rulers appears to have been appropriated by the rulers themselves.

To perform the ceremony adverted to, of "raising up" sachems, and of confirming the investiture of such chiefs as had been previously raised up by a nation, the Mourning council was instituted. Its name, *Hen-nun-do-nuh'-seh*, signifies, with singular propriety, "a mourning council;" as it embraced the two-fold object of lamenting the deceased with suitable solemnities, and of establishing a successor in the sachemship made vacant by his demise.

Upon the death of a sachem, the nation in which the loss had occurred had power to summon a council, and designate the day and place. If the Oneidas, for example, had lost a ruler, they sent out runners at the earliest convenient day, with " belts of invitation" to the sachems of the League, and to the people at large, to assemble around their national council-fire at *Gä-no-a-lo'-häle*. The invitation was circulated in the same manner, and with the same celerity as in convoking a civil council. These belts or the strings of wampum, sent out on such occasions, conveyed a laconic message: " the name" of the deceased " calls for a council." It also announced the place and the time.

The name and the appeal fell not in vain upon the ear of the Iroquois. There was a potency in the name itself which none could resist. It penetrated every seclusion of the forest; and reached every *gä-no-sote'* upon the hillside, on the margin of the lakes, or in the deep solitudes of the wood. No warrior, wise man or chief failed to hear, or could withstand the call. A principle within was addressed, which ever responded; respect and veneration for the sachems of the League.

For these councils, and the festivities with which they were concluded, the *Ho-de'-no-sau-nee* ever retained a passionate fondness. No inclemency of season, nor remoteness of residence, nor frailty of age or of sex offered impassable obstructions. To that hardy spirit which led the Iroquois to traverse the war-paths of the distant south and west, and to leave their hunting trails upon the Potomac and Ohio, the distance to a council within their imme-

diate territories would present inconsiderable hin-
drances. From the Mohawk to the Genesee, they
forsook their hunting-grounds, and their encampments, and put themselves upon the trail for the
council-fire. Old men with gray hairs and totter-
ing steps, young men in the vigor of youth, warriors inured to the hardships of incessant strife,
children looking out, for the first time, upon life,
and women, with their infants encased in the _gă-ōs'-_
_hă_, all performed the journey with singular rapidity and endurance. From every side they bent
their footsteps towards the council; and when the
day arrived, a large concourse of warriors, chiefs,
wise men and sachems, from the most remote as
well as the subjacent parts of their territory, greeted
each other beside the council-fire of the Oneidas.

This council, although entirely of a domestic
character, was conducted with many ceremonies.
Before the arrival of the day announced by the
belt, the several nations entered the country of the
Oneidas in separate bands, and encamped at a distance from the council-house. To advance at once,
would have been a violation of Iroquois usages.
Runners were sent on by the approaching nation to
announce its arrival, and it remained encamped
until the Oneidas had signified their readiness for
its reception. On the day appointed, if the necessary arrangements had been perfected, a rude reception ceremony opened the proceedings. The
several nations in separate trains, each one preceded
by its civil and military dignitaries, drew simul-

taneously towards the council-fire, and were received and welcomed by the Oneidas in a ceremonious manner. The latter advanced to meet them at a distance from the village, where a temporary council-fire was kindled; after which the chief personages of the advancing bands walked around the fire, singing the songs of mourning designed for the occasion. When the songs were finished, the pipe of peace was circulated. Speeches were exchanged between the parties, and the belts of wampum, with which the council had been called, were returned. The several bands, upon the completion of these ceremonies, advanced in file, a funeral procession, and singing the mourning songs, to the general council-fire at the Indian village, where the people arrayed themselves in two divisions. The Mohawks, Onondagas and Senecas, who, as elsewhere stated, were brother nations to each other, and fathers to the other three, seated themselves upon one side of the fire. On the other side were arranged the Oneidas, Cayugas and Tuscaroras, who, in like manner, were brothers to each other, but children to the three first. By their peculiar customs, if the deceased sachem belonged to either of the three elder nations, he was mourned as a father by the three junior; and it became the duty of the latter to perform the ceremony of lamentation prescribed by their usages for the deceased, and afterwards that of raising up his successor. If, on the contrary, the departed ruler belonged to either of the junior nations, as in the case supposed, it cast upon the elder nations the duty of lamenting his death as a child, in the customary form, and of installing a successor in the vacant sachemship.

These observances were performed with the accustomed gravity and earnestness of the red man; and were, in themselves, neither devoid of interest, nor unadapted to impress the mind. The lament was a tribute to the virtues, and to the memory of the departed sachem, a mourning scene, in which not only the tribe and nation of the deceased, but the League itself participated. Surely, a more delicate testimonial of affection than would have been looked for among our Indian predecessors. The ceremony of raising up a successor, which followed, was a succession of musical chants, with choruses, intermingled with speeches and responses. Upon the whole scene, rendered wild and picturesque by the variety of costumes, there rested a spirit of silence and solemnity which invested it with singular interest.

A prominent part of the ceremonial consisted in the repetition of their ancient laws and usages, and an exposition of the structure and principles of the League, for the instruction of the newly-inducted rulers. In the midst of each division, the chief personages of the elder and junior nations were grouped together. Between the two groups of sachems, the wise-man who conducted the observances walked to and fro, repeating those traditionary lessons, and unfolding those regulations, which had been handed down from the foundation of the Confederacy.

Some of th   tive, while
the most we   rethought.
Among th(*we'-dä*, the
founder of the League, there was one designed to
impress upon their minds the necessity of union and
harmony. It was clothed in a figurative dress, as is
the custom of the red man when he would produce
a vivid impression. He enjoined them to plant a
tree with four roots, branching severally to the north,
south, east and west. Beneath its shade the sachems of the League must sit down together in perpetual unity, if they would preserve its stability, or
secure the advantages it was calculated to bestow.
If they did so, the power of the *Ho-dé'-no-sau-nee*
would be planted as firmly as the oak, and the
blasts of adverse fortune would rage against it in
vain.

The laws explained at different stages of the ceremonial, were repeated from strings of wampum,[1]
into which they "had been talked" at the time of
their enactment. In the Indian method of express-

---

[1] The original wampum of the Iroquois, in which the laws of the League
were recorded, was made of spiral
fresh-water shells, *Ote-ko'-ă,* which
were strung on deer skin strings, or
sinew, and the strands braided into
belts, or simply united into strings.
This species of wampum has been for
many years out of use; but all wampum still bears this name. Hubbard
thus speaks of wampum in general:
"It is of two sorts, white and purple.
The white is worked out of the inside
of the great conchs, into the form of
a bead, and perforated to string on
leather. The purple is worked out
of the inside of the muscle shell.
They are wove as broad as one's hand,
and about two feet long. These they
call belts, and give and receive at
their treaties as the seals of their
friendship." Nar. Ind. Wars, New
Eng., p. 40. It was first known in
New England as Wampumpeag,
(Baylies' New Plymouth, p. 37 ;) and
the art of making it was obtained
from the Dutch, according to Hutch-
inson about 1627.

ing the idea, the string, or the belt can tell, by means of an interpreter, the exact law or transaction of which it was made, at the time, the sole evidence. It operates upon the principle of association, and thus seeks to give fidelity to the memory. These strings and belts were the only visible records of the Iroquois; and were of no use except by the aid of those special personages who could draw forth the secret records locked up in their remembrance.

It is worthy of note, that but little importance was attached to a promise or assurance of a foreign power, unless belts or strings were given to preserve it in recollection. Verbal propositions, or those not confirmed by wampum, were not considered worthy of special preservation.[1] As the laws and usages of the Confederacy were intrusted to the guardianship of such strings, one of the Onondaga sachems, *Ho-no-we-nă'-to*, was constituted "Keeper of the Wampum." and was required to be versed in its interpretation.

On these occasions, the wise-man who officiated interpreted strings from time to time, and carried them from one division of sachems to the other. In reply, as many others were subsequently returned with similar forms and explanations. In this manner, with a multitude of forms and ceremonies, con-

---

[1] "It is obvious to all who are the least acquainted with Indian affairs, that they regard no message or invitation, be it of what consequence it will, unless attended or confirmed by strings or belts of wampum, which they look upon as we our letters, or rather bonds." Letter of Sir W. Johnson, 1753. Doc. Hist. N. Y., vol. ii. p. 624.

suming the greater part of a day in their repetition, were their sachems raised up. The proceedings were closed with a presentation of the newly-invested rulers to the people, under the names of their respective sachemships, which, from that day forth, they were permitted to assume.

Up to this stage of the Council, neither gaiety nor mirthfulness were exhibited by the old or young. The people were in mourning for the deceased, and rendering the last acts of public respect. When, however, these offices had been performed, and the places left vacant among the rulers had been filled, the reasons for lamentation had disappeared, and with them disappeared the outward signs. The evening was given up to feasting, and to their religious and domestic dances. It was not uncommon to spend several days in these festivities; devoting the days in succession to athletic games, and the evenings to the feast, and to the social dance.

The succession, under these simple regulations, was rendered entirely free from turmoil and strife; and became not only an easy transaction, but an imposing, and, to them, instructive ceremonial. Upon the sachems was bestowed sufficient control over the transmission of the sachemships for their own protection; while the still more important power of naming those to be raised up, and of deposing the unfaithful, which was retained by the tribes, secured the people from oppression and misgovernment.

A wider dissimilarity, than subsists between the

institutions of our Indian predecessors and our own, cannot be easily conceived. They are as unlike as the races themselves in their essential characteristics. If, however, a correct impression is desired of the state of society, political and social, in which the Iroquois have existed, and in which they have developed whatever of character they possessed, it must be sought in their customs and institutions; it must be furnished by the practical operation of that stupendous system of inter-relationships by which they were bound together, and from which every act in their social intercourse received a tinge.

The degree of social intercourse between the nations of the League was much greater than would at first be suggested. In the pursuits of the chase and of conquest, and in attendance upon councils, they traversed the whole territory far and near. Their trails penetrated the forest in every direction, and their main thoroughfares were as well beaten, as the highways now passing over the same lines. With their habits of traveling over the whole area of the State, they were doubtless more familiar than ourselves with its hills and plains, rivers and lakes, its wild retreats and forest concealments. Much of their social intercourse, especially between the nations, was around their council-fires. The Councils themselves formed a bond of union, and drew them together instinctively. They furnished the excitements and the recreations of Indian life, as well as relieved the monotony of peace. It was here they recounted their exploits upon the war-path, or listened to the eloquence of favorite chiefs. Here they offered tributes of respect to those deceased sachems who had rendered themselves illustrious by public services; or listened to the laws and regulations of their ancestors, which were explained by their sages in the ceremonial of raising up successors. It was here, also, that they celebrated their athletic games with Olympic zeal; and joined in those national dances, some of which were indescribably beautiful and animated.

Custom required the particular tribe in which sachems had been raised up, to furnish a daily entertainment to the multitude during the continuance of the council. The pursuits of the day were suspended as the shades of evening began to fall, and they all sat down to a common repast, which the matrons of the tribe had prepared. After the business upon which the council convened had been consummated, each day in succession was devoted to the simple but diversified amusements of Indian life, the twilight to the feast, and the evening to the dance. The wild notes of their various tunes, accompanied by the turtle-shell rattle and the drum; the rattles, which entered into the costumes of the warriors, and the noise of the moving throng, all united, sent forth a "sound of revelry" which fell with strange accents in the hours of night upon the solemn stillness of the woods. This sound of pleasure and amusement was continued from day to day, until "pleasure itself became satiety," and amusement had lost its power to charm.

When the spirit of festivity had become exhausted, the fire of the *Hen-nun-do-nuh'-seh* was raked together, and the several nations bent their way homeward through the forest. Silence once more resumed her sway over the deserted scene, as the sounds of merriment subsided, and the lingering hum of the dissolving council died insensibly away. Obscurity next advanced with stealthy mien, and quickly folding the incidents of this sylvan pageant in her dusky mantle, she bore them, with their associations, their teachings, and their remembrances, into the dark realm of Oblivion; from which their recall would be as hopeless as would be the last shout which rang along the valley.

* The celebration of their religious festivals was through the instrumentality of councils, and these form the third class. But as they are described in the succeeding pages, no further mention of them will now be made, except to notice them as one of the species into which the councils of the Iroquois are properly divisible. In addition to the religious councils which were held at the period of their festivals, the mourning council was always made an occasion for religious and moral instruction. Many of its exercises were of a strictly religious character, and it would be more proper to designate it as a religious council, than by any other name, but for the circumstance that its object was to raise up rulers, and its ceremonies were entirely distinct from those at the regular festivals.

The influence of the civil, mourning and religious

councils upon the people, would, of itself, furnish an extensive subject of inquiry. Like all the pursuits of Indian life, they changed but little from age to age, and were alike in their essential characteristics, in their mode of transacting business, in their festivities, and in the spirit by which they were animated. From the frequency of their occurrence, and the deep interest with which they were regarded, it is evident that they exercised a vast influence upon the race. The intercourse and society which they afforded, had, undoubtedly, a power to humanize and soften down the asperities of character, which their mode of life was calculated to produce.

CHAPTER VI.

The Ruling Body of the League, with its powers, and the tenure of office of its members—the division of the people into tribes, with the cross-relationships between them—the laws of succession with their incidents—and the councils of the Iroquois with their mode of proceeding, spirit and effects, have severally been brought under consideration.

Upon the facts derived from these sources of investigation, the true character of the Iroquois government must be settled. If it is referable to any determined species, the constituent parts and general features of the League, which have formed the subjects of the preceding chapters, will determine its position in the scale of civil organizations established by political writers.

In their original, well-developed institutions, and in their government, so systematic in its construction, and so liberal in its administration, there is much to enforce a tribute of respect to the intelligence of our Indian predecessors. Without such institutions, and without that animating spirit which they nourished and diffused, it would be difficult to account for the production of such men as have sprung up among the Iroquois. The development of national intellect depends chiefly upon external, reciprocal influences, and is usually proportionate to the vitality and motive which the institutions of a people possess and furnish.

To illustrate, substantially, the nature of their government, it will be necessary to notice the several species which have been instituted among men, the natural order of their origination, the relations in which they mutually stand to each other, and their general characteristics. In no other way can a clear conception be obtained of the character of the Iroquois government, and the relation which it sustains to other political fabrics. No apology, therefore, will be necessary for the digression.

Aristotle, and other Grecian political writers, recognized but three species of government: the monarchical, the aristocratical, and the democratical; the rule of "one," the "few," and the "many." Every other variety was regarded as the wreck, or perversion, of one of the three. If, for example, the first was corrupted, it became a tyranny; if the second degenerated, it was styled an oligarchy; and if the last became tumultuous, it was called an ochlocracy. A polity, or the rule of a large body of select citizens, was a milder form of oligarchy. This classification admits of a qualification to the definition of an aristocracy and oligarchy, hereafter to be noticed.

Modern political writers also recognize three species, as laid down by Montesquieu: the despotic, the monarchical, and the republican. The aristocratic and democratic forms of the Greeks are included in the republican form of modern times: while the monarchical government of the present day—"the rule of a single person by fixed laws"— was entirely unknown to the ancient Greeks. It is further observable that a despotism, as defined by Montesquieu, corresponds precisely with the monarchy of Aristotle.

The order of their origination suggests an important general principle; that there is a regular progression of political institutions, from the monarchical, which are the earliest in time, on to the democratical, which are the last, the noblest, and the most intellectual. This position can be established by the rise and development of the Grecian institutions, and may be further illustrated by the progressive change in the spirit and nature of other governments.

An unlimited monarchy, or "the rule of a single individual according to his own will," is the form of government natural to a people when in an uncivilized state, or when just emerging from barbarism. In the progress of time, by the growth and expansion of civil liberty, the monarchy becomes liberalized or limited, and a few steps forward introduce universal democracy. Hence it is noticeable in the rise of all races, and in the formation of all states, that the idea of chief and follower, or sovereign and people, is of spontaneous suggestion. This notion may be regarded as inherent to society in its primitive state.

It will be remembered that when the Hellenic tribes came down from Thessaly, and finally settled themselves upon the shores of the Mediterranean, their political relations were those of chief and follower. After they had become subdivided into a large number of petty states, and migrations and intermixtures had subsided, leaving each principality under its own ruler, and to the formation of its own institutions, the monarchical form of government became fully established. The small territory of Greece was parcelled out between nearly twenty petty kingdoms. During the Heroic ages, which are understood to have commenced with this inundation of the Grecian territory by the Hellenes, and to have terminated with the Trojan war, a period of about two hundred years, the kingly government was the only one among the Greeks.

At the close of the Heroic ages, a new state of affairs became apparent. Around the reigning families in the several kingdoms, there had sprung up a class of Eupatrids, or nobles, who were in possession of most of the landed estates. Having elevated themselves far above the mass of the people, in the social scale, they gradually absorbed political powers which had before been vested in the kings. By the silent but natural growth of this aristocracy, continued encroachments were made upon the prerogatives of royalty, until at last the kings were brought down to a level with their Eupatrids. An aristocracy was thus substituted for monarchy; and nearly all the states of Greece, in their political progress towards democracy, passed out of the monarchical into the aristocratical form of government.

This form, although indicative of more liberality than the former, and adapted to the state of civil society then existing, pressed heavily upon the people; and while it existed, was unfavorable to the elevation of the race. The Demos, or common people, were free, but were excluded from all political privileges; hence, with the increase of their intelligence, would be excited jealousies of the incumbent class. At times, the very existence of the aristocracy depended upon the forcible subjection of the Demos; for when the great and just sentiment of "political equality" began to be coupled with that of "personal liberty," no form of government could rest in permanent security, which limited the one, or denied the other. The Grecian mind was eminently progressive. No power could subdue or enslave that native energy, which had exemplified itself in the hardy enterprises of the Heroic ages. Nothing could repress or lastingly fetter that majestic intellect, out of which, even then, had sprung a system of mythology destined to infuse itself into the literature of all generations, and to quicken the intellects of every clime—a system so remarkable as an exhibition of the unguided devotional nature of man, and so brilliant as a creation of the imagination, that it may be characterized as the greatest production of genius and credulity which ever emanated from the mind of man.

In the progress of events, the aristocracies were successfully invaded by an uprising of men of wealth, or of capacity, from among the common people. These ambitious plebeians demanded a place in the ruling body, and if refused, they became the champions of the people, and engaged in measures for the overthrow of the government. Such difficulties were usually avoided by admitting these new families to a place among the Eupatrids, and to a participation in the administration. In this way the aristocracy of wealth and talent was in a measure placed upon an equality with that of birth; and by the act the government itself was widened, or liberalized.

These inroads upon the aristocracy, which generally resulted in the infusion of the popular element, may be regarded as the introduction or commencement of the oligarchy. The difference between the two species is to be sought in the spirit by which each respectively was actuated, and not in their forms; for the same body of aristocrats usually became oligarchs by a change in the spirit of the government. When an aristocracy became corrupt and odious to the people, and sought only to perpetuate its own power, it became, in the Grecian sense, a faction, an oligarchy. It ceased to be the rule of the "best men," (ἄριστοι,) and became the rule of the "few" (ὀλίγοι.) This definition admits of a qualification. When an aristocracy became widened or liberalized, by the admission of men of capacity to an equal position, and the government assumed a milder spirit, the aristocracy would, in effect, be changed, but not into a faction. It would be as unlike a rigorous aristocracy as an oligarchical faction, and may be denominated a simple or liberal oligarchy. The government of the Iroquois falls under this precise definition. It cannot be called an aristocracy, because the sachems of the League possessed no landed estates, which, it is well known, are the only true foundation of an aristocracy; neither were their titles or privileges hereditary, in the strict sense, which is another important element of an aristocracy. Their government, however, was the rule of "the few." It was an aristocracy liberalized, until it stood upon the very verge of democracy. It answers to the idea of an oligarchy, which is the last form of government but one, in the progressive series.

The governments of the Grecian states appear to have oscillated for centuries between the rigorous aristocracies, oligarchical factions, and milder oligarchies. These forms were rather transition than permanent conditions of their civil institutions. During the period of their prevalence, the people, who, as before remarked, were personally free, but debarred from political privileges, were gradually improving their condition by the accumulation of

wealth, and consolidating their strength by the up-
rearing of flourishing cities.   With the increase of
their respectability, and the expansion of their
power, the struggle with the incumbent class was
continued with greater and still greater success.
Principles of government became better understood,
and more enlarged views of the rights of man continued to quicken the Grecian mind.   Every successive age added to the popular intelligence; and
the people gradually, but constantly, continued to
repossess themselves of their original authority.
The growth of liberty and free institutions among
the Greeks was slow, but irresistible.   The struggle
of the people for emancipation lasted from generation to generation, from century to century; until,
having emerged from the darkness of barbarism,
and worked their way through every species of government ever devised by the genius of man, they
achieved at last a triumph; and their institutions,
which had been planted and nourished during this
march of ages, finally ripened into universal democracy.

In the history of the States of Greece, there is
noticeable in the midst of a wide diversity of events,
a great uniformity of progress—with a difference in
the period of the development of political changes,
a marked tendency to the same results.   Every
change in their institutions, from the era of absolute
monarchy, made them more liberal; but it required
upward of seven centuries to liberalize them into a
" finished democracy which fully satisfied the Greek

notion; a state in which every attribute of sovereignty might be shared, without respect to rank or property, by every freeman."[1] The Greeks began with monarchy, and having passed through all the intermediate species and shades of government in the progressive series, they finally developed their highest capacities, their most brilliant genius, under the bounding pulse of an extreme, even enthusiastic democracy. How truthful the exclamation of Herodotus : " Liberty is a brave thing."

The same tendency of institutions towards democracy, as races elevate themselves in the scale of civilization, can be observed in the progressive improvement of British institutions. No people have been subjected to such tests, civil and religious; and issued from the throes of revolution with more character, more civilization, more majesty of intellect, for achievements in legislation, science and learning, than our parent, Anglo-Saxon race. Their career, with all its vicissitudes, from the union of the Heptarchies under Egbert, down to the final settlement of the government on the expulsion of the second James, is full of instruction—full of

---

[1] The Trojan war closed 1184 B. C., and the States of Greece soon afterwards passed out of the monarchical form of government. At Athens it was abolished in 1068 B. C. But not until about the year 470 B. C., when Aristides the Just removed the last aristocratical features from the Athenian institutions, could Athens be called a "finished democracy." He broke up the distinctions between the classes which Solon had established, and opened all the dignities of the State to every citizen. Between the Trojan war and this last period, the Athenians had passed through Monarchy, Tyranny, Aristocracy, Faction, Anarchy, Oligarchy, Polity, and limited Democracy. With the legislation of Aristides commenced the rapid elevation of the city of Minerva, and of that noble, unequalled race.

great lessons.   They have tested monarchy in all its degrees of strength and weakness, of popularity and odium, of oppression and dependence.   Their nobles have enjoyed all the privileges, immunities, and powers, which possession of the landed estates, the vassalage of the people, and independence of the crown could secure; while in turn they have been humble and submissive, even servile, under the arbitrary sway of tyrannous kings.   The people, before the time of Edward the First, were cyphers in the State.   Since then, they have suffered religious bondage, and the oppression of a feudal aristocracy.   In the progress of events, however, they have constantly enlarged the quantity of their liberty, and strengthened the guarantees of personal security.   But if they finally achieved that personal freedom which the Grecian citizen never lost, they never have secured that "equality of privileges" which was the constant aspiration of the Greek until attained, which was the watchword in the struggle for American freedom, and which now lies at the foundation of our own political edifice.

The British government has been liberalized from age to age, until it may now be said to stand intrenched upon the borders of free institutions.

Returning from this digression, which was designed to illustrate the position, not very recondite, of a progression of institutions, from the monarchical, the earliest form of political society, on to the democratical, the last, and most truly enlightened; we can now take up the government of the Iroquois,

and determine the position which it occupies between the two extremes of monarchy on the one hand,
and democracy on the other.

The Iroquois had passed out of the earliest form
of government, that of chief and follower, which is
incident both to the hunter and nomadic states, into
the oligarchical form.   It is obvious that the hunter
life is incompatible with monarchy, except in its
miniature form of chief and follower; and the *Ho-
de'-no-sau-nee*, in improving upon this last relation,
passed over the monarchical, into the rule of "the
few." Several tribes first united into one nation.
The people mingled by intermarriage, and the power
of the chiefs ceased to be several, and became joint.
This gave to the nation an aristocratical, or oligarchical form of government, according to the spirit by
which it was actuated.   By a still higher effort of
legislation, several nations were united in a league
or confederacy; placing the people upon an equality,
and introducing a community of privileges.   The
national rulers then became in a united body the
rulers of the League.   In this manner would be constituted oligarchies within an embracing oligarchy,
imperium in imperio, presenting the precise government of the Iroquois, and with great probability the exact manner of its origination, growth
and final settlement.

The Grecian oligarchies do not furnish an exact
type of that of our Indian predecessors.   In its
construction the latter was more perfect, systematic
and liberal than those of antiquity.   There was in

the Indian fabric more of fixedness, more of dependence upon the people, more of vigor. It would be difficult to find a fairer specimen of the government of *the few*, than the one under consideration. In the happy constitution of its ruling body, and in the effective security of the people from misgovernment it stands unrivalled. In assigning to this government its specific name, it will be sufficient to adopt the etymology of the word oligarchy, *the rule of the few*, rejecting the usual Grecian acceptation of the term, *a degenerated aristocracy*. The substitution of the female line for the male, effecting thereby the disinheritance of the son, the partially elective character of the sachemships, the absence of all landed estates, and the power of deposing lodged with the tribes, are reasons conclusive for regarding the government of the Iroquois as an oligarchy rather than an aristocracy.

The spirit which prevailed in the nations and in the Confederacy was that of freedom. The people appear to have secured to themselves all the liberty which the hunter state rendered desirable. They fully appreciated its value, as is evinced by the liberality of their institutions. The red man was always free from political bondage, and, more worthy still of remembrance, his " free limbs never wore a shackle." His spirit could never be bowed in servitude. In the language of Charlevoix, the Iroquois were " entirely convinced that man was born free, that no power on earth had any right to make any attempts against his liberty, and that nothing could make him amends for its loss." It would be difficult to describe any political society, in which there was less of oppression and discontent, more of individual independence and boundless freedom. The absence of family distinctions, and of all property, together with the irresistible inclination for the chase, rendered the social condition of the people peculiar to itself. It secured to them an exemption from the evils, as well as denied to them the refinements, which flow from the possession of wealth, and the indulgence of the social relations.

At this point the singular trait in the character of the red man suggests itself, that he never felt the "power of gain." The *auri sacra fames* of Virgil, the *studium lucri* of Horace, never penetrated his nature. This great passion of civilized man, in its use and abuse his blessing and his curse, never roused the Indian mind. It was doubtless the great reason of his continuance in the hunter state; for the desire of gain is one of the earliest manifestations of progressive mind, and one of the most powerful passions of which the mind is susceptible. It clears the forest, rears the city, builds the merchantman— in a word, it has civilized our race.

All things considered, the Iroquois oligarchy excites a belief of its superiority over those of antiquity. Those of Greece were exceedingly unstable, and therefore incline us to regard them as transition states of their institutions; while that of the *Ho-dé'-no-sau-nee* was guarded in so many ways for the resistance of political changes, that it would have required a very energetic popular movement for its overthrow. The former retained many elements of aristocracy, while the latter had become so far liberalized as to be almost entirely free. Without the influence of cities, which no people construct who live in the hunter state, and the important consequences which result from the aggregation of society into large communities, the government of the Iroquois would doubtless have retained its oligarchical form through many generations. It would have lasted until the people had abandoned the hunter state; until they had given up the chase for agriculture, the arts of war for those of industry, the hunting-ground and the fishing encampment for the village and the city.

It will not be necessary to extend the inquiry, to exhibit more fully the gradual changes in the government of the Iroquois, by which it was brought upon the verge of free institutions. The creation of the class of chiefs furnishes the clearest evidence of the development of the popular element. The proofs of its extreme liberality have been sufficiently exhibited in the structure of the government itself. Reflections could be multiplied upon its spirit, its influence upon the people, its operative force in the development of talent, and its adaptation to produce its historical results; but it is not deemed necessary to carry forward reflections of this description. An outline of the structure of the League has been drawn, and from its general characteristics its principles can be easily deduced.

Under this simple but beautiful fabric of Indian construction arose the power of the Iroquois, reaching, at its full meridian, over a large portion of our republic. In their Long House, which opened its door upon Niagara, they found shelter in the hour of attack, resources for conquest in the season of ambitious projects, and happiness and contentment in the days of peace. In adaptation to their mode of life, their habits and their wants, no scheme of government could have been devised better calculated for their security against outward attack, their triumph upon the war-path, and their internal tranquillity. It is, perhaps, the only league of nations ever instituted among men, which can point to three centuries of uninterrupted domestic unity and peace.

The institutions which would be expected to exist under such a political system as that of the Iroquois, would necessarily be simple. Their mode of life and limited wants, the absence of property in a comparative sense, and the infrequency of crime dispensed with a vast amount of the legislation and machinery incident to the protection of civilized society. While, therefore, it would be unreasonable to seek those high qualities of mind which result from ages of cultivation, in such a rude state of existence, it would be equally irrational to regard the Indian character as devoid of all those higher characteristics which ennoble the human race. If he has never contributed a page to science, nor a discovery to art; if he loses in the progress of generations as much as he gains; still there are certain

qualities of his mind which shine forth in all the
lustre of natural perfection. His simple integrity,
his generosity, his unbounded hospitality, his love
of truth, and, above all, his unshaken fidelity—a
sentiment inborn, and standing out so conspicuously
in his character, that it has not untruthfully become
its characteristic: all these are adornments of humanity, which no art of education can instil, nor
refinement of civilization can bestow. If they exist
at all, it is because the gifts of the Deity have never
been perverted.

There was, however, a fatal deficiency in Indian
society, in the non-existence of a progressive spirit.
The same rounds of amusement, of business, of
warfare, of the chase, and of domestic intercourse
continued from generation to generation. There was
neither progress nor invention, nor increase of political wisdom. Old forms were preserved, old customs
adhered to. Whatever they gained upon one point
they lost upon another, leaving the second generation but little wiser than the first. The Iroquois, in
some respects, were in advance of their red neighbors. They had attempted the establishment of
their institutions upon a broader basis, and already
men of high capacity had sprung up among them,
as their political system unfolded. If their Indian
empire had been suffered to work out its own results, it is still problematical whether the vast power they would have accumulated, and the intellect
which would have been developed by their diversified affairs, would not, together, have been suffi-

ciently potent to draw the people from the hunter into the agricultural state. The hunter state is the zero of human society, and while the red man was bound by its spell, there was no hope of his elevation.

In a speculative point of view, the institutions of the Iroquois assume an interesting aspect. Would they, at maturity, have emancipated the people from their strange infatuation for a hunter life; as those of the Toltecs and Aztecs had before effected the disenthralment of those races in the latitudes of Mexico? It cannot be denied that there are some grounds for the belief that their institutions would eventually have ripened into civilization. The Iroquois, at all times, have manifested sufficient intellect to promise a high degree of improvement, if it had once become awakened and directed to right pursuits. Centuries, however, might have been requisite to effect the change.

But their institutions have a real, a present value, for what they were, irrespective of what they might have become. The Iroquois were our predecessors in the sovereignty. Our country they once called their country, our rivers and lakes were their rivers and lakes, our hills and intervales were also theirs. Before us, they enjoyed the beautiful scenery spread out between the Hudson and Niagara, in its wonderful diversity from the pleasing to the sublime. Before us, were they invigorated by our climate, and were nourished by the bounties of the earth, the forest and the stream. The tie by which we are thus connected carries with it the duty of doing justice to their memory, by preserving their name and deeds, their customs and their institutions, lest they perish from remembrance. We cannot wish to tread ignorantly upon those extinguished council-fires, whose light, in the days of aboriginal dominion, was visible over half the continent.

The political structures of our primitive inhabitants have, in general, proved exceedingly unsubstantial. Isolated nations, by some superiority of institutions, or casual advantage of location, sprang up with an energetic growth, and for a season spread their dominion far and wide. After a brief period of prosperity, they were borne back by adverse fortune into their original obscurity; thus rendering these boundless territories the constant scene of human conflict, and of the rise and fall of Indian sovereignties. It was reserved for the Iroquois to rest themselves upon a more durable foundation, by the establishment of a League. This alliance between their nations they cemented by the imperishable bands of tribal relationship. At the epoch of Saxon occupation, they were rapidly building up an empire, which threatened the absorption or extermination of the whole Indian family east of the Mississippi. Their power had become sufficient to set at defiance all hostile invasions from contiguous nations; and the League itself, while it suffered no loss of numbers by emigrating bands, was endued with a capacity for indefinite expansion. At the periods of their separate discovery, the Aztecs on the south, and the Iroquois in the north were the only Indian races upon the continent, whose institutions promised, at maturity, to ripen into civilization. Such were the condition and prospects of this Indian League, when Hendrick Hudson, more than two centuries since (1609,) sailed up the river which constituted their eastern boundary. This silent voyage of the navigator may be regarded as the opening event in the series, which resulted in reversing the political prospects of the *Ho-de'-no-sau-nee*, and in introducing into their Long House an invader, more relentless in his purposes, and more invincible in arms, than the red man against whose assaults it had been erected.

Their council-fires, so far as they are emblematical of civil jurisdiction, have long since been extinguished, their empire has terminated, and the shades of evening are now gathering thickly over the scattered and feeble remnants of this once powerful League. Race has yielded to race, the inevitable result of the contact of the civilized with the hunter life. Who shall relate with what pangs of regret they yielded up, from river to river, and from lake to lake, this fair broad domain of their fathers. The Iroquois will soon be lost as a people, in that night of impenetrable darkness in which so many Indian races have been enshrouded. Already their country has been appropriated, their forests cleared, and their trails obliterated. The residue of this proud and gifted race, who still linger around their native seats, are destined to fade away, until they become eradicated as an Indian stock. We shall ere long look backward to the Iroquois, as a race blotted from existence; but to remember them as a people whose sachems had no cities, whose religion had no temples, and whose government had no record.

BOOK SECOND.

SPIRIT OF THE LEAGUE.

Richd H. Pease.

GÄ-HAH-NO

A Seneca Indian Girl,

In the Costume of the Irequois.

BOOK II.

SPIRIT OF THE LEAGUE.

CHAPTER I.

FAITH OF THE IROQUOIS. — BELIEF IN THE GREAT SPIRIT. — THE EVIL-MINDED, HE´-NO, THE THUNDERER. — GÄ´-O, SPIRIT OF THE WINDS. — THE THREE SISTERS. — THE INVISIBLE AIDS. — WITCHES. — LEGENDARY LITERATURE. — IMMORTALITY OF THE SOUL. — FUTURE PUNISHMENTS. — MORAL SENTIMENTS. — BURIAL CUSTOMS. — ABODE OF THE GREAT SPIRIT. — WASHINGTON. — SPIRITUALITY OF THEIR FAITH. — ITS INFLUENCE.

THE mind is, by nature, full of religious tendencies. Man, when left to the guidance of his own inward persuasions, searches after the Author of his being, and seeks to comprehend the purposes of his existence, and his final destiny. In every age and condition of society, the best thoughts of the most gifted intellects have been expended upon religious subjects. The conclusions reached by reflective mind, under the inspiration of the works of nature, are propagated from generation to generation, until they grow, by natural enlargement, into a system of fixed Beliefs. Upon them is afterwards engrafted a system of Worship. The two flourish side by side with perpetual vigor. They become interwoven with the civil and social institutions of men, and by nurture and habit acquire such a firm hold upon the affections, that they form a part of the living, thinking, acting mind. Without a knowledge, therefore, of the religious life of a people, their institutions, and their political and domestic transactions would be wholly inexplicable.

Remarkable features are exhibited in the religious system of the Iroquois, when contrasted with other systems of similar origin. Emanating from the mind of man alone, originating in the simplest form of human society, it would naturally be encumbered by the vagaries of fancy, and be upheld by affection, rather than logic. But man, shut out from the light of revelation, and left to construct his own theology, will discover some part of the truth, as shadowed forth by the works of nature. This will illuminate his footsteps, in proportion to his appreciation of its excellence, and his faithful adherence to its divine monitions. The faith and worship of the Iroquois are entitled to a favorable consideration, by reason of the principles of belief which they recognized, and the fundamental truths which they inculcated. Established upon some of those luminous principles which lie at the foundation of sound theology, the blemishes in their spiritual edifice are compensated, in some degree, by the purity of its elements.

The Greeks discovered the traces of divinity in every object in nature; in the affections and passions, in the elements of earth and air, in the rivulet, the mountain and the sea. Ascending from these types to their several supposed originals, they grasped at Deity in a multitude of fragments, as proclaimed by the divided works of creation. Failing, with all the acumen and inspiration of their marvellous intellect, to raise their mental vision above Olympus, and to ascend from united nature up to the indivisible and Eternal One, they perfected and beautified that stupendous production of genius and credulity, the polytheism of the ancient world.

Between the popular belief of the ancients and that of the Iroquois there are some coincidences. This similarity of ideas is observable in a portion of their legends and fables, but more especially in their notions of the spiritual world. Like the ancients, they peopled the invisible world with spiritual existences. In their inferior spiritualities, they fell infinitely below the splendid creations of the ancient mythology; but in their knowledge of the Supreme Being, they rose, in many respects, far above the highest conceptions of the ancient philosophy. It will be at once conceded, that the Supreme Intelligence announced by Anaxagoras, Socrates and Plato, the *Numen Præstantissimæ Mentis* of the ancient philosophical religionists, was in itself a more vague and indefinite conception, than that divine Being worshipped by the entire red race under the appellation of the Great Spirit.

Upon the first great question in theology, the Stoic, the Epicurean, and the other sects of philosophers equally reached the same fundamental conclusion, *esse Deos*, "the Gods exist." This truth, they affirmed, was not only revealed by the works of nature, but it was also innate, and written in the mind of man.[1] But in a multitude of Gods, each clothed with separate and distinct offices and powers, and all subject to a gradation in rank, the popular belief reposed. The idea of one Supreme Being was a sublime induction of philosophy, and far above the level of popular intelligence. This great truth, therefore, failed to become even feebly incorporated with the overshadowing mythology of antiquity. With the red race, however, the belief not only prevailed that a Great Spirit existed, but they made the same induction from the works of nature the foundation of their religious system.

There is also a coincidence of belief in relation to the origin of spiritual existences. The ancient mythology taught, that the Gods were born, *nativos esse Deos*, and furnished, at the same time, their genealogy, with all the minuteness of legendary license. The Iroquois, also, believed that the Great Spirit was born; and tradition has handed down the narrative, with embellishments of fancy which Hesiod himself would not have disdained.[2]

---

[1] Omnibus enim innatum est et in animo quasi insculptum, esse Deos. Cicero De Natura Deorum, Lib. ii. cap. iv. Solus enim vidit, (Epicurus,) primum esse Deos, quod in omnium animis eorum notionem impressisset ipsa natura. Ib. Lib. i. c. xvi. Quid enim potest esse tam apertum tamque perspicuum, quum cælum suspexi-mus, cælestiaque contemplati sumus, quam esse aliquod numen præstantissimæ mentis, quo hæc segantur ? Ib. Lib. ii. c. ii.

[2] The tradition of the birth of the Good Spirit and the Evil Spirit is much the same among the numerous Indian races within the Republic. It is not peculiar to the Iroquois.

Whether the Gods ruled the universe, and were interested in the affairs of men, was a disputed question in the ancient schools. The Epicureans taught that they were unmindful of all human transactions, and spent their existence in ease and pleasure.[1] But the Stoics took the opposite view, and not only affirmed their constant supervision and intervention in human affairs, but also their active administration of the works of nature.[2] This was also the popular belief. The notions of the Iroquois approached nearest to the latter. In error in ascribing to the Great Spirit a finite origin, and with feeble conceptions of his attributes, they yet believed him to be their creator, ruler and preserver; and that in him was the residuum of power.

The creation of the world was also a subject which divided the ancient schools. In a belief in the eternity of matter, they, in general, concurred. Plato and the Stoics, however, taught that the visible universe was fashioned and constructed by the direct agency of God. This opinion, not of the creation of matter, but of the formation of the world, encountered the ridicule of the Epicureans.[3] This

[1] Nihil enim agit: nullis occupationibus est implicatus : nulla opera molitur : sua sapientia et virtute gaudet : habet exploratum, fore se semper tum in maximis, tum in æternis voluptatibus.   Hunc Deum rite beatum dixerimus. Cic. De. Nat. Deo. Lib. i. cap. xix.

[2] Sunt autem alii philosophi, et hi quidem magni atque nobilis, qui Deorum mente atque ratione omnem mundum administrari et regi censeant :

neque vero id solum, sed etiam ab iisden vitæ hominum consuli et provideri. Id. Lib. i. cap. ii.

[3] Quibus enim oculis animi intueri potuit vester Plato fabricam illam tanti operis, qua construi a Deo atque ædificari mundum facit ? Quæ molitio? quæ ferramenta ? qui rectes ? quæ machinæ ? qui ministri tanti muneris fuerunt ? Quemadmodum autem obedire et parere voluntati architecti aër, ignis, aqua, terra potuerunt.   Id. l. i. c. viii.

is one of those questions with which human wisdom is unable to cope. In their religious system, the Iroquois have but little to do with the creation of the visible universe. According to the tradition, the earth grew miraculously, a self-prepared abode for the Great Spirit. Concerning the universe which existed before the advent of the Great Spirit, they pretend to no knowledge. To the Great Spirit, however, the Iroquois ascribed creative power. He created not only the animal and vegetable world, but also adapted the elements, and the whole visible universe to the wants of man.

That the Indian, without the aid of revelation, should have arrived at a fixed belief in the existence of one Supreme Being, has ever been matter of surprise and admiration. In the existence of the Great Spirit, an invisible but ever-present Deity, the universal red race believed. His personal existence became a first principle, an intuitive belief, which neither the lapse of centuries could efface, nor inventions of man could corrupt. By the diffusion of this great truth, if the Indian did not escape the spell of superstition, which resulted from his imperfect knowledge of the Deity, and his ignorance of natural phenomena; yet he was saved from the deepest of all barbarisms, an idolatrous worship. The Iroquois believed in the constant superintending care of the Great Spirit. He ruled and administered the world, and the affairs of the red race. As Moses taught that Jehovah was the God of Abraham, Isaac and Jacob, and of his chosen

people, so the Iroquois regarded the Great Spirit as
the God of the Indian alone. They looked up to
him as the author of their being, the source of
their temporal blessings, and the future dispenser
of the felicities of their heavenly home. To him
they rendered constant thanks and homage for the
changes in the seasons, the fruits of the earth, the
preservation of their lives, and for their social
privileges, and political prosperity; and to him they
addressed their prayers for the continuance of his protecting care. Their knowledge of the attributes of
the Great Spirit was necessarily limited and imperfect. Of his goodness and beneficence they had a
full impression, and some notions, also, of his justice and perfection. But they could not fully con-
ceive of the omnipresence of the Great Spirit, except through the instrumentality of a class of inferior spiritual existences, by whom he was surrounded.
His power was evidenced by the creation of man.
He was also believed to be self-existent, and immortal. The ennobling and exalting views of the Deity which are now held by enlightened and christian
nations would not be expected among a people excluded from the light of revelation. In the simple
truths of natural religion they were thoroughly in-
doctrinated, and many of these truths were held in
great purity and simplicity. Such is the power of
truth over the human mind, and the harmony of all
truth, that the Indian, without the power of logic,
reached some of the most important conclusions of

philosophy, and drew down from heaven some of the highest truths of revelation.

While the religious system of the Iroquois taught the existence of the Great Spirit *Hä-wen-ne'-yu*,[1] it also recognized the personal existence of an Evil Spirit, *Hä-ne-go-ate'-geh*, the Evil-minded. According to the legend of their finite origin, they were brothers, born at the same birth, and destined to an endless existence. To the Evil Spirit, in a limited degree, was ascribed creative power. As the Great Spirit created man, and all useful animals, and products of the earth, so the Evil Spirit created all monsters, poisonous reptiles, and noxious plants. In a word, while the former made everything that was good and subservient, the latter formed everything that was bad and pernicious to man. One delighted in virtue, and in the happiness of his creatures, to which end he exercised over them his unceasing protection. The other was committed to deeds of evil, and was ever watchful to scatter discord among men, and multiply their calamities. Over the Evil-minded the Great Spirit exercised no positive authority, although possessed of the power to overcome him, if disposed to its exertion. Each ruled an independent kingdom, with powers underived. Man's free agency stood between them, with which, in effect, he controlled his own destiny. A life of trust and confidence in the Great Spirit, and of obedience to his commands, afforded a refuge and

[1] This is an original uncompounded word, and in the Seneca dialect. It signifies simply " A Ruler."

a shelter to the pious Indian against the machinations of the Evil-minded.

Inferior spiritual beings were also recognized in the theology of the Iroquois. Though not as accurately described and classified as those of the ancient mythology, they yet exhibit with them some singular coincidences; although these coincidences, real or imaginary, show nothing but the similarity of human ideas in similar conditions of society. They were classified into good and evil, the former being the *assistants* and *subordinates* of the Great Spirit, while the latter were the *emissaries* and *dependents* of the Evil-minded. To some of them was assigned a bodily form, a " local habitation, and a name." To the former class of these spiritual existences, they were wont to render their acknowledgments at their annual festivals for imagined favors, and to supplicate of the Great Spirit the continuance of their watchful care. In the creation of these subordinate beings, the Iroquois manifested their knowledge of the necessity of an Omnipresent Ruler; and at the same time they exhibited their limited comprehension of infinite power. Through these instrumentalities, they believed the Great Spirit was enabled, with ease and convenience, to administer the affairs of nature, and of man.

To *He'-no*, he committed the thunderbolt; at once the voice of admonition, and the instrument of vengeance. He also intrusted to him the formation of the cloud, and the gift of rain. By *He'-no*, was the earth to be cooled and refreshed, vegetation sustained, the harvest ripened, and the fruits of the earth matured. The terror of the Thunderer was held over evil-doers, but especially over witches. With power to inflict the most instantaneous and fearful punishment, he was regarded as the avenger of the deeds of evil. He is represented as having the form of a man, and as wearing the costume of a warrior. Upon his head he wore a magical feather, which rendered him invulnerable against the attacks of the Evil-minded. On his back he carried a basket filled with fragments of chert rock, which he launched at evil spirits and witches, whenever he discovered them, as he rode in the clouds. In the spring-time when the seeds were committed to the ground, there was always an invocation of *He'-no*, that he would water them, and nourish their growth. At the harvest festival they returned thanks to *He'-no* for the gift of rain. They also rendered their thanks to the Great Spirit for the harvest, and supplicated him to continue to them the watchful care of the Thunderer. There is a fanciful legend in relation to *He'-no*, to the effect that he once made his habitation in a cave under Niagara Falls, behind the sheet, where he dwelt amid the grateful noise and din of waters. The Great Spirit gave to him three assistants, who have continued nameless, to enable him to maintain a more vigilant supervision over the important interests committed to his guardianship. One of these, the legend declares, was partly of human, and partly of celestial origin.[1]   To bring *He'-no* nearer to their affections, the Iroquois always addressed him under the appellation of Grandfather, and styled themselves his grandchildren.   In every act of his, however, they recognized the hand of *Hä-wen-ne'-yu*.

Another of the spiritual creations of the Iroquois is recognized in *Gä'-oh*, the Spirit of the Winds. He is, also, a mere instrumentality, through whom the Great Spirit moves the elements.   Having a human form, with the face of an old man, *Gä'-oh* is represented as sitting in solitary confinement, surrounded by a tangle of discordant winds, and ever impatient of restraint.   His residence, *Da-yo-dä'-do-*

---

[1] The legend is as follows: A young maiden residing at *Gä'-u-gwa*, a village above Niagara Falls, at the mouth of Cayuga creek, had been contracted to an old man of ugly manners and disagreeable person. As the marriage was hateful to her, and, by the customs of the nation, there was no escape, she resolved upon self-destruction. Launching a bark canoe into the Niagara, she seated herself within it, and composing her mind for the frightful descent, directed it down the current. The rapid waters soon swept them over the falls, and the canoe was seen to fall into the abyss below, but the maiden had disappeared. Before she reached the waters underneath, she was caught in a blanket by *He'-no* and his two assistants, and carried without injury to the home of the Thunderer, behind the fall. Her beauty attracted one of the dependents of *He'-no*, who willingly joined them in marriage.

For several years before this event,

the people at *Gä'-u-gwa* had been troubled with an annual pestilence, and the source of the scourge had baffled all conjecture. *He'-no*, at the expiration of a year, revealed to her the cause, and out of compassion to the people, sent her back to them, to make known the cause, and the remedy. He told her that a monstrous serpent dwelt under the village, and made his annual repast upon the bodies of the dead which were buried by its side. That to insure a bountiful feast, he went forth once a year, and poisoned the waters of the Niagara, and also of the Cayuga creek, whereby the pestilence was created. The people were directed to move to the Buffalo creek. He also gave her careful directions touching the education of the child, of which she was to become the mother. With these directions she departed on her mission.

After the people had removed as directed, the great serpent, disappointed of his food, put his head *go-wä*, the " Great Home of the Winds," is stationary, in a quarter of the heavens toward the west. Surrounded and compressed by the elements, he ever and anon struggles to free himself from their entanglement. When perfectly quiescent, the winds are at rest. A slight motion sends forth the breeze, which is wafted gently over the face of the earth. When he struggles with restlessness and impatience, the strong wind goes forth to move the clouds, ruffle the waters, and shake the foliage of the forest. But when his restlessness mounts up to frenzy, he puts forth his utmost strength to shake off the confining element. These mighty throes of *Gä'-oh* send forth

above the ground to discover the reason, and found that the village was deserted. Having scented their trail, and discovered its course, he went forth into the lake, and up the Buffalo creek, in open search of his prey. While in this narrow channel, *He'-no* discharged upon the monster a terrific thunderbolt which inflicted a mortal wound. The Senecas yet point to a place in the creek where the banks are semicircular on either side, as the spot where the serpent, after he was struck, turning to escape into the deep waters of the lake, shoved out the banks on either side. Before he succeeded in reaching the lake, the repeated attacks of the Thunderer took effect, and the monster was slain.

The huge body of the serpent floated down the stream, and lodged upon the verge of the cataract, stretching nearly across the river. A part of the body arched backwards near the northern shore in a semicircle. The raging waters thus dammed up by the body broke through the rocks behind; and thus the whole verge of the fall upon which the body rested was precipitated with it into the abyss beneath. In this manner, says the legend, was formed the Horse-Shoe fall.

Before this event there was a passage behind the sheet from one shore to the other. This passage-way was not only broken up, but the home of *He'-no* was also destroyed, in the general crash. Since then his habitation has been in the west.

The child of the maiden grew up to boyhood, and was found to possess the power of darting the lightning at his will. It had been the injunction of *He'-no* that he should be reared in retirement, and not be allowed to mingle in the strifes of men. On a certain occasion having been beset by a playmate with great vehemence, he transfixed him with a thunderbolt. *He'-no* immediately translated him to the clouds, and made him the third assistant Thunderer.

the blasts which sweep the plain, lay low the oak upon the mountain side, and dash the waters against the sky. *Gä'-oh* is represented, however, as a beneficent being, ever mindful of the will of the Great Spirit, and solicitous to fulfil his commands.[1]

Perhaps the most beautiful conception in the mythology of the Iroquois, is that in relation to the Three Sisters, the Spirit of Corn, the Spirit of Beans, and the Spirit of Squashes. These plants were regarded as the special gift of *Hä-wen-ne'-yu*; and they believed that the care of each was intrusted, for the welfare of the Indian, to a separate Spirit. They are supposed to have the forms of beautiful females, to be very fond of each other, and to delight to dwell together. This last belief is illustrated by the natural adaptation of the plants themselves to grow up together in the same field, and perhaps from the same hill. Their apparel was made of the leaves of their respective plants; and in the growing season they were believed to visit the fields, and dwell among them. This triad is known under the name of *De-o-ha'-ko*, which signifies Our Life, or Our Supporters. They are never mentioned separately, except by description, as they have no individual names. There is a legend in relation to corn, that it was originally of easy cultivation, yielded abundantly, and had a grain exceedingly rich with oil. The Evil-minded, being

[1] Æolus naturally suggests himself to the reader, although the analogy is slight.

"Hic vasto rex Æolus antro
Luctantes ventos, tempestatesque sonoras
Imperio premit, ac vinclis et carcere fraenat."
Æneid, Lib. i. 52.

envious of this great gift of *Hä-wen-ne'-yu* to man, went forth into the fields, and spread over it a universal blight. Since then it has been harder to cultivate, yields less abundantly, and has lost its original richness. To this day, when the rustling wind waves the corn leaves with a moaning sound, the pious Indian fancies that he hears the Spirit of Corn, in her compassion for the red man, still bemoaning, with unavailing regrets, her blighted fruitfulness.

Among the inhabitants of the spiritual world, with which the Iroquois surrounded themselves, may be enumerated the Spirits of medicine, of fire, and of water, the Spirit of each of the different species of trees, of each of the species of shrubs bearing fruit, and of the different herbs and plants. Thus there was the Spirit of the oak, of the hemlock, and of the maple, of the whortleberry and of the raspberry, and also of the spearmint, and of tobacco. Most of the objects in nature were thus placed under the watchful care of some protecting Spirit. Some of them were made tangible to the senses, by giving to them a bodily form and specific duties; as the Spirit of springs, and of each of the several fruit trees. But the most of them were feebly imagined existences. In their worship, the Iroquois were accustomed to return their thanks to these subordinates of *Hä-wen-ne'-yu*, under the general name of *Ho-no-che-no'-keh*. This term signifies "the Invisible Aids," and included the whole spiritual world, from *He'-no* the Thunderer, down to the

Spirit of the strawberry. But few of them had specific names, or were mentioned in their worship, except conjointly. The Iroquois appear to have had but a faint conception of the omnipresence of the Great Spirit, as elsewhere observed; or of any individual power sufficiently potent to administer, unassisted, the stupendous works of creation, and the complicated affairs of man. In part from this cause, undoubtedly, they believed that the Great Spirit had surrounded himself with subordinate spiritual beings of his own creation, to whom he intrusted the immediate supervision of the various works of nature. He thus rendered himself, in a limited sense, omnipresent, and ruled and regulated, with ease and convenience, the works of creation. These Spirits were never objects of worship. The Iroquois regarded them merely as the unseen assistants of *Hä-wen-ne'-yu*, and the executors of his will.

Evil spirits were believed to be the creations of *Hä-ne-go-ate'-geh*. Pestilence and disease were supposed to be the work of evil spirits. Witches and enchanters were believed to be possessed with them. There were also the Spirits of poisonous plants and roots. All the agencies of evil were brought into existence by, and held under the dominion of the Evil-minded. To counteract their machinations, the efforts of the Great Spirit and his spiritual host were incessantly put forth. At their religious festivals, the Iroquois invoked *Hä-wen-ne'-yu* to shield them against their secret designs. " Great Spirit, master of all things, visible and invisible; Great Spirit, master of other spirits, whether good or evil; command the good spirits to favor thy children; command the evil spirits to keep at a distance from them." [1]

The Iroquois believed that tobacco was given to them as the means of communication with the spiritual world. By burning tobacco they could send up their petitions with its ascending incense, to the Great Spirit, and render their acknowledgments acceptably for his blessings. Without this instrumentality, the ear of *Hä-wen-ne'-yu* could not be gained. In like manner they returned their thanks at each recurring festival to the Invisible Aids, for their friendly offices, and protecting care. It was also their custom to return thanks to the trees, shrubs and plants, to the springs, rivers and streams, to the fire and wind, and to the sun, moon and stars; in a word, to every object in nature, which ministered to their wants, and thus awakened a feeling of gratitude. But this was done without the intervention of the incense of tobacco. They addressed the object itself.

A belief in witches is to this day, and always has been, one of the most deeply-seated notions in the minds of the Iroquois. The popular belief on this subject rose to the most extravagant degree of the marvellous, and the supernatural. Any person, whether old or young, male or female, might become possessed of an evil spirit, and be transformed

[1] La Hontan.

into a witch. A person thus possessed could assume, at pleasure, the form of any animal, bird or reptile, and having executed his nefarious purpose, could resume his original form, or, if necessary to escape pursuit, could transmute himself into an inanimate object. They were endued with the power of doing evil, and were wholly bent upon deeds of wickedness. When one became a witch, he ceased to be himself. According to the current belief, he was not only willing to take the life of his nearest friend, but such an one was the preferred object of his vengeance. The means of death employed was an unseen poison. Such was the universal terror of witches, that their lives were forfeited by the laws of the Iroquois. Any one who discovered the act, might not only destroy the witch, but could take to himself the dangerous power of deciding who it was. To this day, it is next to impossible, by any process of reasoning, to divest the mind of a Seneca of his deep-seated belief in witches.[1]

There is a current belief among the Iroquois, that these demons are banded together in a secret and systematic organization, which has subsisted for ages ; that they have periodical meetings, an initiation ceremony, and a novitiate fee. These meetings were held at night, and the fee of the neophyte was

[1] But a year since a woman was shot on the Allegany (Seneca) reservation, on the pretence of witchcraft. Such instances have been frequent among the Senecas within the last fifty years. Not the least singular feature of the case is that they sometimes confess the act. There may be some foundation for this strange delusion in the phenomena of nature.

the life of his nearest and dearest friend, to be taken with poison, on the eve of his admission.

The proneness of the Indian mind to superstitious beliefs is chiefly to be ascribed to their legendary literature. The fables which have been handed down from generation to generation, to be rehearsed to the young from year to year, would fill volumes. These fabulous tales, for exuberance of fancy, and extravagance of invention, not only surpass the fireside stories of all other people, but to their diversity and number there is apparently no limit. There were fables of a race of pigmies who dwelt within the earth, but who were endued with such herculean strength as to tear up by its roots the forest oak, and shoot it from their bows; fables of a buffalo of such huge dimensions as to thresh down the forest in his march; fables of ferocious flying-heads, winging themselves through the air; of serpents paralyzing by a look; of a monster musquito, who thrust his bill through the bodies of his victims, and drew their blood in the twinkling of an eye. There were fables of a race of stone giants who dwelt in the north; of a monster bear, more terrific than the buffalo; of a monster lizard, more destructive than the serpent. There were tales of witches, and supernatural visitations, together with marvellous stories of personal adventure. Superadded to the fables of this description, were legends upon a thousand subjects, in which fact was embellished with fiction. These legends entered into the affairs of private life, and of individuals, and were explanatory of a multitude of popular beliefs. Mingled up with this mass of fable, were their historical traditions. This branch of their unwritten literature is both valuable and interesting. These traditions are remarkably tenacious of the truth, and between them all there is a striking harmony of facts. Any one who takes occasion to compare parts of these traditions with concurrent history, will be surprised at their accuracy, whether the version be from the Oneida, the Onondaga, the Seneca, or the Mohawk. The embellishments gained by their transmission from hand to hand are usually separable from the substance, and the latter is entitled to credence. With these fables, legends and traditions the Indian youth was familiarized from infancy. His mind became stored and crowded with bewildering fictions. Without books, and without employment, in the intervals between the hunt, the council, and the warlike expedition, the mind naturally fell back upon this unwritten literature of the wilderness. The rehearsal of these marvellous tales furnished the chief entertainment at the fireside in the Indian village, and also at the lodge far hid in the depths of the forest. The credulity of youth would know no limits, when the narrator himself credited the tale he was relating. Growing into manhood under such intellectual influences, the young warrior would not readily discriminate between that which was too marvellous for belief and that which was consistent with truth, but would adopt the whole as equally veritable. That early and constant familiarity with such a mass of uncorrected fancies should beget a permanent tendency of mind to fall into superstitious beliefs, is far less surprising than would be an exemption from all such delusions.

From a vague and indefinable dread, these fables were never related in the summer season, when the imagination was peculiarly susceptible. As soon as the buds had opened on the trees, these stories were hushed, and their historical traditions substituted. But when the leaves began to fall, their rehearsal again furnished the chief amusement of the hours of leisure in Indian society.

The immortality of the soul was another of the fixed beliefs of the Iroquois. This notion has prevailed generally among all the red races, under different forms, and with different degrees of distinctness. "The happy home beyond the setting sun," had cheered the heart, and lighted the expiring eye of the Indian, before the ships of Columbus had borne the cross to this western world. This sublime conclusion is another of those truths, written, as it were, by the Deity, in the mind of man, and one easily to be deciphered from the page of nature by unperverted reason. This truth has always been taught among the Iroquois, as a fundamental article of faith.

In connection with the immortality of the soul, must be placed their belief in future punishments. This is maintained to have been a part of their ancient faith, but with how much truth it is difficult to determine. It is now taught by the unchristianized portion of the Iroquois, as an essential part of their belief.

The worship of the Iroquois, it is believed, has undergone no important change for centuries. It is the same, in all respects, at this day, that it was at the commencement of their intercourse with the whites. But their faith appears to have suffered some enlargement. They seem to have silently adopted such thoughts of the missionaries as could be interwoven harmoniously with their own creed, while at the same time they firmly and constantly excluded all those beliefs which were inconsistent with their own religious system, as a whole. The principal illustration of this position is to be found in their present views of the nature and office of punishment. They believe that the wicked, after death, pass into the dark realm of *Hä-ne-go-ate'-geh*, there to undergo a process of punishment for their evil deeds. Those who are not consumed by the degree of punishment inflicted, are, after this purification, translated to the abode of the Great Spirit, and to eternal felicity. Evil deeds in this life are neutralized by meritorious acts. After the balance is struck between them, if the good predominate, the spirit passes direct to *Hä-wen-ne'-yu-geh;* but if the bad overbalance, it goes at once to *Hä-nis-ha-o-no'-geh*, the dwelling-place of the Evil minded, where punishments are meted out to it in proportion to the magnitude of its offences. Certain crimes, like those of witchcraft and murder, were punished eternally, but others temporarily. The resemblance between this system of punishment and the purgatory of the Catholic church leads to the inference, that they derived from the Jesuits some of their ideas of the nature and office of punishment, and of its limitations. While, therefore, the Iroquois may have obtained more systematic and enlarged views upon these subjects from without, at the same time, as they affirm, they may always have believed that the wicked were excluded from heaven, and sent to a place of infelicity. Their traditions tend to establish a belief in future punishments, as a tenet of their ancient faith.

There is another practice, now universal among the Iroquois, which appears still more decisively to be of Jesuit origin. It is the confession of sins. Before each of their periodical religious festivals, there is made a general and public confession. Several days before the time designated for the festival, the people assemble by appointment, and each one in turn, who has a confession to make, rising, and taking a string of white wampum in his hand, acknowledges his faults and transgressions, and publicly professes a purpose of amendment. The white wampum is the emblem of purity and sincerity. With it he confirms and records his words. The absolution or forgiveness of sins formed no part of the motive or object in the confession. It had reference to the future conduct exclusively. One who was willing to confess a fault from a sense of religious duty, would, by the act, strengthen his mind against future temptation. This custom has prevailed so long among them, that they have lost its origin. It contains no such analogy to the practices of any Christian community as to compel us to ascribe it to external influences, but yet it has about it so much of the fragrance of Christianity, that it awakens in the mind a doubt of its Indian origin. It is by no means certain, however, but that it is one of their own primitive religious customs, under a modified form.

Reverence for the aged was also one of the precepts of the ancient faith. Among the roving tribes of the wilderness, the old and helpless were frequently abandoned, and, in some cases, hurried out of existence, as an act of greater kindness than desertion. But the Iroquois, at the epoch of the formation of the League, resided in permanent villages, which afforded a refuge for the aged. One of the prominent aims of their first lawgiver, *Da-gä-no-we'-dä*, was to bind the people together by the family ties of relationship, and thus create among them an universal spirit of hospitality, and a lasting desire of social intercourse. After the establishment of the Confederacy, certainly, these practices never prevailed among the Iroquois. On the contrary, their religious teachers inculcated the duty of protecting their aged parents, as divinely enjoined. "It is the will of the Great Spirit that you reverence the aged, even though they be as helpless as infants."[1]

The obedience of children, their instruction in

---

[1] *Sose-ha'-wä*, (Johnson.)

virtuous principles, kindness to the orphan, hospitality to all, and a common brotherhood, were among the doctrines held up for acceptance by their religious instructors. These precepts were taught as the will of the Great Spirit, and obedience to their requirements as acceptable in his sight. "If you tie up the clothes of an orphan child, the Great Spirit will notice it, and reward you for it." "To adopt orphans, and bring them up in virtuous ways, is pleasing to the Great Spirit." "If a stranger wander about your abode, welcome him to your home, be hospitable towards him, speak to him with kind words, and forget not always to mention the Great Spirit."[1]

Respect for the dead was another element of their faith. At various periods of their history, it has manifested itself under different and very singular forms. The burial customs of every people interest the mind. Death is the great catastrophe of humanity. And whether man has reached the highest intellectual elevation, or still sits beside the forest streamlet, in the infancy of his mental growth, this event seizes upon his mind with solemn and absorbing earnestness. With the Iroquois different customs have prevailed, in relation to the mode of burial. At one period they buried in a sitting posture, with the face to the east. Skeletons are still found in this position, in various parts of the State, with a gun barrel resting against the shoulder; thus fixing the period of their sepulture subsequent to

[1] Johnson.

the first intercourse of this people with the whites. It is supposed that this custom was abandoned at the persuasion of the missionaries, although there is a tradition ascribing it to a different cause. Another and more extraordinary mode of burial anciently prevailed among them. The body of the deceased was exposed upon a bark scaffolding, erected upon poles, or secured upon the limbs of trees, where it was left to waste to a skeleton. After this had been effected by the process of decomposition in the open air, the bones were removed, either to the former house of the deceased, or to a small bark house by its side, prepared for their reception. In this manner the skeletons of the whole family were preserved from generation to generation, by the filial or parental affection of the living. After the lapse of a number of years, or in a season of public insecurity, or on the eve of abandoning a settlement, it was customary to collect these skeletons from the whole community around, and consign them to a common resting-place. To this custom, which was not confined to the Iroquois, is doubtless to be ascribed the burrows and bone mounds, which have been found in such numbers in various parts of the country. On opening these mounds, the skeletons are usually found arranged in horizontal layers, a conical pyramid, those in each layer radiating from a common centre. In other cases they are found placed promiscuously.[1]

[1] There are Senecas now residing at Tonawanda and Cattaraugus, who   remember having seen, about sixty years ago, at the latter place, these

The religious system of the Iroquois taught, that it was a journey from earth to heaven of many days' duration. Originally, it was supposed to be a year, and the period of mourning for the departed was fixed at that term. At its expiration, it was customary for the relatives of the deceased to hold a feast; the soul of the departed having reached heaven, and a state of felicity, there was no longer any cause for mourning. The spirit of grief was exchanged for that of rejoicing. In modern times the mourning period has been reduced to ten days, and the journey of the spirit is now believed to be performed in three. The spirit of the deceased was supposed to hover around the body for a season, before it took its final departure; and not until after the expiration of a year according to the ancient belief, and ten days according to the present, did it become permanently at rest in heaven. A beautiful custom prevailed in ancient times, of capturing a bird, and freeing it over the grave on the evening of the burial, to bear away the spirit to its heavenly rest. Their notions of the state of the soul when disembodied, are vague and diversified; but they all agree that, during the journey, it required the same nourishment as while it dwelt in the body. They, therefore, deposited beside the deceased his bow and arrows, tobacco and pipe, and necessary food for the journey. They also painted the face

bark scaffoldings, on which bodies were then exposed. The custom still prevails among the Sioux upon the upper Mississippi, and among some of the tribes in the far west.

and dressed the body in its best apparel. A fire was built upon the grave at night, to enable the spirit to prepare its food. With these tokens of affliction, and these superstitious concernments for the welfare of the deceased, the children of the forest performed the burial rites of their departed kindred.[1] The wail and the lamentation evidenced the passionate character of their grief.[2] After the mourning period had expired, the name of the deceased was never mentioned, from a sense of delicacy to the tender feelings of his friends.

Unless the rites of burial were performed, it was believed that the spirits of the dead wandered for a time upon the earth, in a state of great unhappiness. Hence their extreme solicitude to procure the bodies of their slain in battle.

Heaven was the abode of the Great Spirit, the final home of the faithful. They believed there was a road down from heaven to every man's door.

---

[1] To this universal custom of the red race, of depositing the valuable articles of the deceased by his side, as well as utensils and vessels to prepare and contain his food, we are indebted for all the relics we possess of the earlier epochs of our aboriginal history. Articles are still disentombed from the soil from year to year, some of which reach back to the era of the Mound Builders.

[2] In ancient times, the practice prevailed of addressing the dead before burial, under the belief that they could hear, although unable to answer. The near relatives and friends, or such as were disposed, approached the body in turn; and after the wail had ceased, they addressed it in a pathetic or laudatory speech. The practice has not even yet fallen entirely into disuse. The following address of an Iroquois mother over the body of her son was made on a recent occasion. Approaching his inanimate remains to look upon him for the last time, her grief for some moments was uncontrollable. Presently, her wailing ceased, and she thus addressed him: "My son, listen once more to the words of thy mother. Thou wert brought into life with her pains. Thou wert nourished with her life. She has attempted to be faithful in

On this invisible way, the soul ascended in its heavenly flight until it reached its celestial habitation. As before observed, the spirit was supposed to linger for a time about the body, and perhaps to revisit it. In consequence of this belief, a superstitious custom prevailed of leaving a slight opening in the grave, through which it might reënter its former tenement. To this day, among a portion of the Iroquois, after the body has been deposited in a coffin, holes are bored through it for the same purpose. After taking its final departure, the soul was supposed to ascend higher and higher on its heavenly way, gradually moving to the westward, until it came out upon the plains of heaven. ☞

The inhabitants of this sinless dwelling-place of *Hä-wen-ne'-yu* were believed to possess a body, and the senses, appetites and affections of the earthly life. They carried their knowledge with them, and the memory of former friends. Sex was in

---

raising thee up. When thou wert young, she loved thee as her life. Thy presence has been a source of great joy to her. Upon thee she depended for support and comfort in her declining days. She had ever expected to gain the end of the path of life before thee. But thou hast outstripped her, and gone before her. Our great and wise Creator has ordered it thus. By his will I am left to taste more of the miseries of this world. Thy friends and relatives have gathered about thy body, to look upon thee for the last time. They mourn, as with one mind, thy departure from among us. We, too, have but a few days more, and our journey shall be ended. We part now, and you are conveyed from our sight. But we shall soon meet again, and shall again look upon each other. Then we shall part no more. Our Maker has called you to his home. Thither will we follow. *Na-ho.'"* After this was over, the wail continued for a few moments, when the body was borne away. The above was furnished to the author by *Hä-sa-no-an'-da*, (Ely S. Parker,) who heard it delivered. See also a specimen of an address to the dead in La Hontan's Voy. North Am. Lond. ed. 1735, vol. ii. p. 54.

effect abolished, but families were reunited, and dwelt together in perpetual harmony. All the powers of the Indian imagination were taxed to picture the glowing beauties of their celestial home. It was fashioned to please the natural senses. A vast plain of illimitable extension, it was spread out with every variety of natural scenery which could please the eye, or gratify the fancy. Forests clothed with ever-living foliage, flowers of every hue in eternal bloom, fruits of every variety in perpetual ripeness, in a word, the meridian charms of nature met the eye in every direction. To form a paradise of unrivalled beauty, the Great Spirit had gathered every object in the natural world which could delight the senses, and having spread them out in vast but harmonious array, and restored their baptismal vestments, he diffused over these congregated beauties of nature the bloom of immortality. In this happy abode, they were destined to enjoy unending felicity. No evil could enter this peaceful home of innocence and purity. No violence could disturb, no passions ruffle the tranquillity of this fortunate realm. In amusement or repose they spent their lives. The festivities in which they had delighted while on the earth were re-celebrated in the presence of the great Author of their being. They enjoyed all the happiness of the earthly life, unencumbered by its ills.

With the Iroquois, heaven was not regarded as a "hunting ground," as it appears to have been by some Indian nations. Subsistence had ceased to be

necessary. When the faithful partook of the spontaneous fruits around them, it was for the gratifica-
tion of the taste, and not for the support of life.

Among the modern beliefs engrafted upon the
ancient faith, there is one which is worthy of particular notice. It relates to Washington.[1] According to their present belief, no white man ever reached the Indian heaven. Not having been created by
the Great Spirit, no provision was made for him in
their scheme of theology. He was excluded both
from heaven, and from the place of punishment.
But an exception was made in favor of Washington. Because of his justice and benevolence to the
Indian, he stood preëminent above all other white
men. When, by the peace of 1783, the Indians
were abandoned by their English allies, and left to
make their own terms with the American government, the Iroquois were more exposed to severe
measures than the other tribes in their alliance. At
this critical moment, Washington interfered in their
behalf, as the protector of Indian rights, and the
advocate of a policy towards them of the most enlightened justice and humanity. After his death,
he was mourned by the Iroquois as a benefactor of
their race, and his memory was cherished with reverence and affection. A belief was spread abroad
among them, that the Great Spirit had received him
into a celestial residence upon the plains of heaven,
the only white man whose noble deeds had entitled

---

[1] His name among the Iroquois was *Hä·no-dä-gä'-ne-ars*, which signifies
"Town Destroyer."

him to this heavenly favor. Just by the entrance of heaven is a walled enclosure, the ample grounds within which are laid out with avenues and shaded walks. Within is a spacious mansion, constructed in the fashion of a fort. Every object in nature which could please a cultivated taste had been gathered in this blooming Eden, to render it a delightful dwelling-place for the immortal Washington. The faithful Indian, as he enters heaven, passes this enclosure. He sees and recognizes the illustrious inmate, as he walks to and fro in quiet meditation. But no word ever passes his lips. Dressed in his uniform, and in a state of perfect felicity, he is destined to remain through eternity in the solitary enjoyment of the celestial residence prepared for him by the Great Spirit.

Surely the piety and the gratitude of the Iroquois have, jointly, reared a monument to Washington above the skies, which is more expressive in its praise, than the proudest recitals on the obelisk, and more imperishable in its duration, than the syenite which holds up the record to the gaze of centuries.

The beliefs of our primitive inhabitants, when brought together in a connected form, naturally call forth an expression of surprise. A faith so purely spiritual, so free from the tincture of human passion, and from the grossness of superstition, can scarcely be credited, when examined under the ordinary estimate of the Indian character. It has been the misfortune of the Indian never to be rightly understood, especially in his social relations. Their religious and moral sentiments, such as they were, exercised as decisive an influence upon Indian society, as the precepts of Christianity do over enlightened communities. They furnished springs of action, rules of intercourse, and powers of restraint. And yet, where is the picture of Indian social life, which reveals the domestic virtues, the generous friendships, the integrity between man and man, the harmony of intercourse, and the sympathies of the heart, which bloomed and flourished in the depths of the forest. We have met the red man upon the war-path, and not at the fireside. We have dealt with him as his oppressor, and not as his friend. His evil traits, ever present with the mind, form the standard of judgment; and when his virtues rise up before us, they create surprise, rather than answer expectation, because the standard of estimation is universally unjust.

The mind of the Iroquois was deeply imbued with religious sentiments, the practical results, the actual fruits of which, unseen for the most part, by those who know the Indian only in his intercourse with the whites, reveal themselves in unexpected beauty, when we examine his social relations, and view him in his domestic life. Their influence upon the Iroquois, in their intercourse with other nations, is necessarily secondary. To judge of their religious system from its direct effects, it is necessary to look into Indian society itself. Here its primary influence, at least, must fall. It would be a grateful task to array the virtues, which sprang into existence in the seclusions of the wilderness, to light up the character of the red man. From the harmony which characterized their political relations under the League, down to the domestic quiet of the sylvan home, the picture is much the same. Peace, hospitality, charity, friendship, harmony, integrity, religious enthusiasm, the domestic affections, found a generous growth and cultivation among the Iroquois. Genius, learning and Christianity change the features of society, and cast over it an artificial garment, but its elements continue the same. It need not awaken surprise that the Indian has rivalled many of the highest virtues of civilized and christianized man; or that in some of the rarest traits in the human character, he has passed quite beyond him.

Whatever excellencies the Iroquois character possessed are to be ascribed, in a great measure, to their beliefs, and above all, to their unfailing faith in the Great Spirit. By adhering to that sublime but simple truth, that there was one Supreme Being, who created and preserved them, they not only escaped an idolatrous worship, but they imbibed a more ennobling and spiritual faith, than has fallen to the lot of any other unchristianized people.

CHAPTER II.

The Iroquois had a systematic worship. It consisted in the celebration of periodical festivals, which were held at stated seasons of the year. These observances were suggested by the changes in the seasons, the ripening of the fruits, and the gathering of the harvest. They were performed annually, with the same established ceremonies, which had been handed down from age to age. The worship of the Iroquois, as before remarked, has undergone no change in centuries. It is still the same, in all essential particulars, that it was at the period of their discovery. Some slight additions, ascribable, doubtless, to missionary instructions, will be detected, but they are too inconsiderable to change the form, or disturb the harmony of the whole. Upon an examination of the principal features of the system, it will become apparent that it was chiefly a thanksgiving worship, although the supplication of the Great Spirit for the continuance of his protection entered into it as an essential element.

Six regular festivals, or thanksgivings, were observed by the Iroquois. The first, in the order of time, was the Maple festival. This was a return of thanks to the maple itself, for yielding its sweet waters. Next was the Planting festival, designed, chiefly, as an invocation of the Great Spirit to bless the seed. Third came the Strawberry festival, instituted as a thanksgiving for the first fruits of the earth. The fourth was the Green Corn festival, designed as a thanksgiving acknowledgment for the ripening of the corn, beans and squashes. Next was celebrated the Harvest festival, instituted as a general thanksgiving to "Our Supporters," after the gathering of the harvest. Last in the enumeration is placed the New Year's festival, the great jubilee of the Iroquois, at which the White Dog was sacrificed.

The principle involved in the formal worship of the Great Spirit at stated periods, and the fidelity with which the Iroquois, in prosperity and in adversity, adhered to these observances from generation to generation, are of much more importance in forming a judgment of their religious sentiments than the mere ceremonies themselves. In this constant recognition of their dependence upon the divine power, there is much to awaken a feeling of sympathy and a sentiment of respect for a people, who, untaught by revelation, had reached such high conclusions. By assembling at periodical seasons to render their thanks to *Hä-wen-ne'-yu* for his gifts, they fully recognized the duty which rested upon them as the recipients of such favors. And, also, by supplicating the continuance of his watchful care, and by invoking his blessing upon their present acts, they manifested the sincerity of their faith, and the fulness of their trust in the great Author of their being. But the ceremonies themselves are not without a peculiar interest. They will convey to the mind a more distinct impression of the nature and simplicity of their worship. No attempt will be made to describe these observances with the minuteness of a picture. An outline of those appropriate to each festival will sufficiently illustrate their general character and purpose.

The question here presents itself as to the religious office or priesthood among the Iroquois. Under the League itself no sacerdotal office was recognized. Sachems were raised up, and invested with their titles by a council of all the sachems of the League. Chiefs were first raised up in the nation to which they belonged, and their title was afterwards confirmed by the same general council. But no religious dignitaries were ever raised up by the council of sachems to fill any priestly station. In each nation, however, there was a select class appointed by the several tribes to take the charge of their religious festivals, and the general supervision of their worship. They were styled *Ho-nun-de'-ont*, or "Keepers of the Faith," as the term literally signifies. In the election of this class, their powers and duties, and the tenure of their office, there are many circumstances to distinguish them as a sacerdotal order. To their number there was no limit, and they were usually about as numerous as the chiefs. The chiefs themselves were *ex officio* keepers of the faith. The office was elective, and continued as long as the individual was faithful to his trust. Suitable persons were selected by the wise men and matrons out of their respective tribes, and advanced to the office. Their original names were then taken away, and new ones assigned, out of a collection of names which belonged to this class. At the first subsequent council of the nation, their appointment and names were publicly announced, which in itself completed the investiture. The number furnished by each tribe was an evidence of its fidelity to the ancient faith. They were, to some extent, censors of the people; and their admonitions were received with kindness, as coming from those commissioned to remonstrate. In some cases they reported the evil deeds of individuals to the council, to make of them an example by exposure. Sometimes they held consultations to deliberate upon the moral condition of the people. It was the duty of every individual to accept the office when bestowed; but he could relinquish it at any moment by laying aside his new name and resuming his old. It was their duty to designate the times for holding the periodical festivals, to make the necessary arrangements for their celebration, and to conduct the ceremonies. Certain ones of their number, by previous appointment, made the opening speech, and the thanksgiving address at the council, and also delivered religious discourses whenever they were deemed advisable. All of the members of this class were equal in authority and privileges. Those animated by the highest zeal and enthusiasm would naturally assume the most active charge; but they had no acknowledged head. The distribution of all powers, duties and offices among a number of equals was the prevailing feature of their civil polity. It was necessary that women as well as men should be appointed keepers of the faith, and about in equal numbers. To the matrons more particularly was intrusted the charge of the feast. The Iroquois never held a mourning or religious council, without preparing an entertainment for all the people in attendance on the evening of each day. None but those matrons who were keepers of the faith could take any part in its preparation. But their duties were not confined to the supervision of the feast. They had an equal voice in the general management of the festivals, and of all of their religious concernments. During a discourse or address, all the keepers of the faith acted, if necessary, as prompters to the speaker, and through him communicated to the people any injunction or precept which they deemed advisable. For this reason, one of their names as a class was that of "prompters."

Notwithstanding the systematic organization of the keepers of the faith, and the precise limitation of their duties, there do not seem to be sufficient reasons for calling this class a religious order, or a priesthood, as these terms are usually understood. They were distinguished by no special privileges, except while in the act of discharging their prescribed duties; they wore no costume, or emblem of office, to separate them from the people. In fact they were common warriors, and common women, and, in every sense, of and among the people. The office was one of necessity, and was without reward, like all Indian offices of every name, and also without particular honor to the individual.

O-TÄ-DE-NONE'-NE-O NA WÄ'-TA; OR, THANKS TO THE MAPLE.

This was the first festival of the spring. It was usually called the Maple Dance. The primary idea of this ceremonial was to return thanks to the maple itself; but at the same time they rendered their thanks to the Great Spirit for the gift of the maple. It lasted but one day. When the sap began to flow, the keepers of the faith announced the time and place for commemorating the recurrence of this event, and summoned the people to assemble for that purpose. Some days before the time appointed for the festival, the people assembled for the mutual confession of their sins, both as an act of religious duty, and as a preparation for the council. This act preceded all the festivals; but it was more general and thorough at the three last, than at the three first, as they were deemed more important, and continued for a greater length of time. This council, *Sa-nun-dät-ha-wä'-tä*, literally " a meeting for repentance," was opened by one of the keepers of the faith, with an address upon the propriety and importance of acknowledging their evil deeds, to strengthen their minds against future temptations. He then took the string of white wampum in his hand, and set the example by a confession of his own faults; after which he handed the string to the one nearest to him, who received it, made his confession in like manner, and passed it to another. In this way the wampum went around from hand to hand; and those who had confessions to make stated wherein they had done wrong, and promised to do better in the future. Old and young, men, women, and even children all united in this public acknowledgment of their faults, and joined in the common resolution of amendment. On some occasions the string of wampum was placed in the centre of the room, and each one advanced in turn to perform the duty, as the inclination seized him. A confession and promise without holding the wampum would be of no avail. It was the wampum which recorded their words, and gave their pledge of sincerity. The object of the confession was future amendment. The Iroquois appear to have had no idea either of the atonement or of the forgiveness of sins. Meritorious acts neutralized evil deeds, but neither the one nor the other, when done, could be recalled, or changed, or obliterated.

The celebration of this festival was not limited to one particular place, but it was observed in all the villages of the several nations of the League, which were too remote to unite around the same council-fire. At the time appointed, the people gathered from the subjacent districts, some to offer religious admonitions, some prepared for the dance, others for the games, and still others for the enjoyment of the feast. It was one of their festive days, awakening the eagerness of expectation in the minds of all. On the morning of the day, the matrons, to whom the duty appertained, commenced the preparation of the customary feast for the people, which was as sumptuous as the season, and the means of the hunter life would afford. Towards meridian, the out-door sports and games, which were common to such occasions, were suspended, and the people assembled in council. An opening speech was then delivered, by one of the keepers of the faith. The following, made at the opening of one of these councils among the Senecas, is in the usual form, and will illustrate their general character:—

"Friends and Relatives:—The sun, the ruler of the day, is high in his path, and we must hasten to do our duty. We are assembled to observe an ancient custom. It is an institution handed down to us by our forefathers. It was given to them by the Great Spirit. He has ever required of his people to return thanks to him for all blessings received. We have always endeavored to live faithful to this wise command.

"Friends and Relatives, continue to listen:—It is to perform this duty that we are this day gathered. The season when the maple tree yields its sweet waters has again returned. We are all thankful that it is so. We therefore expect all of you to join in our general thanksgiving to the maple. We also expect you to join in a thanksgiving to the Great Spirit, who has wisely made this tree for the good of man. We hope and expect that order and harmony will prevail.

"Friends and Relatives:—We are gratified to see so many here, and we thank you all that you have thought well of this matter. We thank the Great Spirit, that he has been kind to so many of us, in sparing our lives to participate again in the festivities of this season. *Na-ho'*."[1]

Other speeches often followed, which were in the nature of exhortations to duty. These occasions were seized upon by their moral teachers, to inculcate anew the precepts of their faith, and to offer admonitions for their spiritual guidance. One of the keepers of the faith, addressing the people at such a time, would inculcate the virtues which became a warrior, and unfold the duties which were incumbent upon them as members of one common brotherhood. The duty of living in harmony and peace, of avoiding evil speaking, of kindness to the orphan, of charity to the needy, and of hospitality to all, would be among the prominent topics brought under consideration. He would remind them that the Great Spirit noticed and rewarded good acts, and that those who hoped for success in the affairs of life, should be ready to do them whenever occasion offered; that those who had done wrong should not be treated harshly; that enmities were not to be contracted, lest a spirit of revenge should be awakened, which would never sleep; and finally,

[1] It is almost the universal custom among the Iroquois to conclude their speeches, on all occasions, with this exclamation. It signifies simply, " I have done."

that those who pursued the right path would never fall into trouble.

When these speeches and exhortations were concluded, the dance, which was a prominent feature of their religious festivals, was announced. It is proper here to observe, that dancing was regarded by the Iroquois as an appropriate mode of worship. They regarded the dance as a perpetual outward ceremonial of thanksgiving to the Great Spirit. A belief prevailed among them that the custom was of divine origin. "The Great Spirit knew the Indian could not live without some amusement, therefore he originated the idea of dancing, which he gave to them."[1]   The dance set apart in a peculiar manner for the worship of the Great Spirit, at their festivals, was one of their own invention; and the most spirited, graceful and beautiful in their list. It is known as the Great Feather Dance, (*O-sto-weh'-go-wä.*) It was performed by a select band, in full costume, and was reserved exclusively for religious councils, and for great occasions. It lasted about an hour, never failing to arouse a deep spirit of enthusiastic excitement. Before the band came in, one of the keepers of the faith made a brief speech, explanatory of its origin, nature and objects; in which the popular belief was interwoven, that this dance would be enjoyed by the faithful in the future life, in the realm of the Great Spirit, to whose worship it was especially consecrated.

[1] *Sose-ha'-wä*, (Johnson.)

After the conclusion of this dance others followed, in which all participated. Before they were
ended, the usual thanksgiving address to the Great
Spirit, with the burning of tobacco, was made. In
ancient times the Maple festival was terminated
with these dances. One of the keepers of the
faith made a closing speech, after which the people partook of the feast, and separated for their respective homes.

There is a popular belief among the Iroquois
that the early part of the day is dedicated to the
Great Spirit, and the after part to the spirits of the
dead ; consequently their religious services should
properly be concluded at meridian. They still retain the theory, and to this day religious discourses
are seldom continued after noon ; but in practice
it was found impossible, from the tardiness of the
people in assembling, to conclude the ceremonies of
the festival before twilight. A further innovation
was made many years ago by devoting the evenings
of these festive days to dancing, for the entertainment of guests from other villages or nations, who
chanced to be with them. This became, in time,
the universal custom, and they now continue the practice for their own amusement. These evening entertainments, however, in strictness, form no part of the
festival, although apparently it is one proceeding
from the opening of the council until late at night,
when the entertainment is ended. A distinction
should constantly be held in view, between their
proper religious exercises, and their amusements,

and also between the ancient mode of celebrating these festivals, and the modern. The regular religious ceremonies at the Maple festival consisted of the opening discourse by one of the keepers of the faith, the exhortations of others, the Feather dance, the thanksgiving address to the Great Spirit, with the incense of tobacco, two or three other dances, the closing speech, and the feast in common.

In ancient times these ceremonies were concluded at meridian, but in modern times at twilight. Formerly all the exercises at these festivals were of a strictly religious character, except certain games which were common to these occasions. But in later times other dances have been added, and also an evening entertainment devoted exclusively to dancing. There were likewise certain games of chance, sports, and athletic games, common to all these festivals, which yet formed no part of their religious ceremonies. They were merely outside diversions for the people. Still the Maple festival, as celebrated at the present day among the descendants of the ancient Iroquois, is the same in its essential features, as at the period of its institution.[1]

A-YENT'-WÄ-TÄ; OR, PLANTING FESTIVAL.

This word signifies " the planting season." When this time arrived another festival was held to cel-

[1] The Iroquois have long been in the habit of manufacturing sugar from the maple. Whether they learned the art from us, or we from them, may be a difficult question; although the former would seem the more probable, from the want of suitable vessels among them for boiling.

ebrate the event. It continued but one day. In its observances there was nothing to distinguish it very materially from the Maple festival. A description is therefore unnecessary, except to point out some peculiarities. The object of this festival was two-fold : to render thanks to the Great Spirit for the return of the planting season, and to invoke his blessing upon the seed which they had committed to the earth, that it might yield an abundant harvest.

The Indian had no Sabbath, no sacred writings to furnish him an inexhaustible fountain of instruction; but his gratitude was awakened by every returning manifestation of divine goodness. When nature had reclothed herself in the vestments of spring, and the teeming earth invited him to commit the seeds to her bosom, he recognized in the event the watchful kindness of the Great Spirit. There is something eminently spiritual and beautiful in this Indian conception of the natural periods of worship. Seizing upon the moment when the most conspicuous evidences of the protecting care of the Deity were before him, he acknowledged both his existence, and his beneficence, and manifested, at the same time, his gratitude, and devotion, by those simple rites which the piety of his heart suggested.

At the time appointed by the keepers of the faith, the people assembled to observe the day. After the speeches were over, the Feather and other dances were performed, as at the Maple festival.

In ancient times, the thanksgiving address, or prayer to the Great Spirit, with the burning of tobacco, was confined to the last three, or the principal festivals; but in later days such a prayer was offered generally at the first three also. As elsewhere observed, when the Iroquois returned thanks to the various objects in nature which ministered to their wants, or when they acknowledged to each other their thankfulness to the Great Spirit, or to the lesser Spirits, they never burned tobacco. In these cases, their thanks were returned to the trees and plants and elements direct, to do which, according to their theology, did not require the use of incense, while, as to the spiritual world, they merely avowed to each other that they returned their thanks. But when they offered a prayer, or called upon the Great Spirit, or his Invisible Aids, they were obliged to use the ascending smoke to put themselves in communication with the spiritual world.

This address occurred at no particular stage in the ceremonies of the day. The keepers of the faith having appointed one of their number to perform this duty, the person designated selected a suitable moment for its delivery. Advancing to the fire prepared for the purpose, he called the attention of the people by an exclamation, which was the known precursor of this address. Having sprinkled a few leaves of Indian tobacco upon the fire, he addressed *Hä-wen-ne'-yu*, as the smoke ascended. The following, delivered at a Planting festival among the

Senecas, will illustrate the general character of these prayers or thanksgiving addresses :—

"Great Spirit, who dwellest alone, listen now to the words of thy people here assembled. The smoke of our offering arises. Give kind attention to our words, as they arise to thee in the smoke. We thank thee for this return of the planting season. Give to us a good season, that our crops may be plentiful.

"Continue to listen, for the smoke yet arises. (Throwing on tobacco.) Preserve us from all pestilential diseases. Give strength to us all that we may not fall. Preserve our old men among us, and protect the young. Help us to celebrate with feeling the ceremonies of this season. Guide the minds of thy people, that they may remember thee in all their actions. *Na-ho'*."

There was nothing further to distinguish this festival from the former.

If, after the planting season, a drought should come upon the land, threatening a failure of the harvest, a special council was frequently called, to invoke *Hé'-no*, the Thunderer, to send rain upon the earth. Before the time appointed for this council, the people assembled, as before other festivals, for mutual confession. They feared, as they expressed it, "that some of their number had done some great wrong, for which the Great Spirit was angry with them, and withheld the rain as a merited punishment." After this special council was opened in the usual form, the Thanksgiving dance, and the *Ah-do'-weh*, hereafter to be described, were introduced, which were supposed to be peculiarly acceptable to *Hé'-no*. At a proper time, in the progress of these ceremonies, the keeper of the faith, who had been appointed as usual, advanced to the fire, and having laid on the leaves of tobacco, and gained the attention of the people, he made the following invocation of the Thunderer, as the incense ascended:—

" *He'-no*, our Grandfather, listen now to the words of thy grandchildren. We feel grieved. Our minds are sorely troubled. We fear Our Supporters will fail, and bring famine upon us. We ask our Grandfather that he may come, and give us rain, that the earth may not dry up, and refuse to produce for our support. Thy grandchildren all send their salutations to their Grandfather, *He'-no*."

Then taking another handful of tobacco, and placing it upon the fire, he changed the address to *Hä-wen-ne'-yu*.

" Great Spirit: listen to the words of thy suffering children. They come to thee with pure minds. If they have done wrong, they have confessed, and turned their minds, (at the same time holding up the string of white wampum with which the confession was recorded.) Be kind to us. Hear our grievances, and supply our wants. Direct that *He'-no* may come, and give us rain, that Our Supporters may not fail us, and bring famine to our homes. *Na-ho'*."

After concluding the dance the assembly was dismissed.

HA-NUN-DÄ'-YO; OR, BERRY FESTIVAL.

In the progress of the seasons, next came the Strawberry, the first fruit of the earth. The Iroquois seized upon this spontaneous gift of nature for their sustenance, as another suitable occasion for a thanksgiving festival. By such ceremonials they habituated their minds to a recognition of the providential care of *Hä-wen-ne'-yu ;* cultivating, at the same time, a grateful spirit for the constant re-¹ turn of his gifts. The observances at this festival were the same as those at the Maple, with a sufficient variation of terms to designate the particular occasion. It was concluded with a feast of strawberries. The berries were prepared with maple sugar, in capacious bark trays, in the form of a jelly; and in this condition the people feasted upon this great luxury of nature.

The ripening of the Whortleberry was often made the occasion of another festival. It was in all respects like the last, the only difference consisting in the fact, that the former was an acknowledgment for the first fruit of plants, and the latter for the first fruit of trees.

AH-DAKE'-WÄ-O; OR, GREEN CORN FESTIVAL.

The word from which this takes its name signifies "a feast." It continued four days, the proceedings of each being different in most particulars, but each one terminating with a feast.

When the green corn became fit for use, the season of plenty with the Indian had emphatically arrived. They made it another occasion of general thanksgiving to the Great Spirit, and of feasting and rejoicing among themselves. Corn has ever been the staple article of consumption among the Iroquois. They cultivated this plant, and also the bean and the squash, before the formation of the

League. From the most remote period to which tradition reaches, the knowledge of the cultivation and use of these plants has been handed down among them.[1] They raised sufficient quantities of each to supply their utmost wants, preparing them for food in a great variety of ways, and making them at least the basis of their sustenance. In their own mode of expressing the idea, these plants are mentioned together, under the figurative name of "Our Life," or "Our Supporters." It cannot, therefore, be affirmed with correctness, that the Indian subsisted principally by the chase. After the formation of the League, they resided in permanent villages, and within certain well-defined territorial limits. The fruits of the chase then became a secondary, although a necessary means of subsistence.[2]

On the first day of this festival, after the introductory speeches had been made, the Feather dance, the thanksgiving address, with the burning of tobacco, and three or four other dances, made up the

---

[1] According to the legend, the corn plant sprang from the bosom of the mother of the Great Spirit, after her burial.

[2] The quantities of corn raised by the Iroquois was a constant cause of remark among those who went earliest among them. The first expedition into the Seneca county, of a warlike character, was made by the Marquis De Nonville, as early as 1687, but a few years after the geographical location of the Iroquois nations became known to the French and English. He thus speaks of the quantity of corn. "We remained at the four Seneca villages until the 24th of July. All that time we spent in destroying the corn, which was in such great abundance, that the loss, including old corn which was in *cache* which we burnt, and that which was standing, was computed according to the estimate afterwards made, at four hundred thousand minots of Indian corn." (1,200,000 bushels.) Documentary Hist. New York, v. i. p. 238. This, however, must be regarded as an extravagant estimate.

principal religious exercises. This address was introduced in the midst of one of the dances which succeeded the first. One more specimen of these brief prayers of the Iroquois, as made by the Senecas, will be furnished. Having placed the leaves of tobacco on the fire, as usual, the keeper of the faith thus addressed *Hä-wen-ne'-yu*:—

"Great Spirit in heaven, listen to our words. We have assembled to perform a sacred duty, as thou hast commanded. This institution has descended to us from our fathers. We salute thee with our thanks, that thou hast preserved so many of us another year, to participate in the ceremonies of this occasion.

"Great Spirit, continue to listen: We thank thee for thy great goodness in causing our mother, the earth, again to bring forth her fruits. We thank thee that thou hast caused Our Supporters to yield abundantly.

"Great Spirit, our words still continue to flow towards thee. (Throwing on tobacco.) Preserve us from all danger. Preserve our aged men. Preserve our mothers. Preserve our warriors. Preserve our children. We burn this tobacco; may its smoke arise to thee. May our thanks, ascending with it, be pleasing to thee. Give wisdom to the keepers of the faith, that they may direct these ceremonies with propriety. Strengthen our warriors, that they may celebrate with pleasure the sacred dances of thy appointment.

"Great Spirit; the council here assembled, the aged men and women, the strong warriors, the women and children, unite their voice of thanksgiving to thee. *Na-ho'*." [1]

Before partaking of the feast, the people went out to witness some of those games which were often introduced, as an amusement, to accompany the other exercises of these festive days.

[1] For a similar address in use   North Am., Lond. Ed. 1735, vol. 2, among the Ottawas, see La Hontan's   p. 34.

The second day commenced with the usual address, after which they had the Thanksgiving dance, *Gä-na'-o-uh*, which was the principal religious exercise of the day. This dance was not necessarily a costume performance, although it was usually given by a select band in full dress. In figure, step and music, it was precisely like the Feather dance, the chief difference between them being the introduction of short thanksgiving speeches between the songs of the dance. This dance is fully explained elsewhere; but it is proper to say, to make it intelligible here, that the music consisted of a series of thanksgiving songs, performed by select singers, who accompanied themselves with turtle-shell rattles, to mark time. Each song lasted about two minutes, during which the band danced around the room, in column, with great animation. When the song ceased, the dancers walked around the council-house, about the same length of time, to the beat of the rattles. The thanksgiving speeches were made during these intervals between the songs. A person arose, and perhaps thanked the Maple as follows: "We return thanks to the Maple, which yields its sweet waters for the good of man." Again the dance was resumed, and another song danced out, after which another speech was made by some other person, perhaps as follows: "We return thanks to the bushes and trees, which provide us with fruit." The dance was then resumed as before. In this manner the thanksgiving speeches, the songs and the dance were continued, until all the prominent objects in nature had been made the subjects of special notice. There were always set speeches introduced with the Thanksgiving dance, at the Green Corn and Harvest festivals, and they formed a conspicuous part of the worship of the Iroquois. These speeches, or the principal ones, may be collected into one, for the purpose of showing the range of subjects taken; yet it must be borne in mind that each object formed the subject of a separate speech, and was followed by a thanksgiving song, adapted to the case, which the band danced through. It may be proper further to add, that these speeches were consolidated to form the principal part of the annual thanksgiving address to the Great Spirit, made at the burning of the White Dog. The following is their natural order.

"We return thanks to our mother, the earth, which sustains us. We return thanks to the rivers and streams, which supply us with water. We return thanks to all herbs, which furnish medicines for the cure of our diseases. We return thanks to the corn, and to her sisters, the beans and squashes, which give us life. We return thanks to the bushes and trees, which provide us with fruit. We return thanks to the wind, which, moving the air, has banished diseases. We return thanks to the moon and stars, which have given to us their light when the sun was gone. We return thanks to our grandfather *He'-no*, that he has protected his grandchildren from witches and reptiles, and has given to us his rain. We return thanks to the sun, that he has looked upon the earth with a beneficent eye. Lastly, we return thanks to the Great Spirit, in whom is embodied all goodness, and who directs all things for the good of his children."

After the conclusion of the Thanksgiving dance, two or three other dances followed, and after them the feast, with which the exercises of the day were concluded.

The third morning was set apart for a thanksgiving concert, called the *Ah-do'-weh*, which constituted the chief ceremony of the day. The council was opened by an introductory speech by one of the keepers of the faith, upon its nature, objects and institution. This novelty in their worship was a succession of short speeches made by different persons, one after another, returning thanks to a great variety of objects, each one following his speech with an appropriate song, the words of which were of his own composing, and oftentimes the music also. In a chorus to each song all the people joined, thus sending forth a united anthem of praise. They passed through the whole range of natural objects, thanking each one directly, as in the Thanksgiving dance; but they were not in the *Ah-do'-weh* confined either to the natural or to the spiritual world. Acts of kindness, personal achievements, political events, in a word, all the affairs of public and private life were open on this occasion to the indulgence of the grateful affections. Oftentimes one or two hours were consumed, before the people had all expressed their thanks to each other for per-

sonal favors, to the works of nature for their constant ministration to their wants, and to the Great
Spirit and the "Invisible Aids" for their protecting
care.   Many of the speeches on these occasions, especially those which referred to objects in the natural world, were the same from year to year.   But
those which grew out of their private relations
would vary with circumstances.   This was esteemed
one of their highest religious exercises, and it always continued to be one of their favorite observances.   When the *Ah-do'-weh* was concluded, two or
three dances were generally introduced before the
enjoyment of the feast, with which, as before remarked, each day's proceedings were terminated.

On the fourth day, the festival was concluded
with the peach-stone game, *Gus-gä'-a*, a game of
chance, on which they bet profusely, and to which
they were extravagantly attached.   It was not in
the nature of a religious exercise, but a favorite entertainment, with which to terminate the Green
Corn ceremonial.   It is elsewhere described.

It should be held in the memory, that at the period of the institution of their religious festivals, they
were concluded at meridian; during the middle
period of their history, they were continued until
towards twilight; but in modern times, an evening
entertainment, in the way of dancing, always follows each day of the festival, so long as it continues,
although it forms no part of their religious observances.   It may be further observed, that at the
present time, this festival lasts but three days, the

proceedings of the third and fourth being completed on the former day.

At the close of each day, the people regaled themselves upon a sumptuous feast of succotash. This was always the entertainment at the green corn season. It was made of corn, beans and squashes, and was always a favorite article of food with the red man. It may be well to state in this connection, that among the Iroquois at the present day, they do not sit down together to a common repast, except at religious councils of unusual interest. The feast, after being prepared at the place of council, is distributed at its close, and carried by the women, in vessels brought for the purpose, to their respective homes, where it is enjoyed by each family at their own fireside. But when the people feasted together after the ancient fashion, as they still do occasionally, they selected the hour of twilight. The huge kettles of soup, or hommony, or succotash, as the case might be, were brought into their midst, smoking from the fire. Before partaking of this evening banquet, they never omitted to say grace, which, with them, was a simple ceremonial, but in perfect harmony with their mode of worship. It was a prolonged exclamation, upon a high key, by the solitary voice of one of the keepers of the faith, followed by a swelling chorus from the multitude, upon a lower note. It was designed as an acknowledgment to each other of their gratitude to the great Giver of the feast.

DA-YO-NUN'-NEO-QUÄ NA DE-O-HA'-KO; OR, HARVEST FESTIVAL.

After the gathering of the harvest, the Iroquois held another general thanksgiving for four days. It was the last in the year, as the New Year's observances were not of the same general character. The name given to this festival signifies "Thanksgiving to Our Supporters." It was instituted primarily to return thanks to the corn, beans and squashes, which are always characterized by the Iroquois under this figurative name. Also, to the triad of Spirits, who are so intimately connected in their minds with the plants themselves, that they are nearly inseparable. The resulting object, however, of all these Indian rites, was the praise of *Hä-wen-ne'-yu*. Nature having matured and poured forth her stores for their sustenance, they instituted this ceremonial as a perpetual acknowledgment of their gratitude for each returning harvest.

In the mode of summoning this council, and in the religious ceremonies, and concluding festivities of each day, it so closely resembled the Green Corn worship, that a separate description is rendered unnecessary.

These religious councils were seasons of animation and excitement. The greater activity in social intercourse among the people, generally awakened by these ceremonies and festivities, contributed largely to keep up the spirit of these occasions. In the evening, as soon as the twilight hour was passed, the people gathered for the dance, as this entertainment, since the innovation before referred to, always follows the religious ceremonies of each day. The Iroquois have numerous dances, and to the practice itself they have always been extravagantly addicted. On such occasions the passion was gratified by a free indulgence, and the hours of the night passed by unheeded. With the Iroquois in their festivities, as with more refined communities, neither the admonition of the setting stars, nor of the fallen dew, " counselled sleep." Not, perhaps, until the faint light of approaching day illumined the east, did the spirit of enjoyment decline, and the last murmur of the dispersing council finally subside.

GI'-YE-WÄ-NO-US-QUÄ-GO-WÄ; OR, NEW YEAR'S JUBILEE.

The name given to this festival literally signifies, " The most excellent faith," or " The supreme belief."[1]

Among the ceremonies incident to the worship of the Iroquois, the most novel were those which ushered in the new year. In mid-winter, usually about the first of February, this religious celebration was held. It continued for seven successive days, revealing, in its various ceremonials, nearly every feature of their religious system. The prominent act which characterized this jubilee, and which, perhaps, indicated what they understood by " The most ex-

---

[1] This word will analyze as follows: Gi'-ye-wä, *faith* or *belief;* no-us'-quä, (superlative,) *excellent* or *best;* and go'-wä, *great* or *supreme.*

cellent faith," was the burning of the White Dog, on the fifth day of the festival. This annual sacrifice of the Iroquois has long been known, attracting at various times considerable attention. But the true principle involved in it, appears not to have been rightly understood. In the sequel, it will be found to be a very simple and tangible idea, harmonizing fully with their system of faith and worship.

Several days before the time appointed for the jubilee, the people assembled for the confession of their sins. On this occasion they were more thorough in the work than at any other season, that they might enter upon the new year with a firm purpose of amendment. This council not unfrequently lasted three days, before all the people had performed this act of religious duty.

The observances of the new year were commenced on the day appointed, by two of the keepers of the faith, who visited every house in and about the Indian village, morning and evening. They were disguised in bear skins or buffalo robes, which were secured around their heads with wreaths of corn-husks, and then gathered in loose folds about the body. Wreaths of corn-husks were also adjusted around their arms and ankles. They were robed in this manner, and painted by the matrons, who, like themselves, were keepers of the faith, and by them were they commissioned to go forth in this formidable attire, to announce the commencement of the jubilee. Taking corn-pounders in their hands, they went out in company, on the morning of the day, to perform their duty. Upon entering a house, they saluted the inmates in a formal manner, after which, one of them, striking upon the floor, to restore silence and secure attention, thus addressed them :—

"Listen, Listen, Listen :—The ceremonies which the Great Spirit has commanded us to perform, are about to commence. Prepare your houses. Clear away the rubbish. Drive out all evil animals. We wish nothing to hinder or obstruct the coming observances. We enjoin upon every one to obey our requirements. Should any of your friends be taken sick and die, we command you not to mourn for them, nor allow any of your friends to mourn. But lay the body aside, and enjoy the coming ceremonies with us. When they are over, we will mourn with you." [1]

After singing a short thanksgiving song, they passed out.

In the afternoon this visit was repeated in the same manner. After saluting the family as before, one of the keepers of the faith thus addressed them :—

"My Nephews, my Nephews, my Nephews :—We now announce to you that the New Year's ceremonies have commenced, according to our ancient custom. You are, each of you, now required to go

[1] This singular injunction exhibits the deep interest taken in the performance of these religious ceremonies. In practice, also, they possessed sufficient self-control to carry out the requirement to the letter. If a person died during this festival, the body was laid aside until it was concluded, and the relatives of the deceased participated both in the religious ceremonies, and in the amusements connected with them, with as much interest and attention as if nothing had happened. Sometimes those festivals were broken up by a bad omen : as if, for instance, a dog should bite one of the keepers of the faith on his visitorial round, they would stop the festival, and appoint a new one.

forth, and participate in their observance. This is the will of the Great Spirit. Your first duty will be to prepare your wooden blades (*Gä-ger-we-sä'*,) with which to stir up the ashes upon your neighbors' hearths. Then return to the Great Spirit your individual thanks for the return of this season, and for the enjoyment of this privilege."

Having sung another song, appropriate to the occasion, they departed finally, and when they had in this way made the circuit of the village, the ceremonies of the first day were concluded.

On the first day, however, the White Dog was strangled. They selected a dog, free from physical blemish, and of a pure white, if such an one could be found. The white deer, white squirrel, and other chance animals of the albino kind, were regarded as consecrated to the Great Spirit. White was the Iroquois emblem of purity and of faith. In strangling the dog, they were careful neither to shed his blood, nor break his bones. The dog was then spotted, in places, over his body and limbs, with red paint, and ornamented with feathers in various ways. Around his neck was hung a string of white wampum, the pledge of their sincerity. In modern times, the dog is ornamented with a profusion of many-colored ribbons, which are adjusted around his body and limbs.[1] The ornaments placed upon the dog were the voluntary offerings of the pious; and for each gift thus bestowed, the giver was taught

[1] The author once (February 6, 1846) counted *nine* different colored ribbons upon a white dog thus hung up during a New Year's celebration among the Senecas at Tonawanda. They were tied around his mouth, neck, legs, body and tail.

to expect a blessing. When the dog had been thus decorated, it was suspended by the neck about eight feet from the ground, on the branching prong of a pole erected for that purpose. Here it hung, night and day, until the morning of the fifth day, when it was taken down to be burned. Oftentimes two dogs were burned, one for each of the four tribes. In this case, the people separated into two divisions, and after going through separate preparatory ceremonies, they united around the same altar for the burning of the dogs, and the offering of the thanksgiving address to the Great Spirit.

On the second day all the people went forth, and visited in turn the houses of their neighbors, either in the morning, at noon, or in the evening. They went in small parties apparelled in their best attire. It was customary, however, for the people to be preceded by the two keepers of the faith who made the recitations the day previous, as a matter of etiquette; the houses not being open to all, until these personages had made their call. At this time was performed the ceremony of stirring the ashes upon the hearth, which appears to have no particular idea attached to it, beyond that of a formal visitation. Putting aside the disguise of the day before, the keepers of the faith assumed the costume of warriors, plumed and painted, in which attire they visited every family three times, in the morning, at noon, and in the evening. Taking in their hands wooden blades or shovels, they entered the lodge and saluted the family. One of them then stirred the ashes, and having taken up a quantity upon the blade of the shovel, and sprinkled them upon the hearth, he thus addressed the inmates, as they were in the act of falling: "I thank the Great Spirit that he has spared your lives again to witness this New Year's celebration." Then repeating the process with another shovel full of ashes, he continued: "I thank the Great Spirit that he has spared my life, again to be an actor in this ceremony. And now I do this to please the Great Spirit." The two then united in a thanksgiving song prepared for the occasion, upon the conclusion of which, they took their departure. Other parties of the people then came in successively, and each went through the same performances. In this manner every house was thrice visited on the second day, by the keepers of the faith in the first instance, and afterwards by the whole community.

The proceedings upon the third and fourth days were alike. Small dancing parties were organized, which visited from house to house, and danced at the domestic fireside. Each set selected a different dance, appointed their own leader, and furnished their own music. One party, for instance, took the Feather dance, another the Fish dance, another the Trotting dance, to give variety to the short entertainments which succeeded each other at every house. It was not uncommon, on such occasions, to see a party of juveniles, about a dozen in number, dressed in full costume, feathered and painted, dancing the War dance, from house to house, with all the zeal and enthusiasm, which this dance was so eminently calculated to excite. In this manner every house was made a scene of gaiety and amusement, for none was so humble or so retired as to remain un-visited.

Another pastime incident to these days, was the formation of a " thieving party," as it was called, a band of mischievous boys, disguised with false faces, paint and rags, to collect materials for a feast. This vagrant company strolled from house to house, accompanied by an old woman carrying a huge basket. If the family received them kindly, and made them presents, they handed the latter to the female carrier, and having given the family a dance in acknowledgment of the present, they retired without committing any depredations. But if no presents were made, or such as were insufficient, they purloined whatever articles they could most adroitly and easily conceal. If detected, they at once made restitution, but if not, it was considered a fair win, On the return of this party from their rounds, all the articles collected were deposited in a place open to public examination ; where any one who had lost an article which he particularly prized, was allowed to redeem it, on paying an equivalent. But no one was permitted to reclaim, as the owner, any article successfully taken by this thieving party on its professional round. Upon the proceeds of this forced collection, a feast was eventually given, together with a dance in some private family.

Guessing dreams was another of the novel practices of the Iroquois, which distinguished these festive days. It is difficult to understand precisely, how far the self-delusion under which the dreamer appeared to act was real. A person with a melancholy and dejected countenance, entering a house, announced that he had a dream, and requested the inmates to guess it. He thus wandered from house to house, until he found a solution which suited him. This was either received as an interpretation of an actual dream, or suggested such a dream as the person was willing to adopt as his own. He at once avowed that his dream had been correctly guessed; and if the dream, as interpreted, prescribed any future conduct, he fulfilled it to the letter at whatever sacrifice. The celebrated Cornplanter, *Gy-ant'-wä-ka*, resigned his chiefship in consequence of a dream.[1] In relation to ˌdreams, the Iroquois had ever been prone to extravagant and supernatural beliefs. They often regarded a dream as

---

[1] The dream of Cornplanter occurred about the year 1810. His influence with the Senecas had been for some years on the wane, which his friends ascribed to his friendly relations with the whites. During a New Year's celebration at his village on the Allegany, he went from house to house for three days, announcing wherever he went that he had had a dream, and wished to find some one to guess it. On the third day, a Seneca told him that he could relate his dream. Seeing him nearly naked and shivering with cold, he said: "You shall henceforth be called O-no'-no," meaning "cold." This signified that his name, *Gy-ant'-wä-ka*, should pass away from him, and with it his title as a chief. He then explained the interpretation to Cornplanter more fully: "That he had had a sufficient term of service for the good of the nation. That he was grown too old to be of much further use as a warrior or as a counsellor, and that he must therefore appoint a successor. That if he wished to preserve the continued good-will of the Great Spirit, he must remove from his house and sight every article of the workmanship or invention of the

a divine monition, and followed its injunctions to the utmost extremity. Their notions upon this subject recall to remembrance the conceit of Homer, that "dreams descend from Jove."

During the first four days the people were without a feast, from the fact that the observances themselves did not require the assembling of the people at the council-house. But entertainments were given in the evenings at private houses, where the night was devoted to the dance. Another amusement at this particular season was the Snow-snake game, which, like all Indian games, was wont to arouse considerable interest.

On the morning of the fifth day, soon after dawn, the White Dog was burned on an altar of wood erected by the keepers of the faith near the council-house. It is difficult, from outward observation, to draw forth the true intent with which the dog was burned. The obscurity with which the object was veiled has led to various conjectures. Among other things, it has been pronounced a sacrifice for sin.

white man." Cornplanter, having listened with earnest attention to this interpretation, confessed that it was correctly guessed, and that he was resolved to execute it. His presents, which he had received from Washington, Adams, Jefferson, and others, he collected together, with the exception of his tomahawk, and burned them up. Among the presents thus consumed was a full uniform of an American officer, including an elegant sword and his medal given him by Washington. He then selected an old and intimate friend to be his successor, and sent to him his tomahawk and a belt of wampum, to announce his resolution and his wishes. Although contrary to their customs, the Senecas, out of reverence for his extraordinary dream, at once raised up as a chief the person selected by Cornplanter, and invested him with the name of *Gy-ant'-wä-ka*, which he bore during his life. Cornplanter after this event, was always known among the Iroquois under the name of *O-no'-no*. This tomahawk, the last relic of Cornplanter, is now in the State Historical Collection at Albany.

In the religious system of the Iroquois, there is no recognition of the doctrine of atonement for sin, or of the absolution or forgiveness of sins. Upon this whole subject, their system is silent. An act once done, was registered beyond the power of change. The greatest advance upon this point of faith was, the belief that good deeds cancelled the evil, thus placing heaven, through good works, within the reach of all. The notion that this was an expiation for sin, is thus refuted by their system of theology itself. The other idea, that the sins of the people, by some mystic process, were transferred to the dog, and by him thus borne away, on the principle of the scapegoat of the Hebrews, is also without any foundation in truth. The burning of the dog had not the slightest connection with the sins of the people. On the contrary, the simple idea of the sacrifice was, to send up the spirit of the dog as a messenger to the Great Spirit, to announce their continued fidelity to his service, and, also, to convey to him their united thanks for the blessings of the year. The fidelity of the dog, the companion of the Indian, as a hunter, was emblematical of their fidelity. No messenger so trusty could be found to bear their petitions to the Master of life. The Iroquois believed that the Great Spirit made a covenant with their fathers to the effect, that when they should send up to him the spirit of a dog, of a spotless white, he would receive it as the pledge of their adherence to his worship, and his ears would thus be opened in a special manner to their petitions. To approach *Hä-wen-ne'-yu* in the most acceptable manner, and to gain attention to their thanksgiving acknowledgments and supplications in the way of his own appointing, was the end and object of burning the dog. They hung around his neck a string of white wampum, the pledge of their faith. They believed that the spirit of the dog hovered around the body until it was committed to the flames, when it ascended into the presence of the Great Spirit, itself the acknowledged evidence of their fidelity, and bearing also to him the united thanks and supplications of the people. This sacrifice was the most solemn and impressive manner of drawing near to the Great Spirit known to the Iroquois. They used the spirit of the dog in precisely the same manner that they did the incense of tobacco, as an instrumentality through which to commune with their Maker. This sacrifice was their highest act of piety.

The burning of the dog was attended with many ceremonies. It was first taken down and laid out upon a bench in the council-house, while the fire of the altar was kindling. A speech was then made over it by one of the keepers of the faith, in which he spoke of the antiquity of this institution of their fathers, of its importance and solemnity, and finally enjoined upon them all to direct their thoughts to the Great Spirit, and unite with the keepers of the faith in these observances. He concluded with thanking the Great Spirit, that the lives of so many of them had been spared through another year.

A chant or song, appropriate to the occasion, was then sung, the people joining in chorus. By the time this was over, the altar was blazing up on every side ready for the offering. A procession was then formed, the officiating keeper of the faith preceding, followed by four others bearing the dog upon a kind of bark litter, behind which came the people in Indian file. A loud exclamation, in the nature of a war-whoop, announced the starting of the procession. They moved on towards the altar, and having marched around it, the keepers of the faith halted, facing the rising sun. With some immaterial ceremonies, the dog was laid upon the burning altar, and as the flames surrounded the offering, the officiating keeper of the faith, by a species of ejaculation, upon a high key, thrice repeated, invoked the attention of the Great Spirit.

" *Quä, quä, quä :*—(Hail, hail, hail.) Thou who hast created all things, who rulest all things, and who givest laws and commands to thy creatures, listen to our words. We now obey thy commands. That which thou hast made is returning unto thee. It is rising to thee, by which it will appear that our words are true."[1]

Several thanksgiving songs or chants, in measured verse, were then sung by the keepers of the faith, the people joining in chorus. After this, was made the great thanksgiving address of the Iroquois. The keeper of the faith appointed to deliver it, invoked the attention of *Hä-wen-ne'-yu* by the same thrice-

[1] Some leaves of tobacco were attached to the wampum around the dog's neck, with the incense of which this invocation was made.

repeated exclamation. As the speech progressed, he threw leaves of tobacco into the fire from time to time, that its incense might constantly ascend during the whole address. The following is the address, as delivered among the Senecas:[1]—

"Hail, Hail, Hail:—Listen now, with an open ear, to the words of thy people, as they ascend to thy dwelling, in the smoke of our offering. Behold thy people here assembled. Behold, they have come up to celebrate anew the sacred rites thou hast given them. Look down upon us beneficently. Give us wisdom faithfully to execute thy commands.

"Continue to listen:—The united voice of thy people continues to ascend to thee. Forbid, by thy wisdom, all things which shall tempt thy people to relinquish their ancient faith. Give us power to celebrate at all times, with zeal and fidelity, the sacred ceremonies which thou hast given us.

"Continue to listen:—Give to the keepers of the faith wisdom to execute properly thy commands. Give to our warriors, and our mothers, strength to perform the sacred ceremonies of thy institution. We thank thee, that, in thy wisdom, thou hast given to us these commands. We thank thee, that thou hast preserved them pure unto this day.

"Continue to listen:—We thank thee, that the lives of so many of thy children are spared, to participate in the exercises of this occasion. Our minds are gladdened to be made partakers in the execution of thy commands.

"We return thanks to our mother, the earth, which sustains us. We thank thee, that thou hast caused her to yield so plentifully of her fruits. Cause that, in the season coming, she may not withhold of her fulness, and leave any to suffer for want.

"We return thanks to the rivers and streams, which run their

---

[1] Taken down by *Hä-sa-no-an'-dä,* (Ely S. Parker) as delivered by his grandfather, *Sose-ha'-wä,* at Tonawanda. This is the ancient address handed down from generation to generation, and unchanged in its essential particulars. *Sose-ha'-wä* has delivered it thus for the past twenty-five years at Tonawanda.

courses upon the bosom of our mother the earth. We thank thee, that thou hast supplied them with life, for our comfort and support. Grant that this blessing may continue.

" We return thanks to all the herbs and plants of the earth. We thank thee, that in thy goodness thou hast blest them all, and given them strength to preserve our bodies healthy, and to cure us of the diseases inflicted upon us by evil spirits. We ask thee not to take from us these blessings.

" We return thanks to the Three Sisters. We thank thee, that thou hast provided them as the main supporters of our lives. We thank thee, for the abundant harvest gathered in during the past season. We ask that Our Supporters may never fail us, and cause our children to suffer from want.

" We return thanks to the bushes and trees which provide us with fruit. We thank thee, that thou hast blessed them, and made them to produce for the good of thy creatures. We ask, that they may not refuse to yield plentifully for our enjoyment.

" We return thanks to the winds, which, moving, have banished all diseases. We thank thee that thou hast thus ordered. We ask the continuation of this great blessing.

" We return thanks to our grandfather *He'-no*. We thank thee, that thou hast so wisely provided for our happiness and comfort, in ordering the rain to descend upon the earth, giving us water, and causing all plants to grow. We thank thee, that thou hast given us *He'-no*, our grandfather, to do thy will in the protection of thy people. We ask that this great blessing may be continued to us.

" We return thanks to the moon and stars, which give us light when the sun has gone to his rest. We thank thee, that thy wisdom has so kindly provided, that light is never wanting to us. Continue unto us this goodness.

" We return thanks to the sun, that he has looked upon the earth with a beneficent eye. We thank thee, that thou hast, in thy unbounded wisdom, commanded the sun to regulate the return of the seasons, to dispense heat and cold, and to watch over the comfort of thy people. Give unto us that wisdom, which will guide us in the path of truth. Keep us from all evil ways, that the sun may never hide his face from us for shame, and leave us in darkness.

"We return thanks to the *Ho-no-che-no'-keh*.[1]   We thank thee, that thou hast provided so many agencies for our good and happiness.

"Lastly, we return thanks to thee, our Creator and Ruler.   In thee are embodied all things.   We believe thou canst do no-evil; that thou doest all things for our good and happiness.   Should thy people disobey thy commands, deal not harshly with them; but be kind to us, as thou hast been to our fathers in times long gone by. Hearken unto our words as they have ascended, and may they be pleasing to thee our Creator, the Preserver and Ruler of all things, visible and invisible.   *Na-ho'*."

After the delivery of this address, the people, leaving the partly consumed offering, returned to the council-house, where the Feather dance was performed.   With this the religious exercises of the day were concluded.   Other dances, however, followed, for the entertainment of the people, and the day and evening were given up to this amusement. Last of all came the feast, with which the proceedings of the day were terminated.

On the morning of the sixth day, the people again assembled at the place of council.   This day was observed in about the same manner as one of their ordinary religious days, at which the Thanksgiving dance was introduced.

[1] The *Ho-no-che-no'-keh* included the whole spiritual world, or subordinate spirits created by *Hä-wen-ne'-yu*.   They were believed by the Iroquois to be mere agencies or instrumentalities through whom the Great Spirit administered the government of the world.   They were also believed to have been created to minister to the happiness and protection of the Indian upon earth.

It should also be noticed that the leading objects in the natural world which are made the subject of their thanks, are designed to include all lesser objects.   Under each head, by a figure of speech, whole classes of objects were included.   Thus "the rivers and streams" include all bodies of water, springs, fishes, &c.; "the wind" includes all the birds of the air.

The seventh and last day was commenced with the *Ah-do'-weh*; after which the Peach-stone game was introduced, with the determination of which ended the New Year's jubilee.

Other incidents and circumstances connected with the worship of the Iroquois might be pointed out, and would be necessary to a full explanation of the details of their religious system ; but sufficient has been presented to exhibit its framework, and the principles upon which it rested. No attempt has been made to furnish a picture of either of these religious councils, by a minute description of their proceedings. All the detail has necessarily been omitted. To realize these festive and religious ceremonials of our primitive inhabitants, it would be necessary to have a delineation of the incidents of each day, step by step, a description of the dances, the several games, and of the preparation of the feast, and also an explanation of their modes of social intercourse and of action, the spirit by which the people were animated, and the general character of the scene.

These festivals have been observed from generation to generation, and at the same seasons of the year, upon the Mohawk, at Oneida, in the valley of Onondaga, on the shore of the Cayuga, and in the several villages of the Senecas. Before the voice of the white man was heard in these peaceful and secluded retreats of the forest, that of the Indian had been lifted up to the Great Spirit with thanksgiving and praise. The origin of these festivals is lost, as well as the date and order of their institution; but the Iroquois believe that they have been observed among them, at least since the formation of the League. They have no tradition, which professes to have taken the custody of these dates and events.

To one who has witnessed these observances from time to time, and learned to comprehend the principles and motives in which they originated, they possess a peculiar but almost indefinable interest. These simple religious rites of a people, sitting, it must be admitted, near the full meridian of natural religion, are calculated to fill the mind with serious impressions. In their earnest and constant efforts to draw near to the great Author of their being, to offer thanks for the unnumbered blessings strewn upon their path, and to supplicate the continuance of that watchful care without which there was no preservation, there is a degree of heart-felt piety which the mind cannot resist. We may derive instruction from the faith of any race, if it rises above the grossness of superstition, into the regions of spiritual meditation. The moral nature of man unfolds with thought; and the Indian, in the shades of the forest, as well as Socrates in the groves of Athens, or Moses upon the skirts of Sinai, may contribute some new lessons to the fund of moral instruction.

In this and the preceding chapter, the design has been to expose the structure of the worship of the Iroquois, and to elucidate the beliefs by which it was upheld. By the standard of Christian judgment, it must be confessed, that the Faith and Worship of the Iroquois make up a system, which, in its approaches to the truth, rises infinitely above the theological schemes of all other races, both ancient and modern, which originated independently of revelation. Having a firm hold upon the great truths of natural religion, they established a ceremonious, but simple worship. Unlike the bloody ritual of the Aztecs, its influence upon the mind, and upon the social life of the Indian, was mild, humanizing and gentle. The fruits of their religious sentiments, among themselves, were peace, brotherly kindness, charity, hospitality, integrity, truth and friendship; and towards the Great Spirit, reverence, thankfulness and faith. More wise than the Greeks and Romans in this great particular, they concentrated all divinity into one Supreme Being; more confiding in the people than the priestly class of Egypt, their religious teachers brought down the knowledge of the "Unutterable One" to the minds of all. Eminently pure and spiritual, and internally consistent with each other, the beliefs and the religious ceremonies of the Iroquois are worthy of a respectful consideration. A people in the wilderness, shut out from revelation, with no tablet on which to write the history of passing generations, save the heart of man, yet possessed of the knowledge of one Supreme Being, and striving, with all the ardor of devotion, to commune with him in the language of thankfulness and supplication, is, to say the least, a most extraordinary spectacle; not less sublime in itself, than the spectacle of the persecuted Puritan, on the confines of the same wilderness, worshipping that God in the fulness of light and knowledge, whom the Indian, however limited and imperfect his conceptions, in the Great Spirit, most distinctly discerned.

Their limited knowledge of the attributes which pertained to a Being endued with creative power, will not appear so surprising, when it is remembered to be the highest achievement of learning and piety, fully to comprehend the marvellous perfections of the Deity. When the complicated structures of Egypt, Greece and Rome are brought under comparison with the simple and unpretending scheme of theology of the children of the forest, there is found reason to marvel at the superior acuteness and profundity of the Indian intellect. It may be safely averred, that if the sustaining faith, and the simple worship of the Iroquois are ever fully explored, and carefully elucidated, they will form a more imperishable monument to the Indian, than is afforded in the purity of his virtues, or in the mournfulness of his destiny.

10*

CHAPTER III.

ABOUT the year eighteen hundred, a new religious
teacher arose among the Iroquois, who professed to
have received a revelation from the Great Spirit,
with a commission to preach to them the doctrines
with which he had been intrusted. This revelation
was received under circumstances so remarkable,
and the precepts which he sought to inculcate contained within themselves such evidences of wisdom
and beneficence, that he was universally received
among them, not only as a wise and good man, but
as one commissioned from *Hä-wen-ne′-yu* to become
their religious instructor. The new religion, as it
has since been called, not only embodied all the
precepts of the ancient faith, and recognized the
ancient mode of worship, giving to it anew the
sanction of the Great Spirit, but it also compre-
hended such new doctrines as came in, very aptly,
to lengthen out and enlarge the primitive system,
without impairing the structure itself. Charges of

GOS-TO-WEH or HEAD DRESS.

GA-DE-US-HA or NECK LACE

imposture and deception were at first preferred against him, but disbelief of his divine mission gradually subsided, until, at the time of his death, the whole unchristianized portion of the Iroquois had become firm believers in the new religion, which, to the present day, has continued to be the prevailing faith.

The singular personage who was destined to obtain such a spiritual sway over the descendants of the ancient Iroquois, was *Gä-ne-o-di'-yo*, or "Handsome Lake," a Seneca sachem of the highest class. He was born at the Indian village of *Gä-no-wau'-ges*, near Avon, about the year 1735, and died at Onondaga in 1815, where he happened to be on one of his pastoral visits. By birth he was a Seneca, of the Turtle tribe, and a half-brother of the celebrated Cornplanter, through a common father. The best part of his life was spent in idleness and dissipation, during which, although a sachem and ruler among the Senecas for many years, and through the most perilous period of their history, he acquired no particular reputation. Reforming late in life, in his future career he showed himself to be possessed of superior talents, and to be animated by a sincere and ardent desire for the welfare of his race. He appears to have adopted the idea of a revelation from Heaven, to give authority and sanction to his projected reformation. At this period, and for a century preceding, the prevailing intemperance of the Iroquois had been the fruitful source of those domestic disorders, which, in connection with their political disasters, seemed then to threaten the speedy extinction of the race. A temperance reformation, universal and radical, was the principal and the ultimate object of the mission which he assumed, and the one upon which he chiefly employed his influence and his eloquence, through the residue of his life. Knowing that argument and persuasion were feeble weapons in a contest with this mighty foe, Handsome Lake had the sagacity to address himself to the religious sentiments and the superstitious fears of the people. To secure a more ready reception of his admonitions, he clothed them with the divine sanction; to strengthen their moral principles, he enforced anew the precepts of the ancient faith; and to insure obedience to his teachings, he held over the wicked the terrors of eternal punishment. Travelling from village to village, among the several nations of the League, with the exception of the christianized Oneidas, and continuing his visits from year to year, this self-appointed apostle to the Indians preached the new doctrine with remarkable effect. Numbers, it is said, abandoned their dissolute habits, and became sober and moral men; discord and contention gave place to harmony and order, and vagrancy and sloth to ambition and industry. What peculiar motives induced him, when past the meridian of life, to change the whole tenor of his past career, and embark in this philanthropic enterprise for the social and moral improvement of the Iroquois, it may be difficult to ascertain. The origination of this project has, at times, been ascribed to

Cornplanter, as a means to increase his own influence; but this is not only improbable, but is expressly denied. The motives by which Handsome Lake claimed to be actuated were entirely of a religious and benevolent character, and in pursuance of the injunctions of his spiritual guides.

At the time of his supernatural visitation, about the year 1800, Handsome Lake resided at *De-o-no-sä-da'-ga*, the village of Cornplanter, on the Allegany river, in the State of Pennsylvania. As he explained the matter to his brethren, having lain ill for a long period, he had surrendered all hope of recovery, and resigned himself to death. When in the hourly expectation of departure, three spiritual beings, in the forms of men, sent by the Great Spirit, appeared before him. Each bore in his hand a shrub, bearing different kinds of berries, which, having given him to eat, he was, by their miraculous power, immediately restored to health. After revealing to him the will of the Great Spirit, upon a great variety of subjects, and particularly in relation to the prevailing intemperance, and having commissioned him to promulgate these doctrines among the Iroquois, they permitted him to visit, under their guidance, the realm of the Evil-minded, and to behold with his mortal eyes the punishments inflicted upon the wicked, that he might warn his brethren of their impending destiny. Like Ulysses and Æneas, he was also favored with a glance at Elysium, and the felicities of the heavenly residence of the virtuous. With his mind thus stored with divine precepts, and with his zeal enkindled by the dignity of his mission, *Gä-ne-o-di'-yo* at once commenced his labors.[1]

After his death, *Sose-ha'-wä* (Johnson) of Tonawanda was appointed his successor, the first and only person ever "raised up" by the Iroquois, and invested with the office of supreme Religious Instructor. A sincere believer in the verity of *Gä-ne-o-di'-yo's* mission, and an eminently pure and virtuous man, *Sose-ha'-wä* has devoted himself with zeal and fidelity to the duties of his office, as the spiritual guide and teacher of the Iroquois. He is a grandson of Handsome Lake, and a nephew of Red Jacket, and was born at the Indian village of *Gä-no-wau'-ges*, near Avon, about the year 1774, and still resides at Tonawanda in the county of Genesee.

At the Mourning and Religious councils of the League, which are still held, at intervals of a few years, among the scattered descendants of the children of the Long House, it has long been customary to set apart portions of two or three days to listen to a discourse from *Sose-ha'-wä* upon the new religion. On these occasions, he explains minutely the circumstances attending the supernatural visitation of Handsome Lake, and delivers the instructions, word for word, which he had been accustomed to

[1] The Iroquois are under the impression that Handsome Lake received a license from Washington to preach. There is no doubt that he applied to the government during the presidency of Jefferson for some recognition of his mission; but the paper which they still call the *license*, now in the possession of Blacksmith, at Tonawanda, is simply a letter from General Dearborn, dated in 1802, commending his teachings. *Sose-ha'-wä* (Johnson) fixes the period of this revelation in June, 1800. This venerable man has preached the doctrine upwards of thirty years.

give during his own ministration. Handsome Lake professed to repeat the messages which were given to him from time to time by his celestial visitants, with whom he pretended to be in frequent communication, and whom he addressed as his spiritual guardians, thus enforcing his precepts as the direct commands of the Great Spirit.

It is singular that the credulity, not only of the people, but of their most intelligent chiefs should have been sufficiently great to give credence to these supernatural pretensions; but yet it is in itself no greater, than that indicated by their belief in witchcraft, or in the omens of dreams. The influence of the new religion has been extremely salutary and preservative, without the restraints of which, the fears of *Gä-ne-o-di'-yo* might have been realized ere this, in the rapid decline, if not extinction of the race. Their downward tendencies were arrested, and their constant diminution of numbers was changed to a gradual increase. Its beneficent effects upon the people doubtless contributed more to its final establishment than any other cause.

At their councils and religious festivals, it was customary for the chiefs and keepers of the faith to express their confidence in the new religion, and to exhort others to strengthen their belief. The late Abraham La Fort, *De-ät-ga-doos'*, an educated Onondaga sachem, thus expressed himself upon this subject at a Mourning council of the Iroquois, held at Tonawanda as late as October, 1847:—

" Let us observe the operations of nature. The year

is divided into seasons, and every season has its fruits. The birds of the air, though clothed in the same dress of feathers, are divided into many classes; and one class is never seen to associate or intermingle with any but its own kind. So with the beasts of the field and woods; each and every class and species have their own separate rules by which they seem to be governed, and by which their actions are regulated. These distinctions of classes and colors the Great Spirit has seen fit to make. But the rule does not stop here; it is universal. It embraces man also. The human race was created and divided into different classes, whch were placed separate from each other, having different customs, manners, laws and religions. To the Indian, it seems that no more religion had originally been given than was to be found in the operations of nature, which taught him that there was a Supreme Being, all powerful and all wise; and on this account, as well as on account of his great goodness, they learned to love and reverence him. But in these latter times, when the restless and ambitious spirit of the white-skinned race had crossed the boundary line, and made inroads upon the manners, customs and primitive religion of the Indian, the Great Spirit determined to, and through his servant *Gä-ne-o-di'-yo* did reveal his will to the Indian. The substance of that will was no more than to confirm their ancient belief that they were entitled to a different religion, a religion adapted to their customs, manners and ways of thinking." [1]

[1] Furnished to the author by *Hä-sa-no-an'dä*, (Ely S. Parker,) from notes taken at the time.

As the discourse delivered by *Sose-ha'-wä*, from time to time, contains a very full exposition of their ancient beliefs, and mode of worship, together with the recent views introduced by Handsome Lake, mingled up in one collection, presenting, probably, a better idea of their ethical and religious system than could be conveyed in any other manner, it is given entire, and will explain itself.[1]

"The Mohawks, the Onondagas, the Senecas, and our children (the Oneidas, Cayugas and Tuscaroras) have assembled here to-day to listen to the repetition of the will of the Great Spirit, as communicated to us from heaven through his servant, *Gä-ne-o-di'-yo.*

"Chiefs, warriors, women and children:—We give you a cordial welcome. The sun has advanced far in his path, and I am warned that my time to instruct you is limited to the meridian sun. I must therefore hasten to perform my duty. Turn your minds to the Great Spirit, and listen with strict attention. Think seriously upon what I am about to speak. Reflect upon it well, that it may benefit you and your children. I thank the Great Spirit that he has spared the lives of so many of you to be present on this occasion. I return thanks to him that my life is yet spared. The Great Spirit looked

---

[1] The subjoined translation was prepared by *Hä-sa-no-an'-dä,* (Ely S. Parker,) from copious notes taken by him at the time of its last delivery in October, 1848, at a general Mourning council of the Iroquois, held at Tonawanda. It is proper to add, that he has listened to its delivery on several occasions, and is perfectly familiar with the subject. With some slight alterations, the language is his own. This discourse, as it is given, was made on the forenoons of the 4th, 5th and 6th days of October, 1848.

down from heaven upon the sufferings and the wan-
derings of his red children. He saw that they had
greatly decreased and degenerated. He saw the
ravages of the fire-water among them. He therefore raised up for them a sacred instructor, who
having lived and travelled among them for sixteen
years, was called from his labors to enjoy eternal
felicity with the Great Spirit in heaven. Be patient
while I speak. I cannot at all times arrange and
prepare my thoughts with the same precision. But
I will relate what my memory bears.

"It was in the month of *O-nike'-ya*, (June,) that
Handsome Lake was yet sick. He had been ill
four years. He was accustomed to tell us that he
had resigned himself to the will of the Great Spirit.
'I nightly returned my thanks to the Great Spirit,'
said he, 'as my eyes were gladdened at evening by
the sight of the stars of heaven. I viewed the ornamented heavens at evening, through the opening
in the roof of my lodge, with grateful feelings to
my Creator. I had no assurance that I should at
the next evening contemplate his works. For
this reason my acknowledgments to him were more
fervent and sincere. When night was gone, and
the sun again shed his light upon the earth, I saw,
and acknowledged in the return of day his continued
goodness to me, and to all mankind. At length I
began to have an inward conviction that my end
was near. I resolved once more to exchange friendly words with my people, and I sent my daugh-
ter to summon my brothers *Gy-ant'-wä-ka*, (Corn-

planter,) and *Ta-wan'-ne-ars*, (Blacksnake.') She
hastened to do his bidding, but before she returned,
he had fallen into insensibility, and apparent death.
Ta-wan'-ne-ars, upon returning to the lodge, hastened to his brother's couch, and discovered that portions of his body were yet warm. This happened
at early day, before the morning dew had dried.
When the sun had advanced half-way to the meridian, his heart began to beat, and he opened his
eyes. *Ta-wan'-ne-ars* asked him if he was in his
right mind ; but he answered not. At meridian he
again opened his eyes, and the same question was
repeated. He then answered and said, ' A man
spoke from without, and asked that some one might
come forth. I looked, and saw some men standing
without. I arose, and as I attempted to step over
the threshold of my door, I stumbled, and should
have fallen had they not caught me. They were
three holy men who looked alike, and were dressed
alike. The paint they wore seemed but one day
old. Each held in his hand a shrub bearing different kinds of fruit. One of them addressing me
said, ' We have come to comfort and relieve you.
Take of these berries and eat ; they will restore you
to health. We have been witnesses of your lengthened illness. We have seen with what resignation
you have given yourself up to the Great Spirit.
We have heard your daily return of thanks. He
has heard them all. His ear has ever been open to
hear. You were thankful for the return of night,
when you could contemplate the beauties of heaven.

You were accustomed to look upon the moon, as she coursed in her nightly paths. When there were no hopes to you that you would again behold these things, you willingly resigned yourself to the mind of the Great Spirit. This was right. Since the Great Spirit made the earth and put man upon it, we have been his constant servants to guard and protect his works. There are four of us. Some other time you will be permitted to see the other. The Great Spirit is pleased to know your patient resignation to his will. As a reward for your devotion, he has cured your sickness. Tell your people to assemble to-morrow, and at noon go in and speak to them.'' After they had further revealed their intentions concerning him they departed.

"At the time appointed Handsome Lake appeared at the council, and thus addressed the people upon the revelations which had been made to him: 'I have a message to deliver to you. The servants of the Great Spirit have told me that I should yet live upon the earth to become an instructor to my people. Since the creation of man, the Great Spirit has often raised up men to teach his children what they should do to please him; but they have been unfaithful to their trust. I hope I shall profit by their example. Your Creator has seen that you have transgressed greatly against his laws. He made man pure and good. He did not intend that he should sin. You commit a great sin in taking the fire-water. The Great Spirit says that you must abandon this enticing habit. Your ancestors have brought great misery and suffering upon you. They first took the fire-water of the white man, and entailed upon you its consequences. None of them have gone to heaven. The fire-water does not belong to you. It was made for the white man beyond the great waters. For the white man it is a medicine; but they too have violated the will of their Maker. The Great Spirit says that drunkenness is a great crime, and he forbids you to indulge in this evil habit. His command is to the old and young. The abandonment of its use will relieve much of your sufferings, and greatly increase the comfort and happiness of your children. The Great Spirit is grieved that so much crime and wickedness should defile the earth. There are many evils which he never intended should exist among his red children. The Great Spirit has, for many wise reasons, withheld from man the number of his days; but he has not left him without a guide, for he has pointed out to him the path in which he may safely tread the journey of life.

"'When the Great Spirit made man, he also made woman. He instituted marriage, and enjoined upon them to love each other, and be faithful. It is pleasing to him to see men and women obey his will. Your Creator abhors a deceiver and a hypocrite. By obeying his commands you will die an easy and a happy death. When the Great Spirit instituted marriage, he ordained to bless those who were faithful with children. Some women are unfruitful, and others become so by misfortune. Such have great opportunities to do much good. There are many orphans, and many poor children whom they can adopt as their own. If you tie up the clothes of an orphan child, the Great Spirit will notice it, and reward you for it. Should an orphan ever cross your path be kind to him, and treat him with tenderness, for this is right. Parents must constantly teach their children morality, and a reverence for their Creator. Parents must also guard their children against improper marriages. They, having much experience, should select a suitable match for their child. When the parents of both parties have agreed, then bring the young pair together, and let them know what good their parents have designed for them. If at any time they so far disagree that they cannot possibly live contented and happy with each other, they may separate in mutual good feeling; and in this there is no wrong. When a child is born to a husband and wife, they must give great thanks to the Great Spirit, for it is his gift, and an evidence of his kindness. Let parents instruct their children in their duty to the Great Spirit, to their parents, and to their fellowmen. Children should obey their parents and guardians, and submit to them in all things. Disobedient children occasion great pain and misery. They wound their parents' feelings, and often drive them to desperation, causing them great distress, and final admission into the place of Evil Spirits. The marriage obligations should generate good to all who have assumed them. Let the married be

faithful to each other, that when they die it may
be in peace. Children should never permit their
parents to suffer in their old age. Be kind to
them, and support them. The Great Spirit requires
all children to love, revere and obey their parents.
To do this is highly pleasing to him. The happiness of parents is greatly increased by the affection
and the attentions of their children. To abandon
a wife or children is a great wrong, and produces
many evils. It is wrong for a father or mother-in-
law, to vex a son or daughter-in-law; but they
should use them as if they were their own children. It often happens that parents hold angry dis-
putes over their infant child. This is also a great
sin. The infant hears and comprehends the angry
words of its parents. It feels bad and lonely. It
can see for itself no happiness in prospect. It concludes to return to its Maker. It wants a happy
home, and dies. The parents then weep because
their child has left them. You must put this evil
practice from among you, if you would live
happy.

"'The Great Spirit, when he made the earth,
never intended that it should be made merchandise;
but he willed that all his creatures should enjoy it
equally. Your chiefs have violated and betrayed
your trust by selling lands. Nothing is now left of
our once large possessions, save a few small reservations. Chiefs, and aged men—you, as men, have no
lands to sell. You occupy and possess a tract in
trust for your children. You should hold that trust

sacred, lest your children are driven from their homes by your unsafe conduct. Whoever sells lands offends the Great Spirit, and must expect a great punishment after death.'"

Sose-ha'-wä here suspended the narration of the discourse of Handsome Lake, and thus addressed the council:—

"Chiefs, keepers of the faith, warriors, women and children:—You all know, that our religion teaches, that the early day is dedicated to the Great Spirit, and that the late day is granted to the spirits of the dead. It is now meridian, and I must close. Preserve in your minds that which has been said. Accept my thanks for your kind and patient attention. It is meet that I should also return my thanks to the Great Spirit, that he has assisted me thus far, in my feeble frame, to instruct you. We ask you all to come up again to-morrow, at early day, to hear what further may be said. I have done."

The next morning, after the council had been opened in the usual manner, *Sose-ha'-wä* thus continued:—

"Relatives, uncover now your heads and listen:— The day has thus far advanced, and again we are gathered around the council-fire. I see around me the several nations of the Long House; this gives me great joy. I see also seated around me my counsellors (keepers of the faith,) who have been regularly appointed, as is the custom of our religion. Greetings have been exchanged with each other. Thanks have been returned to *Gä-ni-o-di'-yo.* Thanks also have been returned to our Creator, by the council now assembled. At this moment the Great Spirit is looking upon this assembly. He hears our words, he knows our thoughts, and is always pleased to see us gathered together for good. The sun is now high, and soon it will reach the middle heavens. I must therefore make haste. Listen attentively, and consider well what you shall hear. I return thanks to our Creator, that he has spared your lives through the dangers of darkness. I salute and return my thanks to the four Celestial beings, who have communicated what I am about to say to you. I return thanks to my grandfather, (Handsome Lake,) from whom you first heard what I am about to speak. We all feel his loss. We miss him at our councils. I now occupy his place before you; but I am conscious that I have not the power which he possessed.

"Counsellors, warriors, mothers and children:— Listen to good instruction. Consider it well. Lay it up in your minds, and forget it not. Our Creator, when he made us, designed that we should live by hunting. It sometimes happens that a man goes out for the hunt, leaving his wife with her friends. After a long absence he returns, and finds that his wife has taken another husband. The Great Spirit says that this is a great sin, and must be put from among us.

"The four Messengers further said, that it was wrong for a mother to punish a child with a rod. It is not right to punish much, and our Creator never intended that children should be punished with a whip, or be used with any violence. In punishing a refractory child, water only is necessary, and it is sufficient. Plunge them under. This is not wrong. Whenever a child promises to do better, the punishment must cease. It is wrong to continue it after promises of amendment are made. Thus they said.

"It is right and proper always to look upon the dead. Let your face be brought near to theirs, and then address them. Let the dead know that their absence is regretted by their friends, and that they grieve for their death. Let the dead know, too, how their surviving friends intend to live. Let them know whether they will so conduct themselves, that they will meet them again in the future world. The dead will hear and remember. Thus they said.

"Continue to listen while I proceed to relate whăt further they said:—Our Creator made the earth. Upon it he placed man, and gave him certain rules of conduct. It pleased him also to give them many kinds of amusements. He also ordered that the earth should produce all that is good for man. So long as the earth remains, it will not cease to yield. Upon the surface of the ground berries of various kinds are produced. It is the will of the Great Spirit, that when they ripen, we should return our thanks to him, and have a public rejoicing for the continuance of these blessings. He made every-thing which we live upon, and requires us to be thankful at all times for the continuance of his favors. When Our Life (corn, &c.) has again appeared, it is the will of the Great Ruler that we assemble for a general thanksgiving. It is his will also that the children be brought and made to participate in the Feather dance. Your feast must consist of the new production. It is proper at these times, should any present not have their names published, or if any changes have been made, to announce them then. The festival must continue four days. Thus they said. Upon the first day must be performed the Feather dance. This ceremony must take place in the early day, and cease at the middle day. In the same manner, upon the second day, is to be performed the Thanksgiving dance. On the third, the Thanksgiving concert, *Ah-do'-weh*, is to be introduced. The fourth day is set apart for the Peach-stone game. All these ceremonies, instituted by our Creator, must be commenced at the early day, and cease at the middle day. At all these times, we are required to return thanks to our Grandfather *Hé'-no* and his assistants. To them is assigned the duty of watching over the earth, and all it produces for our good. The great Feather and Thanksgiving dances are the appropriate ceremonies of thanksgiving to the Ruler and Maker of all things. The Thanksgiving concert belongs appropriately to our Grandfathers. In it, we return thanks to them. During the performance of this ceremony, we are required also to give them the smoke of tobacco. Again, we must at this time return thanks to our mother the earth, for she is our relative. We must also return thanks to Our Life and its Sisters. All these things are required to be done by the light of the sun. It must not be protracted until the sun has hid his face, and darkness surrounds all things.

"Continue to listen:—We have a change of seasons. We have a season of cold. This is the hunting season. It is also one in which the people can amuse themselves. Upon the fifth day of the new moon, *Nis-go-wuk'-na*, (about Feb. 1st,) we are required to commence the annual jubilee of thanksgiving to our Creator. At this festival all can give evidence of their devotion to the will of the Great Spirit, by participating in all its ceremonies.

"Continue to listen:—The four Messengers of the Great Spirit have always watched over us, and have ever seen what was transpiring among men. At one time, Handsome Lake was translated by them to the regions above. He looked down upon the earth and saw a great assembly. Out of it came a man. His garments were torn, tattered and filthy. His whole appearance indicated great misery and poverty. They asked him how this spectacle appeared to him. He replied that it was hard to look upon. They then told him that the man he saw was a drunkard. That he had taken the fire-water, and it had reduced him to poverty. Again he looked, and saw a woman seated upon the ground. She was constantly engaged in gathering up and secreting about her person her worldly effects. They said, the woman you see is inhospitable. She is too selfish to spare anything, and will never leave her worldly goods. She can never pass from earth to heaven. Tell this to your people. Again he looked, and saw a man carrying in each hand large pieces of meat. He went about the assembly giving to each a piece. This man, they said, is blessed, for he is hospitable and kind. He looked again, and saw streams of blood. They said, thus will the earth be, if the fire-water is not put from among you. Brother will kill brother, and friend friend. Again they told him to look towards the east. He obeyed, and as far as his vision reached, he saw the increasing smoke of numberless distilleries arising, and shutting out the light of the sun. It was a horrible spectacle to witness. They told him that here was manufactured the fire-water. Again he looked, and saw a costly house, made and furnished by the pale-faces. It was a house of confinement, where were fetters, ropes and whips. They said that those who persisted in the use of the fire-water would fall into this. Our Creator commands us to put this destructive vice far from us. Again he looked, and saw various assemblages. Some of them were unwilling to listen to instruction. They were riotous, and took great pride in drinking the strong waters. He observed another group who were half inclined to hear, but the temptations to vice which surrounded them allured them back, and they also revelled in the fumes of the fire-water. He saw another assemblage which had met to hear instructions. This they said was pleasing to the

Great Spirit. He loves those who will listen and obey. It has grieved him that his children are now divided by separate interests, and are pursuing so many paths. It pleases him to see his people live together in harmony and quiet. The fire-water creates many dissensions and divisions among us. They said that the use of it would cause many to die unnatural deaths; many will be exposed to cold, and freeze; many will be burned, and others will be drowned while under the influence of the fire-water.

"Friends and Relatives:—All these things have often happened. How many of our people have been frozen to death; how many have been burned to death; how many have been drowned while under the influence of the strong waters. The punishments of those who use the fire-water commence while they are yet on the earth. Many are now thrown into houses of confinement by the pale faces. I repeat to you, the Ruler of us all requires us to unite and put this evil from among us. Some say that the use of the fire-water is not wrong, and that it is food. Let those who do not believe it wrong, make this experiment. Let all who use the fire-water assemble and organize into a council; and those who do not, into another near them. A great difference will then be discovered. The council of drunkards will end in a riot and tumult, while the other will have harmony and quiet. It is hard to think of the great prevalence of this evil among us. Reform, and put it from among you. Many resolve to use the fire-water until near death, when they will repent. If they do this, nothing can save them from destruction, for then medicine can have no power. Thus they said.

" All men were made equal by the Great Spirit; but he has given to them a variety of gifts. To some a pretty face, to others an ugly one; to some a comely form, to others a deformed figure. Some are fortunate in collecting around them worldly goods. But you are all entitled to the same privileges, and therefore must put pride from among you. You are not your own makers, nor the builders of your own fortunes. All things are the gift of the Great Spirit, and to him must be returned thanks for their bestowal. He alone must be acknowledged as the giver. It has pleased him to make differences among men; but it is wrong for one man to exalt himself above another. Love each other, for you are all brothers and sisters of the same great family. The Great Spirit enjoins upon all, to observe hospitality and kindness, especially to the needy and the helpless; for this is pleasing to him. If a stranger wanders about your abode, speak to him with kind words; be hospitable towards him, welcome him to your home, and forget not always to mention the Great Spirit. In the morning, give thanks to the Great Spirit for the return of day, and the light of the sun; at night renew your thanks to him, that his ruling power has preserved you from harm during the day, and that night has again come, in which you may rest your wearied bodies.

"The four Messengers said further to Handsome Lake:—Tell your people, and particularly the keepers of the faith, to be strong-minded, and adhere to the true faith. We fear the Evil-minded will go among them with temptations. He may introduce the *fiddle*. He may bring *cards*, and leave them among you. The use of these are great sins. Let the people be on their guard, and the keepers of the faith be watchful and vigilant, that none of these evils may find their way among the people. Let the keepers of the faith preserve the law of moral conduct in all its purity. When meetings are to be held for instruction, and the people are preparing to go, the Evil-minded is then busy. He goes from one to another, whispering many temptations, by which to keep them away. He will even follow persons into the door of the council, and induce some, at that time, to bend their steps away. Many resist until they have entered, and then leave it. This habit, once indulged, obtains a fast hold, and the evil propensity increases with age. This is a great sin, and should be at once abandoned. Thus they said.

"Speak evil of no one. If you can say no good of a person, then be silent. Let not your tongues betray you into evil. Let all be mindful of this; for these are the words of our Creator. Let all strive to cultivate friendship with those who surround them. This is pleasing to the Great Spirit.

"Counsellors, warriors, women and children:—I shall now rest. I thank you all for your kind and patient attention. I thank the Great Spirit, that he has spared the lives of so many of us to witness this day. I request you all to come up again to-morrow at early day. Let us all hope, that, until we meet again, the Creator and Ruler of us all may be kind to us, and preserve our lives. *Na-ho'.*"

The council, on the following day, was opened with a few short speeches, from some of the chiefs or keepers of the faith, returning thanks for the privileges of the occasion, as usual at councils; after which *Sose-ha'-wä*, resuming his discourse, spoke as follows:—

"Friends and Relatives, uncover now your heads:—Continue to listen to my rehearsal of the sayings communicated to Handsome Lake by the four Messengers of the Great Spirit. We have met again around the council-fire. We have followed the ancient custom, and greeted each other. This is right, and highly pleasing to our Maker. He now looks down upon this assembly. He sees us all. He is informed of the cause of our gathering, and it is pleasing to him. Life is uncertain. While we live let us love each other. Let us sympathize always with the suffering and needy. Let us also always rejoice with those who are glad. This is now the third day, and my time for speaking to you is drawing to a close. It will be a long time before we meet again. Many moons and seasons will have passed, before the sacred council-brand shall be again uncovered. Be watchful, therefore, and remember faithfully what you may now hear.

"In discoursing yesterday upon the duties of the keepers of the faith, I omitted some things important. The Great Spirit created this office. He designed that its duties should never end. There are some who are selected and set apart by our Maker, to perform the duties of this office. It is therefore their duty to be faithful, and to be always watching. These duties they must ever perform during their lives. The faithful, when they leave this earth, will have a pleasant path to travel in. The same office exists in heaven, the home of our Creator. They will take the same place when they arrive there. There are dreadful penalties awaiting those keepers of the faith, who resign their office without a cause. Thus they said.

"It was the original intention of our Maker, that all our feasts of thanksgiving should be seasoned with the flesh of wild animals. But we are surrounded by the pale-faces, and in a short time the woods will be all removed. Then there will be no more game for the Indian to use in his feasts. The four Messengers said, in consequence of this, that we might use the flesh of domestic animals. This will not be wrong. The pale-faces are pressing you upon every side. You must therefore live as they do. How far you can do so without sin, I will now tell you. You may grow cattle, and build yourselves warm and comfortable dwelling-houses. This is not sin; and it is all that you can safely adopt of the customs of the pale-faces. You cannot live as they do. Thus they said.

"Continue to listen:—It has pleased our Creator to set apart as our Life, the Three Sisters. For this special favor, let us ever be thankful. When you have gathered in your harvest, let the people assemble, and hold a general thanksgiving for so great a good. In this way you will show your obedience to the will and pleasure of your Creator. Thus they said.

"Many of you may be ignorant of the Spirit of Medicine. It watches over all constantly, and assists the needy whenever necessity requires. The Great Spirit designed that some men should possess the gift of skill in medicine. But he is pained to see a medicine man making exorbitant charges for attending the sick. Our Creator made for us tobacco. This plant must always be used in administering medicines. When a sick person recovers his health, he must return his thanks to the Great Spirit by means of tobacco; for it is by his goodness that he is made well. He blesses the medicine; and the medicine man must receive as his reward whatever the gratitude of the restored may tender. This is right and proper. There are many who are unfortunate, and cannot pay for attendance. It is sufficient for such to return thanks to the medicine man upon recovery. The remembrance that he has saved the life of a relative, will be a sufficient reward.

"Listen further to what the Great Spirit has been pleased to communicate to us:—He has made us, as a race, separate and distinct from the pale-face. It is a great sin to intermarry, and intermingle the blood of the two races. Let none be guilty of this transgression.

"At one time the four Messengers said to Handsome Lake, lest the people should disbelieve you, and not repent and forsake their evil ways, we will now disclose to you the House of Torment, the dwelling-place of the Evil-minded. Handsome Lake was particular in describing to us all that he witnessed; and the course which departed spirits were accustomed to take on leaving the earth. There was a road which led upwards. At a certain point it branched; one branch led straight forward to the Home of the Great Spirit, and the other turned aside to the House of Torment. At the place where the roads separated were stationed two keepers, one representing the Good, and the other the Evil Spirit. When a person reached the fork, if wicked, by a motion from the Evil keeper, he turned instinctively upon the road which led to the abode of the Evil-minded. But if virtuous and good, the other keeper directed him upon the straight road. The latter was not much travelled; while the former was so frequently trodden, that no grass could grow in the pathway. It sometimes happened that the keepers had great difficulty in deciding which path the person should take, when the good and bad actions of the individual were nearly balanced. Those sent to the House of Torment sometimes remain one day, (which is there one of our years.) Some for a longer period. After they have atoned for their sins, they pass to heaven. But when they have committed either of the great sins, (witchcraft, murder, and infanticide,) they never pass to heaven, but are tormented forever. Having conducted Handsome Lake to this place, he saw a large and dark-colored mansion covered with soot, and beside it stood a lesser one. One of the four then held out his rod, and the top of the house moved up, until they could look down upon all that was within. He saw many rooms. The first object which met his eye, was a haggard-looking man; his sunken eyes cast upon the ground, and his form half consumed by the torments he had undergone. This man was a drunkard. The Evil-minded then appeared, and called him by name. As the man obeyed his call, he dipped from a caldron a quantity of red-hot liquid, and commanded him to drink it, as it was an article he loved. The man did as he was directed, and immediately from his mouth issued a stream of blaze. He cried in vain for help. The Tormentor then requested him to sing and make himself merry, as was his wont while on earth, after drinking the fire-water. Let drunkards take warning from this. Others were then summoned. There came before him two persons, who appeared to be husband and wife. He told them to exercise the privilege they were so fond of while on the earth. They immediately commenced a quarrel of words. · They raged at each other with such violence, that their tongues and eyes ran out so far they could neither see nor speak. This, said they, is the punishment of quarrelsome and disputing husbands and wives. Let such also take warning, and live together in peace and harmony. Next he called up a woman who had been a witch. First he plunged her into a caldron of boiling liquid. In her cries of distress, she begged the Evil-minded to give her some cooler place. He then immersed her in one containing liquid at the point of freezing. Her cries then were, that she was too cold. This woman, said the four Messengers, shall always be tormented in this manner. He proceeded to mention the punishment which awaits all those who cruelly ill-treat their wives. The Evil-minded next called up a man who had been accustomed to beat his wife. Having led him up to a red-hot statue of a female, he directed him to do that which he was fond of while he was upon the earth. He obeyed, and struck the figure. The sparks flew in every direction, and by the contact his arm was consumed. Such is the punishment, they said, awaiting those who ill-treat their wives. From this take seasonable warning. He looked again and saw a woman, whose arms and hands were nothing but bones. She had sold fire-water to the Indians, and the flesh was eaten from her hands and arms. This, they said, would be the fate of rum-sellers. Again he looked, and in one apartment he saw and recognized *Ho-ne-yä'-wus*, (Farmer's Brother,) his former friend. He was engaged in removing a heap of sand, grain by grain; and although he labored continually, yet the heap of sand was not diminished. This, they said, was the punishment of those who sold land. Adjacent to the house of torment was a field of corn filled with weeds. He saw women in the act of cutting them down; but as fast as this was done, they grew up again. This, they said, was the punishment of lazy women. It would be proper and right, had we time, to tell more of this place of torment. But my time is limited, and I must pass to other things.

"The Creator made men dependent upon each other. He made them sociable beings; therefore, when your neighbor visits you, set food before him. If it be your next door neighbor, you must give him to eat. He will partake and thank you.

"Again they said:—You must not steal. Should you want for anything necessary, you have only to tell your wants, and they will be supplied. This is right. Let none ever steal anything. Children are often tempted to take things home which do not belong to them. Let parents instruct their children in this rule.

"Many of our people live to a very old age. Your Creator says that your deportment towards them must be that of reverence and affection. They have seen and felt much of the misery and pain of earth. Be always kind to them when old and helpless. Wash their hands and face, and nurse them with care. This is the will of the Great Spirit.

"It has been the custom among us to mourn for the dead one year. This custom is wrong. As it causes the death of many children, it must be abandoned. Ten days mourn for the dead, and not longer. When one dies, it is right and proper to make an address over the body, telling how much you loved the deceased. Great respect for the dead must be observed among us.

"At another time the four Messengers said to Handsome Lake, they would now show him the 'Destroyer of Villages,' (Washington,[1]) of whom you have so frequently heard. Upon the road leading to heaven he could see a light, far away in the distance, moving to and fro. Its brightness far exceeded the brilliancy of the noonday sun. They told him the journey was as follows: First, they came to a cold spring, which was a resting-place. From this point they proceeded into pleasant fairy grounds, which spread away in every direction. Soon they reached heaven. The light was dazzling. Berries of every description grew in vast abundance. Their size and quality were such, that a single berry was more than sufficient to appease the appetite. A sweet fragrance perfumed the air. Fruits of every kind met the eye. The inmates of this celestial abode spent their time in amusement and repose. No evil could enter there. None in heaven ever transgress again. Families were reunited, and dwelt together in harmony. They possessed a bod-

[1] Washington was named by the Iroquois *Hä-no-dä-gä'-ne-ars*, which signifies the Destroyer of Villages. The Presidents have ever since been called by this name. They named the Governors of all the provinces with which they had intercourse, and afterwards continued the names to their successors.

ily form, the senses, and the remembrances of the earthly life. But no white man ever entered heaven. Thus they said. He looked, and saw an inclosure upon a plain, just without the entrance of heaven. Within it was a fort. Here he saw the ' Destroyer of Villages,' walking to and fro within the inclosure. His countenance indicated a great and a good man. They said to Handsome Lake: the man you see is the only pale-face who ever left the earth. He was kind to you, when on the settlement of the great difficulty between the Americans and the Great Crown, (*Go-wek'-go-wä,*) you were abandoned to the mercy of your enemies. The Crown told the great American, that as for his allies, the Indians, he might kill them if he liked. The great American judged that this would be cruel and unjust. He believed they were made by the Great Spirit, and were entitled to the enjoyment of life. He was kind to you, and extended over you his protection. For this reason, he has been allowed to leave the earth. But he is never permitted to go into the presence of the Great Spirit. Although alone, he is perfectly happy. All faithful Indians pass by him as they go to heaven. They see him, and recognize him, but pass on in silence. No word ever passes his lips.

" Friends and Relatives:—It was by the influence of this great man, that we were spared as a people, and yet live. Had he not granted us his protection, where would we have been? Perished, all perished.

" The four Messengers further said to Handsome

Lake, they were fearful that, unless the people repented and obeyed his commands, the patience and forbearance of their Creator would be exhausted; that he would grow angry with them, and cause their increase to cease.

"Our Creator made light and darkness. He made the sun to heat, and shine over the world. He made the moon, also, to shine by night, and to cool the world, if the sun made it too hot by day. The keeper of the clouds, by direction of the Great Spirit, will then cease to act. The keeper of the springs and running brooks will cease to rule them for the good of man. The sun will cease to fulfil its office. Total darkness will then cover the earth. A great smoke will rise, and spread over the face of the earth. Then will come out of it all monsters, and poisonous animals created by the Evil-minded; and they, with the wicked upon the earth, will perish together.

"But before this dreadful time shall come, the Great Spirit will take home to himself all the good and faithful. They will lay themselves down to sleep, and from this sleep of death, they will rise, and go home to their Creator. Thus they said.

"I have now done. I close thus, that you may remember and understand the fate which awaits the earth, and the unfaithful and unbelieving. Our Creator looks down upon us. The four Beings from above see us. They witness with pleasure this assemblage, and rejoice at the object for which it is gathered. It is now forty-eight years since we first began to listen to the renewed will of our Creator. I have been unable, during the time allotted to me, to rehearse all the sayings of *Gä-ne-o-di'-yo*. I regret very much, that you cannot hear them all.

"Counsellors, Warriors, Women and Children:— I have done. I thank you all for your attendance, and for your kind and patient attention. May the Great Spirit, who rules all things, watch over and protect you from every harm and danger, while you travel the journey of life. May the Great Spirit bless you all, and bestow upon you life, health, peace and prosperity; and may you, in turn, appreciate his great goodness *Na-hó*."

CHAPTER IV.

SUFFICIENT has been said in the preceding pages
to convey an impression of the uses of the Dance
among the Iroquois. It remains to notice the several dances themselves, to point out some of the
characteristics of each, and also to exhibit more
fully the spirit of this amusement, and its power
over the minds of the people.

With the Iroquois, as with the red race at large,
dancing was not only regarded as a thanksgiving
ceremonial, in itself acceptable to the Great Spirit,
but they were taught to consider it a divine art, designed by *Hä-wen-ne'-yu* for their pleasure, as well
as for his worship. It was cherished as one of the
most suitable modes of social intercourse between
the sexes, but more especially as the great instrumentality for arousing patriotic excitement, and for
keeping alive the spirit of the nation. The popular
enthusiasm broke forth in this form, and was nourished and stimulated by this powerful agency.
These dances sprang, as it were, a living reflection

from the Indian mind. With their wild music of songs and rattles, their diversities of step and attitude, their graces of motion, and their spirit-stirring associations, they contain within themselves both a picture and a realization of Indian life. The first stir of feeling of which the Indian youth was conscious was enkindled by the dance; the first impulse of patriotism, the earliest dreams of ambition were awakened by their inspiring influences. In their patriotic, religious and social dances, into which classes they are properly divisible, resided the soul of Indian life. It was more in the nature of a spell upon the people than of a rational guiding spirit. It bound them down to trivial things, but it bound them together; it stimulated them to deeds of frenzy, but it fed the flame of patriotism.

The Iroquois had thirty-two distinct dances, out of which number twenty-six were claimed to be wholly of their own invention. Twenty-one of these are still in use among the present Iroquois. To each a separate history and object attached, as well as a different degree of popular favor. Some were costume dances, and were performed by a small and select band; some were designed exclusively for females, others for warriors alone; but the greater part of them were open to all of both sexes who desired to participate. Many of these dances, without doubt, have been handed down among the Iroquois for centuries, transmitted from generation to generation, until their origin is lost even to tradition. Others spread throughout the

whole Indian family, and were known and used
from Maine to Oregon. Indian amusements, as well
as arts, were eminently diffusive, as Indian life was
much the same from ocean to ocean. They are better described by their effects, than by a minute examination of the mode, manner and circumstances
of each in detail. It is to their influence, as a
means of action, that they owe their chief importance. And it is to the zeal and enthusiasm with
which they were cherished and performed, that attention should principally be directed. Their over-
powering influence in arousing the Indian spirit,
and in excluding all thoughts of a different life, and
their resulting effect upon the formation of Indian
character cannot be too highly estimated.

The tenacity with which the Iroquois have always
adhered to these dances furnishes the highest evidence of their hold upon the affections of the people. From the earliest days of the Jesuit missions,
the most unremitted efforts of the missionaries have
been put forth for their suppression. Christian
parties were organized at an early day in each nation, of such as were willing to abandon the dance,
and their religious festivals, and lead a different life.
These parties, down to the present time, have always been largely in the minority, except among
the unexpatriated Oneidas, who are now entirely
denationalized, and, perhaps, the Tuscaroras, who
are partially so; but the body of the Senecas, Onondagas and Cayugas, upon their several reservations, still cling to their ancient customs, and glory

GA-KA-AH or KILT

GISE-HĂ, OR MALE LEGGIN

in the dance as ardently as did their forefathers. When it loses its attractions, they will cease to be Indians.[1]

The Feather dance and the War dance were the two great performances of the Iroquois. One had a religious, and the other a patriotic character. Both were costume dances. They were performed by a select band, ranging from fifteen to twenty-five, who were distinguished for their powers of endurance, activity and spirit. Besides these, there were four other costume dances. In the residue, the performers, who were the people at large, appeared in their ordinary apparel, and sometimes participated to the number of two or three hundred at one time. The Iroquois costume may be called strictly an apparel for the dance. This was the chief occasion on which the warrior was desirous to appear in his best attire. Before describing these dances, it will be proper to notice the various articles of apparel which made up the full dress costume of the Iroquois.

One of the most prominent articles of apparel was the Kilt, *Gä-kä'-ah*, (see plate, page 262,) which was

---

[1] A Mourning council of the Iroquois was held at Tonawanda, in October, 1846, to raise up sachems. There were about six hundred Iroquois in attendance, representing all of the Six Nations. On the second day the Great Feather Dance was performed by a select band of Onondaga and Seneca dancers. The author then first had occasion to realize the magical influence which these dances have upon the Indian. It was impossible even for the spectator to resist the general enthusiasm. It was remarked to *Da-ät'-ga-dose,* (Abraham La Fort,) an educated Onondaga sachem, that they would be Indians forever, if they held to these dances. He replied, that he knew it, and for that reason he would be the last to give them up.

secured around the waist by a belt, and descended to the knee. In ancient times this was made of deer-skin. It was fringed and embroidered with porcu-pine quill-work. Some of these kilts would excite admiration by the exactness of their finish and ad-justment, and the neatness of the material. In mod-ern times various fabrics have been substituted for the deer-skin, although the latter is still used.

Upon the head-dress, *Gus-to'-weh*, (see plate, page 226,) the most conspicuous part of the costume, much attention was bestowed. The frame consisted of a band of splint, adjusted around the head, with a cross-band arching over the top, from side to side. A cap of net-work, or other construction, was then made to enclose the frame. Around the splint, in later times, a silver band was fastened, which completed the lower part. From the top, a cluster of white feathers de-pended. Besides this, a single feather of the largest size, was set in the crown of the head-dress, inclin-ing backwards from the head. It was secured in a small tube, which was fastened to the cross-splint, and in such a manner as to allow the feather to re-volve in the tube. This feather, which was usually the plume of the eagle, is the characteristic of the Iroquois head-dress.

Next was the Leggin, *Gise'-hă*, (see plate, page 263,) which was fastened above the knee, and de-scended upon the moccason. It was also made origi-nally of deer-skin, and ornamented with quill-work upon the bottom and side, the embroidered edge being worn in front. In later times, red broadcloth,

AH -TA-QUA-O-WEH OR MOCCASON

FOR MALE

GÄ-GEH-TÄ. OR BELT.

embroidered with bead-work, as represented in the plate, has been substituted for deer-skin in most cases. Much ingenuity and taste were displayed in the designs, and in the execution of the work upon this article of apparel. The warrior might well be proud of this part of his costume.

The Moccason, *Ah-tä-quä-o'-weh*, (see plate, page 264,) was also made of deer-skin. In the modern moccason, represented in the plate, the front part is worked with porcupine quills after the ancient fashion, while the part which falls down upon the sides, is embroidered with bead-work according to the present taste.

Not the least important article was the belt, *Gä-geh'-tä*, (see plate, page 265,) which was prized as highly as any part of the costume. The one represented in the plate is of Indian manufacture. These belts were braided by hand, the beads being interwoven in the process of braiding. Belts of deer-skin were also worn. These belts were worn over the left shoulder, and around the waist.

Arm Bands, Knee Bands, and Wrist Bands, made of various articles and ornamented in divers ways, were likewise a part of the costume. Sometimes they were made of deer-skin, sometimes of white dog-skin, and in later times of red and blue velvet, embroidered with bead-work, as represented in the plate, page 392.

In addition to the knee-bands, Knee Rattles of deers' hoofs, as shown in the figure, and in modern times, of strips of metal, or of bells, made a necessary part of the costume. Personal ornaments of various kinds, together with the war-club, the tomahawk, and the scalping-knife, completed the attire.

KNEE RATTLE OF DEERS' HOOFS.

The war-club used in the dance, was usually a light article, of which the following is a representation.

GÄ-JE'-WÄ, OR WAR-CLUB.

The various articles of apparel which now make up the costume of the Iroquois, are precisely the same that they were at the epoch of the discovery. No change has been made in the articles themselves, although there have been changes in the materials of which they were made. The deer-skin, in later days, has been laid aside for the broadcloth, and the porcupine quill for the bead. By making a resubstitution of material, the original costume would be recovered in full.

In preparing for the dance, all the articles above

described were not necessarily used by each individual. Those strictly needful were the head-dress, the belt and kilt, to which each wearer added such ornaments and rattles as he was disposed. Usually they were nude down to the waist, and also below the knees, to give greater freedom to their limbs. A great diversity could be seen in their costumes when brought together in the dance, in consequence of the different fabrics of which they were composed, and the variety in their personal ornaments, notwithstanding every article of apparel was of the same pattern. Specimens of full Iroquois costumes, both male and female, are given in the engravings which are introduced as frontispieces. These, and the several plates which are given to illustrate the male costume in detail, will save the necessity of any further description.

GÄ-NO-JO'-O, OR INDIAN DRUM.

1 foot.

The two dances mentioned before this digression were the highest in the popular favor. One was of original invention, the other imported; one was of a strictly religious character, and the other of a patriotic; but both were equally effective to arouse the enthusiasm of the people. All things considered, however, the last of the two, the War dance, *Wä-sä'-seh*, was the favorite. It was the mode of enlistment for a perilous expedition, the dance which preceded the departure of the band, and with which they celebrated their return. It was the dance at the ceremony of raising up sachems, at the adoption of a captive, at the entertainment of a guest, the first dance taught to the young. It was not of Iroquois origin, but was adopted from the Sioux, as its name imports, reaching back through them to a remote antiquity.[1] The characteristic feature of this dance is to be found in the speeches which were made by those surrounding the band of dancers between each tune, or at each break in the dance. From this source the people derived as much entertainment, as they did excitement from the performance itself. It was the only dance in which speeches and replies were appropriate, or ever introduced; and in this particular, it was a novelty, leading oftentimes to the highest amusement. By these

[1] The name of the Sioux in the Seneca dialect is *Wä-sä'-seh-o-no*. By contraction and usage, the word *Wä-sä'-seh* is now used for the Sioux dance, the name by which the War dance has always been known among the Iroquois. This dance has been ascribed by some to the Shawnees, and called *Sa-wä-no'-o-no*, or the Shawnee dance, this being the Seneca name of the Shawnees. One of the Iroquois names of this dance is *Ne-ja'*; but *Wä-sä'-seh* is the customary name.

speeches, which both relieved the performers and diverted the people, the dance was lengthened out to two, and even three hours, before the spirits of the company were expended.

The War dance was usually performed in the evening. It was only brought out on prominent occasions, or at domestic councils of unusual interest. Fifteen made a full company, but oftentimes twenty-five, and even thirty participated. After the business of the day was disposed of, and the dusk of evening had crept in, preparations began for the dance. The people gathered within the council-house, usually in increased numbers, because of this expected entertainment, and arranging themselves in favorable positions, they quietly awaited the approach of the dancers. The arrangements were made, including the selection of the number, the appointment of the leader, and of the singers of the war-songs, by the keepers of the faith. In an adjacent lodge, the band assembled to array themselves in their costumes, and to paint and decorate their persons for the occasion. The war-whoop ever and anon broke in upon the stillness of the evening, indicating to the listening and expectant throng within the council-house, that their preparations were progressing to a completion. A keeper of the faith, in the mean time, occupied the attention of the people with a brief speech upon the nature and objects of this dance. Presently, a nearer war-whoop ringing through the air, announced that the band were approaching. Preceded by their leader, and marching in file to the beat of the drum, they drew near to the council-house. As they came up, the crowd gave way, the leader crossed the threshold, followed quickly by his feathered band, and immediately opened the dance. In an instant they grouped themselves within a circular area, standing thick together, the singers commenced the war-song, the drums beat time, and the dancers made the floor resound with their stirring feet. After a moment the song ceased, and with it the dance; the band walking around a common centre to the beat of the drum at half time. Another song soon commenced, the drums quickened their time, and the dance was resumed. In the middle of the song there was a change in the music, accompanied with a slight cessation of the dance, after which it became more animated than before, until the song ended, and the band again walked to the beat of the drum. Each tune or war-song lasted about two minutes, and the interval between them was about as long. These songs were usually recited by four singers, using two drums of the kind represented in the figure, to mark time, and as an accompaniment. The drums beat time about twice in a second, the voices of the singers keeping pace, thus making a rapid and strongly accented species of music.[1]

[1] These war songs are in a dead language, or, at all events, the Iroquois are unable to interpret them. They are in regular verses, or measured sentences, and were learned by them with the dance originally. Charlevoix has furnished a translation of some of these songs as follows: "I am brave and intrepid. I do not fear death, nor any kind of torture. Those who fear them are cowards. They are less than women. Life is nothing to those who have courage. May my enemies be confounded with

It would be difficult, if not impossible, to describe the step, except generally. With the whites, the dancing is entirely upon the toe of the foot, with rapid changes of position, and but slight changes of attitude. But with the Iroquois, it was chiefly upon the heel, with slow changes of position, and rapid changes of attitude. The heel is raised and brought down with great quickness and force, by muscular strength, to keep time with the beat of the drum, to make a resounding noise by the concussion, and at the same time to shake the knee-rattles, which contributed materially to the "pomp and circumstance" of the dance. In the War dance, the attitudes were those of the violent passions, and consequently were not graceful. At the same instant of time, in a group of dancers, one might be seen in the attitude of attack, another of defence; one in the act of drawing the bow, another of striking with the war-club; some in the act of throwing the tomahawk, some of listening, or of watching an opportunity, and others of striking the foe. These violent motions of the body, while they, perhaps, increased the spirit and animation of the dance, led to disagreeable distortions of the countenance, as well as to uncouth attitudes. But, at the same time, the striking costumes of the dancers, their erect forms at certain stages of the figure, their suppleness and activity, the wild music, the rattle of the

despair and rage." These songs were sung by captives at the torture; and doubtless those used in the War dance are of the same general character.

dance, together with the excitable and excited throng around them, made up a scene of no common interest.

In this dance, the war-whoop and the response always preceded each song. It was given by the leader, and answered by the band. A description of this terrific outbreak of human voices is scarcely possible. It was a prolonged sound upon a high note, with a decadence near the end, followed by an abrupt and explosive conclusion, in which the voice was raised again to the same pitch. The whole band responded in a united scream upon the same key with which the leader concluded, and at the same instant.[1]

In this celebrated dance, therefore, which has doubtless been used for centuries, and been performed throughout the whole area of the American republic, we find this simple succession of acts: the war-whoop and responses, the simultaneous commencement of the war-song and the dance, the slight cessation at the middle of the tune, with a change in the music, the renewal of the dance with redoubled animation, and the final conclusion of the war-song in perhaps less than two minutes from its

[1]

Solo. . . . .

Ah - - - - - ah.

An attempt is here made to represent this wild cry. It is given by the Indian with wide open mouth. His voice slides down the descending notes, when he pauses an instant to take a new inspiration, all which is to be expended in the sudden and far reaching yell with which the piece concludes. On this last note, the whole band join in chorus, using the syllables "ah um," connected in one, or something like it.

commencement; and lastly, the walk at the beat of the
drum around a central point for about two minutes,
until the war-whoop again sounded, and another war-
song was introduced. This round was continued, until
the spirit of the dancers began to flag, and the desires of the people had been reasonably gratified.
Without any speeches between the tunes to relieve
the band, it usually lasted about an hour; but with
speeches, it often continued for three hours, with
unabated animation.

Any one present was at liberty to make a speech
at any stage of the dance. His desire was manifested by a rap. At the sound the dance ceased, or, if
finished, and the band were walking, they were required to stop, and all present, as well as the music,
to be silent. The only condition affixed to the right
of making a speech, was that of bestowing a present
at its close upon the dancers, or upon the one to
whom it was addressed. After the speech was concluded, and the present delivered, the war-whoop
and responses were again sounded, the drums beat,
the song and the dance commenced, and were ended
as before. Then followed another speech, and still
others, alternating with the songs, or suspending
the dance at the moment of its highest animation,
at the pleasure of the speaker. In this manner the
War dance was continued until the spirit of enjoyment began to subside, when the final war-whoop
put an end to the dance, and the band retired.

These speeches were often pleasantries between
individuals, or strictures upon each other's foibles,

or earnest exhortations, or perchance patriotic ebul-
litions of feeling, according to the fancy of the person and of the moment. Some of them were received with rounds of applause, some with jeers,
and others with seriousness and deference. They
usually lasted but two or three minutes. The Indian
has a keen appreciation of wit, and is fond of both
jest and repartee, as well as of ridicule.

To convey a fuller impression of the character of
these speeches, and of the nature of the dance itself,
a few specimens will be introduced. These speeches
are short and rather unmeaning, when separated
from the occasion, and the connection in which they
were called forth. Those most interesting would
require an explanation of collateral circumstances to
be understood, and they are therefore excluded.
Those to be given are not particularly interesting;
but they explain themselves, and will answer the
purpose for which they are introduced as fully as if
they sparkled with wit.

After the band came in and opened the War dance,
several songs were performed before any one was
disposed to interrupt them. All eyes were turned
upon the several costumes of the band, upon the
spirit and activity of individuals in the dance, and
the animation and enthusiasm of the party. Round
after round followed, until the spirit of the company
was fully aroused, when it began to expend itself in
speeches and witticisms. The first rap was made
by *To-no-ai'-o*, a humorous old chief. Silence being
restored, he spoke as follows: "Friends and Rela-

tives—I am occasionally fond of a drink of the strong waters. I do not know how it is with *Tä-yä-dä-o-wuh'-kuh*, (the guest to whom the War dance was given;) but presume it is something the same with him, and therefore I send him a sixpence to buy a drink with on his way home." Gives the money. Again the drum sounded, the war-whoop and responses were given, and the music and the dance were resumed. At the end of the tune another rap restored silence. *Hä-sque'-sa-o*, another chief, and one somewhat noted for his fondness for the fire-water, spoke as follows: "Friends and Relatives—I am much pleased with the dance, and hope it will continue to be well sustained. I return my thanks to the war-dancers for the spirit with which they perform their duty. I wish them all prosperity and long life. If any one should look at me, they will find that I keep my eye fixed upon the dancers, and furthermore, that I have a good eye, so much so, that one would think I wore glasses. I take from my pocket a shilling for the dancers." Gives the money. The dance was then resumed. At the end of the song, the speech of *Hä-sque'-sa-o* called out a reply from *Sä-de-wä'-na*, as follows: "Friends and Relatives—We have just heard some one on the other side of the house announce, that he had an eye so bright that one would think he wore spectacles. But as he has a pair of red eyes, we must, I suppose, conclude that he uses red spectacles." Gives tobacco to the dancers. This hit at *Hä-sque'-sa-o's* infirmity was received with applause. Again the dance goes on as usual. Among the dancers were men of all sizes, figures and heights. There was one warrior, especially, of such herculean proportions, that he might be called a giant. He furnished a theme for the next speech, which was made by *Hä-sa-no-an'-da*, the dance having ceased, as follows: "Friends and Relatives—I admire the ease and grace with which *Hä-ho'-yäs* manages his wonderful proportions. He has every reason to be proud of his size and dignity. I propose to give him a present of two plugs of tobacco, supposing that it will be sufficient for *one quid.*" Gives the tobacco. *Hä-ho'-yäs* received the tobacco with seeming pleasure, and the people the jest with considerable merriment. At the conclusion of the next song, he thus replied: "Friends and Relatives—I return my thanks to *Hä-sa-no-an'-da* for his present. I assure him that my intellectual capacities correspond very justly with my physical dimensions. I hope my brother will publish my fame from the rising to the setting sun." Again the war-whoop sounded, the music opened, and the dance was renewed.

Other speeches were made from time to time, some of which called forth applause, and in due time a reply adapted to the case. After a number had thus spoken, *Sä-de-wä'-na* rapped again. When the music and the dancers were still, he thus said: "Friends and Relatives—I have made another strike. I desire to make a present to the women who have assisted in preparing the feast. But as I cannot give presents to all, I wish to see the one who has to-day eaten the most beef, and is considered the most greedy. I request her to come forward and receive the present." One of them, *Gi-an'-ok*, advanced and received the money, good-naturedly, which the people applauded. After a few more courses of the dance, a speech was made by *O-no'-sä*, of a more serious cast, as follows: "Friends and Relatives—We have reason to glory in the achievements of our ancestors. I behold with sadness the present declining state of our noble race. Once the warlike yell, and the painted band were the terror of the white man. Then our fathers were strong, and their power was felt and acknowledged far and wide over the American continent. But we have been reduced and broken by the cunning and rapacity of the white-skinned race. We are now compelled to crave, as a blessing, that we may be allowed to live upon our own lands, to cultivate our own fields, to drink from own springs, and to mingle our bones with those of our fathers. Many winters ago, our wise ancestors predicted that a great monster, with white eyes, would come from the east, and, as he advanced, would consume the land. This monster is the white race, and the prediction is near its fulfilment. They advised their children, when they became weak, to plant a tree with four roots, branching to the north, the south, the east and the west; and then collecting under its shade, to dwell together in unity and harmony. This tree, I propose, shall be this very spot. Here we will gather, here live, and here die." Gives tobacco to the dancers. The dance was then resumed as before, and continued until a rap announced another speech from *To-no-ai'-o*, the first speaker, who, after silence was restored, addressed the dancers: "In my view of the dance you do not do it as well as it can be done; although you doubtless have done as well as you know how. When I was a young man, I was the greatest dancer of my time. I did not know any one who could surpass me in the War dance. Furthermore, I was considered the best singer of the war-songs. I hope, however, you will continue to do the best you can, even though you fail to perform this dance as well as it can be done. I have another piece of the leaf which I will turn over to the singers. I wish them to swallow the juice, as it will make their voices clear, and help their singing." Gives the tobacco. Again the dance was resumed. After the next tune, this speech called out a reply from *Jä-ese'*, as follows: "Friends and Relatives—We have just heard a speaker, on the other side of the house, boasting of what he had done in his younger days. I do not like to hear such high speaking of one's self. I should like to see *To-no-ai'-o* come out and show the people what he can do, or what he used to do in his younger days." Gives money to the dancers. Again the war-whoop sounded, the responses followed, and the music and the dance made the house resound. In this manner was this famous dance conducted by our primitive inhabitants around their domestic council-fires.

These illustrations will suffice to exhibit the general character of these speeches, as well as of the dance itself. In the numerous addresses and witticisms which the War dance called forth, the Iroquois took the highest delight. They served the double purpose of relieving the dancers themselves, who would soon have been exhausted by continuous exertion, and of entertaining the people in the interval. This was the secret of its great popularity as a dance, and of its universal adoption. To this day, a well-conducted War dance is the highest entertainment known among the Iroquois.

GUS-DÄ'-WA-SÄ, OR RATTLE.

Second in the public estimation, but first intrinsically, stood the great Feather dance, *O-sto-weh'-go-wä*, sometimes called the Religious dance, because it was specially consecrated to the worship of the Great Spirit. The invention, or at least the introduction of this dance, is ascribed to the first *To-do-däʹ-ho*, at the period of the formation of the League. In its Iroquois origin, they all concur. It was performed by a select band, ranging from fifteen to thirty, in full costume, and was chiefly used at their religious festivals, although it was one of the prominent dances on all great occasions in Indian life. This dance was the most splendid, graceful and remarkable in the whole collection, requiring greater powers of endurance, suppleness and flexibility of person, and gracefulness of deportment, than either of the others. The *saltandi ars*, or dancing art, found in the Feather dance its highest achievement, at least in the Indian family; and it may be questioned whether a corresponding figure can be found among those which are used in refined communities, which will compare with it in those particulars which make up a spirited and graceful dance.

The music was furnished by two singers, seated in the centre of the room, each having a turtle-shell rattle of the kind represented in the figure.[1] It consisted of a series of songs or measured verses, which required about two minutes each for their recitation. They were all religious songs, some of them in praise of the Great Spirit, some in praise of various objects in nature which ministered to their wants, others in the nature of thanksgivings to *Hä-wen-né'-yu*, or supplications of his continued protection. The rattles were used to mark time, and as an accompaniment to the songs. In using them, they were struck upon the seat as often as twice or thrice in a second, the song and the step of the dancers keeping time, notwithstanding the rapidity of the beat.

The band arrayed themselves in their costumes in an adjacent lodge, came into the council-house,

---

[1] To make this rattle they remove the animal from the shell, and after drying it, they place within it a handful of flint-corn, and then sew up the skin which is left attached to the shell. The neck of the turtle is then stretched over a wooden handle.

and opened in all respects as in the case last described. Instead of grouping, however, within the area of a circle, they ranged themselves in file, and danced slowly around the council-house. When the music ceased, the dance also was suspended, and the party walked in column to the beat of the rattles. After an interval of about two minutes, the rattles quickened their time, the singers commenced another song, and the warriors, at the same instant, the dance. The leader, standing at the head of the column, opened, followed by those behind. As they advanced slowly around the room, in the dance, they gestured with their arms, and placed their bodies in a great variety of positions, but, unlike the practice in the War dance, always keeping their forms erect. None of the attitudes in this dance were those of the violent passions, but rather of the mild and gentle feelings. Consequently, there were no distortions either of the countenance or the body; but all their movements and positions were extremely graceful, dignified and imposing. The step has the same general peculiarities as that in the dance last described, but yet is quite distinct from it. Each foot in succession is raised from two to eight inches from the floor, and the heel is then brought down with great force as frequently as the beat of the rattles. Frequently one heel is brought down twice or three times before it alternates with the other. This will convey an impression of the surprising activity of this dance, in which every muscle of the body appears to be strung to its highest degree of tension. The concussion of the foot upon the floor served the double purpose of shaking the rattles and bells, which form a part of the costume, and of adding to the noise and animation of the dance.

The dancers were usually nude down to the waist, with the exception of ornaments upon their arms and necks, as represented in the engraving, thus exposing their well-formed chests, finely rounded arms, and their smooth, evenly colored skins, of a clear and brilliant copper color. This exposure of the person, not in any sense displeasing, contributed materially to the beauty of the costume, and gave a striking expression to the figure of the dancer. Such was the physical exertion put forth in this dance, that before it closed, the vapor of perspiration steamed up, like smoke, from their uncovered backs. No better evidence than this need be given, that it was a dance full of earnestness and enthusiasm. One of their aims was to test each other's powers of endurance. It not unfrequently happened that a part of the original number yielded from exhaustion before the dance was ended. Nothing but practice superadded to flexibility of person and great muscular strength would enable even an Indian to perform this dance. When the popular applause was gained by one of the band for spirited or graceful dancing, he was called out to stand at the head of the column, and lead the party: in this way several changes of leaders occurred before the final conclusion of the figure.

In this dance the women participated, if they

were disposed. They wore, however, their ordinary apparel, and entered by themselves at the foot of the column. The female step is entirely unlike the one described. They moved sideways in this figure, simply raising themselves alternately upon each foot from heel to toe, and then bringing down the heel upon the floor, at each beat of the rattle, keeping pace with the slowly advancing column. With the females dancing was a quiet, and not ungraceful amusement.

As a scene, its whole effect was much increased by the arrangement of the dancers into column. In this long array of costumes, the peculiar features of each were brought more distinctly into view, and by keeping the elliptical area around which they moved, entirely free from the pressing throng of Indian spectators, a better opportunity was afforded to all to witness the performance. To one who has never seen this dance, it would be extremely difficult to convey any notion of its surprising activity, and its inspiring influence upon the spectators. Requiring an almost continuous exertion, it is truly a marvellous performance.

The Thanksgiving dance, *Gä-na'-o-uh*, was likewise a costume dance, and given by a select band. It resembles the one last described so closely, both in step and plan, that it is not necessary to describe it.

One of the most simple figures among the Iroquois, was called the Trotting dance, *Gä-dä'-shote*. It was usually the opening dance at councils, and at private entertainments, when no costume figures were introduced. A person appointed to act as leader, followed by a few others, took the floor and began. Others joined in as the column passed around the room.

The music was entirely vocal, and furnished by those who danced. It consisted of about twenty different songs, each lasting something less than two minutes. In this dance the tune was the mere repetition of one exclamation by those at the head of the column, followed by a response, in chorus, from the residue. Three specimens are given in illustration. The leader, in concert with those nearest him, sang the following syllables: *Yä-hä'we-yä-hä'*, to which all the others responded, *Hä-hä'*. This would be repeated and responded to, for about two minutes, the pronunciation of the syllables being subjected to a musical variation each time. When the tune ended, the band walked for about the same length of time. The next song might consist of the syllables *Gä-no'-oh-he-yo'*, with the response *Wä-hä'-ah-he-yo'*. This would be continued, and the key varied, in the same manner as the last. After this was ended, and the dancers had refreshed themselves by walking, perhaps the next song would consist of the following syllables: *Yu-wä'-na-he-yo'*, and the response *Wä-hä'-ah-ha'*.

As to the step it was very simple, being nearly a trot, or alternate step on each foot. In dancing, those engaged stood close to each other, and advanced slowly around the council-house. The women participated, but they were by themselves at

the foot of the column. As this dance was extremely simple, it was not uncommon to see two
and even three hundred engaged in it at one time,
moving around in three or four concentric lines.

Another figure, in very general use, was called
the Fish dance, *Ga-so-wä'-o-no.* It was of foreign
origin. The music consisted of singing, accompanied with the drum, and the squash-shell rattle;
the two singers seating themselves in the centre of
the room facing each other, and using the drum
and rattle to mark time, and increase the volume of
the music. The step was merely an elevation from
heel to toe, twice repeated upon each foot alternately; bringing down the heel each alternate time
with considerable force, to mark time and make the
floor resound.

The dance was commenced by the leader, who
took the floor, followed by others, and walked to
the beat of the drum. When the song commenced,
each alternate dancer faced round, thus bringing
the column into sets of two each, face to face, those
who turned dancing backwards, but the whole band
moving around the room, as in other cases. Each
song, or tune lasted about three minutes. At the
end of the first minute there was a break in the
music, and the sets turned, thus reversing their positions; at the end of the second there was another
change in the music, in the midst of which the sets
turned again, which brought them back to their
original positions. Through the third and last subdivision of the time, the dance was continued with

increased animation. At the close of it, those who had been dancing backwards faced around, and the whole column walked about two minutes, to the beat of the drum. Another tune was then commenced and finished in the same manner.

The peculiarity of this dance was the opportunity which it afforded the Indian maiden to select whoever she preferred as a partner. In this particular the custom of refined communities was reversed. The warrior never solicited the maiden to dance with him; that privilege was accorded to her alone. In the midst of the dance, the females present themselves in pairs between any set they may select, thus giving to each a partner. This rule prevails in all Indian dances; so that the Indian maiden at her own convenience "gracefully presents her personage to the one she designs to favor, and thus quietly engages herself in the dance." In none of the changes of position in this dance do the partners join hands. This figure usually continues less than an hour. Sometimes, as a mark of respect to a guest, or distinguished chief, two women presented themselves before him, as partners in the dance.

The Passing dance, *Ga-no'-ga-yo*, was also in high favor. It is similar to the last, the column being divided into sets of two each, the women engaging in whichever set they please. At a certain stage of the song, the woman passed her partner, and took the next, her place being supplied from behind. They danced around the room, facing each other in pairs, the men moving backwards. The music and the step were about the same as in the dance last described.

An occasional and very singular figure was called the Dance for the Dead. It was known as the *O-ke'-wä*. It was danced by the women alone. The music was entirely vocal, a select band of singers being stationed in the centre of the room. To the songs for the dead, which they sang, the dancers joined in chorus. It was plaintive and mournful music. This dance was usually separate from all councils, and the only dance of the occasion. It commenced at dusk, or soon after, and continued until towards morning, when the shades of the dead, who were believed to be present and participate in the dance, were supposed to disappear. This dance was had whenever a family, which had lost a member, called for it, which was usually about a year after the event. In the spring and fall, it was often given for all the dead indiscriminately, who were believed then to revisit the earth and join in the dance.

One of their performances was called the Buffalo dance, *Da-ge'-yä-go-o-an'-no*. It was designed for males alone. The music consisted of singing, accompanied with the drum and the rattle. Its principal feature was the attempt to imitate the actions of the buffalo. According to tradition, this dance originated in a warlike expedition of the Iroquois against the Cherokees. When they had proceeded as far as the Kentucky salt lick, they heard, for the first time, the buffaloes, " singing their favorite songs," (bellowing and grumbling.)   From this bellowing the music, and from their actions the plan of the dance, were made.

GUS-DÄ'-WA-SÄ, OR SQUASH-SHELL RATTLES.

In connection with the dances of the Iroquois, may be mentioned their concerts, which occupy a conspicuous place in their amusements.   But one will be noticed of the four, which make up the number of kinds. It was called the *O-ee-dose'*. It was given in the night, in a dark room, and no women were allowed to be present.   Those engaged in the concert were seated on benches around the room, in a continuous row, each one holding in his hand a rattle, of the kind represented in the figure.   These rattles were made to give each one a different note, by means of different-sized shells, and holes bored in them to emit the sound. Among twenty of them, rattled together at such a concert, no two would give the same sound.   Corn was placed inside the shell.   When the parties were ready, one of their number sang a song, to which they all beat time with their rattles, and at certain intervals, all joined in the song in chorus.   Another then commenced a song, which was continued and finished in the same manner. After each one in turn had sung his song, which, with the accompaniments and the choruses, made a not unpleasant entertainment, the concert was ended.[1]

The other three are the Medicine concert, *Gä-no-dä'-yo-suh;* the Female concert, *O-e-un'-do-tä;* and the Thanksgiving concert, *Ah-do'-weh*, before described.

It will not be necessary to describe the remaining dances. Sufficient, at least, has been presented, to give a general idea of the Dance among the Iroquois. A few of them have been given in detail, as they seemed calculated to furnish a glimpse of Indian society. These amusements of our primitive inhabitants are not, in themselves, devoid of interest, although they indicate a tendency of mind unbefitting rational men. A hunter by nature and by inclination, averse to cities, and impatient of labor, the chase, the war-path, and the council-fire, with the dance, furnished the three great employments of his life. Who shall tell how much the hopes, the friendships, the happiness, and even the virtues of the

---

[1] The Indian appears to have had a good perception of time, and to have measured it, in his music and dances, with considerable exactness; but in tune he was sadly deficient. He knew nothing of the natural intervals of tones and semi-tones. There runs always through his music one predominant and constantly recurring sound, from which the others vary by all kinds of irregular intervals and fractions of intervals. The tunes of the Iroquois, if the name may be given to their rude minstrelsy, were both numerous and varied, and capable, also, of inspiring enthusiasm or sadness. In their occasional songs, as in the *Ah-do'-weh*, the music, as well as the words, was often *impromptu*. The Indian voice, especially that of the female, is musical, and highly capable of cultivation.

Indian, were bound up in indissoluble connection with the Dance. With it the Iroquois kindled the flame of patriotism which glowed in his breast, while vindicating the prowess of his race upon the hills of New England, on the prairies of the Mississippi, or in the trackless forests of the South. With it he celebrated his victories, and in the days of peace cultivated his social affections. And with it, also, at stated seasons of the year, he offered up his praise and homage to the Great Spirit, the ever present Author of his being.[1]

[1] SCHEDULE OF IROQUOIS DANCES.

1 O-sto-weh'-go-wä,‡	Great Feather Dance.	For both sexes.
2 Gä-na'-o-uh,‡	Great Thanksgiving Dance.	"
3 Da-yun'-da-nes-hunt-hä,	Dance with Joined Hands.	"
4 Gä-dä'-shote,*	Trotting Dance.	"
5 O-to-wa'-ga-kä,* †	North Dance.	"
6 Je-hä'-yä,	Antique Dance.	"
7 Gä'-no-jit'-ga-o,	Taking the Kettle out.	"
8 Ga-so-wä'-o-no,*	Fish Dance.	"
9 Os-ko-dä'-tä,	Shaking the Bush.	"
10 Ga-no'-ga-yo,‡	Rattle Dance.	"
11 So-wek-o-an'-no,*	Duck Dance.	"
12 Jä-ko'-wä-o-an'-no,	Pigeon Dance.	"
13 Guk-sä'-gä-ne-a,†	Grinding Dishes.	"
14 Gä-so'-ä,†	Knee Rattle Dance.	"
15 O-ke'-wä,	Dance for the Dead.	For Females.
16 O-as-ka-ne'-a,	Shuffle Dance.	"
17 Da-swä-da-ne'-a,	Tumbling Dance.	"
18 Gä-ne-ä'-seh-o,†	Turtle Dance.	"
19 Un-dä-da-o-at'-hä,†	Initiation Dance for Girls.	"
20 Un-to-we'-sus,	Shuffle Dance.	"
21 Da-yo-dä'-sun-dä-e'-go,	Dark Dance.	"
22 Wä-sä'-seh,* ‡	Sioux, or War Dance.	For Males.
23 Da-ge'-yä-go-o-an'-no,	Buffalo Dance.	"
24 Ne-ä'-gwi-o-an'-no,*	Bear Dance.	"
25 Wä-a-no'-a,†	Striking the Stick.	"
26 Ne-ho-sä-den'-da,†	Squat Dance.	"
27 Gä-na-un'-dä-do,† ‡	Scalp Dance.	"
28 Un-de-a-ne-suk'-tä,† ‡	Track Finding Dance.	"
29 Eh-nes'-hen-do,†	Arm Shaking Dance.	"
30 Gä-go'-sä,	False Face Dance.	"
31 Gä-je'-sa,	" " "	"
32 Un-da-de-a-dus'-shun-ne-at'-hä,†	Preparation Dance.	"

Those marked thus *, are of foreign origin; thus †, are now obsolete; and thus ‡, are costume dances.

CHAPTER V.

IN their national games is to be found another fruitful source of amusement in Indian life. These games were not only played at their religious festivals, at which they often formed a conspicuous part of the entertainment, but special days were frequently set apart for their celebration. They entered into these diversions with the highest zeal and emulation, and took unwearied pains to perfect themselves in the art of playing each successfully. There were but six principal games among the Iroquois, and these are divisible into athletic games, and games of chance.

Challenges were often sent from one village to another, and were even exchanged between nations, to a contest of some of these games. In such cases the chosen players of each community or nation were called out to contend for the prize of victory. An intense degree of excitement was aroused, when the champions were the most skilful players of rival villages, or adjacent nations.[1] The people en-

[1] Tradition relates that the war which ended in the expulsion of the Eries, about the year 1653, from the western part of New York, originated

listed upon their respective sides, with a degree of enthusiasm, which would have done credit, both to the spectators and the contestants, at the far-famed Elian games. For miles, and even hundreds of miles, they flocked together at the time appointed to witness the contest.

Unlike the prizes of the Olympic games, no chaplets awaited the victors. They were strifes between nation and nation, village and village, or tribes and tribes; in a word parties against parties, and not champion against champion. The prize contended for was that of victory; and it belonged, not to the triumphant players, but to the party which sent them forth to the contest.

When these games were not played by one community against another, upon a formal challenge, the people arranged themselves on two sides, according to their tribal divisions. By an organic provision of the Iroquois, as elsewhere stated, the Wolf, Bear, Beaver and Turtle tribes were brothers to each other, as tribes, and cousins to the other four. In playing their games they always went together, and formed one party or side. In the same manner the Deer, Snipe, Heron and Hawk tribes were brothers to each other, as tribes, and cousins to the four first named. These formed a second, or opposite party. Thus in all Indian games, with the exceptions first mentioned, the people divided themselves into two sections, four of the

in a breach of faith or treachery on the part of the Eries, in a Ball game to which they had challenged the Senecas.

tribes always contending against the other four. Father and son, husband and wife, were thus arrayed in opposite ranks.

Betting upon the result was common among the Iroquois. As this practice was never reprobated by their religious teachers, but, on the contrary, rather encouraged, it frequently led to the most reckless indulgence. It often happened that the Indian gambled away every valuable article which he possessed; his tomahawk, his medal, his ornaments, and even his blanket. The excitement and eagerness with which he watched the shifting tide of the game, was more uncontrollable than the delirious agitation of the pale-face at the race-course, or even at the gaming-table. Their excitable temperament and emulous spirits peculiarly adapted them for the enjoyment of their national games.

These bets were made in a systematic manner, and the aticles then deposited with the managers of the game. A bet offered by a person upon one side, in the nature of some valuable article, was matched by a similar article, or one of equal value, by some one upon the other. Personal ornaments made the usual gaming currency. Other bets were offered and taken in the same manner, until hundreds of articles were sometimes collected. These were laid aside by the managers, until the game was decided, when each article lost by the event was handed over to the winning individual, together with his own, which he had risked against it.

GÄ'-NE-Ä, OR BALL BAT, 5 FEET

With the Iroquois, the Ball game, *O-tä-dä-jish'-quä-äge*, was the favorite among their amusements of this description. This game reaches back to a remote antiquity, was universal among the red races, and was played with a degree of zeal and enthusiasm which would scarcely be credited. It was played with a small deer-skin ball, by a select band, usually from six to eight on a side, each set representing its own party. The game was divided into several contests, in which each set of players strove to carry the ball through their own gate. They went out into an open plain or field, and erected gates, about eighty rods apart, on its opposite sides. Each gate was simply two poles, some ten feet high, set in the ground about three rods asunder. One of these gates belonged to each party: and the contest between the players was, which set would first carry

GA-KA or BREECH CLOTH

the ball through its own a given number of times. Either five or seven made the game, as the parties agreed. If five, for example, was the number, the party which first carried, or drove the ball through its own gate this number of times, won the victory. Thus, after eight separate contests, the parties might stand equal, each having won four; in which case the party which succeeded on the ninth contest would carry the game. The players commenced in the centre of the field, midway between the gates. If one of them became fatigued or disabled during the progress of the game, he was allowed to leave the ranks, and his party could supply his place with a fresh player, but the original number were not at any time allowed to be increased. Regular managers were appointed on each side to see that the rules of the game were strictly and fairly observed. One rule forbade the players to touch the ball with the hand or foot.

In preparing for this game, the players denuded themselves entirely, with the exception of the waist-cloth,[1] (see plate, page 295.) They also underwent, frequently, a course of diet and training, as in a preparation for a foot-race.

When the day designated had arrived, the people gathered from the whole surrounding country, to witness the contest. About meridian they assem-

---

[1] The *Gä'-kä*, or waist-cloth, was a strip of deer-skin or broadcloth, about a quarter wide and two yards long, ornamented at the ends with bead or quill-work. It was passed between the limbs, and secured by a deer-skin belt, passing around the waist, the embroidered ends falling over the belt, before and behind, in the fashion of an apron.

bled at the appointed place, and having separated
themselves into two companies, one might be seen
upon each side of the line, between the gates, arranged
in scattered groups, awaiting the commencement of
the game. The players, when ready, stationed
themselves in two parallel rows, facing each other,
midway on this line, each one holding a ball bat,
of the kind represented in the figure, and with which
alone the ball was to be driven. As soon as all the
preliminaries were adjusted, the ball was dropped
between the two files of players, and taken between
the bats of the two who stood in the middle of each
file, opposite to each other. After a brief struggle
between them, in which each player endeavored,
with his bat, to get possession of the ball, and give
it the first impulse towards his own gate, it was
thrown out, and then commenced the pursuit. The
flying ball, when overtaken, was immediately surrounded by a group of players, each one striving to
extricate it, and, at the same time, direct it towards
his party gate. In this way the ball was frequently
imprisoned in different parts of the field, and an
animated controversy maintained for its possession.
When freed, it was knocked upon the ground, or
through the air; but the moment a chance presented,
it was taken up upon the deer-skin network of the
ball bat, by a player in full career, and carried in a
race towards the gate. To guard against this contingency, by which one contest of the game might
be determined in a moment, some of the players
detached themselves from the group contending

around the ball, and took a position from which to intercept a runner upon a diagonal line, if it should chance that one of the adverse party got possession of the ball. These races often formed the most exciting part of the game, both from the fleetness of the runners, and the consequences which depended upon the result. When the line of the runner was crossed, by an adversary coming in before him upon a diagonal line, and he found it impossible, by artifice or stratagem, to elude him, he turned about, and threw the ball over the heads of both of them, towards his gate; or, perchance, towards a player of his own party, if there were adverse players between him and the gate. When the flight of the ball was arrested in any part of the field, a spirited and even fierce contest was maintained around it; the players handled their bats with such dexterity, and managed their persons with such art and adroitness, that frequently several minutes elapsed before the ball flew out. Occasionally in the heat of the controversy, but entirely by accident, a player was struck with such violence, that the blood trickled down his limbs. In such a case, if disabled, he dropped his bat and left the field, while a fresh player from his own party supplied his place. In this manner was the game contested: oftentimes with so much ardor and skill, that the ball was recovered by one party at the very edge of the adverse gate; and finally, after many shifts in the tide of success, carried in triumph through its own. When one contest in the game was thus decided,

the prevailing party sent up a united shout of rejoicing.

After a short respite for the refreshment of the
players, the second trial was commenced, and continued like the first. Sometimes it was decided in
a few moments, but more frequently it lasted an
hour, and sometimes much longer, to such a system
had the playing of this game been reduced by skill
and practice. If every trial was ardently contested,
and the parties continued nearly equal in the number decided, it often lengthened out the game, until
the approaching twilight made it necessary to take
another day for its conclusion.

On the final decision of the game, the exclamations of triumph, as would be expected, knew no
bounds. Caps, tomahawks and blankets were
thrown up into the air, and for a few moments the
notes of victory resounded from every side. It was
doubtless a considerate provision, that the prevailing
party were upon a side of the field opposite to, and
at a distance from, the vanquished, otherwise such
a din of exultation might have proved too exciting
for Indian patience.

In ancient times they used a solid ball of knot.
The ball bat, also, was made without network, having a solid and curving head. At a subsequent day,
they substituted the deer-skin ball and the network
ball bat in present use. These substitutions were
made so many years ago, that they have lost the
date.

The game of Javelins, *Gä-na'-gä-o*, was very simple, depending upon the dexterity with which the javelin was thrown at a ring, as it rolled upon the

GÄ-GEH'-DÄ, OR JAVELIN.

ground. They frequently made it a considerable game, by enlisting skilful players to prepare for the contest, and by betting upon the result. The people divided by tribes, the four brothers playing against their four cousin tribes, as in the last case, unless the game was played on a challenge between neighboring communities.

The javelin was five or six feet in length, by three fourths of an inch in diameter, and was usually made of hickory or maple. It was finished with care, sharpened at one end, and striped as shown in the figure. The ring was about eight inches in diameter, made either into a hoop or solid like a wheel, by winding with splints. Sometimes the javelin was thrown horizontally, by placing the forefinger against its foot, and supporting it with the thumb and second finger; in other cases it was held in the centre, and thrown with the hand raised above the shoulder.

On either side, from fifteen to thirty players were arranged, each having from three to six javelins, the number of both depending upon the interest in the game, and the time they wished to devote to the contest. The javelins themselves were the forfeit, and the game was gained by the party which won them.

Among the preliminaries to be settled by the managers, was the line on which the ring was to be rolled, the distance of the two bands of players from each other, and the space between each and the line itself. When these points were adjusted, and the parties stationed, the ring was rolled by one party on the line, in front of the other. As it passed the javelins were thrown. If the ring was struck by one of them, the players of the adverse party were required, each in turn, to stand in the place of the person who struck it, and throw their javelins in succession at the ring, which was set up as a target, on the spot where it was hit. Those of the javelins which hit the target when thus thrown were saved; if any missed they were passed to the other party, and by them were again thrown at the ring from the same point. Those which hit were won, finally, and laid out of the play, while the residue were restored to their original owners. After this first contest was decided, the ring was rolled back, and the other party, in turn, threw their javelins. If it was struck, the party which rolled it was required, in the same manner, to hazard their javelins, by throwing them at the target. Such as missed were delivered to the other party, and those which hit the target when thrown by them, were won also, and laid out of the play. In

this manner the game was continued, until one of
the parties had lost their javelins, which, of itself,
determined the contest.

There was another game of javelins, *Gä-ga-dä-yan'-
duk*, played by shooting them through the air.   In
this game, the javelin used was made of sumac, because of its lightness, and was of the same length
and size as in the former.   This game was divided
into contests, as the Ball game, and was won by the
party which first made the number agreed upon.
The game was usually from fifteen to twenty, and
the number of players on a side ranged from five to
ten.   When the parties were ready, the one which
had the first throw selected the object upon which
the javelin was to be thrown, to give it an upward
flight, and also its distance from the standing point.
If, for example, it was a log, at the distance of a
rod, the player placed his forefinger against the
foot of the javelin, and, supporting it with his thumb
and second finger, he threw it in such a manner, that
it would strike the upper side of the log, and thus
be thrown up into the air, and forward, until its
force was spent.   In this manner all the players, in
turn, threw their javelins.   The one which was
thrown the greatest distance won a point.   If another, upon the same side, was in advance of all
upon the opposite side, it counted another, and so
on for every one which led all those upon the opposite side.   In the next contest, the second party
chose the object over which to throw the javelin,
and the distance.   The game was thus continued,

until the number of points were gained which were agreed upon for the game.

GUS-GA-E-SA′-TÄ, OR DEER-BUTTONS.

This was strictly a fireside game, although it was sometimes introduced as an amusement at the season of religious councils, the people dividing into tribes, as usual, and betting upon the result. Eight buttons, about an inch in diameter, were made of elk-horn, and having been rounded and polished, were slightly burned upon one side to blacken them. When it was made a public game, it was played by two at a time, with a change of players, as elsewhere described in the Peach-stone game. At the fireside, it was played by two or more, and all the players continued in their seats until it was determined. A certain number of beans, fifty perhaps, were made the capital, and the game continued until one of the players had won them all. Two persons spread a blanket, and seated themselves upon it. One of them shook the deer-buttons in his hands, and then threw them down. If six turned up of the same color, it counted two, if seven, it counted four, and if all, it counted twenty, the winner taking as many beans from the general stock, as he made points by the throw. He also continued to throw as long as he continued to win. When less than six came up, either black or white, it counted nothing, and the throw was passed to the other player. In this manner the game was continued until the beans were taken up between the two players. After that the one paid to the other out of his own winnings, the game ending as soon as the capital in the hands of either player was exhausted. If four played, each had a partner, or played independently, as they were disposed; but when more than two played, each one was to pay to the winner the amount won. Thus, if four were playing independently, and after the beans were distributed among them, in the progress of the game, one of them should turn the buttons up all black, or all white, the other three would be obliged to pay him twenty each; but if the beans were still in bank, he took up but twenty. The deer-buttons were of the same size. In the figure they are represented at different angles.

GA-WA'-SA, OR SNOW-SNAKE.

Among the amusements of the winter season, in Indian life, was the game with Snow-snakes. It was primarily designed as a diversion for the young; but it was occasionally made a public game between the tribes like the other, and aroused a great degree of spirit, and the usual amount of betting. The snake was thrown with the hand by placing the forefinger against its foot, and supporting it with the thumb and remaining fingers. It was thus made to run upon the snow crust with the speed of an arrow, and to a much greater distance, sometimes running sixty or eighty rods. The success of the player depended upon his dexterity and muscular strength.

The snakes were made of hickory, and with the most perfect precision and finish. They were from five to seven feet in length, about a fourth of an inch in thickness, and gradually diminishing from about an inch in width at the head, to about half an inch at the foot. The head was round, turned up slightly, and pointed with lead to increase the momentum of the snake.

This game, like that of ball, was divided into a number of separate contests; and was determined when either party had gained the number of points agreed upon, which was generally from seven to ten. The players were limited and select, usually not more than six. A station was determined upon, with the line, or general direction in which the snake was to be thrown. After they had all been thrown by the players on both sides, the next question was to determine the count. The snake which ran the greatest distance was a point for the side to which it belonged. Other points might be won on the same side, if a second or third snake was found to be ahead of all the snakes upon the adverse side. One count was made for each snake which outstripped all upon the adverse side. These contests were repeated until one of the parties had made the requisite number of points to determine the game.

WÄ-A'-NO, OR BOW.

GÄ'-NO, OR ARROW.

In archery the Indian has scarcely been excelled. With a quick eye and a powerful muscle, he could send the arrow as unerringly as the archers of Robin Hood. It cannot be called, in strictness, a game, but trials of skill were common in ancient times; successful archery raising the individual into high repute.

The Indian bow was usually from three and a half to four feet in length, with such a difficult spring, that an inexperienced person could scarcely bend it sufficiently to set the string. To draw the string back, when set, an arm's length, could only be done by practice, superadded to the most powerful muscular strength. An arrow thus sent would strike its object with fearful velocity. The arrow was about three feet in length, and feathered at the small end with a twist, to make it revolve in its flight. It gave to its motion horizontality and precision, doubtless suggesting, at a later day, the idea of the twist in the rifle barrel, by which the ball is made to revolve in the same manner. The English and Scottish archers feathered their arrows, but without this peculiarity. Three feathers were also used by them, which were set parallel with the arrow, and with each other. But they were set upon one side of the arrow at its three quarters, and in such a way that the three parallel feathers formed obtuse angles with each other. The Indian used but two feathers, which passed around the opposite sides of the arrow in a twist, as shown in the figure. For this purpose, the feather was stripped off from the quill and tied to the arrow with sinew. Originally, the Indian arrow was pointed with a flint or chert-head, which would enable it to penetrate deeply any object at which it was directed. With such an arrow, it was an easy matter to bring down the deer, the wild fowl, or the warrior himself. Skeletons have been disentombed, having the skull penetrated with an arrow-head of, this description, with the flint-head itself still in the fracture, or entirely within the skull. In Oregon and on the upper Mississippi, the Indian arrow is still pointed with flint. Thus it was with the Iroquois, until the bow was laid aside for the rifle. Arrow-heads of this description are still found scattered over the whole surface of the State. With Indian youth, the bow and the arrow is still a favorite source of amusement.

Foot-races furnished another pastime for the Iroquois. They were often made a part of the entertainment with which civil and mourning councils were concluded. In this athletic game the Indian excelled. The exigencies, both of war and peace, rendered it necessary for the Iroquois to have among them practiced and trained runners. A spirit of emulation often sprang up among them, which resulted in regular contests for the palm of victory. In these races, the four tribes put forward their best runners against those of the other four, and left the question of superiority to be determined by the event of the contest. Before the time appointed for the races, they prepared themselves for the occasion by a process of training. It is not necessary to describe them. They dressed in the same manner for the race as for the game of ball. Leaping, wrestling and the other gymnastic exercises appear to have furnished no part of the public amusements of our primitive inhabitants.

An ancient and favorite game of the Iroquois, *Gus-kä'-eh*, was played with a bowl and peach-stones. It was always a betting game, in which the people divided by tribes. By established custom, it was introduced as the concluding exercise on the last

GUS-KÄ'-EH, OR PEACH STONES.

GA-JIH, OR BOWL.

day of the Green Corn and the Harvest festivals, and also of the New Year's jubilee. Its introduction among them is ascribed to the first *To-do-dä'-ho*, who flourished at the formation of the League. A popular belief prevailed, that this game would be enjoyed by them in the future life, in the realm of the Great Spirit; which is, perhaps, but an extravagant way of expressing their admiration for the game.

A dish, about a foot in diameter at the base, was carved out of a knot, or made of earthen. Six peach-stones were then ground, or cut down into an oval form, reducing them in the process about half in size, after which the heart of the pit was removed, and the stones themselves were burned upon one side, to blacken them. The above representation will exhibit both the bowl and the peach-stones; the latter being drawn in different positions to show the degree of their convexity.

It was a very simple game, depending, in part, upon the dexterity of the player, but more upon his good fortune. The peach-stones were shaken in the bowl by the player, the count depending upon the number which came up of one color, after they had ceased rolling in the dish. It was played in the public council-house by a succession of players, two at a time, under the supervision of managers appointed to represent the two parties, and to conduct the contest. Its length depended somewhat upon the number of beans which made the bank, usually one hundred, the victory being gained by the side which finally won them all.

A platform was erected a few feet from the floor and spread with blankets. When the betting was ended, and the articles had been delivered into the custody of the managers, they seated themselves upon the platform in the midst of the throng of spectators, and two persons sat down to the game between the two divisions into which they arranged themselves. The beans, in the first instance, were placed together in a bank. Five of them were given to each player, with which they commenced. Each player, by the rules of the game, was allowed to keep his seat until he had lost this outfit, after which he surrendered it to another player on his own side selected by the managers of his own party. And this was the case, notwithstanding any number he might have won of his adversary. Those which he won were delivered to his party managers. The six peach-stones were placed in the bowl and shaken by the player; if five of them came up of one color, either white or black, it counted one, and his adversary paid to him the forfeit, which was one bean; the bean simply representing a unit in counting the game. On the next throw, which the player having won, retained, if less than five came up of the same color, it counted nothing, and he passed the bowl to his adversary. The second player then shook the bowl; upon which, if they all came up of one color, either white or black, it counted five. To pay this forfeit required the whole outfit of the first player, after which, having nothing to pay with, he vacated his seat, and was succeeded by another of his own side, who received from the bank the same number of beans which the first had. The other player followed his throw as long as he continued to win; after which he repassed the bowl to his adversary. If a player chanced to win five, and his opponent had but one left, this was all he could gain. In this manner the game continued, with varying fortune, until the beans were divided between the two sides in proportion to their success. After this the game continued in the same manner as before, the outfit of each new player being advanced by the managers of his own party; but as the beans or counters were now out of sight, none but the managers knew the state of the game with accuracy. In playing it there were but two winning throws, one of which counted one and the other five. When one of the parties had lost all their beans, the game was done.

There were some other peculiarities and variations in this game which would be necessary to a full understanding of it, but sufficient has been given to illustrate its general character. As they began to play this game about meridian, it often happened that it was necessary to take another day for its conclusion. It was made a long game by its constitution, as it was carefully guarded against the extreme fickleness of most games of chance. It so happens that games of this description do not depend for their interest upon the striking combinations involved in their construction. This is dependent very much upon practice, habit and association. Oftentimes the most simple game in its contrivance, is the most attractive and absorbing to the practiced player. This game, as simple as it may appear, was productive of a great degree of excitement, and when finally decided, the exultation of the victors broke forth in vehement rejoicings. Having intently watched, for hours, the ever-changing tide of the game, when the long suspense was over, and the tension of the mind was ended, its rebound, under the impulse of victory, exhibited itself in extravagant exclamations.

A brief description of the plan of these games will no more exhibit their hidden sources of entertainment, than a volume descriptive of chess would reveal the fascinations of the game itself. These games all depend, for their interest, upon circumstances. The Olympic, Pythian and other games of the Greeks, and the Apollinarian, Circensian and other games of the Romans, consisted chiefly, as is well known, of running, leaping, wrestling, riding and chariot-racing. Aside from the last, they were not, intrinsically, much superior to the games of the Iroquois. But in the hands of the Greeks, especially, they were made the most extraordinary entertainments of the ancient world. Among the Iroquois, in the celebration of their national games, as far as they went, is to be found the same species of enthusiasm and emulation which characterized the celebration of the games of antiquity. Although the national games, like the popular songs of one people, may be incapable of exciting the enthusiasm or awakening the patriotic spirit of another; yet they are not, for this reason, devoid of interest. If it be asked what interest for us can attach to these games of the Iroquois, one answer at least may be given;—they show that the American wilderness, which we have been taught to pronounce a savage solitude until the white man entered its borders, had long been vocal in its deepest seclusions, with the gladness of happy human hearts.

CHAPTER VI.

NOTWITHSTANDING the simplicity of Indian life,
and its barrenness of those higher social enjoyments
which pertain to refined communities, Indian society
was bound together by permanent institutions, governed by fixed laws, and impelled and guided by
well-established usages and customs. The diversified
powers, motives and restraints embraced within
them, exercised an important influence upon their
social life, and therefore they present fruitful and
interesting subjects of investigation. To form a
judgment of the Indian character, which is founded
upon a knowledge of his motives and principles of
action, he must be seen in his social relations. But
it is not deemed advisable to consider these topics
minutely.

The Iroquois resided in permanent villages. Not
knowing the use of wells, they fixed their residences
upon the banks of rivers and lakes, or in the vicinity
of copious springs. About the period of the formation of the League, when they were exposed to

the inroads of hostile nations, and the warfare of migratory bands, their villages were compact and stockaded. Having run a trench several feet deep, around five or ten acres of land, and thrown up the ground upon the inside, they set a continuous row of stakes or palisades in this bank of earth, fixing them at such an angle that they inclined over the trench. Sometimes a village was surrounded by a double, or even triple row of palisades. Within this enclosure they constructed their bark-houses, and secured their stores. Around it was the village field, consisting, oftentimes, of several hundred acres of cultivated land, which was subdivided into planting lots; those belonging to different families being bounded by uncultivated ridges. *Nun-da-wä'-o*, at the head of Canandaigua lake, the oldest village of the Senecas, was stockaded; so also were *Skä-hase'-gă-o* on the site of Lima, and two or three other of their oldest towns.

But at the commencement of the seventeenth century, which may be called the middle period of the history of the Iroquois, when their power had become consolidated, and most of the adjacent nations had been brought under subjection, the necessity of stockading their villages in a measure ceased, and with it the practice. At the period of the discovery of the inland Iroquois, about the year 1640,[1] few, if any, of the villages of the Senecas,

[1] The Franciscan Le Caron, passed through the country of the Iroquois in 1616, (Brancroft's Hist. U. S. 3. 120.) But little, however, was known of them prior to 1640.

Cayugas, or Onondagas were surrounded with palisades; but the Oneidas and Mohawks continued to stockade their villages for many years afterwards, in consequence of the inroads of the French. At this period, also, their villages were compactly built.

The modern village was a cluster of houses, planted like the trees of the forest, at irregular intervals, and over a large area. No attempt was made at a street, or at an arrangement of their houses in a row; two houses seldom fronting the same line. They were merely grouped together sufficiently near for a neighborhood.

As their villages, at an early day, were reckoned by the number of houses, it is important to remark the difference between the *Gä-no'-sote*, or Bark-house of the middle and the modern period, to arrive at an estimate of the number of inhabitants. When the village was scattered over a large area, the houses were single, and usually designed for one family; but when compact, as in ancient times, they were very long, and subdivided, so as to accommodate a number of families. The long house was generally from fifty to a hundred and thirty feet in length, by about sixteen in width, with partitions at intervals of about ten or twelve feet, or two lengths of the body. Each apartment was, in fact, a separate house, having a fire in the centre, and accommodating two families, one upon each side of the fire. Thus a house one hundred and twenty feet long, would contain ten fires and twenty families.

A Mr. Greenhalgh, in 1677, visited the Seneca village of *Dä-yo-de-hok'-to*, signifying " a bended creek," situated upon a bend of the Honeoye outlet, west of Mendon, in the county of Monroe. Under the name of " Tiotohatton," he thus speaks of it :—
" Tiotohatton lies on the brink or edge of a hill; has not much cleared ground; is near the river Tiotohatton, which signifies bending. It lies to the westward of Canagorah," probably *Nun-da-wä'-o*, " about thirty miles, containing about 120 houses, being the largest of all the houses we saw, (the ordinary being from fifty to sixty feet long,) with from twelve to thirteen fires in one house. They have good store of corn, growing about a mile to the northward of the town."[1] The Marquis De Nonville, in 1687, captured this, with three other villages of the Senecas, at the time of his invasion of the Seneca territory. In the *Acté*, executed at this village, by which the French took formal possession of the territories of the Seneca-Iroquois, on behalf of France, it is written "Totiakton," and is called " the largest of the Seneca villages."[2] It is not im-

[1] Documentary Hist. New York, i. 13. He further states that Canagorah contained 150 houses; Onondaga, 140; Oneida village, 100; ib. 12–13.

[2] Doc. Hist. N. Y., i. 242. The three other villages taken by De Nonville were Gannagaro, as it is called in the acté, or *Gä-o-sä-gä'-o*, signifying " in the Basswood country," situated a short distance south-east of Victor in the county of Ontario, Gannondata and Gannongaraę, one of which was doubtless *Gä-nun-dä'-gwa*, " place selected for a settlement," upon the site of the present village of Canandaigua. De Nonville estimated the population of the four villages at 15,000, and the Indian corn destroyed by his troops at 400,000 minots, (Doc. Hist. i. 239.) Doubtless, both of these estimates were exaggerations.

probable that the largest villages of the Iroquois contained 3000 inhabitants.

The *Gä-no'-sote*, or Bark-house, (see plate, page 3,) was a simple structure. When single, it was about twenty feet by fifteen upon the ground, and from fifteen to twenty feet high. The frame consisted of upright poles firmly set in the ground, usually five upon the sides, and four at the ends, including those at the corners. Upon the forks of these poles, about ten feet from the ground, cross-poles were secured horizontally, to which the rafters, also poles, but more numerous and slender, were adjusted. The rafters were strengthened with transverse poles, and the whole were usually so arranged as to form an arching roof. After the frame was thus completed, it was sided up, and shingled with red elm or ash bark, the rough side out. The bark was flattened and dried, and then cut in the form of boards. To hold these bark boards firmly in their places, another set of poles, corresponding with those in the frame, were placed on the outside; and by means of splints and bark rope fastenings, the boards were secured horizontally between them. It usually required four lengths of boards, and four courses from the ground to the rafters to cover a side, as they were lapped at the ends, as well as clapboarded; and also in the same proportion for the ends. In like manner, the roof was covered with bark boards, smaller in size, with the rough side out, and the grain running up and down; the boards being stitched through and through with fastenings, and thus held between the frames of poles, as on the sides. In the centre of the roof was an opening for the smoke, the fire being upon the ground in the centre of the house, and the smoke ascending without the guidance of a chimney. At the two ends of the house were doors, either of bark hung upon hinges of wood, or of deer or bear-skins suspended before the opening; and however long the house, or whatever the number of fires, these were the only entrances. Over one of these doors was cut the tribal device of the head of the family. Within, upon the two sides, were arranged wide seats, also of bark boards, about two feet from the ground, well supported underneath, and reaching the entire length of the house. Upon these they spread their mats of skins, and also their blankets, using them as seats by day and couches at night. Similar berths were constructed on each side, about five feet above these, and secured to the frame of the house, thus furnishing accommodations for the family. Upon cross-poles, near the roof, was hung, in bunches, braided together by the husks, their winter supply of corn. Charred and dried corn, and beans were generally stored in bark barrels, and laid away in corners. Their imple-ments for the chase, domestic utensils, weapons, ar-ticles of apparel, and miscellaneous notions,[1] were stowed away, and hung up, whenever an unoccupied place was discovered. A house of this description

[1] For some account of their fabrics, implements and utensils, see Book iii. ch. i.

would accommodate a family of eight, with the limited wants of the Indian, and afford shelter for their necessary stores, making a not uncomfortable residence. After they had learned the use of the axe, they began to substitute houses of hewn logs, but they constructed them after the ancient model. Many of the houses of their modern villages in the valley of the Genesee were of this description.

There was another species of house occasionally constructed, either for temporary use or for a small family. It was triangular at the base, the frame consisting of three poles on a side, gathered at the top, but with space sufficient between them for a chimney opening. They were sided up in the same manner as the rectangular *Gä-no'-sote*. During the hunt, bark-houses of this description were often erected as a shelter.

The Iroquois were accustomed to bury their surplus corn, and also their charred green corn, in caches, in which the former would preserve uninjured through the year, and the latter for a much longer period. They excavated a pit, made a bark bottom and sides, and having deposited their corn within it, a bark roof, water tight, was constructed over it, and the whole covered up with earth. Pits of charred corn are still found near their ancient settlements. Cured venison and other meats were buried in the same manner, except that the bark repository was lined with deer-skins.

In this connection, the marriage customs of the Iroquois naturally suggest themselves. They exhibit novel, if not distinctive features. Marriage was not founded upon the affections, which constitute the only legitimate basis of this relation in civilized society, but was regulated exclusively as a matter of physical necessity. It was not even a contract between the parties to be married, but substantially between their mothers, acting oftentimes under the suggestions of the matrons and wise-men of the tribes to which the parties respectively belonged. In a general sense, therefore, the subject of marriage was under the supervision of the older members of each tribe; but practically, it was under maternal control. With the improvement and elevation of the race, changes were gradually introduced in relation to the marriageable age, and the disparity of age between the sexes. In ancient times, the young warrior was always united to a woman several years his senior, on the supposition that he needed a companion experienced in the affairs of life. The period was also deferred on his part until twenty-five, that he might first become inured to the hardships of the war-path and of the chase, before his freedom was curtailed and his responsibilities were increased by the cares of a family, light as these cares seem to have been under their social system. Thus, it often happened that the young warrior at twenty-five was married to a woman of forty, and oftentimes a widow; while the widower at sixty was joined to the maiden at twenty. But these were their primitive customs; the ages of the parties afterwards drew nearer to an equality, and the marriageable age was, in time, reduced to twenty, and even below it.

When the mother considered her son of a suitable age for marriage, she looked about her for a maiden, whom, from report, or acquaintance, she judged would accord with him in disposition and temperament. A negotiation between the mothers ensued, and a conclusion was speedily reached. Sometimes the near relatives and the elderly persons of the 'tribes to which each belonged were consulted; but their opinions were of no avail, independently of the wishes of the mothers themselves. Not the least singular feature of the transaction, was the entire ignorance in which the parties remained of the pending negotiation; the first intimation they received being the announcement of their marriage, without, perhaps, ever having known or seen each other. Remonstrance or objection on their part was never attempted; they received each other as the gift of their parents. As obedience to them in all their requirements was inculcated as a paramount duty, and disobedience was followed by disownment, the operative force of custom, in addition to these motives, was sufficient to secure acquiescence. The Indian father never troubled himself concerning the marriage of his children. To interfere would have been an invasion of female immunities; and these, whatever they were, were as sacredly regarded by him, as he was inflexible in enforcing respect for his own.

When the fact of marriage had been communicated to the parties, a simple ceremonial completed the transaction. On the day following the announcement, the maiden was conducted by her mother, accompanied by a few female friends, to the home of her intended husband. She carried in her hand a few cakes of unleavened corn bread, which she presented on entering the house, to her mother-in-law, as an earnest of her usefulness and of her skill in the domestic arts. After receiving it, the mother of the young warrior returned a present of venison, or other fruit of the chase, to the mother of the bride, as an earnest of his ability to provide for his household. This exchange of presents ratified and concluded the contract, which bound the new pair together in the marriage relation. Thus simple was the formation of the nuptial bond among our primitive inhabitants.

From the very nature of the marriage institution among the Iroquois, it follows that the passion of love was entirely unknown among them. Affection after marriage would naturally spring up between the parties from association, from habit, and from mutual dependence; but of that marvellous passion which originates in a higher development of the powers of the human heart, and is founded upon a cultivation of the affections between the sexes, they were entirely ignorant. In their temperaments, they were below this passion in its simplest forms. Attachments between individuals, or the cultivation of each other's affections before marriage, was entirely unknown; so also were promises of marriage. The fact that individuals were united in this relation, without their knowledge or consent, and perhaps without even a previous acquaintance, illustrates and confirms this position. This invasion of the romances of the novelist, and of the conceits of the poet, upon the attachments which sprang up in the bosom of Indian society, may, perhaps, divest the mind of some pleasing impressions; but these are entirely inconsistent with the marriage institution as it existed among them, and with the facts of their social history.

Intercourse between the sexes was restrained by circumstances, and by inclination. Indian habits and modes of life divided the people socially into two great classes, male and female. The male sought the conversation and society of the male, and they went forth together for amusement, or for the severer duties of life. In the same manner the female sought the companionship of her own sex. Between the sexes there was but little sociality, as this term is understood in polished society. Such a thing as formal visiting was entirely unknown. When the unmarried of opposite sexes were casually brought together, there was little or no conversation between them. No attempts by the unmarried to please or gratify each other by acts of personal attention, were ever made. At the season of councils and religious festivals, there was more of actual intercourse and sociality, than at any other time; but this was confined to the dance, and was, in itself, limited. A solution of this singular problem is, in part, to be found in the absence of equality in the sexes. The Indian regarded woman as the inferior, the dependent, and the servant of man, and from nurture and habit, she actually considered herself to be so. This absence of equality in position, in addition to the force of custom, furnishes a satisfactory explanation of many of the peculiarities characteristic of Indian society. In the cultivation of the affections between the sexes, and in the development of kindred sentiments, is to be found the origin of the amenities and the mitigation of the asperities of life.

In intimate connection with the subject of marriage, is that of divorce. Polygamy was forbidden among the Iroquois, and never became a practice; but the right to put away the wife, or of voluntary separation, was allowed to all. The mothers of the married pair were responsible for their concord and harmony. If differences arose between them, it became their duty to effect a reconciliation, and by advice and counsel, to guard against a repetition of the difficulty. But if disturbances continued to follow reconciliations, and their dispositions were found to be too incongruous for domestic peace, a separation followed, either by mutual consent or the absolute refusal of one of the parties longer to recognize the marriage relation. As such a rupture in ancient times was regarded as discreditable to the parties, and brought them under the pressure of public censure, they were then unfrequent. In later days, however, the inviolability of the nuptial con-

tract was less sacredly regarded, and the most friv-
olous reasons, or the caprice of the moment, were
sufficient for breaking the marriage tie.

The husband and wife were never of the same
tribe, as has been elsewhere more fully explained;
and the children were of the tribe of their mother.
No right in the father to the custody of their persons, or to their nurture, was recognized.   As, after
separation, he gave himself no farther trouble concerning them, nor interested himself in their future welfare, they became estranged as well as separated.   Parental affection was much weaker, as is
usually the fact, on the part of the father than on
that of the mother.   The Indian father seldom
caressed his children, or by any outward acts manifested the least solicitude for their welfare; but
when his sons grew up to maturity, he became more
attached to them, making them his companions in
the hunt, and upon the war-path.   The care of their
infancy and childhood was intrusted to the watchful
affection of the mother alone.

By the laws of the Iroquois, the nationality as
well as the tribe of the individual was never lost, or
merged in another.   If a Cayuga woman married a
Seneca, her children were Cayugas, and her descendants in the female line, to the latest posterity, continued to be Cayugas, although they resided with
the Senecas, and by intermarriage with them had
lost nearly every particle of Cayuga blood.   In the
same manner, if a Mohawk married a Delaware woman, her children were not only Delawares, but

aliens, unless they were regularly adopted and christened as Mohawks, and the fact of adoption was announced in open council.

Property, both in amount and variety, was exceedingly limited; as would naturally be expected
among a people living a hunter and semi-agricultural life, and making a mere subsistence the limit of
their wants, and of their ambition. But inconsiderable as it was in the aggregate, it was held, and
subject to distribution, under fixed laws. Having
neither currency nor trade, nor the love of gain,
their property consisted merely of planting lots,
orchards, houses, implements of the chase, weapons,
articles of apparel, domestic utensils, personal ornaments, stores of grain, skins of animals, and those
miscellaneous fabrics which the necessities of life
led them to invent. The rights of property, of both
husband and wife, were continued distinct during
the existence of the marriage relation; the wife
holding, and controlling her own, the same as her
husband, and in case of separation, taking it with
her. No individual could obtain the absolute title
to land, as that was vested by the laws of the
Iroquois in all the people; but he could reduce
unocccupied lands to cultivation, to any extent he
pleased; and so long as he continued to use them,
his right to their enjoyment was protected and secured. He could also sell his improvements, or
bequeath them to his wife or children. If the wife,
either before or after marriage, inherited orchards,
or planting lots, or reduced land to cultivation, she

could dispose of them at her pleasure, and in case
of her death, they were inherited, together with
her other effects, by her children.   The rule of descent, on the death of the father, was different. His
children, not being of his tribe, were out of the line
of inheritance ; for by their laws, property could
not, by descent, pass out of the tribe.   If he gave
his planting lots, or any articles of property to his
wife or children, in the presence of a witness, they
were allowed to hold them.   But if he made no
disposition of his effects, they were handed over
upon his decease, to the near relatives in his own
tribe, who usually assigned to the family the house,
and such other articles as they deemed advisable,
and distributed the residue among themselves, as
personal mementos of the deceased.

One of the most attractive features of Indian society was the spirit of hospitality by which it was
pervaded.   Perhaps no people ever carried this
principle to the same degree of universality, as did
the Iroquois.   Their houses were not only open to
each other, at all hours of the day, and of the
night, but also to the wayfarer, and the stranger.
Such entertainment as their means afforded was
freely spread before him, with words of kindness
and of welcome.   The Indian had no regular meal
after the morning repast, but he allayed his appetite
whenever the occasion offered.   The care of the
appetite was left entirely with the women, as the
Indian never asked for food.   Whenever the husband returned, at any hour of the day, it was the

duty and the custom of the wife to set food before
him.   If a neighbor or a stranger entered her dwelling, a dish of hommony, or whatever else she had
prepared, was immediately placed before him, with
an invitation to partake.   It made no difference at
what hour of the day, or how numerous the calls,
this courtesy was extended to every comer, and was
the first act of attention bestowed.   This custom
was universal, in fact one of the laws of their social
system; and a neglect on the part of the wife to
observe it, was regarded both as a breach of hospitality, and as a personal affront.   A neighbor, or a
stranger, calling from house to house, through an
Indian village, would be thus entertained at every
dwelling he entered.   If the appetite of the guest
had thus been fully satisfied, he was yet bound in
courtesy to taste of the dish presented, and to return the customary acknowledgment, *Hi-ne-ä'-weh*,
" I thank you;" an omission to do either being esteemed a violation of the usages of life.   A stranger
would be thus entertained without charge, as long
as he was pleased to remain; and a relation was entitled to a home among any of his kindred, while
he was disposed to claim it.   Under the operation
of such a simple and universal law of hospitality,
hunger and destitution were entirely unknown
among them.   This method of dealing with the
human appetite strikes the mind as novel; but it
was founded upon a principle of brotherhood, and
of social intercourse, not much unlike the common
table of the Spartans.   The abounding supplies of

corn yielded, with light cultivation, by their fruitful
fields, and the simple fare of the Indian, rendered
the prevailing hospitality an inconsiderable burden.
It rested chiefly upon the industry, and therefore
upon the natural kindness of the Indian woman;
who, by the cultivation of the maize, and their other
plants, and the gathering of the wild fruits, provided the principal part of their subsistence, for the
warrior despised the toil of husbandry, and held all
labor beneath him. But it was in exact accordance
with the unparalleled generosity of the Indian
character. He would surrender his dinner to feed
the hungry, vacate his bed to refresh the weary,
and give up his apparel to clothe the naked. No
test of friendship was too severe, no sacrifice to re-
pay a favor too great, no fidelity to an engagement
too inflexible for the Indian character. With an innate knowledge of the freedom and the dignity of
man, he has exhibited the noblest virtues of the
heart, and the kindest deeds of humanity in those
sylvan retreats, which we are wont to look back
upon as vacant and frightful solitudes.[1]

In their subsistence there was but a limited variety from the necessity of the case. Their prin-

[1] Canassatego, a distinguished On-
onadaga chief, who flourished about
the middle of the last century, thus
cuttingly contrasted the hospitality of
the Iroquois with that of the whites,
in a conversation with Conrad Weiser,
an Indian interpreter. "You know
our practice. If a white man, in
travelling through our country, enters
one of our cabins, we all treat him as
I do you. We dry him if he is wet,
we warm him if he is cold, and give
him meat and drink that he may allay
his hunger and thirst; and we spread
soft furs for him to rest and sleep on.
We demand nothing in return. But
if I go into a white man's house at
Albany, and ask for victuals and
drink, they say, 'Where is your
money?' And if I have none, they
say, '*Get out, you Indian dog.*'"

cipal articles of food were cracked corn, and skinned corn hommony, two or three varieties of corn bread, venison and other game, soups, succotash, charred and dried green corn prepared in different ways, wild fruit, ground nuts, (*apios tuberosa*,) resembling wild potatoes, beans and squashes. These were the staples of their consumption, furnishing a considerable diversity of dishes, but a limited range to the appetite. They had also several kinds of tea. A favorite beverage was made from the tips of hemlock boughs boiled in water, and seasoned with maple sugar. Maple tea was prepared by boiling sap, and seasoning it with sassafras root; and spice tea, by steeping a species of wild spice.

Crimes and offences were so unfrequent under their social system, that the Iroquois can scarcely be said to have had a criminal code. Yet there were certain misdemeanors which fell under the judicial cognizance of the sachems, and were punished by them in proportion to their magnitude. Witchcraft was punishable with death. Any person could take the life of a witch when discovered in the act. If this was not done, a council was called, and the witch arraigned before it, in the presence of the accuser. A full confession, with a promise of amendment, secured a discharge. But if the accusation was denied, witnesses were called and examined concerning the circumstances of the case; and if they established the charge to the satisfaction of the council, which they rarely failed to do, condemnation followed, with a sentence of death. The witch was then delivered over to such executioners as volunteered for the purpose, and by them was led away to punishment. After the decision of the council, the relatives of the witch gave him up to his doom without a murmur.

Adultery was punished by whipping; but the punishment was inflicted upon the woman alone, who was supposed to be the only offender. A council passed upon the question, and if the charge was sustained, they ordered her to be publicly whipped by persons appointed for the purpose. This was the ancient custom, when such transgressions were exceedingly rare.

The greatest of all human crimes, murder, was punished with death; but the act was open to condonation. Unless the family were appeased, the murderer, as with the ancient Greeks, was given up to their private vengeance. They could take his life whenever they found him, even after the lapse of years, without being held accountable. A present of white wampum, sent on the part of the murderer to the family of his victim, when accepted, forever obliterated and wiped out the memory of the transaction. Immediately on the commission of a murder, the affair was taken up by the tribes to which the parties belonged, and strenuous efforts were made to effect a reconciliation, lest private retaliation should lead to disastrous consequences. If the criminal belonged to one of the first four tribes, and the deceased to one of the second four, these tribes assembled in separate councils, to inquire into all the facts of the case. The question of the guilt or innocence of the accused was generally an easy matter to determine, when the consequences of guilt were open to condonation. The first council then ascertained whether the offender was willing to confess his crime, and to make atonement. If he was, the council immediately sent a belt of white wampum, in his name, to the other council, which contained a message to that effect. The latter then endeavored to pacify the family of the deceased, to quiet their excitement, and to induce them to accept the wampum in condonation. If this was not sent in due time, or the family resisted all persuasions to receive it, then their revenge was allowed to take its course. Had it chanced that both parties belonged to one of the four brother tribes, a council of this division alone would convene, to attempt an adjustment among themselves. If, however, the family continued implacable, the further interference of mutual friends was given over, leaving the question to be settled between the murderer and the kindred of his victim, according to the ancient usage. If the belt of wampum was received before the avenger had been appointed, and had left the lodge on his mission, it was usually accepted as a condonation, but if he had gone forth, the time for reparation had passed. The family then either took upon themselves jointly the obligation of taking what they deemed a just retribution, or appointed an avenger, who resolved never to rest until life had answered for life. In such cases, the murderer usually fled.

As all quarrels were generally reconciled by the relatives of the parties, long-cherished animosities, and consequently homicides, were unfrequent in ancient times. The present of white wampum was not in the nature of a compensation for the life of the deceased, but of a regretful confession of the crime, with a petition for forgiveness. It was a peace-offering, the acceptance of which was pressed by mutual friends, and under such influences that a reconciliation was usually effected, except, perhaps, in aggravated cases of premeditated murder.

Theft, the most despicable of human crimes, was scarcely known among them. In the days of their primitive simplicity, a mercenary thought had not entered the Indian mind. After the commencement of their intercourse with the whites, the distribution of presents and of ardent spirits among them, and the creation of new kinds of property by the pursuits of trade, so far corrupted the habits of the Indian, that in some instances the vagrant and intemperate were led to the commission of this offence. But in justice to them it must be acknowledged, that no people ever possessed a higher sense of honor and self-respect in this particular, or looked down with greater disdain upon this shameful practice, than did the Iroquois. To this day, among their descendants, this offence is almost unknown. No locks, or bolts, or private repositories were ever necessary for the protection of property among themselves. The lash of public indignation, the severest punishment known to the red man, was the only penalty attached to this dereliction from the path of integrity.

These were the four principal crimes against society among our primitive inhabitants. The introduction of ardent spirits among them, in modern times, has changed the face of Indian society, and proved the fruitful source of all their calamities; aggravating those disorders which were incident to their social system, and introducing new ones entirely unknown in the days of their sylvan independence. Against this infamous traffic, their wise and good men, from the earliest period of their intercourse with us, have put forth incessant but unavailing protestations. The power of self-control, in this particular, was much weaker with the red man than the white; and the consequences of indulgence more lamentable and destructive. The "fire-water," as they have fitly termed it, has been a more invincible and devouring enemy than civilization itself, to both of which causes, about in equal degrees, they owe their displacement. It filled their villages with vagrancy, violence and bloodshed: it invaded the peace of the domestic fireside, stimulated the fiercest passions, introduced disease, contention and strife; thus wasting them away by violence, poverty and sickness, and by the casualties of hunger and cold. If there is any one act in our past intercourse with the Iroquois, for which we are more reprehensible than another, it was the permission, short of the penalty of hanging, of this most nefarious and inhuman traffic. A Mohawk chief, in 1754, thus addressed the governor of the province of New York upon this subject: "There is an affair about which our hearts tremble; this is the selling of rum in our castles. It destroys many both of the old and young people. We request of all the governors here present, that it may be forbidden to carry it among any of the Five Nations."[1] About the same time a representation was made to the British government, as follows: "They are supplied with rum by the traders, in vast and almost incredible quantities, the laws of the colonies now in force being insufficient to restrain the supply; and the Indians of every nation are frequently drunk, and abused in their trade, and their affections thereby alienated from the English. They often wound and murder each other in their liquor, and to avoid revenge flee to the French; and perhaps more have been lost by these means than by the French artifices."[2]

The love of truth was another marked trait of the Indian character. This inborn sentiment flourished in the period of their highest prosperity, in all the freshness of its primeval purity. On all occasions, and at whatever peril, the Iroquois spoke the truth without fear and without hesitation. Dissimulation was not an Indian habit. In fact, the language of the Iroquois does not admit of double speaking, or of the perversion of the words of the speaker. It is simple and direct, not admitting of those shades of meaning and those nice discriminations which pertain to polished languages. Subse-

[1] Doc. Hist. N. Y. ii. 591.   [2] Ib. ii. 610.

quent to their discovery, in their intercourse with the whites, their native truthfulness was sometimes corrupted by traffic and intemperance, but, as a people, they have preserved to this day the same elevation of sentiment in this particular which characterized their ancestors.

To the faith of treaties the Iroquois adhered with unwavering fidelity. Having endured the severest trials of political disaster, this faith furnishes one of the proudest monuments of their national integrity. They held fast to the " covenant chain" with the British until they were themselves deserted, and their entire country became the forfeit of their fidelity. In their numerous transactions with the several provinces formed out of their ancient territories, no serious cause of complaint was found against them for the non-fulfilment of treaty stipulations, although they were shorn of their possessions by treaty after treaty, and oftentimes made the victims of deception and fraud. In their intercourse with Indian nations, they frequently entered into treaties, sometimes of amity and alliance, sometimes of protection only, and in some instances for special purposes. All of these national compacts were " talked into" strings of wampum, to use the Indian expression, after which these were delivered into the custody of *Ho-no-we-nă'-to*, the Onondaga sachem, who was made hereditary keeper of the Wampum, at the institution of the League; and from him and his successors, was to be sought their interpretation from generation to generation. Hence the expression—" This belt preserves my words," so frequently met with at the close of Indian speeches, on the presentation of a belt. Indian nations, after treating, always exchanged belts, which were not only the ratification, but the memorandum of the compact.

There was an ancient treaty between the Senecas and the *Gä-quä-ga'-o-no*,[1] or Eries, who resided upon the southern shore of Lake Erie, to the effect that the Genesee river should be the boundary between them, and that when a hostile band of either nation re-crossed this river into its own territories, it should be safe from further pursuit. An infraction of this treaty was one of the reasons of the long-cherished animosity of the Iroquois against them. A similar compact was once made with the *O-ya-dä'-go-o-no*,[2] or Cherokees, by which the Tennessee river was the limit of pursuit. If a war-party of the latter had returned and re-crossed the Tennessee before they were overtaken by the pursuing Iroquois, they were as safe from their attack, as if intrenched behind an impregnable rampart. The Iroquois band could still invade, if disposed, the territory of the enemy,

---

[1] This was the Iroquois name of the Erie nation, who were expelled by them about the year 1655. They were an offshoot of the Iroquois stock, and spoke a dialect of their language. Charlevoix calls them the "Cat Nation." Vol. ii. p. 62. It is a singular fact that the Neuter Nation, who dwelt on the banks of the Niagara river, and who were expelled by the Iroquois about the year 1643, was known among them as the *Je-go'-sä-sa*, or Cat Nation. The word signifies a wild-cat; and from being the name of a woman of great influence among them, it came to be the name of the nation. Charlevoix also speaks of the Neuter Nation, vol. i. p. 377. It is quite probable that he transposed or confounded their aboriginal names.

[2] *O-ya-dä'-go-o-no*, the Iroquois name of the Cherokees, signifies, "The people who dwell in caves."

but they passed the camp of the retreating war-party without offering the slightest molestation.

The Iroquois prided themselves upon their sacred regard for the public faith, and punished the want of it with severity when an occasion presented. An example is to be found in the case of the *Sag-a-na'-gä*, or Delawares. After they had been subdued, and had acknowledged their dependence by send-ing the tributary wampum, they made an inroad upon a western nation under the protection of the Iroquois, notwithstanding their knowledge of the treaty, and a prohibition against its infringement. A deputation of Iroquois chiefs went immediately into the country of the Delawares, and having assembled the people in council, they degraded them from the rank of even a tributary nation. Having reproved them for their want of faith, they forbade them from ever after going out to war, divested them of all civil powers, and declared that they should hence-forth be as women. This degradation they signified in the figurative way of putting upon them the *Gä-kä'-ah*, or skirt of the female, and placing in their hands a corn-pounder, thus showing that their busi-ness ever after should be that of women. The Del-awares never emancipated themselves, after this act of denationalization.[1]

[1] The Delawares, about the year 1742, having sold some of their lands upon the Delaware river to Penn-sylvania, without the knowledge or consent of the Iroquois, Canassetego, the Onondaga chief before mentioned, reproved them in a speech, from which some extracts are subjoined in further illustration of the lordly man-ner in which the Iroquois conducted themselves towards subjugated na-tions. "Let this belt of wampum serve to chastise you. * * How came you to take upon you to sell land at

After war had been declared against any nation, either by the congress of sachems at Onondaga, or by an individual nation against a neighboring enemy, the existence of the war was indicated by a tomahawk painted red, ornamented with red feathers, and with black wampum, struck in the war-post in each village of the League. Any person was then at liberty to organize a band, and make an invasion. This was effected in a summary manner. Dressed in full costume, the war-chief who proposed to solicit volunteers and conduct the expedition, went through the village sounding the war-whoop to announce his intentions; after which he went to the war-post, *Gä-on-doté*, and having struck into it his red tomahawk, he commenced the war-dance. A group gathered around him, and as their martial ardor was aroused by the dance, they enlisted, one after the other, by joining in its performance. In this manner a company was soon formed; the matrons of the village prepared their subsistence while the dance was performing; and at its close, while they

all? We conquered you; we made women of you; you know you are women, and can no more sell land than women; nor is it fit that you should have the power of selling lands, since you would abuse it. * * We therefore assign you two places to go, either to Wyoming or Shamokin. You may go to either of these places, and then we shall have you more under our eye, and shall see how you behave. Don't deliberate, but remove, and take this belt of wampum." * * Then taking another belt he continued. "After our just reproof,

and absolute order to depart from the land, you are now to take notice of what we have further to say to you. This string of wampum serves to forbid you, your children and your grand-children to the latest posterity forever, meddling in land affairs; neither you, nor any who shall descend from you, are ever hereafter to presume to sell any land. For which purpose you are to preserve this string, in memory of what your uncles have this day given you in charge." Colden's Hist. Five Nations, Lond. Ed. 1750, page 80–81.

were yet fired with enthusiasm for the enterprise, they immediately left the village, and turned their footsteps towards the country of the enemy. If the movement was simultaneous in several villages, these parties joined each other on their march, but each band continued under the direction of its own war-chief. Their subsistence was usually charred corn, parched a second time, pounded into fine flour, and mixed with maple-sugar, thus reducing it in bulk and lightness to such a degree, that the warrior could carry without inconvenience in his bear-skin pocket a sufficient supply for a long and perilous expedition. The band took the war-path in single file, and moved with such rapidity that it was but five days' journey to the country of the Cherokees, upon the southern banks of the Tennessee. At their night encampments, they cut upon the trees certain devices to indicate their numbers and destination. On their return, they did the same, showing also the number of captives, and the number slain. When the returning war-party reached the outskirts of their village, they sounded the war-whoop to announce their approach, and to summon the people to assemble for their reception. Then leading their captives, they entered the village in a dancing procession, as they had shortly before gone out. After they had reached the war-post in the centre of the place, a wise-man addressed them in a speech of welcome and congratulation; in reply to which, a speech was made by one of the band, descriptive of their adventures, after which the war-dance was again enjoyed.

The Iroquois never exchanged prisoners with Indian nations, nor ever sought to reclaim their own people from captivity among them. Adoption or the torture were the alternative chances of the captive. A distinguished war-chief would sometimes be released by them from admiration of his military achievements, and be restored to his people, with presents and other marks of favor. No pledges were exacted in these occasional instances of magnanimity, but the person thus discharged esteemed himself bound in honor never again to take the war-path against his generous enemy. If adopted, the allegiance and the affections of the captive were transferred to his adopted nation. When the Indian went forth to war, he emphatically took his life in his hand, knowing that if he should be taken it was forfeited by the laws of war; and if saved by adoption, his country, at least, was lost forever. From the foundation of the Confederacy, the custom of adoption has prevailed among the Iroquois, who carried this principle farther than other Indian nations. It was not confined to captives alone, but was extended to fragments of dismembered tribes, and even to the admission of independent nations into the League. It was a leading feature of their policy to subdue adjacent nations by conquest, and having absorbed them by naturalization, to mould them into one common family with themselves. Some fragments of tribes were adopted

and distributed among the nations at large; some
were received into the League as independent members, as the Tuscaroras, while others were taken
under its shelter, like the Mohekunnucks, and assigned a territory within their own. The fruit of
this system of policy was their gradual elevation to
a universal supremacy; a supremacy which was
spreading so rapidly at the epoch of their discovery,
as to threaten the subjugation of all the nations
east of the Mississippi.

A regular ceremony of adoption was performed
in each case, to complete the naturalization. With
captives, this ceremony was the gantlet, after which
new names were assigned to them; and at the next
religious festival, their names, together with the
tribe and family into which they were respectively
adopted, were publicly announced. Upon the return of a war-party with captives, if they had lost
any of their own number in the expedition, the
families to which these belonged were first allowed
an opportunity to supply from the captives the
places made vacant in their households. Any family could then adopt out of the residue any who
chanced to attract their favorable notice, or whom
they wished to save. At the time appointed, which
was usually three or four days after the return of
the band, the women and children of the village
arranged themselves in two parallel rows just without the place, each one having a whip with which
to lash the captives as they passed between the
lines. The male captives, who alone were required

to undergo this test of their powers of endurance, were brought out, and each one was shown in turn the house in which he was to take refuge, and which was to be his future home, if he passed successfully through the ordeal. They were then taken to the head of this long avenue of whips, and were compelled, one after another, to run through it for their lives, and for the entertainment of the surrounding throng, exposed at every step, undefended, and with naked backs, to the merciless inflictions of the whip. Those who fell from exhaustion, were immediately despatched as unworthy to be saved; but those who emerged in safety from this test of their physical energies, were from that moment treated with the utmost affection and kindness. The effects of this contrast in behavior upon the mind of the captive must have been singular enough. During the slow progress of these arrangements, how many captives have listened to every sound, and watched every motion with the most intense solicitude. Carried into the heart of the country of the enemy, far away from all hope of succor, the question was about to be decided whether the clemency of their captors would bestow upon them the rights of citizenship, or their warlike frenzy lead them away to the torture. Its decision depended upon the most fickle impulses. Who shall relate our sylvan history! To the red man compassion has seldom been ascribed, but yet these scenes in the forest oftentimes revealed the most generous traits of character. Admiration for the chivalric bearing of a captive, the recollection of a past favor, or a sudden impulse of compassion, were sufficient to decide the question of adoption. When the perils of the gantlet, which was an enviable lot compared with the fate of the rejected, were over, he ceased to be an enemy, and became an Iroquois. Not only so, but he was received into the family by which he was adopted with all the cordiality of affection, and into all the relations of the one whose place he was henceforth to fill. By these means all recollections of his distant kindred were gradually effaced, bound as he was by gratitude to those who had restored a life which was forfeited by the usages of war. If a captive, after adoption, became discontented, which is said to have been seldom the case, he was sometimes restored, with presents, to his nation, that they might know he had lost nothing by his captivity among them.

The rejected captives were then led away to the torture, and to death. It is not necessary to describe this horrible practice of our primitive inhabitants. It is sufficient to say that it was a test of courage. When the Indian went out upon the warpath, he prepared his mind for this very contingency, resolving to show the enemy, if captured, that his courage was equal to any trial, and above the power of death itself. The exhibitions of heroism and fortitude by the red man under the sufferings of martyrdom, almost surpass belief. They considered the character of their nation in their keeping, and the glory of the race as involved and illustrated in the manner of their death.

A slight notice of a few of their customs in relation to the hunt, will close this desultory chapter. The deer, the elk, the moose, the bear, and several species of wild fowl, furnish their principal game. At certain seasons of the year, the female of all animals was spared, by the provisions of their game-laws, lest there should be a diminution of the supply. Not having a species of dog adapted to the chase, they were obliged to resort to the still hunt, and seize the opportunity whenever it presented; thus rendering it necessary to success that the hunter should become well versed in the habits of animals. Sometimes they trapped both deer and bear, and spread nets for quails and other small fowl. One species of deer-trap was attached to a young tree bent over, and so adjusted that the springing of the trap fastened a loop around the hind legs of the deer, and at the same time released the tree, which drew him up, and held him suspended in the air. They practiced another method of taking deer, in herds. A large party of hunters was formed, and a brush fence was built in the shape of the letter V, two or three miles in length on each side. The woods were then fired in the rear at some miles' distance, so as to drive the deer towards the opening, into which they were guided by parties stationed upon either side. They followed the fence down to the angle, where the arrows of the unseen hunters soon brought them down one after the other.

Sometimes a hundred were thus taken at one time. In the bear-hunt it was customary to tire out the animal by a long chase, as when fresh and vigorous he was too formidable to attack with the bow and arrow, or the hunting tomahawk; but when wearied out it was an easy matter to overcome him. The hunter selected the choice pieces of venison, and having removed the bone, and dried and cured the flesh before a fire, he packed it in small bark barrels, and thus carried it home upon his back. It was so much reduced in weight and bulk by the process of curing, that a hunter could thus transport, with ease, the substance of a dozen deer. Their skins were also dried and packed, and carried home in the same manner. When deer or bear were taken in winter, within a day's journey of their villages, bark sledges were prepared, on which they were drawn home, undressed, upon the snow crust.

Hunting was a passion with the red man. He pursued it for the excitement and employment it afforded, as well as for subsistence, frequently making long and toilsome expeditions. The Senecas, for example, in the season of the fall hunt, would leave their villages in small parties; some turning south, would encamp upon the Chemung river, and traverse the whole adjacent country; others, descending the Allegany, penetrated the inland regions of Ohio, which was a favorite hunting-ground, not only of the Senecas, but also of the other nations of the League; while still others encamped within the Niagara peninsula, which was formerly a place of great resort for the beaver-hunt. The Cayugas turned to the Susquehanna, which furnished them an inexhaustible store. They also ranged Pennsylvania; and with parties from the other nations, they not unfrequently roamed as far as the Potomac, which was within their ancient domain. Parties of the Onondagas descended the Chenango to the Susquehanna, or turning northward, perchance, crossed over into Canada. The Oneidas, for the fall hunt, descended the Unadilla, and also went northward, into the regions watered by the Black river. Lastly, the Mohawks, leaving their valley, found well-stocked hunting-grounds upon the head-waters of the Delaware and Susquehanna, and also in the wild and rugged regions of the north, and around lake Champlain.

About midwinter these widely scattered parties began to find their way back to their villages for the celebration of their annual jubilee; after which they surrendered themselves for a season to idleness, or to the amusements of the winter life. With the spring came the fishing season, in which for a time they found employment. The summer again was a season of repose, except when enlivened by councils, by their religious festivals, or by the adventures of the war-path.

In this round of occupations the Iroquois glided through the year. The progress of the seasons suggested their appropriate employments, if not marked in the exuberance of unsubdued nature, by the same attractive changes which pursue each other in regions beautified by cultivation. While with the fullest appreciation he enjoyed the grandeur of nature in her wild attire, and surrendered himself to her deepest inspirations, he yet knew nothing of her inexhaustible fruitfulness, or of those more delicate features of beauty which are revealed only by the hand of art. Aspiring to a freedom as boundless as the forest, satisfied with the martial pursuits, the amusements, the friendships and the social privileges of Indian life, and proud of their military achievements and of the fame of the League among Indian nations, the Iroquois measured out their days with all the happiness which these considerations could secure, and with all the contentment which could result from knowing no higher destiny.

BOOK THIRD.

INCIDENT TO THE LEAGUE.

GÄ-Ó-WO
or
BARK CANOE.

BOOK III.

INCIDENT TO THE LEAGUE.

CHAPTER I.

Fabrics of the Iroquois. — Their Artisan Intellect. — Indian Pottery. — Earthen Vessels. — Moccason. — War Club. — Tomahawk. — Rope Making. — Bark Vessels. — Bark Canoe. — Corn Mortar.—Maize.—Tobacco.—Snow Shoe.—Indian Saddle. —Miscellaneous Inventions. — Basket Making. — Costumes. — Baby Frame. — Diffusion of Indian Arts. — Improvement of the Iroquois.

THE fabrics of a people unlock their social history. They speak a language which is silent, but yet more eloquent than the written page. As memorials of former times, they commune directly with the beholder, opening the unwritten history of the period they represent, and clothing it with perpetual freshness. However rude the age, or uncultivated the people from whose hands they come, the products of human ingenuity are ever invested with a peculiar and even solemn interest. It is greatly to be regretted that so few remains of the skill and industry of the Iroquois have come down to the present age, to illustrate the era of Indian occupation. Although their fabrics are indicative of a low state of the useful arts, the artificial contrivances by which they were surrounded are yet the indices of their social condition, and for this reason are not devoid of instruction. Further than this, it is but just to them to save from oblivion the fruits of their inventive intellect, however unpretending they may seem, that, in the general judgment pronounced upon their memory, they may not be defrauded of even their humblest inventions.

Since the commencement of European intercourse, and especially within the last century, great changes have been wrought among the Iroquois. Their primitive fabrics have mostly passed away, and with them, many of their original inventions. The introduction of articles of more skilful manufacture has led to the gradual disuse of many of their simple arts. At the present moment, therefore, much of the fruit of their inventive capacity is entirely lost. Fragments, it is true, are frequently disentombed from the resting-places to which they had been consigned by their burial rites, but they are mere vestiges of the past, and afford but a slight indication of their social condition, or of the range of their artisan intellect. It would now be extremely difficult to furnish a full description of their implements, domestic utensils, and miscellaneous fabrics. Many of the inventions of the earlier Iroquois are still preserved among their descendants now residing within our limits and in Canada; but that portion of them which would especially serve to illustrate the condition of the hunter life have passed beyond our reach.

The remains of Indian art which are found scattered over the soil of New York are of two distinct kinds, and to be ascribed to widely different periods. The first class belong to the ante-Columbian period, or the era of the " Mound Builders," whose defensive works, mounds, and sacred enclosures are scattered so profusely throughout the west.[1]   With the second period may be connected the name of the Iroquois. It will also include the remains of the fugitive races, who, since the extermination of the " Mound Builders," have displaced each other in succession, until the period of the Iroquois commenced.

In the fabrics of the Iroquois a wide range is observable. It reaches from the rudest specimens of pottery of the ancient, to the most delicate needlework of the modern Iroquois. Since the era of the discovery, and the commencement of their intercourse with Europeans, a gradual revolution has been effected. Their social condition has changed greatly, and is changing from day to day. With equal pace their simple arts have been dropping from their hands, one after the other, as they have taken up agricultural pursuits, until at the present epoch the fabrics of the Iroquois contrast very

[1] The remains of this period indicate a semi-civilization of the most imposing character, including a considerable development of the art of agriculture. Exclusive of the mounds and enclosures, they have left implements of copper and chert, of stone, porphyry and earthen, some of which are elaborately and ingeniously wrought. The fugitive specimens belonging to this period, which are occasionally found within the limits of our State, are much superior to any of the productions of the earlier Iroquois.

strangely with those of their ancestors. In their present advanced condition, a large proportion of their articles are of a mixed character. They rather exhibit the application of Indian ingenuity to fabrics of foreign manufacture, as shown in their reduction into use, than originality of invention. But this class of articles are not without a peculiar interest. They furnish no slight indication of artisan capacity, and will serve as a species of substitute for those articles which they have displaced, and those inventions which they have hurried into forgetfulness.

One of the most ancient Indian arts was that of pottery. It was carried to considerable perfection by the Iroquois at an early day, as is shown by the specimens which are still occasionally disentombed from the burial-places, where they were deposited beside the dead; but the art itself has been so long disused, that it is now entirely lost. Pipes, and earthen pots of various designs and sizes, are the principal articles thus found. Some of these specimens of black pottery, which is the best variety, are of so fine a texture as to admit of a tolerable polish, and so firm as to have the appearance of stone. Their common pottery is of a clay color, and is a compound of common clay and pulverized quartz.

This pipe is of black pottery, well finished, and nearly as hard as marble, and is also represented at its actual size. In some specimens the bowl is fronted with a human face, or with a wolf or dog's

head.   Frequently these imitations are delicately,
even exquisitely made.   Another species of pipe, in

AH-SO-QUA'-TÄ, OR IROQUOIS PIPE, LIMA, LIV. CO., N. Y.

use among the Iroquois in later times, was cut out
of soap-stone, which yields readily to metallic instru-
ments.   A representation of one of these pipes of

Seneca manufacture, will be found in the plate (see page 104.)   It is fronted with a human face, and designed to be used with a stem-piece of reed.   The other, in the same plate, is also a modern Iroquois pipe, made of Catlinite, or the red Missouri pipe-stone.   Pipes of this description are used chiefly among the Sioux, by whom they were introduced into use, and other western Indians; and were rather accidental, than common among the Iroquois.

BOTTOM OF PIPE.

PIPE OF THE MOUND BUILLERS, VALLEY OF THE GENESEE.

This pipe is anomalous. It is of black marble, highly polished, with the bowl and stem bored with great precision. Doubtless it is a relic of the "Mound Builders," which, having found its way into the hands of a Seneca, was finally buried by his side in the valley of the Genesee, to be again brought to light upon the excavation of the Valley canal. Like the pipes of that era, it has the bowl in the central part of the stone. In material, also, and in finish, it is unlike, and superior to the pipes of the Iroquois.

GÄ-JIH,' OR EARTHEN VESSEL.

Earthen pots of this description are frequently found beside the remains of the Iroquois. They are usually of sufficient capacity to contain from two to six quarts. On exposure to the air, after disinterment, they are apt to crumble, being usually, if not always, of the light-colored common pottery, which is less firm and coherent than the black. In these earthen vessels it was customary to deposit food for the departed, while journeying to the realm of the Great Spirit. These earthen dishes are still found in Indian burial-places, where, perhaps, they had lain for centuries; and the fragments of those which have been broken by the plough, are also mingled with the soil.

Metallic implements were unknown among them, as they had not the use of metals. Rude knives of chert were used for skinning deer, and similar purposes. For cutting trees and excavating canoes, and corn mortars, in a word, for those necessary purposes for which the axe would seem to be indispensable, the Iroquois used the stone chisel, *Uh'-ga-o-gwät'-hä*. In cutting trees, fire was applied at the foot, and the chisel used to clear away the coal. By a repetition of the process, trees were felled and cut to pieces. Wooden vessels were hollowed out by the same means. Fire and the chisel were the substitutes for the axe. The chisel was usually about six inches long, three wide, and two thick; the lower end being fashioned like the edge of an axe. Stone gouges in the form of a convex chisel, were also used when a more regular concavity of the vessel was desired. Stone mortars for pounding corn, grinding mineral paint, and for pulverizing roots and barks for medicines, were also among their utensils.

Arrow-heads of chert, or flint, were so common, that it is scarcely necessary to refer to them. Occasionally they are found with a twist to make the arrow revolve in its flight. It is well known that the Indian always feathered his arrow for the same purpose. It is not uncommon to find the places where these arrow-heads were manufactured, which

AH - TA - QUA - O - WEH, OR MOCCASON.

FOR FEMALE.

is indicated by the fragments of chert which had been made by cleavage. In the western mounds rows of similar chert heads have been found lying side by side, like teeth, the row being about two feet long. This has suggested the idea that they were set in a frame and fastened with thongs, thus making a species of sword. Their discovery in those mounds also establishes the great antiquity of the art.

O-SQUE'-SONT, OR STONE TOMAHAWK

In ancient times the Iroquois used the stone toma-hawk. It was fashioned something like an axe, but in place of an eye for the helve, a deep groove was cut around the outside, by means of which the handle was firmly attached with a withe or thong. Oval stones, with groves around their greatest cir-cumference, were also secured in the head of war-clubs, and thus made dangerous weapons. Other implements and utensils of stone, some of which were very ingeniously worked, were in use among the Iroquois; and also personal ornaments of the same material, but a sufficient number have been brought under notice.

The moccason (see plate, page 359,) is preëmi-nently an Indian invention, and one of the highest antiquity. It is true to nature in its adjustment to the foot, beautiful in its materials and finish, and durable as an article of apparel. It will compare favorably with the best single article for the protection and adornment of the foot ever invented, either in ancient or modern times. With the sanction of fashion, it would supersede among us a long list of similar inventions. Other nations have fallen behind the Indian, in this one particular at least. The masses of the Romans wore the calceus ligneus, or wooden shoe; the masses of Germany and Ireland, and of many of the European nations, formerly wore the same. With the cothurnus and sandal of the ancients, and the boot of the moderns, the moccason admits of no unfavorable comparison. It deserves to be classed among the highest articles of apparel ever invented, both in usefulness, durability and beauty.

The moccason is made of one piece of deer-skin. It is seamed up at the heel, and also in front, above the foot, leaving the bottom of the moccason without a seam. In front the deer-skin is gathered, in place of being crimped; over this part porcupine quills or beads are worked, in various patterns. The plain moccason rises several inches above the ankle, like the Roman cothurnus, and is fastened with deer strings; but usually this part is turned down, so as to expose a part of the instep, and is ornamented with bead-work, as represented in the plate. A small bone near the ankle joint of the deer, has furnished the moccason needle from time immemorial; and the sinews of the animal the thread. These bone needles are found in the mounds of the West, and beside the skeletons of the Iroquois, where they were deposited with religious care. This isolated fact would seem to indicate an affinity, in one art at least, between the Iroquois and the Mound Builders, whose name, and era of occupation and destiny are entirely lost.

In ancient times the Iroquois used another shoe, made of the skin of the elk. They cut the skin above and below the gambrel joint, and then took it off entire. As the hind leg of the elk inclines at this joint, nearly at a right angle, it was naturally adapted to the foot. The lower end was sewed firmly with sinew, and the upper part secured above the ankle with deer strings.

In connection with this subject is the art of tanning deer-skins; as they still tan them after the ancient method. It is done with the brain of the deer, the tanning properties of which, according to a tradition, were discovered by accident. The brain is mingled with moss, to make it adhere sufficiently to be formed into a cake, which is afterwards hung by the fire to dry. It is thus preserved for years. When the deer-skin is fresh, the hair, and also the grain of the skin are taken off, over a cylindrical beam, with a wooden blade or stone scraper. A solution is then made by boiling a cake of the brain in water, and the moss, which is of no use, being removed, the skin is soaked in it for a few hours. It is then wrung out and stretched, until it becomes dry and pliable. Should it be a thick one, it would be necessary to repeat the process until it becomes thoroughly penetrated by the solution. The skin is still porous and easily torn. To correct both, a smoke is made, and the skin placed over it in such a manner as to enclose it entirely. Each side is smoked in this way until the pores are closed, and the skin has become thoroughly toughened, with its color changed from white to a kind of brown. It is then ready for use.

They also use the brain of other animals, and sometimes the back-bone of the eel, which, pounded up and boiled, possesses nearly the same properties for tanning. Bear-skins were never tanned. They were scraped and softened, after which they were dried, and used without removing the hair, either as an article of apparel, or as a mattrass to sleep upon.

GÄ-JE'-WÄ, OR WAR-CLUB.

Before the tomahawk came into use among the Iroquois, their principal weapons were the bow, the stone tomahawk, and the war-club. The *Gä-je'-wä* was a heavy weapon, usually made of ironwood, with a large ball of knot at the head. It was usually about two feet in length, and the ball five or six inches in diameter. In close combat it would prove a formidable weapon. They wore it in the belt, in front.

GÄ-NE-U'-GA-O-DUS-HA, OR DEER-HORN WAR-CLUB.

This species of war-club was also much used. It was made of hard wood, elaborately carved, painted and ornamented with feathers at the ends. In the lower edge, a sharp-pointed deer's horn, about four inches in length, was inserted. It was thus rendered a dangerous weapon in close combat, and would inflict a deeper wound than the former. They wore it in the girdle. At a later period they used the same species of club, substituting a steel or iron blade resembling a spearhead, in the place of the horn. War-clubs of this description are still to be found among the Iroquois, preserved as relics of past exploits. It is not probable, however, that these two varieties were peculiar to them; they were doubtless common over the continent.

The tomahawk succeeded the war-club, as the rifle did the bow. With the invention of this terrible implement of warfare the red man had nothing to do, except in having it so fashioned as to be adapted to his taste and usage. The tomahawk is

known as widely as the Indian, and the two names
have become apparently inseparable. They are

O-SQUE'-SONT, OR TOMAHAWK.

made of steel, brass, or iron. The choicer articles
are surmounted by a pipe-bowl, and have a perforated handle, that they may answer the double
purpose of ornament and use. In such the handle,
and often the blade itself, are richly inlaid with silver. It is worn in the girdle, and behind the back,
except when in actual battle. They used it in close
combat with terrible effect, and also threw it with
unerring certainty at distant objects, making it revolve in the air in its flight. With the Indian, the
tomahawk is the emblem of war itself. To bury it,
is peace; to raise it, is to declare the most deadly
warfare.

Rope-making, from filaments of bark, is also an
Indian art. The deer string answers a multitude of
purposes in their domestic economy; but it could
not supply them all. Bark-rope, (*Gä-a'-sken-dä,*)
has been fabricated among them from time immemorial. In its manufacture, they use the bark of

the slippery-elm, the red-elm, and the bass-wood.
Having removed the outer surface of the bark, they
divide it into narrow strips, and then boil it in ashes
and water. After it is dried it is easily separated
into small filaments, the strings running with the
grain several feet without breaking. These filaments are then put up in skeins and laid aside for
use. Slippery-elm makes the most pliable rope; it
is soft to the touch, can be closely braided, and is

GUS-HA'-ÄH, OR BURDEN-STRAP.

very durable. The burden-strap is worn around
the forehead, and lashed to a litter, which is borne
by Indian women on their back. It is usually
about fifteen feet in length, and braided into a belt
in the centre, three or four inches wide. Some of
them are entirely covered upon one side with porcupine quill-work, after various devices, and are in
themselves remarkable products of skilful industry.
The braiding or knitting of the bark threads is effected with a single needle of hickory. In other
specimens, the quill-work is sprinkled over the belt
for ornament, the quills in all cases being of divers
colors. Of all their fabrics, there is no one, per-

haps, which surpasses the porcupine-quill burden-strap, in skill of manufacture, richness of material, or beauty of workmanship. In this species of work, the Iroquois female excelled. They also made a common bark rope for ordinary uses, which consisted of three strands, hard twisted; a single rope being frequently forty or fifty feet in length. The art of rope-making, like many others, has mostly fallen into disuse among the present Iroquois. But few Indian families now provide themselves with skeins of bark thread, or make any ropes of this description.

Bark vessels and dishes of various kinds were in common use among them. The bark barrel, *Gä-no'-quă*, was of the number. It was made of the inner rind of red-elm bark, the grain running around the barrel. Up the side it was stitched firmly, and had a bottom and a lid secured in the same manner. Such barrels were used to store charred corn, beans, dried fruit, seeds, and a great variety of articles. They were very durable, and when properly taken care of would last a hundred years.

GÄ-O-WO', OR BARK TRAY.

Trays of this description are found in every Indian family. They serve a variety of purposes, but are chiefly used for kneading, or rather preparing corn bread. A strip of elm-bark, of the requisite dimensions, was rounded and gathered up at the ends, so as to form a shallow concavity. Around the rim, both outside and in, splints of hickory were adjusted, and stitched through and through with the bark. These trays were of all sizes, from those of sufficient capacity to contain one, to those large enough for ten pecks. The rough bark was removed from the outside, and the vessel within became smooth with usage. They made durable and convenient articles for holding corn meal, for preparing corn bread, and for many other purposes.

GA-SNÄ' GÄ-O-WO'; OR, BARK CANOE.

In the construction of the bark canoe, the Iroquois exercised considerable taste and skill. The art appears to have been common to all the Indian races within the limits of the republic, and the mode of construction much the same. Birch bark was the best material; but as the canoe birch did not grow within the home territories of the Iroquois, they generally used the red-elm, and bitternut-hickory. The canoe figured in the plate, (see page 351,) is made of the bark of the red-elm, and consists of but one piece. Having taken off a bark of the requisite length and width, and removed the rough outside, it was shaped in the canoe form.

Rim pieces of white-ash, or other elastic wood, of
the width of the hand, were then run around the
edge, outside and in, and stitched through and
through with the bark itself.   In stitching, they
used bark thread or twine, and splints.   The ribs
consisted of narrow strips of ash, which were set
about a foot apart along the bottom of the canoe,
and having been turned up the sides, were secured
under the rim.   Each end of the canoe was fashioned alike, the two side pieces inclining towards
each other until they united, and formed a sharp
and vertical prow.   In size, these canoes varied
from twelve feet, with sufficient capacity to carry
two men, to forty feet with sufficient capacity for
thirty.   The one figured in the plate is about twenty-
five feet in length, and its tonnage estimated at two
tons, about half that of the ordinary bateau.
Birch bark retained its place without warping, but
the elm and hickory bark canoes were exposed to
this objection.   After being used, they were drawn
out of the water to dry.   One of the chief advantages of these canoes, especially the birch bark,
was their extreme lightness, which often became a
matter of some moment from the flood wood and
water-falls, which obstructed the navigation of the
inland rivers.   Two men could easily transport
these light vessels around these obstacles, and even
from one river to another when the portage was not
long.

For short excursions one person usually paddled
the canoe, standing up in the stern; if more than

two, and on a long expedition, they were seated at equal distances upon each side alternately. In the fur trade these canoes were extensively used. They coasted lakes Erie and Ontario, and turning up the Oswego river into the Oneida lake, they went from thence over the carrying place into the Mohawk, which they descended to Schenectady. They would usually carry about twelve hundred pounds of fur. At the period of the invasions of the Iroquois territories by the French, large fleets of these canoes were formed for the conveyance of troops and provisions. With careful usage they would last several years.

GÄ-O-WO', OR BARK SAP-TUB.

Our Indian population have been long in the habit of manufacturing sugar from the maple. Whether they learned the art from us, or we received it from them, is uncertain. One evidence, at least, of its antiquity among them, is to be found in one of their ancient religious festivals, instituted to the maple, and called the Maple dance. The sap-tub is a very neat contrivance, and surpasses all other

articles of this description.   Our farmers may safely
borrow, in this one particular, and with profit substitute this Indian invention for the rough and
wasteful one of their own contrivance.

A strip of bark about three feet in length by two
in width, makes the tub.   The rough bark is left
upon the bottom and sides.   At the point where
the bark is to be turned up to form the ends, the
outer bark is removed; the inner rind is then
turned up, gathered together in small folds at the
top, and tied around with a splint.   It is then ready
for use, and will last several seasons.   Aside from
the natural fact that the sap would be quite at home
in the bark tub, and its flavor preserved untainted,
it is more durable and capacious than the wooden
one, and more readily made.

The Senecas use three varieties of corn : the
White, (*O-na-o'-ga-ant*,) the Red, (*Tic'-ne*,) and
the White Flint, (*Ha-go'-wä*.)   Corn is, and always
has been, their staple article of food.   When ready
to be harvested, they pick the ears, strip down the
husks, and braid them together in bunches, with
about twenty ears in each.   They are then hung up
ready for use.   The white flint ripens first, and is
the favorite corn for hommony ; the red next, and
is used principally for charring and drying ; the
white last, and is the corn most esteemed by the Indians.   It is used for bread, and supplies the same
place with them that wheat does with us.   They
shell their corn by hand, and pound it into flour in
wooden mortars.   In two hours from the time the

GÄ-NE′-GÄ-TÄ, OR CORN MORTAR.

Mortar, 2 feet in diameter. Pounder, 4 feet in length.

corn is taken from the ear it is ready to eat, in the form of unleavened bread.   It is hulled in the first instance, by boiling in ashes and water; after the skin is thus removed from each kernel, it is thoroughly washed, and pounded into flour or meal in a mortar, of which a representation will be found above.   Having been passed through a sieve basket, to remove the chit and coarser grains, it is made into loaves or cakes about an inch in thickness, and six inches in diameter; which are cooked by boiling them in water.   Upon bread of this description, and upon the fruits of the chase, the Indian has principally subsisted from time immemorial.

The practice of charring corn is of great antiquity among the red races.   In this condition it is preserved for years without injury.   Caches or pits of charred corn have been found in various parts of the country.   The Iroquois were in the habit of charring corn to preserve it for domestic use.   The Senecas still do the same.   For this use the red corn is preferred.   When green the corn is picked, and roasted in the field before a long fire, the ears being set up on end in a row.   It is not charred or blackened entirely, but roasted sufficiently to dry up the moisture in each kernel.   The corn is then shelled and dried in the sun.   In this state it is chiefly used by hunting parties, and for subsistence on distant excursions.   Its bulk and weight having been diminished about half by the two processes, its transportation became less burdensome.   The red races seldom formed magazines of grain to guard against distant wants. It is probable, therefore, that these pits of charred corn owe their origin to the sudden flight of the inhabitants, who buried their dried corn because they could not remove it, rather than to a desire to provide against a failure of the harvest.

There was another method of curing corn in its green state, quite as prevalent as the former. The corn was shaved off into small particles, and having been baked over the fire in pans or earthen dishes, it was then dried in the sun. In this condition it was preserved for winter use.

A favorite article of subsistence was prepared from the charred corn. It was parched a second time, after which, having been mixed with about a third part of maple sugar, it was pounded into a fine flour. This was carried in the bear-skin pocket of the hunter, and upon it alone he subsisted for days together.

This noble grain, one of the gifts of the Indian to the world, is destined, eventually, to become one of the staple articles of human consumption. More than half of our republic lies within the embrace of the tributaries of the Mississippi. Upon their banks are the corn-growing districts of the country; and there, also, at no distant day, will be seated the millions of our race. Experience demonstrates that no people can rely wholly upon exchanges for the substance of their bread-stuffs, but that they must look chiefly to the soil they cultivate. This law of production and consumption is destined to intro-duce the gradual use of corn flour, as a partial substitute at least, for its superior rival, in those districts where it is the natural product of the soil. In the southern portions of our country this principle is already attested, by the fact that corn bread enters as largely into human consumption as wheaten. Next to wheat, this grain, perhaps, contains the largest amount of nutriment. It is the cheapest and surest of all the grains to cultivate; and is, also, the cheapest article of subsistence known among men. Although wheat can be cultivated in nearly all the sections of the country; although its production can be increased to an unlimited degree by a higher agriculture; we have yet great reason to be thankful for this secondary grain, whose reproductive energy is so unmeasured as to secure our entire race, through all coming time, against the dangers of scarcity, or the pressure of want.

O-YEH'-GWÄ-Ä-WEH; OR, INDIAN TOBACCO.

Tobacco is another gift of the Indian to the world; but a gift, it must be admitted, of questionable utility. We call both corn and tobacco the legacy of the red man; as these indigenous plants, but for his nurture and culture through so many ages, might have perished, like other varieties of the fruits of the earth. Many of our choicest fruits owe their origin to vegetable combinations entirely fortuitous. They spring up spontaneously, flourish for a season, and become extinct, but for the watch-

ful care of man. Nature literally pours forth her
vegetable wealth, and buries beneath her advancing
exuberance the products of the past. But few of
the fruits and plants and flowers of the ancient
world, have come down to us unchanged; and still
other plants, perhaps, have perished, unknown, in
the openings of the forest, which contained within
their shrivelled and stinted foliage, the germ of
some fruit, or grain, or plant, which might have
nourished or clothed the whole human family. We
may therefore, perchance, owe a debt to the Indian,
in these particulars, beyond our utmost acknowledgments.

The Senecas still cultivate tobacco. Its name signifies " *The only Tobacco*," because they considered
this variety superior to all others. It is raised from
the seed, which is sown or planted in the spring,
and requires but little cultivation. The leaves are
picked early in the fall, when their color first
changes with the frost, and when dried are ready
for use. After the first year it grows spontaneously,
from the seed shed by the plant when fully ripened. If the plants become too thick, which is frequently the case, from their vigorous growth, it becomes necessary to thin them out, as the leaves diminish in size with their increase in number. This
tobacco is used exclusively for smoking. The custom of chewing the article appears to have been derived from us. Although this tobacco is exceedingly
mild, they mingle with it the leaves of the sumac,
to diminish its stimulating properties. The sumac

has been used by the Indian to temper tobacco from time immemorial.

Several varieties of the bean and of the squash were also cultivated by the Iroquois, and were indigenous in the American soil. They regarded the corn, the bean, and the squash as the special gift of the Great Spirit, and associated them together under the name of the Three Sisters. They also used the ground-nut (*apios tuberosa*,) as a species of potato, gathering it in its wild state.

GA-WEH'-GÄ, OR SNOW-SHOE.

2 feet 10 inches.

The snow-shoe is an Indian invention. Upon the deep snows which accumulate in the forest, it would be nearly impossible to travel without them. They were used in the hunt, and in warlike expeditions undertaken in the season of winter.

The snow-shoe is nearly three feet in length, by about sixteen inches in width. A rim of hickory, bent round with an arching front, and brought to a point at the heel, constituted the frame, with the addition of cross pieces to determine its spread. Within the area, with the exception of an opening for the toe, was woven a net-work of deer strings, with interstices about an inch square. The ball of the foot was lashed at the edge of this opening with thongs, which passed around the heel for the support of the foot. The heel was left free to work up and down, and the opening was designed to allow the toe of the foot to descend below the surface of the shoe, as the heel is raised in the act of walking. It is a very simple invention, but exactly adapted for its uses. A person familiar with the snow-shoe can walk as rapidly upon the snow, as without it upon the ground. The Senecas affirm that they can walk fifty miles per day upon the snow-shoe, and with much greater rapidity than without it, in consequence of the length and uniformity of the step. In the bear-hunt, especially, it is of the greatest service, as the hunter can speedily overtake the bear, who, breaking through the crust, is enabled to move but slowly.

AH-DÄ'-DÄ-QUÄ; OR, INDIAN SADDLE.

This is an Indian invention, but came originally from the west. It closely resembles the saddle of the native Mexicans in its general plan, but its pommel is not as high, and its side-pieces are longer. It is still used among the Iroquois, and among the Indian tribes of the west. The frame is made of four pieces of wood, firmly set together, over which is a

covering of raw hide. The side-pieces are about
eighteen inches in length, six in width, and about

an inch in thickness, at the centre, but terminating
in a sharp edge above and below. In front the
pommel rises about five inches above the side-pieces.
It is made of a stick having a natural fork, which
is so adjusted as to embrace the side-pieces, and determine the spread of the saddle. Another piece,
in the same manner, embraced the side-pieces at
the opposite end, rising several inches above, and

descending nearly to their lower edges. These side-pieces at the top are about three inches apart, leaving a space for the back-bone of the horse. The fastenings of the saddle, including those of the stirrup, were originally of ropes, made of buffalo's hair. Triangular stirrups of wood completed the trappings of the saddle. As the Iroquois seldom made use of the Indian horse, the saddle with them was rather an accidental, than a usual article. The specimen above represented is of Seneca manufacture.

GÄ-GA-AN-'DÄ, OR AIR-GUN ; AND GÄ-NO', OR ARROW.

Air-gun, 6 feet.   Arrow, 2 feet.

The air-gun is claimed as an Indian invention. It is a simple tube or barrel, about six feet in length, and an inch in diameter, and having a half-inch bore. It is made of alder, and also of other wood, which is bored by some artificial contrivance. A very slender arrow, about two feet in length, with a sharp point, is the missile. Upon the foot of the arrow, the down or floss of the thistle is fastened on entire, with sinew. This down is soft and yielding, and when the arrow is placed in the barrel, fills it air-tight. The arrow is then discharged by blowing. It is used for bird-shooting.

YA-O'-DÄ-WAS-TÄ, OR INDIAN FLUTE.

1½ feet.

This instrument is unlike any known among us, but it clearly resembles the clarionet. Its name signifies "a blow pipe." It is usually made of red cedar, is about eighteen inches in length, and above an inch in diameter. The finger holes, six in number, are equidistant. Between them and the mouthpiece, which is at the end, is the whistle, contrived much upon the same principle as the common whistle. It makes six consecutive notes, from the lowest, on a rising scale. The seventh note is wanting, but the three or four next above are regularly made. This is the whole compass of the instrument. As played by the Indians, it affords a species of wild and plaintive music. It is claimed as an Indian invention.

YUN-GA'-SA, OR TOBACCO POUCH.

The tobacco pouch is made of the skin of some small animal, which is taken off entire. It was anciently an indispensable article, and was worn in the girdle. They were usually made of white weasel, mink, squirrel, and fisher skin.

DA-YA-YÄ-DÄ-GÄ´-NEÄ-TÄ.

This is an Indian invention, and of great antiquity.
Its rudeness may excite a smile, in this day of lucifer
matches, but yet the step backward to the steel and
flint is about the same, as from the latter to the
contrivance in question. Not knowing the use of
metals or of chemicals, it was the only method of
creating fire known to the red man. It consisted
of an upright shaft, about four feet in length, and
an inch in diameter, with a small wheel set upon
the lower part, to give it momentum. In a notch
at the top of the shaft was set a string, attached to
a bow about three feet in length. The lower point

rested upon a block of dry wood, near which are placed small pieces of punk. When ready to use, the string is first coiled around the shaft, by turning it with the hand. The bow is then pulled downwards, thus uncoiling the string, and revolving the shaft towards the left. By the momentum given to the wheel, the string is again coiled up in a reverse manner, and the bow again drawn up. The bow is again pulled downwards, and the revolution of the shaft reversed, uncoiling the string, and recoiling it as before. This alternate revolution of the shaft is continued, until sparks are emitted from the point where it rests upon the piece of dry wood below. Sparks are produced in a few moments by the intensity of the friction, and ignite the punk, which speedily furnishes a fire.

O-NO-NEÄ GOS-HA'-DÄ, OR CORN-HUSK SALT BOTTLE.

In the art of basket-work, in all its varieties, the Indian women also excel. Their baskets are made with a neatness, ingenuity and simplicity, which de-

serve the highest praise. Splint is the chief material, but they likewise use a species of flag, and also
corn-husks. Among these various patterns, which
are as diversified as convenience or ingenuity could
suggest, the most perfectly finished is the sieve basket. It is designed for sifting corn meal to remove
the chit, and coarser particles, after the corn has been
pounded into flour. The bottom of the basket is
wove in such fine checks as to answer very perfectly
all the ends of the wire sieve. Another variety of
open basket was made of corn-husks and flags, very
closely and ingeniously braided. In their domestic
economy, the basket answered a multitude of purposes. Bottles for salt were made of corn-husks in
the forms represented in the figures.

Their wooden implements were often elaborately
carved. Those upon which the most labor was expended were the ladles, *Ah-do-quä'-să*, of various sizes,
used for eating hommony and soup. They were
their substitute for the spoon, and hence every Indian family was supplied with a number. The end
of the handle was usually surmounted with the figure of an animal, as a squirrel, a hawk, or a beaver,
some of them with a human figure in a sitting posture, others with a group of such figures in various
attitudes, as those of wrestling or embracing.
These figures are carved with considerable skill and
correctness of proportion. Upon the hommony-
stirrer, *Got'-go-ne-os-hă'*, similar ornaments were
bestowed. Bowls, pitchers and other vessels of
knot are common in Indian families, and are worked

out with great labor and care. In ancient times, the aged and infirm were wont to assist themselves in walking with a simple staff, but in later times the cane, *Ah-dä'-dis-hă*, has been substituted. Like their other utensils of wood, the modern cane is elaborately carved.

GÄ-KA'-ÄH, or SKIRT.—See Plate, page 384.

The modern female costume of the Iroquois is both striking and graceful. Some of them would excite admiration by the exactness of their adjustment and the delicacy, even brilliancy of their bead-work embroidery. They use, to this day, the same articles of apparel in form and fashion, as in ancient times, but they have substituted materials of foreign manufacture. The porcupine quill has given place to the bead, and the skins of animals to the cotton fabric and the broadcloth. Much taste is exhibited in the bead-work, which is so conspicuous in the female costume. The colors are blended harmoniously, and the patterns are ingeniously devised and skilfully executed. It is sufficiently evident, from the specimens of their handiwork, that the Indian female can be taught to excel with the needle. The *Gä-kä'-ah*, or Skirt, of one of which the plate is an accurate copy, is usually of blue broadcloth, and elaborately embroidered with bead-work. It requires two yards of cloth, which is worn with the selvedge at the top and bottom; the skirt being secured about the waist, and descending nearly to the

GA-KÄ-AH or SKIRT.

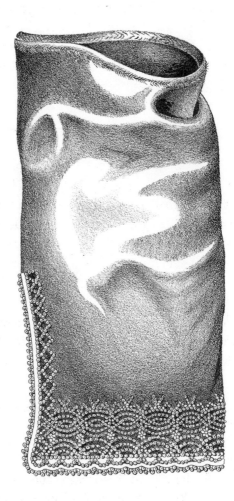

GISE-HĂ or FEMALE LEGGIN.

moccason. Around the lower edge, and part way up the centre in front, it is tastefully and beautifully embroidered. In one of the angles a figure is worked representing a tree or flower. The cloth skirt is universally worn among the present Iroquois, but they are not usually as richly embroidered, or of as fine material as the one represented in the plate. This is of Seneca workmanship, and is a rare specimen of Indian needlework.

GISE'-HĂ, OR PANTALETTE.—<small>See Plate, page 385.</small>

This article of female apparel is also universally worn. It is usually made of red broadcloth, and ornamented with a border of bead-work around the lower edge, and also part way up the side at the point which becomes the front of the pantalette. It is secured above the knee, and falls down upon the moccason. In ancient times the *Gise'-hă* was made of deer-skin and embroidered with porcupine quill work. As the moccason is elsewhere described, nothing further need be said in relation to it as a part of the female costume.

AH-DE-A'-DA-WE-SA, OR OVER-DRESS.—<small>See Plate, page 386.</small>

The over-dress is usually of muslin or calico of the highest colors. It is loosely adjusted to the person, gathered slightly at the waist, and falls part way down the skirt. Around the lower edge is a narrow border of bead-work. In front it is generally

buttoned with silver broaches, arranged as represented in the plate.   They are usually larger in size,
and arranged in parallel rows, as represented in the
female costume in the frontispiece.   The Indian female delights in a profusion of silver ornaments,
consisting of silver broaches of various patterns and
sizes, from those which are six inches in diameter,
and worth as many dollars, down to those of the
smallest size, valued at a sixpence.   Silver ear-rings
and finger-rings of various designs, silver beads, hat
bands and crosses, are also found in their parapher-
nalia.   These crosses, relics of Jesuit influence, are
frequently eight inches in length, of solid silver, and
very valuable, but they are looked upon by them
simply in the light of ornaments.

E'-YOSE, OR BLANKET.

This indispensable and graceful garment is of
blue or green broadcloth, of which it requires two
yards.   It falls from the head or neck in natural
folds the width of the cloth, as the selvedges are at
the top and bottom, and it is gathered round the
person like a shawl.   It is worn very gracefully by
the Indian female, and makes a becoming article of
apparel.

By some singular impulse of fancy, the fur hat
has been appropriated by the women as a part of
the female costume, until among the modern Iroquois it is more common to see this part of the
white man's apparel upon the head of the Indian

AH-DE-A-DÄ-WE-SÄ ᴏʀ OVER-DRESS.
FRONT

AH-DE-A-DÄ-WE-SÄ or OVER DRESS.

BACK.

female than upon that of the warrior. Hat bands of silver, or of broaches strung together, or of long silver beads, are indispensable ornaments on public occasions. Sometimes, but rarely, clusters of feathers are attached to the hat.

GÄ'-TE-AS-HÄ', OR NECKLACE.—See Plate, page 226.

The necklace is made of silver and wampum beads, and has a silver cross suspended. The beads usually worn by Indian women are of common glass. In ancient times it was customary to wear necklaces of the teeth of animals, but such barbarous ornaments were long since repudiated by the Iroquois. A species of shoulder ornament in the nature of a necklace made of a fragrant marsh grass, called by the Senecas *Gä-a-o'-tä-ges*, is very generally worn. Several strands or cords are braided from this grass, of the requisite length, and tied into one string. At intervals of three or four inches, small round discs, made of the same material, sometimes covered upon the upper face with bead-work, are attached. It thus makes a conspicuous ornament, and emits an agreeable odor, furnishing a substitute for perfumery. Wampum beads are rarely worn, as they are scarce and held at high rates. These beads are used chiefly for religious purposes, and to preserve laws and treaties. They are made of the conch shell, which yields both a white and a purple bead, the former of which is used for religious, and the latter for political purposes. A full string of wampum is usually three feet long, and contains a dozen or more strands. In ancient times, six of these strands was the value of a life, the amount paid in condonation for a murder. When sold, they were counted and reckoned at half a cent a bead. Wampum belts were made by covering one side of a deer-skin belt with these beads, arranged after various devices, and with most laborious skill. As a belt four or five feet long by four inches wide would require several thousands of these beads, they were estimated at a great price.

ONT-WIS'-DÄ-GA-DUST-HÄ', OR SILVER MEDAL.

The government has long been in the habit of presenting silver medals to the chiefs of the various Indian tribes at the formation of treaties, and on the occasion of their visit to the seat of government. These medals are held in the highest estimation. Red Jacket, Corn Planter, Farmers'

GÄ-YÄ-AH or WORK BAG.

YA-WA-O-DÄ-QUÄ or NEEDLE BOOK.

Brother, and several other distinguished Seneca chiefs have received medals of this description. Washington presented a medal to Red Jacket in 1792. It is an elliptical plate of silver, surrounded by a rim, as represented in the figure, and is about six inches in its greatest diameter. On each side it is engraved with various devices. The medal is now worn by *Sose-ha'-wä*, (Johnson,) a Seneca chief.

GÄ-NUH'-SÄ, OR SEA-SHELL MEDAL.

Medals of sea-shell, inlaid with silver, as represented in the figure, were also worn suspended from the neck as personal ornaments. They were made of the conch-shell, and were highly valued.

A few plates further to illustrate the handiwork of the Indian female in bead-work are introduced at the end of this chapter. The figures themselves will dispense with the necessity of any description, although they should be colored to give a full impression of their character. The patient industry of the Indian female is quite remarkable, when seen in contrast with the impatience of labor in the warrior himself. In the work of their reclamation and gradual induction into industrial pursuits, this fact furnishes no small degree of encouragement.

GÄ-OSE'-HÄ; OR, BABY-FRAME.—See Plate, page 390.

This is likewise an Indian invention. It appears to have been designed rather as a convenience to the Indian mother for the transportation of her infant, than, as has generally been supposed, to secure an erect figure. The frame is about two feet in length, by about fourteen inches in width, with a carved foot-board at the small end, and a hoop or bow at the head, arching over at right angles. After being enclosed in a blanket, the infant is lashed upon the frame with belts of bead-work, which firmly secure and cover its person, with the exception of the face. A separate article for covering the face is then drawn over the bow, and the child is wholly protected. When carried, the burden-strap attached to the frame is placed around the forehead of the mother, and the *Gă-ose'-hă* upon her back. This frame is often elaborately carved, and its ornaments are of the choicest description. When cultivating the maize, or engaged in any out-door occupation, the *Gă-ose'-hă* is hung upon a limb of the nearest tree, and left to swing in the breeze. The patience and quiet of the Indian child in this close confinement are quite remarkable. It will hang

GA-ON-SEH. or BABY FRAME.

YA-WA-O-DÄ-QUÄ or PIN CUSHION.

thus suspended for hours, without uttering a complaint.

Many other articles might be introduced further to illustrate the social life of the Iroquois, did space permit, but sufficient has been given to exhibit the general character of their fabrics, implements and utensils. A portion of them, which appeared particularly calculated to exhibit their artisan intellect, have been noticed minutely, for it is in this view that they are chiefly interesting.

Such is the diffusion of Indian arts and Indian inventions among the red races, that it is impossible to ascertain with what nation or tribe they in fact originated. Many of them were common to all, from Maine to Oregon, and from the St. Lawrence to the peninsula of Florida. To this day Indian life is about the same over the whole republic. If we wished to discover the inventions of the Iroquois, we might expect to find them as well among the Sioux of the upper Mississippi, as among the descendants of the Iroquois themselves. It is for this reason, that in describing the fabrics which illustrate the era of Indian occupation, we should take in the whole range of Indian life, from the wild tribes dwelling in the seclusions of Oregon, to the present semi-agricultural Iroquois who reside among ourselves. They have passed through all the intermediate stages, from extreme rudeness to comparative civilization. If we wish to connect the fabrics of the former with those of our own primitive inhabitants, we may find that connection in the fact, that similar implements and similar fabrics, at no remote period, were in the hands, and of the manufacture of the Iroquois themselves. Many of the relics disentombed from the soil of New York relate back to the period of the Mound Builders of the west, and belong to a race of men and an age which have passed beyond the ken of Indian tradition. Our first Indian epoch is thus connected with that of the Mound Builders. In the same manner, the fabrics of the Iroquois are intimately connected with those of all the tribes now resident within the republic. One system of trails belted the whole face of the territory from the Atlantic to the Pacific; and the intercourse between the multitude of nations who dwelt within these boundless domains was constant, and much more extensive than has ever been supposed. If any one, therefore, desires a picture of Iroquois life before Hendrick Hudson sailed up the river upon whose banks rested the eastern end of their "Long House," he should look for it in Catlin's Scenes at the skirts of the Rocky Mountains. There are diversities, it is true, but Indian life is essentially the same.

In the fabrics of the modern Iroquois, there is much to inspire confidence in their teachableness in the useful arts. When their minds are unfolded by education, and their attention is attracted by habit to agricultural pursuits, as has already become the case, to some extent, there is great promise that a portion, at least, of this gifted race will be reclaimed, and raised, eventually, to a citizenship among our-

GÄ-GEH-TÄ, YEN-CHE-NO-HOS-TA-TÄ

OR KNEE BAND

YEN-NIS-HO-QUÄ-HOS-TÄ

OR WRIST BAND.

GA-GEH-TA YEU-NIS-HÄ-HOS-TA

OR ARM BAND.

GOT-GWEN-DÄ or POCKET BOOK.

selves.   It would be a grateful spectacle, yet to behold the children of our primeval forests cultivating
the fields, over which their fathers roamed in sylvan
independence.

CHAPTER II.

The language of the Iroquois, like all unwritten languages, is imperfect in its construction, and scarcely admits of comparison, except on general principles, with those which have been systematized and perfected. It would doubtless be characterized by the schoolman as a barbarous jargon, although entitled to some portion of the indulgence which is due to all primitive or uncompounded languages, in the early stages of their formation. To us, however, there is an interest incident to these dialects, which rises above mere literary curiosity. Through all generations, their language will continue to be spoken in our geographical terms: "their names are on our waters, we may not wash them out." The face of nature, indeed, changes its appearance, *mutat terra vices*, but its landmarks remain essentially the same. Within our borders, the Iroquois have written them over with such a permanent imprint, that to the most distant ages will our hills and vales and ever-flowing rivers speak

"Their dialect of yore."

The Hodénosaunee were eminently fortunate in engrafting their names upon the features of nature, if they were desirous of a living remembrance. No one can turn to the lake, or river, or streamlet, to which they have bequeathed an appellation, without confessing that the Indian has perpetuated himself by a monument more eloquent and imperishable than could be fabricated by human hands.

From considerations of this description, there arises a sufficient interest in the language of our predecessors, to invite an inquiry into its principal features.

Of the six dialects in which it is now spoken, the Mohawk and Oneida have a close resemblance to each other; the Cayuga and Seneca the same; while the Onondaga and Tuscarora are not only unlike each other, but are also distinguished from the other four by strong dialectical differences. In the estimation of the Iroquois, the Onondaga dialect is the most finished and majestic, and the Oneida the least vigorous in its expressions; but to the American ear, the former is harsh and pointed, and the latter is liquid, harmonious, and musical. The Tuscarora is admitted to be a dialect of the Iroquois language, but it has not such a close affinity to either of the remaining five, as the latter have to each other. In conversation they are all able to understand each other with readiness, unless words intervene which have been naturalized into one of their dialects from foreign languages. A comparison of these dialects will be found in the table.

NAMES.	SENECA DIALECT.	CAYUGA DIALECT.	ONONDAGA DIALECT
Albany.	Skä-neh'-tä-de.	Skä'-na-tä-de.	Skä-na'-tä-de.
Utica.	Nun-da-dä'-sis.	De-o'-nun-da-dä'-sis.	None-da-dä'-sis.
Auburn.	Dwas-co'.	Was'-co.	Os'-co.
Geneva.	Gä-nun-dä-sa'-ga.	Gä-na-dä-sa'-ga.	Gä-nä-dä-sa'-ga.
Canandaigua.	Gä-nun-dä'-gwa.	Gä-na-dä'-gwa.	Cä-nä-dä'-quä.
Rochester.	Gä-sko'-sä-go.	Gä-sko-sä'-go.	Gä-sko'-sä-go'-w
Tonawanda.	Tä'-nä-wun-da.	Tä-no-wun'-da.	Tä-no-wä'-da.
Buffalo.	Do-sho'-weh.	De-o-tro'-weh.	De-o-sa'-weh.
Niagara River.	Ne-ah'-gä.	O-ne-ä'-gä.	Ne-ah'-gä.
Honeoye Lake.	Hä-ne-ä'-yeh.	Hä-ne-ä'-ha.	Hä-ne-ä'-ya.
Hemlock Lake.	O-neh'-dä.	De-o-neh'-dä-eh.	O-nä'-dä.
Skaneateles Lake.	Skä'-ne-o'-dice.	Skä-ne-a'-dice.	Skä-ne-o'-dice.
Chautauque Lake.	Chä-dä'-gweh.	Chä-dä'-qua.	Chä-dä'-quä.
Waterloo.	Sä'-yase.	Skoi'-yase.	Sä'-yase.
Herkimer.	Dä-yä-o'-geh.	Da-ä-o'-ga.	Te-o-gun'.
Conhocton River.	Gä-hä'-to.	Gä-hä'-tro.	Gä-hä'-to.
Oriskany Creek.	O-his'-heh.	O-his'-ha.	O-his'-kä.
Oswego.	Swa-geh'.	Swa-geh'.	Swa-geh'.
Canajoharie.	Cä-na'-jo-hä.		Cä-na-jo-hä'-ga.
Montezuma.	Te-kä'-jik-ha'-do.	T'car-jik-ha'-do.	Te-skä-jik-ha'-d
Schenectady.	Ho-no'-ä-go-neh'.		No-wä-go'-na.
Black River.	Gä-hun'-go-wä.	Gä-hun-go'-wä.	Kä-hu-wä-go'-nä
Oneida Castle.	Gä-no'-ä-o-hä.	Gä-no-ä-o'-ä.	Gä-no-wi'-hä.
Allegany River.	O-hee'-yo.	O-hee'-yo.	O-hee'-yu.

The number of their elementary sounds, as at present ascertained, is below that of the English language, but twenty-three having been determined in the Seneca tongue, while in the former it is well known that there are thirty-eight. A more critical analysis would doubtless discover additional sounds, as in the guttural and nasal tones they take a wider range than the English voice.

In illustrating the parts of speech by a cursory examination, and in elucidating the declensions and conjugations, the words introduced as specimens will be taken from the Seneca language.

It is supposed by those who have inquired philosophically into the formation of language, that the noun substantive would be the first part of speech in the order of origination, inasmuch as the objects in nature must be named, and perhaps classed, before relations between them are suggested, or actions concerning them are expressed. Much of the beauty of a language depends upon this part of speech. Nouns of one syllable are rarely, if ever, found in either of the dialects; those of two syllables are not very numerous; those of three and four syllables embrace the great mass of words which belong to this part of speech. As specimens of the language, the following examples are given:—

NOUNS OF TWO SYLLABLES.

An-da′,	Day.	Gă-ee′,	Tree.
So-a′,	Night.	Hă-ace′,	Panther.
Gă-o′,	Wind.	Je-yeh′,	Dog.
Gus-no′,	Bark.	Gen-joh′,	Fish.

NOUNS OF THREE SYLLABLES.

Ah-wä'-o,	Rose.	O-o'-zä,	Bass-wood.
O-gis'-tä,	Fire.	O-äne'-dä,	Shrub.
O-we'-zä,	Ice.	O-nä'-tä,	Leaf.
O-dus'-hote,	A spring.	Gä-ha'-neh,	Summer.
Gä-hä'-dä,	Forest.	O-gäs'-ah,	Evening.
O-eke'-tä,	Thistle.	Gä-o'-wo,	Canoe.

NOUNS OF FOUR SYLLABLES.

O-na-gä'-nose,	Water.	Ong-wa-o'-weh,	Indian.
Gä-a-nun'-da,	Mountain.	Gä-gä-neäs'-heh,	Knife.
Gä-gwe-dake'-neh,	Spring.	O-gwen-nis'-hä,	Copper.
Sä-da'-che'-ah,	Morning.	Ah-tä-gwen'-dä,	Flint.
Gä-a-o'-dä,	Gun.		

NOUNS OF FIVE SYLLABLES.

Sä-da'-wä-sun-teh,	Midnight.	So-a'-kä-gä-gwä,	Moon.
O-wis'-tä-no-o,	Silver.	Gä-ne-o'-us-heh,	Iron.
An-da'-kä-gä-gwä,	Sun.	O-dä'-wä-an-do,	Otter.

In most, if not all languages, the idea of singular and plural is conveyed by an inflection of the word itself, or by some addition. To illustrate from the language under consideration, which forms the plural in several ways by inflection, the subjoined examples are introduced.

Singular.		Plural.	
O-on'-dote,	A tree.	O-on-do'-do,	Trees.
Gä-no'-sote,	A house.	Gä-no-so'-do,	Houses.
Gä-ne-o'-wa-o,	A brook.	Gä-ne-o-wa-o'-neo,	Brooks.
Je-dä'-o,	A bird.	Je-dä-o'-suh-uh,	Birds.
O-an'-nuh,	A pole.	O-an'-nuh-suh,	Poles.
Ga-hun'-da,	A creek.	Ga-hun-da'-neo,	Creeks.

There are several other terminations by which the plural is indicated.

It is said that the dual number originated in the difficulty of inventing the numerals, one, two, three,

&c., which are in themselves extremely abstract conceptions. The ideas of *one*, *two* and *more*, which correspond with singular, dual and plural, would be far more easily formed in the mind, than the idea of number in general; and the most simple mode of expressing them would be by a variation of the word itself. Hence in the Hebrew and Greek, which are original or uncompounded languages, in the general sense, the dual is found to exist, while in the Latin, and in modern languages, which are compounds, and were formed subsequent to the invention of numerals, the dual number is discarded. The Iroquois, so far as we know, is an original and uncompounded language, and it has the dual number, both in its verbs and nouns.

Gender was very happily indicated in the Latin and Greek by final letters or terminations. In the English, by giving up the ancient declensions, this mode of designating gender was also laid aside, and two or three modes substituted; thus, that of varying the word itself, as tiger, tigress, of giving the same animal names entirely different, as buck and doe, and more frequently still that of prefixing words which signify male and female. The Iroquois nouns have three genders, which are indicated in the manner last mentioned. Unlike the provisions of other languages, all inanimate objects, without distinction, were placed in the neuter gender.

In some respects the adjective would be a simple part of speech to invent, as quality is an object of external sense, and is always in concrete with the subject. But to discover and adopt a classification, founded upon the similitudes of objects, would be more difficult, since both generalization and abstraction would be required. The dialects of the *Ho-de'-no-sau-nee* appear to be amply furnished with this part of speech, on which so much of the beauty of a language is known to depend, to express nearly every shade of quality in objects. Comparison, of which they have the three degrees, is effected by adding another word, and not by an inflection of the word itself, in the following manner:

Positive.		Comparative.	Superlative.
Great,	Go-wä-na',	Ah-gwus'-go-wä-na,	Ha-yo-go-sote'-go-wä-na.
Good,	We-yo',	Ah-gwus'-we-yo,	Ha-yo-go-sote'-we-yo.
Sweet,	O-gä-uh',	Ah-gwus'-o-gä-uh,	Ha-yo-go-sote'-o-gä-uh.
Small,	Ne-wä-ah',	Ah-gwus'-ne-wä-ah,	Ha-yo-go-sote'-ne-wä-ah.

But in connecting the adjective with the noun, the two words usually enter into combination, and lose one or more syllables. This principle, or species of contraction, is carried throughout the language, and to some extent prevents prolixity. The language has but few primitive words, or ultimate roots; and when these are mastered, their presence is readily detected and understood, through all the elaborate and intricate combinations in which they are used. To illustrate the manner of compounding the adjective with the substantive, the following examples may be taken: *O-yä'*, fruit; *O-gä-uh'*, sweet; *O-yä'-gä-uh*, sweet fruit; *O*, the first syllable of sweet, being dropped. Again, *E'-yose*, a blanket; *Gä'-geh-ant*, white; *Yose-ä-geh'-ant*, white blanket; *Gä-no'-sote*, a house; *We-yo'*, good; *Gä-no'-se-yo*, a good house; literally fruit sweet, blanket white, and house good, illustrative of that natural impulse in man which leads him to place the object before the quality. In other instances the adjective is divided, and one part prefixed and the other suffixed to the noun thus: *Ga-nun'-dä-yeh*, a village; *Ne-wä'-ah*, small; *Ne-gä-nun-dä'-ah*, a small village; *Ah-tä'-quä-o-weh*, a moccason; *Ne-wä'-tä-quä-ah*, a small moccason. The adjective is also frequently used uncompounded with the noun, as *Ga-nä'-dike-ho E'-yose*, a green blanket.

The indefinite article *a* or *an*, is entirely unknown in the language of the Iroquois. There are numerous particles, as in the Greek, which, without significance in themselves separately, are employed for euphony, and to connect other words. These particles qualify and sometimes limit the signification of words; but yet if they should be submitted to a critical examination, none of them would answer the idea of the article *a*, or *an*. The existence in completeness of this refined part of speech would indicate a greater maturity and finish, than the dialects of the Iroquois possessed. But the definite article *na*, *the*, is found in the language. It is not as distinctly defined, and perfectly used, as in more polished languages, but it is usually prefixed to substantives, as with us, to indicate the thing intended.

Of the adverb nothing need be introduced, except to remark that the language is furnished with the usual variety. A few specimens may be added.

Nake-ho', here ; *O-nă'*, now ; *Ta-dă'*, yesterday ; *Skă-no'*, well.

The preposition is allowed to be so abstract and metaphysical in its nature, that it would be one of the last and most difficult parts of speech to invent. It expresses relation "considered in concrete with the correlative object;" and is of necessity very abstruse. The prepositions, *of*, *to*, and *for*, are regarded as the most abstract, from the character of the relations which they indicate. Declension, it is supposed, was resorted to by the Greeks, and adopted by the Latins, to evade the necessity of inventing these prepositions ; as it would be much easier to express the idea by the variation of the noun, than to ascertain some word which would convey such an abstract relation as that indicated by *of* or *to*. By the ancient cases, this difficulty was surmounted, and the preposition was blended with the correlative object, as in *Sermonis*, of a speech ; *Sermoni*, to a speech. Modern languages have laid aside the ancient cases, for the reason, it is said, that the invention of prepositions rendered them unnecessary. In the Iroquois language, the prepositions above mentioned are not to be found ; neither have its nouns a declension, like the Greek and Latin. Some traces of a declension are discoverable ; but the cases are too imperfect to be compared with those of the ancient languages, or to answer fully the ends of the prepositions. This part of speech is the most imperfectly developed of any in the language ; and the contrivances resorted to to express such of these relations as were of absolute necessity, are too complex to be easily understood.

The language, however, contains the simple prepositions, as *Da-ga'-o*, across; *No'-gă*, after; *Nă'-ho*, at; *O'-an-do*, before; *Dose-gă'-o*, near, &c. It must be inferred that the framers of the language had no distinct idea of the relations conveyed by the deficient prepositions, otherwise they would be found in the language. From the number of particles employed in the language, and the complexity of their combinations, it would be impossible to analyze the word, or phrase, for example, in which *on* occurs, and take out the specific fragment which has the force of the preposition.

In the imperfect declensions through which the Iroquois substantives are passed, pronouns, as well as prepositions, are interwoven by inflection. These declensions are not reduceable to regular forms, but admit of great diversities, thus rendering the language itself, like all simple and original languages, exceedingly intricate in its inflections. The following examples will exhibit the ordinary variations of the noun.

Gä-no'-sote,	A house.
Ho-no'-sote,	His house.
Hä-to-no'-sote,	Of, to, from, or at his house.
Ho-no'-sa-go,	In his house.
A-so'-gwä-tä,	A pipe.
Ho-so'-gwä-tä,	His pipe.
Na-no-so'-gwä-tä,	Of his pipe.
Ho-so'-gwä-tä-go,	In his pipe.
O-on-dote',	A tree.
Ho-on-dä',	His tree.
Hä'-to-de-on-dote,	Of, to, from, or at his tree.

O-yä',	Fruit.
Ho-yä',	His fruit.
Ho-dä-yä',	Of, to, from, or at his fruit.

Wä-nis'-heh-da,	Day.
Dwen-nis'-heh-dake,	At a day past.
Dwen-nis'-heh-deh,	At a day future.
Sä-wen-nis'-hät,	With the day.

Wä-sun'-dä-da,	Night.
Dwä-sun'-dä-dake,	At a night past.
Dwä-sun'-dä-da,	At a night future.
Sä-wä-sun'-dart,	With the night.

Of the pronouns but little need be added, except that they are very defective: thus *E* signifies I, we, me, and us; *Ese*, thou, ye or you, and thee. *He* and *they*, are wanting, except as expressed in the verb by its inflection. The personal pronouns make the possessive case very regularly, thus: *Ah-gä-weh'*, mine; *Sä-weh'*, thine; *Ho-weh'*, his; *Go-weh'*, hers; *Ung-gwä-weh'*, ours; *Swä-weh'*, yours; *Ho-nau-weh'*, theirs. Similar variations can be made on some of the relative pronouns.

Interjections are extremely numerous in this language, and appear to be adapted to all the passions. It has also the ordinary conjunctions.

Next and last, the verb presents itself. This part of speech, in the nature of things, must have been one of the first invented, as without its aid, there could be no affirmation, no expression of action or passion. Among primitive languages, the conjugation of the verb is extremely complex. Grammarians assign as a reason, that the tenses and moods of the verb would be more easily indicated by its inflection, than by contriving or inventing the substantive verb, I am; the possessive verb, I have; and the auxiliaries, do, will, would, shall, can, and may; all of which are necessary in the conjugation of an English verb. It will be remembered that the Englisn verb admits of but three variations in itself, as *press, pressed, pressing*; and its conjugation is completed by the auxiliary verbs above-mentioned; while the Greek, Latin, and Iroquois verbs are conjugated, except some part of the passive voice in Latin, by the variations throughout of the verb itself; thus, *Legeram*, I had read; *Che-wä'-ge-yä-go*, I had shot; *Legero*, I shall have read; *A-wä-ge'-yä-go*, I shall have shot. In this manner, the conjugation not only dispensed with the pronouns I, thou, and he, with their plurals, but also with the auxiliary verbs, which have introduced such prolixity into modern languages. The Iroquois verbs are conjugated with great regularity and precision, making the active and passive voices, all the moods, except the infinitive, and all the tenses, numbers, and persons, common to the English verb. Some part of the optative mood can also be made.

But the participles are wanting. It is difficult to determine upon what principle the absence of this part of speech, which in a written language would be a serious blemish, shall be accounted for; and much more difficult to ascertain the nature of the substitute in a verbal language. A substitute for the infinitive mood is found in the present tense of the subjunctive mood, together with a pronoun, as in the following passage: "Direct that *He'-no* may come

and give us rain;" see the invocation entire on
page 197;) instead of saying, "Direct *Hé-no* to come,
and give us rain." In correctly translated Indian
speeches this form of expression will frequently appear, from the influence which this idiomatic peculiarity of all Indian languages will exercise upon
the translator.

The origin of the dual number has been adverted to. In the active voice of Iroquois verbs, the
dual number is well distinguished; but in the passive voice, the dual and the plural are the same.
The presence of this number is indicative of the intricate nature of their conjugations.

To convey a distinct notion of the mutations
through which an Iroquois verb passes in its conjugation, and to furnish those who are curious, as lin-
guists, with a specimen for comparison with the
conjugations of other languages, one of their verbs,
with its inflections, is subjoined in Appendix, No. 2.
Its great regularity, even harmony of inflection,
conveys a favorable impression of the structure of
the language; but it does not, nor would it be expected to possess the elegance and beauty of the
Greek, or the brevity and solidity of the Latin conjugations. The principal parts of a few verbs are
given as specimens.

ACTIVE VOICE.

Pres. Indic.	Future Indic.	Perfect Indic.	
Ge'-yäse,	Eh-ge'-yäke,	Ah-ge'-yä-go,	To shoot.
O-gee'-a,	Eh-ge'-a,	Ah-ge'-a-go,	To die.
Gä-geh',	Eh-gä-geh',	Ah'-gä-geh,	To see.
Ga-go'-ace,	Eh-gä-go'-ake,	Ah-ga'-go-a-go,	To strike.
Ah-got'-hun-da,	Eh-gä'-ouk,	Ah-gä'-o-geh,	To hear.
Kna-ga-hä',	Enk-na'-ga-ä,	Kna-ga'-huk,	To drink.

It has been laid down as a maxim, that "the more simple any language is in its composition, the more complex it must be in its declensions and conjugations, and on the contrary, the more simple it is, in its declensions and conjugations, the more complex it must be in its composition." The position is thus illustrated: when two people, by uniting or otherwise, blend their languages, the union always simplifies the structure of the resulting language, while it introduces a greater complexity into its materials. The Greek which is uncompounded, and is said to have but three hundred primitives, is extremely intricate in its conjugations. On the other hand, the Latin, which is a compound language, laid aside the middle voice and the optative mood, which are peculiar to the Greek, and also the dual number. This simplified its conjugations. In its declensions, the Latin, although it has an additional case in the ablative, is yet much more simple than the Greek, as it has no contract nouns. The English, which is a mixture of several languages, is more simple than either in its declensions, which are made by the aid of prepositions alone ; and in its conjugations, which are made by other verbs. With this principle in mind, the regularity, fulness and intricacy of the Iroquois conjugations are not particularly remarkable. Its primitive words, as before remarked, are few, and their language has been formed out of them by a complex and elaborate system of combinations.

The language of the *Ho-de'-no-sau-nee* has the

substantive or neuter verb, *E-neh'-ga*, I am, although imperfect in some of its tenses. This verb is regarded by philologists as extremely difficult of invention, as it simply expresses being. Impersonal verbs are also very numerous in the language, as *O-geon'-de-o*, it snows ; *O-nä-yose'-don-de-o*, it hails ; *Gä-wä'-no-däs*, it thunders. It is supposed by those who have inquired into the formation of language, that most of the verbs in primitive tongues originally took the impersonal form, for the reason that such a verb expresses in itself an entire event, while the division of the event into subject and attribute, involves some nice metaphysical distinctions.

Before closing upon this subject it will be proper to notice a few of the peculiarities of the language. In the first place it has no labials, consequently the Iroquois, in speaking, never touch their lips together. This fact may be employed as a test in the pronunciation of their words and names. Their language possesses the numerals firstly, secondly, thirdly, &c., also the numbers one, two, three, ascending, by various contrivances, to about one hundred. For sums above this, their mode of enumeration was defective, as mathematical computation ceased, and some descriptive term was substituted in its place.

The voices of the *Ho-de'-no-sau-nee* are powerful, and capable of reaching a high shrill key. In conversation its natural pitch is above the English voice, especially with the female, whose voice by a natural transition, frequently rises in conversation an octave above its ordinary pitch, and sounds upon a tone to which the English voice could not be elevated and retain a distinct articulation. It also passes up and down, at intervals, from octave to octave, the voice retaining upon the elevated key a clear and musical intonation.

In verbal languages the words appear to be literally strung together in a chain, if the one under inspection may be taken as a specimen. Substantives are mingled by declension with pronouns, and sometimes with the substantive verb, or compounded with the adjective, thus forming a new word. Particles are then conjoined, varying or adding to the signification of the compound, until the word, by the addition of the verb, becomes so far extended as to embrace a perfect sentence. The principles upon which these combinations are effected are too much involved to be systematized or generalized. The most which can be said is, that the general result is accomplished by conjugations and declensions, which, although regular in general, are diversified and intricate. To illustrate the manner in which words are made up, the following example may be given. *Nun-da-wä-o*, the radix of the name of the Senecas, signifies " a great hill ;" by suffixing *o-no*, which conveys the idea of " people at," *Nun-da-wä'-o-no*, results literally, " the people at the great hill." Next, by adding the particle *ga*, itself without significance, but when conjoined, conveying the idea of " place" or " territory," it gives the compound *Nun-da-wä'-o-no-ga'*, " the territory of the people at the great hill." A more perfect specimen of the language, as a whole, may be found in the following version of the Lord's Prayer in the Seneca dialect.

Gwä-nee' gă-o-yä'-geh che-de-oh'; sä-sa-no-do'-geh-teek; gä-o' ne-dwa na' sa-nunk-tä; na-huk' ne-yä-weh' na yo-an'-jä-geh ha'-ne-sä-ne-go'-dă ha ne-de-o'-dă na' gă-o-yä'-geh. Dun-dä-gwä-e'-wä-să-gwus na' ong-wi-wä-na-ark-seh' na' da-yä'-ke-wä-să-gwä'-seh na' onk-ke-wä-na'-ä-ge. Dä-ge-o'-na-geh'-wen-nis'-heh-da na' ong-wä-quä'. Să-nuk' na-huh' heh'-squä-ä ha' gä-yeh na' wä-ate-keh' na-gwä' na' dä-gwä-yä-duh'-nuh-onk ha' gä-yeh na' wä-ate-keh'; na' seh-eh' na ese' sä-wă na' o-nuk-ta' kuh' na' gă-hus-ta-seh' kuk' na' da-gä-ă-sä-uh'. Na-huh'-ne-yä-weh.[1]

Names of places as well as of persons, form an integral part of their language, and hence are all significant. It furnishes a singular test of their migrations, for accurate descriptions of localities become

---

[1] If an attempt should be made to give a literal translation of each word, or phrase, it would render transposition necessary, and change the formation of the words in some respects, as the following will exhibit.

Gwä-nee', che-de-oh' gă-o'-yä-geh, gä-sa-nuh', ese' sä-nuk-tä' gä-oh'
Our Father, which art in heaven, hallowed be thy name, thy kingdom come,

ese' sne'-go-eh ne-yä-weh' yo an-jä'-geh ha' ne-de-o'-deh gă-o'-yä-geh.
thy will be done on earth as it is in heaven.

Dun-dä-gwä-e'-wä-să-gwus ong-wä-yeh'-his-heh' da-yä-ke'-a-wä-
Forgive us our debts as we

să-gwus-seh' ho-yeh'-his. Dä-ge-oh' ne' na-geh' wen-nis'-heh-deh e' na-hä-
forgive our debtors. Give us this day our

da-wen-nis'-heh-geh o-ä'-qwa. Hă-squä'-ah e' să-no' ha' wä-ate-keh', na-gwä'
daily bread. Lead us not into temptation, but

dä-gwä-yä-dan'-nake ne' wä-ate-keh', na-seh'-eh nees' o-nuk'-tä na-kuh'
deliver from us evil, for thine is the kingdom, and

na gä-hus'-tes-heh, na-kuh' da-gä-ă-sä-oh'.
the power, and the glory.

Na-huh'-se-yä-weh.

in this manner incorporated into their dialects. The Tuscaroras still adduce proof from this source to establish a common origin with the Iroquois, and pretend to trace their route from Montreal, *Do-te-ä'-co*, to the Mississippi, *O-nau-we-yo'-kä*, and from thence to North Carolina, out of which they were driven in 1712. The era of their separation from the parent stock, and of this migration, they have entirely lost; but they consider the names of places on this extended route, now incorporated in their language, a not less certain indication of a common origin than the similarity of their languages. Indian languages are exceedingly tenacious of traditionary facts intrusted to their preservation.

CHAPTER III.

OUR Indian geography is a subject of inquiry peculiar in its interest and in its character. Many of
the names bestowed by our predecessors having become incorporated into our language, will be transmitted to distant generations, and be familiar after
their race, and perhaps ours, have passed away.
There is still attainable a large amount of geographical information pertaining to the period of Indian
occupation, which, estimated at its true value, would
amply remunerate for its collection ; and which, if
neglected, must fade, ere many years, from remembrance. The features of nature were first christened by the red man. These baptismal names, the
legacy of the Indian, it were prodigality to cast
away. To the future scholar this subject will com-
mend itself, when, perchance, the dusky mantle of
obscurity has enshrouded it, and research itself cannot penetrate the covering.

In an antiquarian aspect, it may be considered
fortunate, that as the villages and settlements of the

Ho-de'-no-sau-nee disappeared, and the cities and villages of the succeeding race were reared upon their sites, all of these ancient names were transferred to these substituted habitations. Yielding step by step, and contracting their possessions from year to year, the Iroquois yet continued in the constant use of their original names, although the localities themselves had been surrendered. If a Seneca, for example, were to refer to Geneva, he would still say *Gä-nun'-dä-sa'-ga;* and the Oneida in like manner would call Utica, *Nun-da-dä'-sis.* All of these localities, as well as our rivers, lakes and streams, still dwell in the memory of the Iroquois by their ancient names, while such places as have sprung up on nameless sites, since they surrendered their domain, have been christened as they appeared. These names, likewise, are significant, and are either descriptive of features of the country, the record of some historical event, or interwoven with some tradition. From these causes their geography has been preserved among them with remarkable accuracy.

The Iroquois method of bestowing names was peculiar. It frequently happened that the same lake or river was recognized by them under several different names. This was eminently the case with the larger lakes. It was customary to give to them the name of some village or locality upon their borders. The Seneca word *Te-car-ne-o-di'*, means something more than "lake." It includes the idea of nearness, literally, "the lake at." Hence, if a Seneca were asked the name of lake Ontario, he would answer, *Ne-ah'-gä Te-car-ne-o-di'*, " the lake at *Ne-ah'-gä.*" This was a Seneca village at the mouth of the Niagara river. If an Onondaga were asked the same question, he would prefix *Swa-geh'* to the word lake, literally, " the lake of Oswego."[1] The same multiplicity of names frequently arose in relation to the principal rivers, where they passed through the territories of more than one nation. It was not, however, the case with villages and other localities.

The principal villages of the Iroquois, in the days of aboriginal dominion, were connected by well-beaten trails. These villages were so situated that the central trail, which started from the Hudson at the site of Albany, passed through those of the Mohawks and Oneidas ; and, crossing the Onondaga valley and the Cayuga country, a few miles north of the chief settlements of these nations, it passed through the most prominent villages of the Senecas, in its route to the valley of the Genesee. After crossing this celebrated valley, it proceeded westward to lake Erie, coming out upon it at the mouth of Buffalo creek, on the present site of Buffalo.

Since this Indian highway passed through the centre of the Long House, as well as through the fairest portions of New York, it is desirable to commence with this trail on the Hudson, and trace it through the State. It will furnish the most conve-

---

[1] Lake Ontario was known at an early day among the English as lake Cataraque. The root of this word, *Ga-dai'-o-que* in Onondaga, *Gä-dä'-loque* in Oneida, and *Gä-da-o'-ka* in Seneca, signifies " A fort in the water."

nient method of noticing such stopping-places as were marked with appropriate names in the dialects of the Iroquois, and also the Indian villages which dotted this extended route.

Albany, at which point the trail started from the Hudson, owes its Iroquois name to the openings which lay between that river and the Mohawk at Schenectady. Long anterior to the foundation of ·the city, this site was well known to our predecessors under the name of *Skä-neh'-tä-de*. The name is given in the Seneca dialect, and signifies " beyond the openings." [1] Out of this name originated that of the Hudson, *Skä-neh'-ta-de Ga-hun'-da*, " the river beyond the openings."

Leaving the Hudson at the site of Albany, the trail took the direction of the old turnpike north of the capitol, and proceeded, mostly on the line of this road, to a spring which issued from a ravine about six miles west. From thence it continued towards Schenectady, and descending the ravine through which the railway passes, it came upon the Mohawk at the site of this city, and crossed the river at the fording-place, where the toll-bridge has since been erected. Schenectady has not only appropriated the Indian name of Albany, but has, by inheritance, one of the most euphonious names in the dialects of the Iroquois, as given by the Oneidas. It was christened *O-no-al'-i-gōne*, which

---

[1] In the Seneca dialect this word is compounded of *Gä-neh'-tä-yeh*, " openings," and *Se'-gwä*, " beyond." In the same manner *Skai'-dä-de*, " be-yond the swamp," is a compound of *Gai'-tä-yeh*, " a swamp," and *Se'-gwä*, " beyond."

ᴜgnifies "in the head," a somewhat fanciful geographical name.

From this fording-place, two trails passed up the
Mohawk, one upon each side. That upon the south
was most travelled, as the three Mohawk castles, as
they were termed, or principal villages, were upon
that side. Following the valley, and pursuing the
windings of the river, the trail crossed the Schoharie creek, *Ose-ho-kar'-lä*, and entered *Te-hon-dä-
lo'-ga*, the lower castle of the Mohawks, situated
upon the west side of this creek, at its junction
with the river. At a subsequent day Fort Hunter
was located near the site of this Indian village.
From thence the trail, continuing up the valley
nearly on the line subsequently pursued by the
canal, crossed the Canajoharie creek, near its junction with the river, and led up to Canajoharie, *Cä-
nä-jo'-hä-e*,[1] or the middle Mohawk castle. This favorite and populous village occupied a little eminence upon the east bank of the *Ot-squä'-go* creek,
and overlooking the present site of Fort Plain.
From Canajoharie, the trail followed up the river to
Gä-ne'-ga-hä'-gä, the upper Mohawk castle, which
was situated in the town of Danube, Herkimer
county, nearly opposite the mouth of the East Canada creek. Leaving this Indian village, the last
in the territory of the Mohawks, the trail pursued

---

[1] This word signifies "washing the
basin." In the bed of the Canajoharie creek there is said to be a basin,
several feet in diameter, with a
symmetrical concavity, washed out
in the rock. Hence the name
Ca-nä-jo'-hä-e. One would naturally
have expected to have found the
Indian village upon this creek, instead of the Ot-squä'-go.

the bank of the river without passing any other stopping-place, until it reached the site of Utica, in the country of the Oneidas.

Near this city, on the east side, the trail passed around the base of a hill, in such a manner as to be noticeable for its singularity. Hence, *Nun-da-dä'-sis*, signifying "around the hill," was bestowed upon this locality, as a name descriptive of the course of the trail. When Utica at a subsequent day sprang up near this spot, the name was transferred, according to the custom of the Iroquois, to the city itself.

From Utica, the trail proceeded up the river, and crossing the Whitesboro creek, at Whitesboro, *Che-gä-queh*, and the Oriskany creek, *Ole-his'-ka*, at Oriskany, it continued up the bank of the Mohawk to Rome, where this river turns to the north.

The site of Rome was an important stopping-place with the Iroquois, both as the terminus of the trails upon the Mohawk, and as a carrying-place for canoes. A narrow ridge at this point forms a division between those waters which flow through the Mohawk and the Hudson, and those which flow through lake Ontario, and the St. Lawrence. The portage from the Mohawk to Wood creek, was about a mile. In the days of aboriginal sovereignty, the amount of navigation, in bark canoes, upon the large lakes, as well as upon the smaller lakes and rivers, was much greater than we would be apt to suspect. Birch-bark canoes would find their way from Detroit, and even beyond to Rome and Schenectady. Others from Kingston, would make their

way into the Cayuga[1] and Seneca lakes, and on to
the old trading-post at the mouth of the Niagara
river. Such was the facility of transportation,
owing to the lightness of the vessel, that the portage made but a slight obstruction. In an hour
after drawing out the canoe from Wood creek, it
was floating again upon the Mohawk; and the cargo
having also been carried over, the frail vessel was
soon re-ladened, and under weigh upon the descending stream.[2] The aboriginal name of this locality,
Da-yä-hoo-wä'-quat, which signifies a "place for carrying boats," has been bestowed upon Rome.

The trail upon the north bank of the Mohawk
ascended the river from Schenectady nearly upon
the line since pursued by the turnpike. At Tribes
Hill, nearly opposite the lower Mohawk castle, a
branch trail crossed the country to Johnstown, *Ko-
lä-ne'-kä*, a few miles north from the river. This
was the name bestowed upon the residence of Sir
William Johnson, the Indian superintendent. From

[1] In 1793, a canoe ladened with
1200 pounds of fur started from Kingston in Canada; and having coasted
the lake to the Great Sodus bay,
Seo-dose', and been transported from
thence over the portage to Clyde
river, it made its way into the Cayuga
lake and up to Aurora, *De-ä-wen'-
dote*; where the furs were tranship-
ped in a bateau for Albany. The
canoe was owned for some years
afterwards by Col. Payne, one of the
first settlers of Aurora.

[2] For many years after the commencement (about 1790) of the settlement of Western New York, the
greater part of the supplies of merchandise from the east, as well as
the immigrants who flocked thither-
ward, with their household goods,
and farming implements, ascended
the Mohawk in bateaus or small river boats as far as Rome. Having
drawn out their vessels at this portage and unladened them, they carried
them over the ridge and launched
them into Wood creek. Descending
to the Oswego river, which is formed
by the outlets of the principal inland
lakes of the State, the whole lake
country was open before them. Like
the Iroquois, they made use of the
natural highways of the country.

the period of the settlement of this distinguished personage in the country of the Mohawks, and more especially after the battle of lake George in 1755, he acquired and maintained, until his death in 1774, a greater personal influence over the Iroquois than was ever possessed by any other individual, or even by any government. A careful scrutiny of his intercourse with the Iroquois, shows that he exercised a watchful care over their welfare, and that his conduct was governed by the most enlightened principles of rectitude and benevolence. To this fact he owed his personal popularity, and the affectionate respect with which the Iroquois ever regarded him. His house at *Ko-lä-ne'-kä* was a favorite place of Indian resort; and the Mohawk and the Seneca, the Oneida and the Cayuga felt as much at ease under the roof of the baronet as beneath the wide-spread shelter of their own forests.

Leaving Johnstown, the trail came down again upon the Mohawk at the small Indian village of *Gä-no'-wau-ga*, near the site of Fonda, where it intersected the river trail. Continuing up the Mohawk, and crossing the East Canada creek, *Date-car'-hu-har'-lo*, and over the site of Little Falls, *Tä-lä-que'-ga*, it came next upon the West Canada creek, *Te-uge'-ga*, and from thence led up to the portage at the site of Rome.

As with lake Ontario, the Mohawk river was known under a multiplicity of names. It is difficult now to determine whether it had any general name running through the several dialects by which it was known to all the nations of the League. Among the Senecas, the West Canada creek was considered the true head of the river, and this stream, together with the Mohawk from Herkimer to the Hudson, was known as one river under the name of *Te-uge'-ga*, while the Mohawk from the junction of the West Canada creek to its source was regarded as a branch under the name of *Da-yä-hoo-wä'-quat*. With the Oneidas and Onondagas it was known under the last name, or the word which, in their respective dialects, signifies the same thing.

From Rome, the main trail, taking a south-west direction, passed through Verona, *Te-o-na-täle'*, and finally came out at Oneida castle. This was the principal village of the Oneidas, called in their dialect *Gä-no-a-lo'-häle*, which is rendered "a head on a pole." In this beautifully situated Indian village, burned the council-fire of one of the nations of the League. The Oneidas were fortunate in the location of their territories, embracing as they did not only some of the finest agricultural districts of the State, but the most attractive localities in its central parts.

Fording the Oneida creek at the Indian village, the trail, continuing west, passed near the site of Canestota, *Kä-ne-to'-tä*, crossed the Canaseraga creek, *Kä-nä-so-wä'-ga*, near the site of the village of the same name, the Chittenango creek, *Chu-de-näng'*, at the site of Chittenango, and from thence led up to the Deep Spring near Manlius, on the boundary line between the territories of the Oneidas and Onondagas. This spring was known under the name of *De-o-sä-dä-ya'-ah*, signifying "the spring in the deep basin," and was a favorite stopping-place of the Iroquois in their journeys upon the great thoroughfare.

Leaving this locality, and continuing west, the trail forded the Limestone creek, *De-ä-o-no'-he*, at the site of Manlius, and proceeding mostly on the line since pursued by the turnpike, it crossed the Jamesville creek, *Gä-sun'-to*, at the site of Jamesville, and from thence descending into the Onondaga valley, it crossed the Onondaga river, *O-nun-dä'-ga*, and entered the Indian village of *Gis-twe-ah'-na*, which occupied the site of the present village of Onondaga Hollow.

The Onondagas made this picturesque and fertile valley their chief place of residence. Here was the Council-Brand of the confederacy, which rendered it the sylvan seat of government of the League. In the estimation of the Iroquois, it was a consecrated vale. Their eloquence, their legendary lore, and their civil history, were all interwoven, by association, with this favorite valley. Here their sachems gathered together in the days of aboriginal supremacy, to legislate for the welfare of the race. Here they strengthened and renewed the bonds of friendship and patriotism, indulged in exultation over their advancing prosperity, and counselled together to arrest impending dangers, or repair the mischances of the past. As it was upon the northern bank of the Onondaga lake that the League was formed,

the united nations habitually turned to the Onondaga valley as the place to brighten the chain of
brotherhood.

Upon the Onondaga river, *O-nun-dä'-ga*, were the
principal villages of the Onondagas. There were
but three of any note; one of them has been mentioned as on the line of the great trail. The chief
village was Onondaga castle, *Kä-nä-tä-go'-wä*, situated upon both sides of the river, about four miles
above *Gis'-twe-ah'-na*. It was quite a populous village in the days of their highest prosperity. Around
the council-brand which burned in this secluded place,
the sachems of the League were wont to meet.
About three miles farther up the river, and upon
the west side, the Indian village of *Nan-ta-sä'-sis*
was situated near the skirts of the hill. There was
another considerable village on the uplands about
four miles east of Onondaga castle, called *Tu-e-a-
das'-so*. Throughout the whole length of the beautiful valley of the Onondaga, the bark houses of
the people were sprinkled.

After crossing the valley, the trail passed up a
small ravine to the top of the hill, where it took a
north-west direction, and crossing the Nine-mile
creek, *Us'-te-ka*, at the site of Camillus, *O-yä'-
han*, it went up to a stopping-place where Carpen-
ter's tavern was subsequently erected, near the site
of Elbridge, *Kä-no-wä'-ya*. From thence fording
the Jordan creek, *Ha-nan'-to*, and passing through
the town of Sennet, the trail came upon the Owasco
outlet, *Was'-co*, at the site of Auburn; and forded

this stream a short distance above the prison, at the point where the "Red Store" was subsequently erected. This locality was in the territory of the Cayugas, and its name signifies "a floating bridge."

The Cayugas had but a few small villages, as the people were scattered around the lake. Their principal village, *Gă-yä-gä-an'-ha*, was situated upon the bank of a creek three miles south of Union Springs, and about a mile and a half back from the lake. Here was the council-house of the nation. There was another village consisting of a few houses, situated upon the site of Union Springs, which was called *Ge-wau'-ga*. Steeltrap, *Hisé'-tă-jee*, a celebrated Cayuga chief, was buried here. On the opposite side of the lake was the village of *Gä-no'-geh*, occupying the site of the present Cannoga. Near this village was the birthplace of Red Jacket. Along the eastern margin of the lake, the former residences of the Cayugas were indicated by the apple and peach orchards which they left behind them. Back from the lake, upon the ridge, similar, but more numerous evidences of Indian occupation were to be found. In 1779, the villages of the Cayugas were destroyed by General Sullivan.

Leaving the site of Auburn, the trail proceeded nearly on the line of the turnpike, half-way to the lake, where it turned out upon the south side and came down upon the lake about half a mile above Cayuga bridge, *Wäs-gwase'*. At the precise point where the trail reached the shore, the original Cayuga ferry was established. The trail, turning down the lake, and following its bank about four miles to the old fording-place near the lower bridge, there crossed the foot of the lake, and came out upon the north bank of the Seneca river, *Swa'-geh*.[1] Following up the north bank of the river, it passed over the site of Waterloo, *Skoi-yase'*, and pursued the stream up to its outlet from the Seneca lake. A shorter route from the east bank of the Cayuga was taken by crossing the lake in canoes at the ferry, and proceeding due west to the river, which the trail came upon at the rapids a little above Seneca Falls. Ascending the river upon the south bank, the trail passed through South Waterloo, *Skoi-yase'*, and continued up the river to the lake, where, crossing the outlet, it intersected the other trail. Having run along the foot of the lake upon the beach to the present site of Geneva, *Gä-nun-dä-sa'-ga*, it turned up the Geneva creek, which it ascended about one and a half miles north-west, to the Indian village of *Gä-nun-dä-sa'-ga*, the first in the territory of the Senecas.

This name, which signifies "a new settlement village," was bestowed upon the lake, the creek, and also upon the outlet. At a subsequent day it was transferred to Geneva. During the destructive in-

---

[1] There is a geographical novelty in the method adopted by the Iroquois to designate the several outlets of the lakes which, united, form the Oswego river. Descending from the Seneca lake to Oswego, the river was called *Swa'-geh* through its whole length. But ascending from Oswego, it was called the Onondaga river, *O-non-dä'-ga*, until you passed the outlet of the Onondaga lake. Then it was called the Cayuga river, *Gwä-u'-gweh*, until you passed the Cayuga outlet. After that it was called the Seneca river, *Gä-nun-dä-sa'-ga*, up to the Seneca lake.

road of General Sullivan, in September, 1779, the Indian village was entirely destroyed. No efforts were ever made subsequently to rebuild it. Many of the old trees in the Indian orchard are still standing and yield fruit, although partially girdled at the time. The artificial burial mound,[1] about one hundred paces in circuit, still remains undisturbed, and also the trenches of a picket enclosure, seventy by forty feet on the ground plan, concerning the erection and uses of which but little can be ascertained.

From *Gä-nun-dä-sa'-ga* the trail proceeded through the towns of Seneca and Hopewell, nearly on the line of the turnpike, to the Indian village of *Gä'-nun-dä'-gwa*, situated at the foot of the lake of the same name. It signifies " a place selected for a settlement." Canandaigua, the fairest of all the villages which have sprung into life upon the central trail of the Iroquois, not only occupies the site of the Indian village, but has accepted and preserved its name with unusual accuracy ; the only legacy which the retiring Seneca could bestow, save the beautiful natural scenery by which it is surrounded, and which induced him " to select it for a settlement."

[1] There is an interesting tradition connected with this mound. The Senecas say that they once had a protector, a mighty giant, taller than the tallest trees, who split the largest hickory for his bow, and used pine-trees for his arrows. He once wandered west to the Mississippi, and from thence east again to the sea. Returning homeward over the mountains along the Hudson, he saw a great bird on the water, flapping its wings as if it wished to get out, so he waded in and lifted it on land. He then saw on it a number of men, who appeared dreadfully frightened, and made signs to him to put them back again. He did so, and they gave him a sword and a musket, with powder and balls, and showed him how to use them, after which the bird swam off and he saw it no more.

Leaving Canandaigua were two trails. One turning south-west, passed through the town of Bristol, and led to the foot of the Honeoye lake, *Hä'-ne-ä-ya'*. After crossing the outlet, it continued west through the town of Richmond, going over the hill in sight of the Hemlock lake, *O-neh'-dä*, and coming out upon the Connesus, *Gä-ne-a'-sos*, near the north end. Following the shore to the foot of the lake, and fording the outlet, it proceeded west, passing over the site of Geneseo, *O-hä'-di*, and crossing the valley and the river Genesee, *Gen-nis'-he-yo*, it led into Little Beards town, *De-o-nun'-dä-gä-a*, the most populous village of the Senecas. It is worthy of remark that the root of the word Genesee was the name of the valley and not of the river, the latter deriving its name from the former. *Gen-nis'-he-yo* signifies "the beautiful valley," a name most fitly bestowed.

The other trail, which was the main highway, leaving Canandaigua, passed along the north road, over the site of West Bloomfield, *Gä-nun'-dä-ok*, and the Honeoye outlet, and proceeded to the Indian village of *Skä-hase'-gä-o*, on the site of Lima. From

Having returned to the Senecas at *Gä-nun-dä-sa'-ga*, he exhibited to them the wonderful implements of destruction, and fired the gun before them. They were exceedingly terrified at the report, and reproached him for bringing such terrible things among them, and told him to take them away again, for they would be the destruction of the Indians, and he was an enemy to their nation who had brought them there. Much grieved at their reproaches, he left the council, taking the dreaded weapons with him, and lay down in a field. The next morning he was found, from some mysterious cause, dead, and this mound was raised over his body where it lay. It is averred by the Onondagas, that if the mound should be opened a skeleton of supernatural size would be found underneath.

thence, proceeding westward nearly on the line since pursued by the State road, it passed over the site of Avon, *Gä-no-wau'-ges*, and, descending into the valley of the Genesee, crossed the river a few rods above the Avon bridge, and followed along its bank up to the Indian village of *Gä-no-wau'-ges*, about a mile above the ford. This word signifies " fetid waters," and was bestowed by the Senecas upon the sulphur springs at Avon, and upon the whole adjacent country.

Departing from the valley of the Genesee, the trail, taking a north-west direction, led to the Caledonia cold spring, *De-o'-na-gä-no*, a well-known stopping-place on the central trail through the territories of the Iroquois. Proceeding westward from thence, it came upon Allen's creek, *O-at'-kä*, at the dam near the rapids, in the village of Le Roy. This fording-place was known under the name *Te-car'-no-wän-ne-dä'-ne-o*, rendered " many falls," which is accurately descriptive of the locality. This name has been conferred upon Le Roy. After turning up the stream about a mile to avoid a marsh near the rapids, the trail again proceeded west, and crossing Black creek, *Jä-go-'o-ga*, near Stafford, it continued in a westerly direction, and finally came out upon the Tonawanda creek, *Tä'-nä-wun-dä*, about a mile above Batavia, to which it led. The ancient name of Batavia, or rather of the locality itself, was *De-o'-on-go-wä*, which signifies " the grand hearing-place." Here the rapids in the Tonawanda creek first began to be heard, and some assert that the distant roar

of Niagara could be heard by the practiced ear of
the Indian, at this point, in certain states of the at-
mosphere.

Descending the creek, the trail passed over the site
of Batavia. At the point where the arsenal now
stands, it turned north-west through the oak-open-
ings to Caryville, and came again upon the creek at
"Washington's fording-place," where it crossed, and
led to the Indian village of *Tä'-nă-wun-dä'*, one of
the present villages of the Senecas, situated upon
the borders of the great swamp which stretches for
many miles along the Tonawanda creek. On leaving
the Indian village the trail branched. One taking a
north-west direction, recrossed the creek at a short
distance below the village, and passing through the
swamp, out of which it emerged near Royalton, it
proceeded direct to *De-o'-na-gä-no*, or the Cold
Spring, about two miles north-east of Lockport, *Tä-
gă'-ote*. From thence continuing north-west, it came
out upon the ridge-road, where it intersected the
Ontario, or ridge trail, and followed this ridge
westward to *Gä-a-no'-ga*, the Tuscarora Indian village on Lewiston Heights. Here was the termina-
tion of one branch of the main trail upon the bank of
the Niagara river. This was the route to Canada.

The other trail, leaving the village of Tonawan-
da, took a south-west direction, and having forded
Murder creek, *De-o-oon-go'-at*, at Akron, and the
Eighteen-mile creek, *Ta--nun-no-ga'-o*, at Clarence
Hollow, it continued west, crossing Ellicott creek,
Gă-dă-o-yä'-deh, at Williamsville, *Gä-sko-sä-dä'-ne-o*,

and leading direct to the Cold Spring, it finally came upon the site of Buffalo at the head of Main street, and descended to the mouth of the creek, within the limits of the city. Here was the western terminus of the central trail; and like its eastern terminus on the Hudson, it has become a point of great commercial importance, and the site of a flourishing city. It is not a little remarkable, that these two geographical points should have been as clearly indicated, as places of departure, by the migrations of the red race, as they have been at a subsequent day, by the migrations of our own.

We have thus followed the great Indian trail, *Wä-a-gwen'-ne-yu*, through the State, from the Hudson to lake Erie; noticing, as far as ascertained, the principal stopping-places on the route. To convey an adequate impression of the forest scenery, which then overspread the land, is beyond the power of description. This trail was traced through the overhanging forest for almost its entire length. In the trail itself there was nothing particularly remarkable. It was usually from twelve to eighteen inches wide, and deeply worn in the ground; varying in this respect from three to six, and even twelve inches, depending upon the firmness of the soil. The large trees on each side were frequently marked with the hatchet. This well-beaten footpath, which no runner, nor band of warriors could mistake, had doubtless been trodden by successive generations from century to century. It had, without question, been handed down from race to race, as

the natural line of travel, geographically considered, between the Hudson and lake Erie. While it
is scarcely possible to ascertain a more direct route
than the one pursued by this trail, the accuracy
with which it was traced from point to point, to
save distance, is extremely surprising. It proved,
on the survey of the country, to have been so judiciously selected, that the turnpike was laid out main-
ly on the line of this trail, from one extremity of the
State to the other. In addition to this, all the
larger cities and villages west of the Hudson, with
one or two exceptions, have been located upon it.
As an independent cause, this forest highway of the
Iroquois doubtless determined the establishment of
a number of settlements, which have since grown
up into cities and villages.

There are many interesting considerations connected with the routes of travel pursued by the aborigines; and if carefully considered, they will be
found to indicate the natural lines of migration suggested by the topography of the country. The
central trail of the Iroquois, which we have been
tracing, after leaving the Mohawk valley, one of
nature's highways, became essentially an artificial
road across the drainage of the country, fording rivers, crossing valleys, and traversing marshes and
dense forests, pursuing its course over hill and plain,
through stream and thicket, as if in defiance of nature, without an aim and without a reason. Yet the
establishment of this trail between two such points
as Albany and Buffalo, exhibits not only the extent

and accuracy of the geographical knowledge of our predecessors, but also indicates the active intercourse which must have been maintained between the various races east of the Mississippi. The tide of population which has poured upon the west, in our generation, mostly along the line of this old trail of the *Ho-dé'-no-sau-nee*, and the extraordinary channel of trade and intercourse which it has become, between the north-western States and the Atlantic, sufficiently and forcibly illustrate the fact that it was and is, and ever must be, one of the great natural highways of the continent.

Having traced the main trail from the Hudson to lake Erie, it remains to notice briefly the lake and river trails, and to locate such Indian villages as were situated upon them. In pursuing this inquiry, the Ontario trail first arrests our attention. Bordering lake Ontario, from Oswego to Lewiston, there is a ridge running, for the entire distance, from three to six miles inland from the shore, and mostly a continuous level. From the shore-marks everywhere conspicuous, it is generally admitted that this ridge was anciently the shore of the lake, the basin of which has been depressed some three hundred feet, or the surrounding country elevated by subterraneous agencies. A natural road is formed by this ancient beach from Oswego to Lewiston. From the valley of Genesee to Niagara, it was extensively travelled by the Iroquois, as one of the routes to Canada.

Oswego, *Swa'-geh*, was a point of considerable im-

portance to our predecessors, both as the terminus
of the trails which descended the river from the
Onondaga and Oneida country, and as the inlet of
intercourse by water from lake Ontario. Com-
mencing at the site of this place, the trail followed
the ridge to the westward, until it came ·upon the
Irondequoit bay, *Nu-dă-on'-dä-quät*, when it turned
up the bay to its head. From the head of the bay,
the trail turned back from the ridge, and proceeded
direct to the Genesee ford, at Rochester, *Gä-sko'-
sä-go*, which crossed the river at the point where
the aqueduct has since been constructed. Turning
down the river to the lower falls, it came again
upon the ridge-road, which it followed westward to
Gä-o-no'-geh, the Tuscarora village near Lewiston.
Here was the principal crossing-place into Canada.

Having now reached the banks of the Niagara,
and the vicinity of the great cataract, the deriva-
tion of the word Niagara suggests itself as a subject for inquiry. Colden wrote it *O-ni-ag-a-ra*, in
1741,[1] and he must have received it from the Mohawks or Oneidas. It was the name of a Seneca
village at the mouth of the Niagara river, located
as early as 1650, near the site of Youngstown. It
was also the place where the Marquis De Nonville
constructed a fort in 1687, the building of which
brought this locality under the particular notice of
the English. The name of this Indian village in
the dialect of the Senecas was *Ne-ah'-gä*, in Tuscarora *O-ne-ä'-kars*, in Onondaga *O-ne-ah'-gä*, in Onei-

---

[1] Colden's History of the Five Nations, ed. of 1741, p. 79.

da *O-ne-ah'-gäle*, and in Mohawk *O-ne-ă'-gä-rä*. These names are but the same word under dialectical changes. It is clear that Niagara was derived from some one of them, and thus came direct from the Iroquois language. The signification of the word is lost, unless it be derived, as some of the present Iroquois suppose, from the word which signifies "neck," in Seneca *O-ne-ah'-ä*, in Onondaga *O-ne-yä'-ä*, and in Oneida *O-ne'-arle*.[1]

The name of this Indian village was bestowed by the Iroquois upon Youngstown; upon the river Niagara, from the falls to the lake; and upon lake Ontario, as has been elsewhere stated.

In bestowing names upon water-falls, the Iroquois custom agrees with the English. The name of the river is connected with the word "fall." In the case of Niagara Falls, however, an adjective is incorporated with the word "fall," as the idea of its grandeur and sublimity appears to have been identified with the fall itself. Thus, in Onondaga it is called *Date-car'-sko-sis*, in Seneca *Date-car'-sko-sase*, the word *Ne-ah'-gä* being understood. It signifies "the highest falls."

In the broad valley of the Genesee, the Senecas established most of their villages. Of great extent, boundless fertility, and easy cultivation, it became their favorite residence, and fully deserved the appellation of "the beautiful valley," which they bestowed upon it. Its situation in **the centre**

---

[1] Bancroft is in error in deriving this word from the language of the Neuter Nation.

of their territories, and the easily forded river which flowed through it, alike invited to its settlement. At the period of their highest prosperity, it became the most thickly peopled district in the country of the Iroquois.

From Rochester there were two trails up the Genesee, one upon each side. That upon the west side, following the bank of the river, first entered the small Indian village of *O-at'-kä*, upon the site of Scottsville; and continuing up the valley upon the flat, it next passed into the Indian village of *Gä-no-wau'-ges*, before mentioned.[1] From thence the trail pursued the winding of the river up to *O-hä'-gi*, a Tuscarora village on the flat, between two and three miles below Cuylerville. Proceeding up the river, it next led up to the Seneca village of *Gä-un-do'-wä-neh*, or "big tree," which was situated upon the hill about one mile north of Cuylerville. Here at a subsequent day was marked off to the Senecas the "Big Tree Reservation," in the same manner as they had reserved a tract around the favorite village of *Gä-no-wau'-ges*. Leaving this village, the trail turned a bend in the river, and entered *De-o-nun'-dä-gä-a*, or Little Beard's town, also before mentioned. It was situated upon the flat immediately in front of Cuylerville, and on the opposite side of the valley from Geneseo. Adjacent to this village, upon the sloping bank, was a small settlement called *Gä-neh'-dä-on-twä*. There was also an Indian vil-

---

[1] Mr. Newbold's farm embraces the site of this ancient village.

lage upon the site of Moscow, *Gä-nun'-dä-sa*. The trail, following up the river, next turned out of this valley, and led up to *Da-yo-it'-gä-o*, or Squakie Hill, opposite Mount Morris. This word signifies "where the river issues from the hills," and it is beautifully descriptive of the emergence of the river from between its rocky barriers into the broad valley of the Genesee.

It is a singular feature of the country, geologically considered, that the valley follows the river from near Rochester to Mount Morris only. At the latter place the river is suddenly confined in a narrow channel cut through the rock, while the valley, which at this place is about three miles wide, follows the Caneseraga creek, *Gä-nose'-gä-go*, up to Dansville, situated at its head. From Mount Morris south, up the Genesee, the valley is narrow and irregular, until at Portage the whole scenery is changed into rugged declivities and picturesque water-falls. On the Caneseraga creek, however, from Dansville down to Mount Morris, the scenery and the valley are quite the same as upon the Genesee from the latter place to Rochester. This "beautiful valley" of the Senecas, varying from one half mile to three miles in breadth, for the distance of forty miles, vies with, if it does not surpass, the more celebrated valley of Wyoming.

Leaving Squakie Hill, the trail continued up the river, crossing the outlet of the Silver lake, *Gä-na'-yät*, and entering the Indian village of *Gä-dä-o'*, situated in the town of Castile, Genesee county.

Here, at a subsequent day, was the Gardow Reservation. From thence the trail continued up the river, and over the site of Portage, to the Indian village of *O-wa-is'-ki*, near the confluence of the creek of the same name with the Genesee. Having crossed this stream, the trail led up the river to *Gä-o-yä-de'-o*, or Caneadea, the last Seneca village upon the Genesee. It was situated in the town of Hume, in the county of Allegany. The name is rendered, "the heavens leaning against the earth." It appears that there was an extensive opening at this locality, on looking through which the heavens and earth appeared to meet, or the sky seemed to rest upon the earth. Subsequently, there was a large reserve retained by the Senecas around this village, which is still marked upon old maps as the "Caneadea Reservation." In this manner may be discovered the favorite residences of the Senecas upon the river. The Genesee trail, which we have been tracing, was one of the routes to the Allegany river, *O-hee'-yo*, for those who sought to descend that stream towards the south-west.

O-hee'-yo, the radix of the word Ohio, signifies "the beautiful river;" and the Iroquois, by conferring it upon the Allegany, or head branch of the Ohio, have not only fixed a name from their language upon one of the great rivers of the continent, but indirectly upon one of the noblest States of our Confederacy.

The trail upon the east side of the Genesee, started from the ford, near the aqueduct, at Rochester, and turning a little back from the river, crossed Mount Hope. To commemorate the fact, one of the principal carriage-ways through the cemetery, which was laid upon the line of the trail, has been named "Indian Trail Avenue." Ascending the Genesee, it followed the windings of the river up to Mount Morris, *So-no'-jo-wau-ga*, where there was a small Indian village, the only one upon the east bank of the river. *So-no'-jo-wau-ga*, or Big Kettle, a Seneca orator, scarcely inferior to Red Jacket in the estimation of the nation, erected his sylvan house upon the site of Mount Morris; and the Senecas bestowed his name upon the cluster of houses which sprung up around him, and at a subsequent day upon Mount Morris itself, one of the most attractive villages in the region of the Genesee.

From thence there were two trails up the Caneseraga creek, *Gä-nose'-gă-go*, one upon each side. They led up to the small Indian village of *Gä-nose'-gă-go*, situate upon the site of Dansville, at the head of the valley.

Leaving the Genesee country, we come next to a system of trails which point to the southward. The Susquehanna and its branches penetrated the country of the Mohawks, Oneidas and Onondagas on the east and north, while the Chemung and its branches flowed through the territory of the Senecas, from near the Genesee, upon the north-west. These rivers, by their junction at Tioga, form as it were a triangle, having Tioga point as its apex, and the central trail through the State, from east to west, as its base. Following the course of these numerous streams from the north-east and north-west, these several trails converged upon Tioga, and descending the Susquehanna, formed the Great Southern trail, or highway of travel and migration into the south. The trails upon the Iroquois lakes, which lay north and south, in a measure connected the Central with the Susquehanna trail. Within this triangle were seated the Mohawk, Oneida, Tuscarora, Onondaga, Cayuga, and a part of the Seneca Nations.

These trails running upon the banks of the rivers, which are the highways fashioned by the hand of nature, need not be minutely traced, as they followed the windings of the streams. A trail descended the Conhocton river, *Gä-hä'-to*, to Tioga, *Tä-yä'-o-ga*. The convergence of so many trails upon this point, preparatory to a descent upon the south, through Pennsylvania, and into Virginia on the west side of the Blue Ridge, rendered it an important and well-known locality among the Iroquois.

From Tioga there were two trails up the Susquehanna, *Gä-wa-no-wä'-nă*. That upon the north bank ascending the river, passed over the site of Owego, *Ah-wa'-ga*, forded the Chenango, *O-che-näng'*, near its mouth, and passing over the site of Binghampton, *O-che-näng'*, continued up the river to the junction of the Unadilla, *De-u-na-dil'-lo*, where it intersected the trail coming down from the Oneida country. Continuing up the Susquehanna to the junction of the Charlotte river, the trail branched.

One ascended to the junction of the Cherry Valley creek, and following up this creek, finally passed over to Canajoharie. The other trail, having ascended the Charlotte river to its head, crossed over to the Cobuskill, *As-ca-lĕ'-ge*, and descended that stream to the Schoharie creek, where it intersected the Schoharie trail, from the lower castle of the Mohawks. From Schoharie, *Ose-ko-har'-lä*, a branch trail turned up Foxes creek, and crossing the Helderberg hills, descended to Albany. Another branch leaving the Schoharie, crossed the town of Middleburg to the Caatskill river, and descended that river to the Hudson.

Many of the early settlers of middle Pennsylvania, and nearly all of our people who located themselves on the fertile tracts spread out upon the Susquehanna, entered the country upon these trails, which were the only roads opened through the forest. They trusted entirely for their route to the well-beaten, well-selected trails of the Iroquois. The same observation applies to the central trail, which, before the opening of regular roads, was traversed by the early pioneers of western New York, with their horses, cattle, and implements of husbandry. For many years this trail was the only route of travel. It guided the early immigrants into the heart of the country, and not a little were they indebted to the Iroquois for thus making their country accessible.

There were also regular beaten trails along the banks of our inland lakes, which were used for hunting purposes, for mutual intercourse, and as routes of communication between the central thoroughfare, and the river trails which converged upon Tioga.

We have thus followed the devious footsteps of the Iroquois, for many hundred miles through their territories, and restored some of the names in use during the era of Indian occupation. Facts of this character may not possess a general interest; but they will find an appropriate place among our aboriginal remains. The trails of our Indian predecessors, indeed, have been obliterated, and the face of nature has been transformed; but all recollection of the days of Indian supremacy cannot as easily pass away. They will ever have "a share in our history."

"The Empire State, as you love to call it," said a Cayuga chief on a recent occasion, "was once laced by our trails from Albany to Buffalo,—trails that we had trod for centuries,—trails worn so deep by the feet of the Iroquois, that they became your roads of travel, as your possessions gradually eat into those of my people. Your roads still traverse those same lines of communication, which bound one part of the Long House to the other. Have we, the first holders of this prosperous region, no longer a share in your history? Glad were your fathers to sit down upon the threshold of the Long House. Had our forefathers spurned you from it, when the French were thundering at the opposite side to get a passage through, and drive you into the sea, whatever has been the fate of other Indians, the Iroquois might still have been a nation, and I, instead of pleading here for the privilege of living within your borders, I—might have had a country." [1]

A brief reference to Indian runners will not be inappropriate in this connection. To convey intelligence from nation to nation, and to spread information throughout the Confederacy, as in summoning councils upon public exigencies, trained runners were employed. But three days were necessary, it is said, to convey intelligence from Buffalo to Albany. Swiftness of foot was an acquirement, among the Iroquois, which brought the individual into high repute. A trained runner would traverse a hundred miles per day. With relays, which were sometimes resorted to, the length of the day's journey could be considerably increased. It is said that the runners of Montezuma conveyed intelligence to him of the movements of Cortes, at the rate of two hundred miles per day; but this must be regarded as extravagant. During the last war, a runner left Tonawanda at daylight in the summer season, for Avon, a distance of forty miles upon the trail. He delivered his message, and reached Tonawanda again about noon. In the night their runners were guided by the stars, from which they learned to keep their direction, and regain it, if perchance they lost their way. During the fall and winter, they determined their course by the Pleiades, or

[1] Peter Wilson, (*Wä-o-wo-wä-no'-onk*) before the New York Historical Society, in May, 1847.

Seven Stars. This group in the neck of Taurus, they called *Got-gwär'-där*. In the spring and summer they ran by another group, which they named *Gwe-o-gä'-ah*, or the Loon, four stars at the angles of a rhombus. In preparing to carry messages they denuded themselves entirely, with the exception of the *Gä-kä'-ah*, or breech cloth, and a belt. They were usually sent out in pairs, and took their way through the forest, one behind the other, in perfect silence.

Upon the accompanying map, the trails which have been traced will be found. Also the names in the several dialects of the Iroquois, of the lakes, rivers, and creeks; of the Indian villages, and ancient localities, known to our immediate predecessors; and the names of our own cities and villages, which have been christened as they appeared.[1] This map is newly designed, to exhibit the Home Country of the *Ho-de'-no-sau-nee*.

The Iroquois were the master spirits of the north. Fortunate in their geographical position, and powerful from the concentration of their strength through the League, the lesser tribes scattered over these vast territories could offer but slight obstruction to their combined attack. Large masses, like the Sioux of the west, or the Cherokees of the south, were alone able to withstand their valor, or resist their invasions. In comparison with other

[1] In the Appendix No. 1, will be found a schedule containing all the names upon the Map, with the signification of each, arranged under their respective counties.

Indian nations, the Iroquois might well exult in the superiority of their institutions; and felicitate themselves upon the high destiny which seemed to await the full development of their civil institutions.

CHAPTER IV.

The future destiny of the Indian upon this continent, is a subject of no ordinary interest. If the fact, that he cannot be saved in his native state, needed any proof beyond the experience of the past, it could be demonstrated from the nature of things. Our primitive inhabitants are environed with civilized life, the baleful and disastrous influence of which, when brought in contact with Indian life, is wholly irresistible. Civilization is aggressive, as well as progressive—a positive state of society, attacking every obstacle, overwhelming every lesser agency, and searching out and filling up every crevice, both in the moral and physical world; while Indian life is an unarmed condition, a negative state, without inherent vitality, and without powers of resistance. The institutions of the red man fix him to the soil with a fragile and precarious tenure; while those of civilized man, in his highest estate, enable him to seize it with a grasp which defies displacement. To uproot a race at the meridian of its intellectual power, is next to impossible; but the expulsion of a contiguous one, in a state of primitive rudeness, is comparatively easy, if not an absolute necessity.

The manifest destiny of the Indian, if left to himself, calls up the question of his reclamation, certainly, in itself, a more interesting, and far more important subject than any which have before been considered. All the Indian races now dwelling within the Republic have fallen under its jurisdiction; thus casting upon the government a vast responsibility, as the administrator of their affairs, and a solemn trust, as the guardian of their future welfare. Should the system of tutelage and supervision, adopted by the national government, find its highest aim and ultimate object in the adjustment of their present difficulties from day to day; or should it look beyond and above these temporary considerations, towards their final elevation to the rights and privileges of American citizens? This is certainly a grave question, and if the latter enterprise itself be feasible, it should be prosecuted with a zeal and energy as earnest and untiring as its importance demands. During the period within which this question will be solved, the American people cannot remain indifferent and passive spectators, and avoid responsibility; for while the government is chiefly accountable for the administration of their civil affairs, those of a moral and religious character, which, at least, are not less important, appeal to the enlightened benevolence of the public at large.

Whether a portion of the Indian family may yet be reclaimed and civilized, and thus saved eventually from the fate which has already befallen so many of our aboriginal races, will furnish the theme of a few concluding reflections. What is true of the Iroquois, in a general sense, can be predicated of any other portion of our primitive inhabitants. For this reason the facts relied upon to establish the hypothesis that the Indian can be permanently reclaimed and civilized, will be drawn exclusively from the social history of the former.

There are now about four thousand Iroquois living in the State of New York. Having for many years been surrounded by civilization, and shut in from all intercourse with the ruder tribes of the wilderness, they have not only lost their native fierceness, but have become quite tractable and humane. In addition to this, the agricultural pursuits into which they have gradually become initiated, have introduced new modes of life, and awakened new aspirations, until a change, in itself scarcely perceptible to the casual observer, but in reality very great, has already been accomplished. At the present moment their decline has not only been arrested, but they are actually increasing in numbers, and improving in their social condition. The proximate cause of this universal spectacle is to be found in their feeble attempts at agriculture; but the remote and the true one is to be discovered in the schools of the missionaries.

To these establishments among the Iroquois, from

the days of the Jesuit fathers down to the present
time, they are principally indebted for all the progress they have made, and for whatever prospect
of ultimate reclamation their condition is beginning
to inspire. By the missionaries they were taught
our language, and many of the arts of husbandry,
and of domestic life; from them they received the
Bible and the precepts of Christianity. After the
lapse of so many years, the fruits of their toil and
devotion are becoming constantly more apparent:
as, through years of slow and almost imperceptible
progress, they have gradually emancipated themselves from much of the rudeness of Indian life.
The Iroquois of the present day, is, in his social condition, elevated far above the Iroquois of the seventeenth century. This fact is sufficient to prove, that
philanthropy and Christianity are not wasted upon
the Indian; and further than this, that the Iroquois,
if eventually reclaimed, must ascribe their preservation to the persevering and devoted efforts of those
missionaries, who labored for their welfare when
they were injured and defrauded by the unscrupu-
lous, neglected by the civil authorities, and oppressed by the multitude of misfortunes which
accelerated their decline.

There are but two means of rescuing the Indian
from his impending destiny; and these are education and Christianity. If he will receive into his
mind the light of knowledge, and the spirit of civilization, he will possess, not only the means of self-
defence, but the power with which to emancipate

himself from the thraldom in which he is held. The frequent attempts which have been made to educate the Indian, and the numerous failures in which these attempts have eventuated, have, to some extent, created a belief in the public mind, that his education and reclamation are both impossible. This enterprise may still, perhaps, be considered an experiment, and of uncertain issue; but experience has not yet shown that it is hopeless. There is now, in each Indian community in the State, a large and respectable class who have become habitual cultivators of the soil; many of whom have adopted our mode of life, have become members of the missionary churches, speak our language, and are in every respect, discreet and sensible men. In this particular class there is a strong desire for the adoption of the customs of civilized life, and more especially for the education of their children, upon which subject they often express the strongest solicitude. Among the youth who are brought up under such influences, there exists the same desire for knowledge, and the same readiness to improve educational advantages. Out of this class Indian youth may be selected for a higher education, with every prospect of success, since to a better preparation for superior advantages, there is superadded a stronger security against a relapse into Indian life. In the attempted education of their young men, the prime difficulty has been to render their attainments permanent, and useful to themselves. To draw an untutored Indian from his forest home, and, when carefully educated, to dismiss him again to the wilderness, a solitary scholar, would be an idle experiment; because his attainments would not only be unappreciated by his former associates, but he would incur the hazard of being despised because of them. The education of the Indian youth should be general, and chiefly in schools at home.

A new order of things has recently become apparent among the Iroquois, which is favorable to a more general education at home, and to a higher cultivation in particular instances. The schools of the missionaries, established as they have been, and are, in the heart of our Indian communities, have reached the people directly, and laid the only true and solid foundation of their permanent improvement. They have created a new society in the midst of them, founded upon Christianity; thereby awakening new desires, creating new habits, and arousing new aspirations. In fact they have gathered together the better elements of Indian society, and quickened them with the light of religion and of knowledge. A class has thus been gradually formed, which, if encouraged and strengthened, will eventually draw over to itself that portion of our Indian population which is susceptible of improvement and elevation, and willing to make the attempt. Under the fostering care of the government, both state and national, and under the still more efficient tutelage of religious societies, great hopes may be justly entertained of the ultimate and permanent civilization of this portion of the Iroquois.

It is, indeed, a great undertaking to work off the Indian temper of mind, and infuse that of another race. It is necessary, to its accomplishment, to commence in infancy, and at the missionary school, where our language is substituted for the Indian language, our religion for the Indian mythology, and our amusements and mode of life for theirs. When this has been effected, and upon a mind thus prepared has been shed the light of a higher knowledge, there is not even then a firm assurance that the Indian nature is forever subdued and submerged in that superior one which civilization creates. In the depths of Indian society there is a spirit and a sentiment to which their minds are attuned by nature; and great must be the power, and constant the influence which can overcome the one, or eradicate the other.

In the education of the Iroquois, New York has recently made a commencement. Prior to 1846 our Indian youth were excluded from the benefits of the common school fund; their want of preparation for such schools, furnishing, to some extent, a sufficient reason. At that time schools were first opened among them under appropriations from the public fund. These schools have not met with encouraging success; but their efficiency would have been much greater if they had been organized upon the boarding-school or missionary plan, instead of that of the common school. The former is the more practicable and successful system of Indian education; and it is greatly to be hoped that it will soon be adopted. To meet the growing demand for a higher education, the State Normal School, within the past year, has not only been opened to a limited number of Indian youth, but a sufficient appropriation made for their maintenance while improving its advantages. These two important events form an interesting era with the modern Iroquois. It remains only to give them permanent boarding-schools at home for the instruction of the mass of their youth, with access to the Normal School for their advanced scholars, and in a few years they will rise in the scale of intelligence, as far above their present level, as their fathers raised themselves, in the days of aboriginal sovereignty, above the level of cotemporary nations.

In addition to the special claim which the residue of the Iroquois have upon the people of the State, every principle of philanthropy pleads for the encouragement of their young men in their efforts to obtain a higher course of instruction than the limited earnings of Indian husbandry can afford. The time has come, in their social progress, when they are capable of a thorough intellectual training, and are able to achieve as high and accurate a scholarship, as many of their white competitors. The time has also arrived when academical attainments will prove a blessing to themselves, and to their families. By the diffusion of knowledge among them the way will be facilitated for the introduction of the mechanic arts, and for their improvement in agricultural pursuits. A small band of educated

young men in each Indian community would find
sufficient employment for their acquired capacities,
in the various stations of teacher, physician, mechanic, and farmer; in each and all of which they
would greatly promote the general welfare. If the
desire for improvement, which now prevails among
them, is met and encouraged, it will require but a
few years to initiate them into the arts of civilized
life, and to prepare them eventually for exercising
those rights of property, and rights of citizenship,
which are common to ourselves. How much more
noble for the State to reclaim and save this interesting and peculiar portion of her people, than to accelerate their extinction by injustice; or to abandon
them to their fate, when they are struggling to
emancipate themselves by taking into their hands
the implements of agriculture, and opening their
minds to the light of knowledge.

There is no want of sympathy for their welfare
among the people of New York; on the contrary,
there is a wide-spread and deep-seated interest in
their future reclamation. Whatever can be done
to ameliorate their condition, and encourage that
portion who have commenced the work of their
own improvement, would receive the warmest com-
mendation. If the Indian puts forth his hand for
knowledge, he asks for the only blessing which we
can give him in exchange for his birthright, which
is worthy of his acceptance.

The education and christianization of the Iroquois
is a subject of too much importance, in a civil as-

pect, to be left exclusively to the limited and fluctuating means of religious societies.   The schools established and sustained among them by private benevolence, are, to the Indian, almost the same as common schools to our own people; and without them the Indian would, in times past, have been denied all means of instruction.   These schools bring together the youth for elementary tuition, as a necessary preparation for moral and religious training.   While there, they adopt, in all respects, the habits of civilized life, are taught our language, and the more simple elementary studies.   In so far, it would be but a just act of public beneficence to allow those pupils to draw the same share of public money which falls to the other children of the State. A system of public Indian education, upon such a plan as their circumstances demand, should either be adopted by the State; or a portion of the public money, bearing some proportion to the number of Indian pupils, should be placed at the disposal of the local missionary, to be expended with an equal portion contributed by private benevolence, or by the Indians themselves.   It is time that our Indian youth were regarded, in all respects, as a part of the children of the State, and brought under such a system of tutelage as that relation would impose.

The vast extent of the religious enterprises of the present day has tended to draw the attention of the Christian world away from the Indian, into fields more distant, and perhaps more attractive. During the past sixty years, the Iroquois have re-

ceived but a small share of the Christian watchful-
ness to which their wants entitled them. Faithful
and zealous missionaries, it is true, have labored
among them, producing results far greater than is
generally believed; but the inadequate scale upon
which these missions were organized, and the fluc-
tuations in their efficiency, which were inseparable
from their irregular and limited supplies, have prevented them from carrying forward their work to
its full completion. But whatever has been done,
is chiefly to be ascribed to them, and to the denom-
inations which they represent.

Too much cannot be said of the teachableness of
the Indian, and of his aptitude to learn, when subjected to systematic discipline. If the same means,
and the same influences which are employed to educate and elevate the mass of our own people, and
without the constant application of which, they
themselves would soon fall into ignorance, were
brought to bear upon our Indian population, they
would rise under it with a rapidity which would
excite both surprise and admiration. Instances are
not wanting, among the present Iroquois, of attainments in scholarship which would do credit to any
student. To give employment to those Indian
youth whose acquired capacities would enable them
to fill stations of trust and profit among ourselves,
is another species of encouragement which com-
mends itself to the generous mind. Both in our
civil and social relations with the red men, we regard them as a distinct and separate class; when in

each of these relations they should not only be regarded as our fellow-men, but as a part of our own
people. Born upon the soil, the descendants of its
ancient proprietors, there is no principle which
should make them aliens in the land of their nativity, or exclude them from any of those advantages
which are reserved to ourselves. So far as they are
able to appreciate and enjoy the same privileges
which pertain to the mass of the people, the claim
for participation which their situation silently puts
forth should not be disregarded.

The lands of the Iroquois are still held in common, the title being vested in the people. Their
progress towards a higher agricultural life, has rendered this ancient tenure a source of inconvenience;
although they are not as yet prepared for their division among the people. Each individual can improve and enclose any portion of their common
domain, and sell or retain such improvements, in the
same manner as with personal property; but they
have no power to transfer the title to the land to
each other, or to strangers. As early as the reign of
James the Second, the right of purchasing Indian
lands was made a government right exclusively, by
royal proclamation, and it proved such a necessary
shield against the rapacity of speculators, that this
humane provision is still retained as a law in all
the States of the Union, and by the national government. When the Iroquois reach such a stable
position, as agriculturists, as to make it safe to divide their lands among the several families of

each nation, with the power of alienation, it will give to them that stimulus and ambition which separate rights of property are so well calculated to produce. The present system has at least the merit of saving all the people from poverty and vagrancy, if it does not enable a portion of them to become thrifty and substantial agriculturists. The first step towards the amelioration of their condition in this particular, would be a division among themselves, with the power of alienation to each other, under such restrictions as would be adapted to the case. This would serve to prepare the way for other changes, until finally they could be restored, with safety to themselves, not only to the full possession of those rights of property which are common to ourselves, but also to the rights and privileges of citizens of the State. When this time arrives, they will cease to be Indians, except in name.

The progressive elevation of our Indian population, here indicated, if carried to a successful result, would save but a portion of the Indian family; but that portion would become, in every respect, as useful and respectable as any other portion of our people. They would neither be wanting in ability, or morality, or public spirit; and perhaps it is not too much to conjecture, that specimens of the highest genius, and of the most conspicuous talent, hereafter destined to figure in the civil history of our Republic, may spring from the ranks of the Indian citizens.

On the other hand, if they are left, unencouraged and unassisted, to struggle against their adverse destiny—or, more fatal still, if they are subjected to a false and unjust system of superintendence, the whole Indian family will ere long fade away, and finally become enshrouded in the same regretful sepulchre, in which the races of New England lie entombed.

The present system of national supervision is evidently temporary in its plans and purposes, and designed for the administration of our Indian affairs with the least possible inconvenience, rather than for their ultimate reclamation, to be followed by the bestowment of citizenship. It carries, upon all its features, the impression, that the presence of the Indian upon this continent is temporary; and that he must inevitably surrender the remainder of his possessions, when he shall have become surrounded by the white man, and the summons be sent in for the customary capitulation. The sentiment which this system proclaims is not as emphatic as that emblazoned upon the Roman policy towards the Carthaginians—*Carthago est delenda,*—" Carthage must be destroyed :" but it reads in not less significant characters—*The destiny of the Indian is extermination.* This sentiment, which is so wide-spread as to have become a general theme for school-boy declamation, is not only founded upon erroneous views, but it has been prejudicial to the Indian himself. If, then, public opinion and the national policy are both wrong upon these great questions, or if there are even strong grounds for suspecting them to be so, it becomes an act of justice, as well as of duty, to correct the one, and change the other. Our Indian relations, from the foundation of the Republic to the present moment, have been administered with reference to the ultimate advantage of the government itself; while the reclamation of the Indian has been a secondary object, if it ever entered into the calculation in the slightest degree. Millions of money, it is true, have been expended, and some show of justice preserved in their complicated affairs; but in all prominent negotiations the profit has been on the side of the government, and the loss on that of the Indian. In addition to this, instances of sharp-sighted diplomacy, of ungenerous coercion, and of grievous injustice, are to be found in the journal of our Indian transactions—a perpetual stigma upon the escutcheon of our Republic. If references are demanded to the paragraphs, the reader may turn to that upon the Seminoles, or to the Georgia Cherokee treaty, executed by the government, or to the more recent treaties with the Iroquois themselves, in which the government bartered away its integrity, to minister to the rapacious demands of the Ogden Land Company.

Jefferson made the civilization of the Indian a subject of profound consideration, and a favorite element of the national policy during his administration. Washington, at a still earlier period, regarded the future welfare of the Indian with deep solicitude. In founding the first system of intercourse and superintendence, he was guided by the most enlightened principles of justice and benevolence; and to such a degree were the Iroquois, in particular, impressed with the goodness and beneficence of his character, that they not only bestowed upon him, in common with other Indian nations, the appellation of *father*, but to this day he is known among them as "the Great American." The aggressive spirit of the people, however, in connection with the slight estimation in which Indian rights were held, has ever been found too powerful an element to be stayed.   It has had free course during the last sixty years, until the whole territory east of the Mississippi, with inconsiderable exceptions, has been swept from the Indian.   This fact renders any argument superfluous, to show, that within this period the reclamation and preservation of the red man has formed no part of the public policy.

But within the same period the moral elements of society have been developed and strengthened to such a degree as to work a change in public sentiment.   A kindlier feeling towards the Indian is everywhere apparent, joined with an unwillingness to allow him to be urged into further extremities. He has been sufficiently the victim of adverse fortune, to be entitled to a double portion of the interest and assistance of the philanthropist; and a new day, it is to be hoped, has already dawned upon his prospects.

It cannot be forgotten, that in after years our Republic must render an account, to the civilized world, for the disposal which it makes of the Indian. It is not sufficient, before this tribunal, to plead inevitable destiny; but it must be shown affirmatively, that no principles of justice were violated, no efforts were omitted, and no means were left untried to rescue them from their perilous position. After all has been accomplished which the utmost efforts of philanthropy, and the fullest dictates of wisdom can suggest, there will still be sufficient to lament, in the unpropitious fate of the larger portion of the Indian family. It is the great office of the American people, first, to shield them against future aggression, and then to mature such a system of supervision and tutelage, as will ultimately raise them from the rudeness of Indian life, and prepare them for the enjoyment of those rights and privileges which are common to ourselves.

To the Indian Department of the national government, the wardship of the whole Indian family is, in a great measure, committed; thus placing it in a position of high responsibility. If any discrimination could be made between the several departments of the government, this should be guided by the most enlightened justice, the most considerate philanthropy. Great is the trust reposed, for it involves the character of the white race, and the existence of the red. May it ever be quickened to duty by a vivid impression of its responsibilities, and never violate, for any consideration, the sacred trust committed to its charge.

The profoundly truthful sentiment of Cicero,

" without the highest justice a republic cannot be governed," furnishes a text eminently worthy of being studied in this connection.   It would form an apt inscription, to be written over the doorway of the Indian Department—

"Sine summa justitia Rempublicam regi non posse."

APPENDIX.

APPENDIX, I.

SCHEDULE EXPLANATORY OF THE INDIAN MAP.[1]

VOWEL MARKS.

ä sounded as in far.	ĕ sounded as in met.
ă " " at.	ī " " pine.
â " " fall.	ō " " tone.

HO-DE'-NO-SAU-NEE'-GA,

TERRITORIES OF THE PEOPLE OF THE LONG HOUSE.

Gä-neă'-ga-o-no'-ga,	Territory of the Mohawks.
O-na'-yote-kä-o-no'-ga,	Territory of the Oneidas.
O-nun'-dä-ga-o-no'-ga,	Territory of the Onondagas.
Gwe-u'-gweh-o-no'-ga,	Territory of the Cayugas.
Nun-da'-wä-o-no'-ga,	Territory of the Senecas.
Dus-ga'-o-weh-o-no'-ga,	Territory of the Tuscaroras.

NUN-DA'-WÄ-O-NO'-GA,

OR THE TERRITORY OF THE SENECAS.

SENECA DIALECT.

CHAUTAUQUE COUNTY.

ENGLISH NAME.	INDIAN NAME.	SIGNIFICATION.
Dunkirk,	Gä-na'-da-wä-o,	Running through the Hemlocks.
Cattaraugus Creek,	{ Gä-dä'-ges-ga-o, { Gä-hun'-da,[2]	} Fetid Banks.
Silver Creek,	Gä-a-nun-dä'-tä, G.	A Mountain levelled down.
Chautauque Creek,	Gä'-no-wun-go, G.	In the Rapids.
Conewango River,	Gä'-no-wun-go, G.	In the Rapids.
Canadawa Creek,	Gä-na'-da-wä-o, G.	Running through the Hemlocks.
Cassadaga Creek,	Gus-dä'-go, G. [di',[2]	Under the Rocks.
Cassadaga Lake,	Gus-dä'-go. Te-car-ne-o-	Under the Rocks.
Chautauque Lake,	Chä-dä'-quĕh, T.	Place where one was lost.
Cattaraugus,	Ga'-dä-ges'-ga-o,	Fetid Banks.

[1] Where the Map and this Schedule are at variance, the latter must govern.
[2] *Gä-hun'-da* and *Te-car-ne-o-di'* are common nouns, signifying, the former "a river" or "creek," and the latter, "a lake." They are always affixed by the Iroquois, in speaking, to the name itself.

Vowel Sounds:

ä ... as in far.

ă ... " " at.

a ... " " mate

ō ... " " tone.

GA-WA-NASE-GEH.

O-NIK-HA-DA-GE-GA.

CATTARAUGUS COUNTY.

ENGLISH NAME.	INDIAN NAME.	SIGNIFICATION.
Allegany River,	O-hee'-yo, G.	The Beautiful River.
Great Valley Creek,	O-dä'-squä-dos-sa, G.	Around the Stone.
Little Valley Creek,	O da'-squä-wa-tĕh', G.	Small Stone beside a large one.
Oil Creek,	Te-car'-nohs, G.	Dropping Oil.
Ischuna Creek,	He'-soh, G.	Floating Nettles.
Oswaya Creek,	O-so'-ä-yeh, G.	Pine Forest.
Burton Creek,	Je'-gä-sa-nek, G.	Name of an Indian.
Lime Lake,	Te-car'-no-wun-do, T.	Lime Lake.
Ellicottville,	De-äs'-hen-dä-quä,	Place for holding Courts.
Burton,	Je'-gä-sa-neh,	Name of an Indian.
Olean,	He'-soh,	Same as Ischuna Creek.
Hasket Creek,	O-so'-ä-went-ha, G.	By the Pines.

INDIAN VILLAGES.

Allegany Village,	De-o'-na-gä-no,	Cold Spring.
" "	Jo'-ne-a-dih,	Beyond the Great Bend.
Oil Spring Village,	Te-car'-nohs,	Dropping Oil.
Bend Village,	Da'-u-de-hok-to,	At the Bend.
Trail of the Eries,	Gä-quä'-ga-o-no, Wä-ä'-gwen-ne-yuh.	

ERIE COUNTY.

Two Sisters Creek,	Te-car'-na-gä-ge, G.	Black Waters.
Caugwa-ga "	Gä'-gwä-ga, G.	Creek of the Cat Nation.
Smokes "	Dä-de-o'-dä-na-suk'-to, G.	Bend in the Shore.
Cazenovia "	Gä-ä'-nun-dĕh-tä, G.	A Mountain flattened down.
Buffalo "	Do'-sho-weh, G.	Splitting the Fork.
Cayuga "	Gä-da'-geh, G.	Through the Oak Openings.
Ellicott "	Gä-dä'-o-yä-deh, G.	Level Heavens.
Grand Island,	Gä-weh'-no-geh,	On the Island.
Eighteen Mile Creek,	Tä-nun'-no-ga-o, G.	Full of Hickory Bark.
Murder Creek,	De'-on-gote, G.	Place of Hearing.
Lake Erie,	Do'-sho-weh, T.	Same as Buffalo Creek.
Buffalo,	Do'-sho-weh,	do.
Black Rock,	De-o'-steh-gä-a,	A Rocky Shore.
Williamsville,	Gä-sko'-sä-dä-ne-o,	Many Falls.
Clarence Hollow,	Tä-nun'-no-ga-o,	Full of Hickory Bark.
Akron,	De'-on-gote,	{ Place of Hearing, (Neuter gender.)
Lancaster,	Gä-squen'-dä-geh,	Place of the Lizard.

INDIAN VILLAGES.

Red Jacket Village,	Te-kise'-da-ne-yout,	Place of the Bell.
Falls Village,	Gä-sko'-sä-da,	The Falls.
Cattaraugus Village,	Gä-dä'-ges-ga-o,	Same as Cattaraugus Creek.
Carrying Place Village,	Gwä'-u-gweh,	{ Place of taking our Boats, or Portage.

GENESEE AND WYOMING COUNTIES.

Tonawanda Creek,	Tä'-nä-wun-da, G.	Swift Water.
Allens "	O'-ät-kä, G.	The Opening,
Black "	Jä'-go-o-geh, G.	{ Place of Hearing. (This is feminine.)

ENGLISH NAME.	INDIAN NAME.	SIGNIFICATION.
Stafford,	Yä'-go-o-geh,	Place of Hearing.
Batavia,	Deo-on'-go-wä,	The Great Hearing Place.
Oakfield,	Te-car'-dä-na-duk,	Place of many Trenches.
Alabama,	Gä'-swä-däk,	By the Cedar Swamp.
Caryville,	Gau'-däk,	By the Plains.
Pine Hill,	Te-cä'-so-ä-a,	Pine lying up.
Attica,	{ Gweh'-tä-ä-ne-te-car'- nun-do-deh,	} The Red Village.
Alexander,	Da-o'-sa-no-geh,	Place without a Name.
Wyoming,	Te-car'-ese-tä-ne-ont,	Place with a Sign-post.
Pembroke,	O-ä'-geh, [ne-o,	On the Road.
Le Roy,	Te-car'-no-wun-na-dä'-	Many Rapids.
Darien,	O-so'-ont-geh,	Place of Turkeys.
Silver Lake,	Gä-na'-yät, T.	Signification lost.
Silver Lake Outlets,	Gä-na'-yät, G.	" "
Caneadea Creek,	Gä-o'-ya-de-o, G.	Same as Caneadea.
Warsaw,	Chi'-nose-heh-geh,	On the Side of the Valley.

INDIAN VILLAGES.

Tonawanda Village,	Tä'-nä-wun-da,	Swift Water.
Gardow,	Gä-dä'-o,	Bank in Front.

ALLEGANY COUNTY.

Genesee River,	Gen-nis'-he-yo, G.	The Beautiful Valley.
Wiskoy Creek,	O-wa-is'-ki, G.	Under the Banks.
Black Creek,	Jä-go'-yo-geh, G.	Hearing Place.
Angelica,	Gä-ne-o'-wĕh-ga-yat,	Head of the Stream.
Caneadea,	Gä-o'-ya-de-o,	{ Where the Heavens lean against the Earth.
Caneadea Creek,	Gä-o'-yä-de-o, G.	{ Where the Heavens rest upon the Earth.
Nunda,	Nun-dä'-o,	Hilly.
Wiskoy,	O-wa-is'-ki,	Under the Banks.

INDIAN VILLAGES.

O-wa-is-ki,	O-wa-is'-ki,	Under the Banks.
Caneadea,	Gä-o'-ya-de-o,	{ Where the Heavens lean against the Earth.

LIVINGSTON COUNTY.

Caneseraga Creek,	Gä-nus'-gä-go, G.	Among the Milkweed.
Connesus Lake,	Gä-ne-ä'-sos, T.	Place of Nanny-berries.
Connesus Outlet,	Gä-ne-ä'-sos, G.	" "
Hemlock Lake,	O-neh'-dä, T.	The Hemlock.
Hemlock Outlet,	O-neh'-dä, G.	" "
Geneseo,	O-hä'-di,	Trees Burned.
Mount Morris,	So-no'-jo-wau-ga,	{ Big Kettle. (Residence of a Seneca Chief.)
Dansville,	Gä-nus'-gä-go,	Among the Milkweed.
Livonia,	De-o'-de-sote,	The Spring.

ENGLISH NAME.	INDIAN NAME.	SIGNIFICATION.
Lima,	Skă-hase′-gă-o,	Once a long Creek.
Avon,	Gä-no′-wau-ges,	Fetid Waters.
Caledonia,	De-o′-na-gä-no,	Cold Water.
Moscow,	Gä-nĕh′-dä-on-tweh,	Where Hemlock was spilled.

INDIAN VILLAGES.

Squakie Hill,	Da-yo′-it-gă-o,	Where the River issues from the Hills.
Site of Moscow,	Gä-nĕh′-dä-on-tweh,	Where Hemlock was spilled.
Little Beard's Town,	De-o-nun′-dä-gä-a,	Where the Hill is near.
Big Tree Village,	Gä-un-do′-wä-na,	A Big Tree.
Tuscarora Village,	O-hä′-gi,	Crowding the Bank.
Ganowauges,	Gä-no′-wau-ges,	Fetid Waters.
Site of Dansville,	Gä-nus′-gä-go,	Among the Milkweed.
Near Livonia,	De-o′-de-sote,	The Spring.
Site of Mt. Morris,	So-no′-jo-wau-ga,	Big Kettle.

MONROE COUNTY.

Irondequoit Bay,	Neo′-dä-ŏn-dä-quät,	A Bay.
Salmon Creek,	Ga′-doke-na, G.	Place of Minnows.
Sandy Creek,	O-nĕh′-chĭ-gĕh, G.	Long ago.
Honeoye Outlet,	Hä′-ne-ä-yeh, G.	Finger Lying.
Rochester,	Gä′-sko-sä-go, [do′-teh,	At the Falls.
Brockport,	Gweh′-ta-a-ne-te-car-nun-	Red Village.
Scottsville,	O′-ăt-kä,	The Opening. (Same as Allen's Creek.) [struction.
Honeoye Falls,	Sko′-sa-is-to, [yu,	Falls rebounding from an obstruction.
Ontario Trail, [Bend,	Ne-ä′-gä Wa-ä-gwen-ne-	Ontario Foot Path.
Indian Village at the	Dä-yo′-de-hok-to,	A Bended Creek.

ORLEANS AND NIAGARA COUNTIES.

Oak Orchard Creek,	Dä-ge-ă′-no-gä-unt, G.	Two Sticks coming together.
Johnson's Creek,	A-jo′-yok-ta, G.	Fishing Creek.
18 mile Creek,	Date-ge-ä′-de-hä-nä-geh,	Two Creeks near together.
Tuscarora Creek, East Branch,	Te-car′-na-ga-ge, G.	Black Creek.
" West Branch,	De-yo′-wuh-yeh, G.	Among the Reeds. [ed.
Albion,	De-o′-wun-dake-no,	Place where Boats were burned.
Medina,	Date-geh′-ho-seh,	One Stream crossing another. (Aqueduct on the canal.)
Middleport,	Te-ka′-on-do-duk,	Place with a Sign-Post.
Lockport,	De-o′-do-sote,	The Spring. (Referring to the Cold Spring.)
Royalton Centre,	O-ge-a′-wä-te-kä′-e,	Place of the Butternut.
Lewiston,	Gä′-a-no-geh,	On the Mountains. [Neck.
Youngstown,	Ne-ah′-gä, [G.	Supposed from O-ne′-ah. A
Golden Creek,	Hate-keh′-neet-ga-on-dä,	Signification lost.
Niagara River,	Ne-ah′-gä, G.	Same as Youngstown.
Lake Ontario,	Ne-ah′-gä, T.	" "
The word Ontario,	Skä-no′-dä-ri-o, T.	The "Beautiful Lake." (This is a Mohawk word, and Ontario is a derivative.)

ENGLISH NAME.	INDIAN NAME.	SIGNIFICATION.
Niagara Falls,	Date-car'-sko-sase,	The Highest Falls.
Niagara Village, [lage,	Date-car-'sko-sase,	" " "
Tuscarora Indian Vil-	Gä'-a-no-geh,	On the Mountains.
Seneca Indian Village,	Gä-u'-gweh,	{ Taking Canoe out. (Carrying Place at the mouth of Tonawanda Creek.)

WAYNE AND ONTARIO COUNTIES.

Mud Creek,	Gä'-nä-gweh, G.	Same as Palmyra.
Flint Creek,	Ah-tä'-gweh-dä-ga, G.	[ment.
Canandaigua,	Gä'-nun-dä-gwa,	A Place selected for a Settle-
Canandaigua Outlet,	Gä'-nun-dä-gwa, G.	" " "
Canandaigua Lake,	Gä'-nun-dä-gwa, T.	" " "
Hemlock Outlet,	O-neh'-dä, G.	Hemlock.
Honeoye Lake,	Hä'-ne-ä-yeh, T.	Finger Lying.
Skaneatice Lake,	Skä'-ne-a-dice, T.	Long Lake.
Sodus Bay,	Seo-dose'. (Seneca.)	{ Ah-slo-dose, (Oneida.) Signification lost.
Little Sodus Bay,	Date-ke-ä'-o-shote,	{ Two Baby Frames. (From Gä-ose'-hä, a Baby Frame.)
Palmyra,	Gä'-nä-gweh,	A Village suddenly sprung up.
Geneva,	Gä-nun'-dä-sa-ga,	New Settlement Village.
Seneca Lake,	Ga-nun'-dä-sa-ga, T.	" " "
West Bloomfield,	Gä-nun'-dä-ok,	Village on the top of a Hill.
Victor,	Gä-o'-sä-ga-o,	In the Basswood Country.
Naples,	Nun'-da-wä-o,	Great Hill.

INDIAN VILLAGES.

Near Geneva,	Gä-nun'-dä-sa-ġa,	New Settlement Village.
Canandaigua,	Gä'-nun-dä-gwa,	Place selected for a Settlement.
Victor,	Gä-o'-sä-ga-o,	In the Basswood Country.
Near Naples,	Nun'-da-wä-o,	Great Hill.

YATES, STEUBEN, AND CHEMUNG COUNTIES.

Crooked Lake,	O-go'-yä-ga, T.	Promontory proj. into the Lake.
" " Outlet,	O-go'-yä-ga, G.	" " " "
Conhocton River,	Gä-hä'-to, G.	A Log in the Water.
Chemung River,	Gä-hä'-to, G.	" " "
Canisteo River,	Te-car'-nase-te-o, G.	Board on the Water.
Bath,	Do-na'-tä-gwen-da,	Opening in an Opening.
Painted Post,	Te-car'-nase-te-o-ah,	A Board Sign.
Elmira,	Skwe'-do-wä,	Great Plain.

GWE-U'-GWEH-O-NO'-GA,

OR THE TERRITORY OF THE CAYUGAS.

(PARTLY CAYUGA AND PARTLY SENECA.)

ENGLISH NAME.	INDIAN NAME.	SIGNIFICATION.
Tioga Point,	Tä-yo'-ga,	At the Forks.
Ithaca,	Ne-o-däk'-he-ät,	At the Head of the Lake
Cayuga Lake,	Gwe-u'-gweh, T.	The Lake at the Mucky Land.
Aurora,	De-ä-wen'-dote,	Constant Dawn.
Canoga,	Gä-no'-geh,	Oil Floating on the Water.
Cayuga Bridge,	Was'-gwas,	A Long Bridge.
Montezuma,	Te-car'-jïk-ha'-do,	Place of Salt.
Howland's Island,	Gä-weh'-no-wä-na,	Great Island.
Waterloo,	Skoi'-yase,	Place of Whortleberries.
Seneca River,	Swa'-geh, G.	Flowing Out. (Some doubt about the Signification.)
Clyde River,	Gä-nä'-gweh, G.	River at a Village suddenly sprung up.
Auburn,	Was'-co,	Floating Bridge.
Otter Lake,	Squä-yen'-na, T.	A great way up.
Muskrat Creek,	Squä-yen'-na, G.	" "
Owasco Outlet,	De-ä-go'-gä-ya, G.	Place where Men were killed.
Owasco Lake,	Dwas'-co, T.	Lake at the Floating Bridge.
North Sterling Creek,	Dats-ka'-he, G.	Hard Talking.
Sodus Bay Creek,	Te-gä-hōne'-sä-o'-tä, G.	A Child in a Baby Frame.

INDIAN VILLAGES.

Site of Canoga,	Gä-no'-geh,	Oil on the Water.
Site of Union Springs,	Ge-wä'-ga,	Promontory running out.
Above Lockwoods Cove,	Gä-yä'-gä-an'-ha,	Inclined downwards.
Site of Ithaca,	Ne-o'-däk-he'-ät,	At the End of the Lake.

O-NUN'-DÄ-GA-O-NO'-GA,

OR THE TERRITORY OF THE ONONDAGAS.

(ONONDAGA DIALECT.)

Susquehanna River,	Gä'-wa-no-wä'-nä-neh, G.	Great Island River.
Owego,	Ah-wa'-ga,	Where the Valley widens.
Owego Creek,	Ah-wa'-ga, G.	" "
Cortland,	O-nan'-no-gi-is'-kä, [hä,	Shagbark Hickory.
Homer,	Te-wis'-ta-no-ont-sa'-ne-ä-	Place of the Silver Smith.
Owasco Inlet,	Kä'-na-kä'-ge, G.	Black Water.
Tionghinoga River,	O-nan'-no-gi-is'-kä, G.	Shagbark Hickory.

ONONDAGA COUNTY.

ENGLISH NAME.	INDIAN NAME.	SIGNIFICATION.
Tully Lake,	Te-kä'-ne-a-dä'-he, T.	A Lake on a Hill.
Tully,	Te-kä'-ne-a-dä'-he,	" "
Apulia,	O-nun'-o-gese,	Long Hickory.
Skaneateles Lake,	Skan-e-a'-dice, T.	Long Lake.
Skaneateles,	Skan-e-a'-dice,	" "
Otisco Lake,	Ga-ah'-na, T.	Rising to the Surface, and again sinking. Legend of a drowning man.
Otisco,	Ga-ah'-na,	do.
Otisco Outlet,	Ga-ah'-na, G.	do.
Lafayette,	Te-kä'-wis-to'-tä,	Tinned Dome.
Pompey Hill,	De-o'-wy-un'-do,	Wind Mill.
Pompey,	De-is'-wä-ga'-hä,	Place of Many Ribs.
Oil Creek,	De-o'-nake-ha'-e, G.	Oily Water.
Onondaga Creek,	O-nun-dä'-ga, G.	On the Hills.
Onondaga West Hill,	Te-ga-che'-qua-ne-on'-ta,	A Hammer Hanging.
Onondaga Hollow,	Te-o-hä'-ha-hen'-wha,	Turnpike Crossing the Valley.
Marcellus,	Us-te'-ka,	Bitternut Hickory.
Nine Mile Creek,	Us-te'-ka, G.	" "
Camillus,	O-yä'-han,	Apples Split Open.
Elbridge,	Kä-no-wä'-ya,	Skull lying on a Shelf.
Jordan Creek,	Ha-nan'-to, G.	Small Hemlock limbs on water.
Jordan,	Ha-nan'-to,	" "
Cross Lake,	U-neen'-do, T.	Hemlock tops lying on water.
Fort Brewerton,	Gä-do'-quat,	(Oneida Dialect. Signification lost.)
Oneida Outlet,	She-u'-ka, G.	(Lost.)
Liverpool,	Gä-nä-wa'-ya,	A Great Swamp.
Liverpool Creek,	Tun-da-dä'-quä, G.	Thrown Out.
Onondaga Lake,	Gä-nun-ta'-ah, T.	Material for Council Fire.
Salina,	Te-gä-jik-ha'-do,	Place of Salt.
Syracuse,	Na-tä'-dunk,	Pine Tree broken with Top hanging down.
Jamesville Creek,	Gä-sun'-to, G.	Bark in the Water.
Jamesville,	Gä-sun'to,	" " " [rises.
Limestone Creek,	De-ä-o'-no-he, G.	Where the Creek suddenly
Manlius,	De-ä-o'-no-he,	do.
Fayetteville,	Gä-che'-a-yo,	Lobster.
Deep Spring,	De-o'-sä-dä-ya'-ah,	Deep Basin Spring.
South Onondaga,	Swe-no'-ga,	A Hollow.
Christian Hollow,	De-o'-nake-hus'-sink,	Never Clean.

INDIAN VILLAGES.

Onondaga Castle,	Kä-nä-tä-go'-wä,	Signification lost.
4 Miles East of Castle,	Tu-e-a-das'-so,	Hemlock Knot in the Water.
Site of Onondaga Hollow,	Gis-twe-ah'-na,	A Little Man.
3 Miles South of Onondaga Castle,	Nan-ta-sä'-sis,	Going Partly Round a Hill.

OSWEGO AND JEFFERSON COUNTIES.

Oswego,	Swa'-geh,	Flowing Out.
New Haven Creek,	Kä-dis-ko'-nä, G.	Long Marsh.
Little Salmon Creek,	Gä-nun-tä-sko'-nä, G.	Large Bark.

ENGLISH NAME.	INDIAN NAME.	SIGNIFICATION.
Grindstone Creek,	He-ah-hä'-whe, G.	Apples in Crotch of Tree.
Big Salmon Creek,	Gä-hen-wä'-ga, G.	A Creek.
Pulaski,	Gä-hen-wä'-ga,	"
Sandy Creek,	Te-kä'-dä-o-gä'-he, G.	Sloping Banks.
Grand Island,	De-ä'-wōne-dä-ga-han'-da,	Signification lost.
Sackets Harbor,	Gä-hu'-ä-go-je-twä-da-a'-lote,	Fort at the Mouth of Great River.

---◆◆◇---

O-NA'-YOTE-KÄ-O-NO'-GA,

OR ONEIDA TERRITORY.

(ONEIDA DIALECT.)

St. Lawrence River,	Gä-nä-wä'-ga, G.	The Rapid River.
Black Lake,	Che'-gwä-ga, T.	In the Hip.
Oswegatchie River,	O'-swa-gatch, G.	Signification lost.
Ogdensburgh,	O'-swa-gatch,	" "
Black River,	Kä-hu-ah'-go, G.	Great, or Wide River.
Watertown,	Kä-hu-ah'-go,	" "
Beaver River,	Ne-hä-sä'-ne, G.	Crossing on a Stick of Timber.
Deer Creek,	Gä-ne'-gä-to'-do, G.	Corn-Pounder.
Moose River,	Te-kä'-hun-di-an'-do, G.	Clearing an Opening.
Otter Creek,	Dä-ween'-net, G.	The Otter.
Indian River,	O-je'-quack, G.	Nut River.

ONEIDA COUNTY.

Mohawk River above Herkimer,	Da-yä'-hoo-wä'-quat, G.	Carrying Place.
Rome,	"	"
Fish Creek,	Ta-gä'-soke, G.	Forked like a Spear.
Wood Creek,	Kä-ne-go'-dick, G.	Signification lost.
Oneida Lake,	Gä-no'-a-lo'-häle, T.	A Head on a Pole.
Scribas Creek,	Gä-sote'-na, G.	High Grass.
Bay Creek,	Te-guä'-no-tä-go'-wä, G.	Big Morass.
West Canada Creek, and Mohawk River,	Te-ah-ō'-ge, G.	At the Forks.
Trenton Village,	Ose'-te-a'-daque,	In the Bone.
Trenton Falls,	Date-wä'-sunt-hä'-go,	Great Falls.
Utica,	Nun-da-dä'-sis,	Around the Hill.
Whitestown Creek,	Che-gä-quat'-kä, G.	Kidneys.
Whitestown,	"	"
Oriskany Creek,	Ole'-hisk, G.	Nettles.
Oriskany,	"	"
Paris Hill,	Gä-nun-do'-glee,	Hills shrunk together.
Clinton,	Kä-dä'-wis'-däg,	White Field.
Sangerfield,	Skä'-nä-wis,	A Long Swamp.
Vernon,	Skä-nu'-sunk,	Place of the Fox.
Vernon Centre,	Skun-an-do'-wä,	Great Hemlock.

ENGLISH NAME.	INDIAN NAME.	SIGNIFICATION.
Oneida Creek,	Gä-no-a-lo′-hale, G.	Head on a Pole.
Verona,	Te-o-na′-täle,	Pine Forest.
Nine Mile Creek,	Te-yä-nun′-soke, G.	A Beech Tree standing up.
Camden,	He-stä-yun′-twä,	Meaning lost.
Oneida Dépôt,	De-ōse-la-ta′-gaat,	Where the Cars go fast.
New Hartford,	Che-ga-quat′-kä,	Kidneys.

INDIAN VILLAGES.

Oneida Castle,	Gä-no-a-lo′-häle,	Head on a Pole.
Site of Camden,	Ho-stä-yun′-twä,	Meaning lost.
On Fish Creek,	Ta-gä′-soke, G.	Forked like a Spear.
Near Oneida Castle,	Gä-nä′-doque,	Empty Village.

MADISON AND CHENANGO COUNTIES.

Canestota,	Kä-ne-to′-tä,	Pine Tree Standing alone.
Lenox,	Skä-wais′-lä,	A Point made by Bushes.
Caneseraga Creek,	Kä-nä′-so-wä′-ga, G.	{ Several Strings of Beads with a String lying across.
Chittenango Creek,	Chu-de-nääng′, G.	Where the Sun Shines Out.
Chittenango,	"	" "
Cazenovia Lake,	Ah-wä′-gee, T.	Perch Lake.
Cazenovia,	Ah-wä′-gee,	"
Hamilton,	Da-ude′-no-sä-gwa-nose,	Round House.
Unadilla River,	De-u-na′-dil-lo, G.	Place of Meeting.
Chenango River,	O-che-näng, G.	Bull Thistles.
Sherburn,	Gä-na′-dä-dele,	Steep Hill.
Norwich,	Gä-na′-so-wä′-di,	Signification lost.
Oxford,	So-de-ah′-lo-wä′-nake,	Thick-necked Giant.
Binghampton, [Village,	O-che-nang′,	Bull Thistles.
Stockbridge Indian	Ah-gote′-sa-ga-näge,	Meaning lost.

———◆ ◆ ◆———

GÄ-NE-Ä′-GA-O-NO′-GA,

OR MOHAWK TERRITORY.

(MOHAWK DIALECT.)

West Canada Creek,	Te-uge′-ga, G.	At the Forks.
Mohawk River	" G.	"
Herkimer,	"	"
Little Falls,	Tä-lä-que′-ga,	Small Bushes.
Fort Plain,	Twä-dä-a-la-ha′-lä,	Fort on a Hill.
Canajoharie Creek,	Gä-na-jo-hi′-e, G.	Washing the Basin.
Canajoharie,	"	"
Johnstown,	Ko-lä-ne′-kä,	Indian Superintendent.
Fonda,	Gä-nä-wä′-da,	On the Rapids.
Fort Hunter,	Te-on-dä-lo′-ga,	Two Streams coming together.
Schoharie Creek,	Sko-har′-le, G.	Flood-wood.
Schoharie,	"	"

ENGLISH NAME.	INDIAN NAME.	SIGNIFICATION.
East Canada Creek,	Te-car'-hu-har-lo'-da, G.	Visible over the Creek.
Otsquago Creek,	O-squa'-go, G.	Under the Bridge.
Amsterdam Creek,	Ju-ta-lä'-ga, G.	Signification lost.
Garoge Creek,	Ga-ro'-ga, G.	"
Schenectady,	O-no-ä-lä-gŏne'-na,	In the Head.
Albany,	Skä'-neh-tä'-de,	Beyond the Openings.
Hudson River,	Skä'-neh-tä'-de, G.	River Beyond the Openings.
Cohoes Falls,	Gä'-hä-oose,	Shipwrecked Canoe. [alect.)
Lake Champlain,	O-ne-ä-dä'-lote, T.	Signification lost. (Oneida di-
Ticonderoga,	Je-hŏne-tä-lo'-ga,	Noisy.
Saratoga,	S'har-la-to'-ga,	Signification lost.
Lake St. Francis,	Gä-na-sä-dä'-ga, T.	Side Hill. (Oneida dialect.)
Salmon River,	Gau-je'-ah-go-nä'-ne, G.	Sturgeon River. "
St. Regis River,	Ah-qùa-sos'-ne, G.	Partridges Drumming.
St. Regis,	"	"
Racket River,	Tä'-na-wä'-deh, G.	Swift Water.

COUNTIES SOUTH OF THE MOHAWK.

Otsego Lake,	Ote-sa'-ga, T.	Signification lost.
Cooperstown,	"	"
Delaware River,	Skä-hun-do'-wä, G.	In the Plains.
Cobus Hill,	As-ca-le'-ge,	Meaning lost.
New York,	Gä-no'-no,	" [lect.)
Long Island,	Gä'-wa-nase-geh,	A Long Island. (Oneida di-
Atlantic Ocean,	O-jik'-ha-dä-ge'-ga,	Salt Water.

INDIAN VILLAGES.

Upper Mohawk Castle,	Gä-ne'-ga-hä'-gä,	Possessor of the Flint.
Middle Mohawk Castle,	Gä-na-jo-hi'-e,	Washing the Basin.
Lower Mohawk Castle,	Te-ah'-ton-ta-lo'-ga.	Two Streams Coming Together.

CANADA.

Quebec,	Ke-a-done-dä-a'-ga,	Two Forts Contiguous.
Montreal,	Do-te-ä'-ga,	Almost Broken.
Kingston,	Gä-dai-o'-que,	Fort in the Water.
Welland River,	Jo-no'-dok, G.	Signification lost.
Grand "	Swa'-geh, G.	Flowing Out.
Burlington Bay,	De-o-na'-sä-de'-o,	Where the Sand forms a Bar.
Queenstown,	Do-che'-hä-o',	{ Where the Mountain dies in the River.
Hamilton,	De-o-na'-sä-de'-o,	See above.
Toronto,	De'-on-do,	Log Floating upon the Water.
Brock's Monument,	Gus-tä'-ote,	
Chippeway,	Jo-no'-däk,	Signification lost.

PENNSYLVANIA.

Erie,	Gus-ha'-wä-ga,	On the Body.
Cornplanter's Village,	De-o-no'-sä-da-ga,	Burned Houses.

APPENDIX, II.

Table exhibiting, in the Seneca dialect, the conjugation of the Verb, Ge'-yäse, "I shoot."

ACTIVE VOICE.

INDICATIVE MOOD.

Present Tense.—*Shoot, or am shooting.*

Singular.	*Dual.*	*Plural.*
1. Ge'-yäse,	1. Och-ne'-yäse,	1. Ah-gwä'-yäse.
2. Sne'-yäse,	2. Sne'-yäse,	2. Swä'-yäse.
3. Hä'-yase,	3. Ne'-yäse,	3. Hä-ne'-yäse.

Imperfect.—*Did shoot, or was shooting.*

1. Ge'-yäse-quä,	1. Ne'-yäse-quä,	1. Dwä'-yäse-quä.
2. Se'-yäse-quä,	2. Sne'-yäse-quä,	2. Swä'-yäse-quä.
3. Hä'-yäse-quä,	3. Ne'-yäse-quä,	3. Hä-ne'-yäse-quä.

Perfect.—*Shot, have shot, or did shoot.*

1. Ah-ge'-yä-go,	1. Unc-ne'-yä-go,	1. Ung-gwä'-yä-go.
2. Sä-yä'-go,	2. Sne'-yä-go,	2. Swä-yä'-go.
3. Ho-yä'-go,	3. Ho-ne'-yä-go,	3. Ho-ne'-yä-go.

Pluperfect.—*Had shot.*

1. Che-wä'-ge-yä-go,	1. Che-unk'-ne-yä-go,	1. Che-yung'-gwä-yä-go.
2. Che-sä'-yä-go,	2. Che-sne'-yä-go,	2. Che-swä-yä-go.
3. Che-o'-yä-go,	3. Che-o'-ne-yä-go,	3. Che-o'-ne-yä-go.

Future.—*Shall, or will shoot.*

1. Eh-ge'-yäke,	1. Och-ne'-yäke-heh,	1. Eh-yä'-gwä-yake.
2. Se-yake'-heh,	2. Eh-sne'-yäke,	2. Eh-swä'-yäke.
3. Hä'-yäke-heh,	3. Eh-ne'-yäke,	3. Eh-ne'-yäke.

Subjunctive Mood.

Present Tense.—*May*, or *can shoot*.

Singular.	*Dual.*	*Plural.*
1. Eh-ge'-yäke-ge'-seh,	1. Eh-ne'-yäke-ge'-seh,	1. Eh-dwä'-yäke-ge'-seh.
2. Eh-se'-yäke-ge'-seh,	2. Eh-sne'-yäke-ge'-seh,	2. Eh-swä'-yäke-ge'-seh.
3. Ha-o'-yäke-ge'-seh,	3. Eh-ne'-yäke-ge'-seh,	3. Eh-ne'-yäke-ge'-seh.

Imperfect.—*Might, could,* or *would shoot*.

1. Ah-ge'-yäke,	1. I-ne'-yäke,	1. I-dwä-yäke.
2. Ah-se'-yäke,	2. I-sne'-yäke,	2. I-swä'-yäke.
3. Ah-ah'-yäke,	3. Ah-ne'-yäke,	3. Ah-an-ne'-yäke.

Perfect.—*May have shot*.

1. Ah-wä-ge'-yä-go-ge'-seh,	1. Ah-yunk-ne'-yä-go-ge'-seh,	1. Ah-yung-gwä'-yä-go-ge'-seh.
2. I-sä'-yä-go-ge-seh,	2. I-sne'-yä-go-ge'-seh,	2. I-swä'-yä-go-ge'-seh.
3. Ah-o'-yä-go-ge'-seh,	3. Ah-o'-ne-yä-go-ge'-seh,	3. Ah-o'-ne-yä-go-ge'-seh.

Pluperfect wanting.

Future.—*Shall have shot*.

1. Ah-wä-ge'-yä-go,	1. Ah-yunk'-ne-yä-go,	1. Ah-yung-guä'-yä-go.
2. I-sä'-yä-go,	2. I-sne'-yä-go,	2. I-swä'-yä-go.
3. Ah-o'-yä-go,	3. Ah-o'-ne-yä-go,	3. Ah-o'-ne-yä-go.

Imperative Mood.

2. Je'-yäke, *Shoot thou.*	2. Sne'-yäke, *Shoot ye two.*	2. Swä'-yäke, *Shoot ye.*
3. Hä'-yäke, *Let him shoot.*	3. Ne'-yäke, *Let them two shoot.*	3. Hä-ne'-yäke, *Let them shoot.*

Infinitive Mood wanting.

Participles wanting.

PASSIVE VOICE.

Indicative Mood.

Present Tense.—*Am shot*.

Singular.	*Plural.*
1. Ung-ge'-yä-go,	1. Unc-ke'-yä-go.
2. A-sä'-yä-go,	2. A-che'-yä-go.
3. Ho-wä'-yä-go,	3. Ho-wen-ne'-yä-go.

Dual.—Same as Plural.

Imperfect.—*Was shot*.

Singular.	*Plural.*
1. Ung-ge'-yä-go'-no,	1. Unc-ke'-yä-go'-no.
2. Sa-yä'-go-no,	2. A-che'-yä-go'-no.
3. Ho-wuh'-yä-go'-no,	3. O-wen'-ne-yä'-go-no.

Perfect.—*Have been shot.*—Same as Imperfect.

Pluperfect wanting.

Future.—*Shall*, or *will be shot.*

1. Eh-yung'-ge-yäke,
2. Eh-yä'-sä-yäke,
3. A-on'-wuh-yäke,

1. Eh-yunk'-ke-yäke.
2. Eh-yä'-che-yäke.
3. A-on'-wen-ne-yäke.

SUBJUNCTIVE MOOD.

Present Tense.—*May be shot.*

1. Eh-yung'-ge-yäke-ge'-seh,
2. Eh-yä'-sä-yäke-ge'-seh,
3. A-o-wuh'-yäke-ge'-seh,

1. Eh-yunk'-ke-yäke-ge'-seh.
2. Eh-yä'-che-yäke-ge'-seh.
3. A-o-wen-ne'-yäke-ge'-seh.

Imperfect wanting.

Perfect.—*May have been shot.*

1. Ah-yung-ge'-yä-gon-no-ge'-seh,
2. Ah-yä-sä-yä'-gon-no-ge'-seh,
3. Ah-o-wuh'-yä-gon-no-ge'-seh,

1. Ah-yunk-ke'-yä-gon-no-ge'-seh.
2. Ah-ya-che'-yä-gon-no-ge'-seh.
3. Ah-o-wen-ne'-yä-go-no-ge'-seh.

Pluperfect.—*Might, could, would*, or *should have been shot.*

1. Ah-yung-ge'-yä-go-no-na-geh,
2. Ah-yä-sä-yä'-go-no-na-geh,
3. Ah-o-wuh-yä'-go-no-na-geh,

1. Ah-yunk-ke'-yä-go-no-na-geh.
2. Ah-yä-che'-yä-go-no-na-geh.
3. Ah-o-wen-ne'-ya-no-na-geh.

Future.—*Shall have been shot.*

1. Ah-yung-ge'-ya-go-no,
2. Ah-yä-sä'-yä-go-no,
3. Ah-o-wuh'-yä-go-no,

1. Ah-yunk-ke'-yä-go-no.
2. Ah-yä-che'-yä-go-no.
3. Ah-o-wen-ne'-yä-go-no.

IMPERATIVE MOOD.

2. Ah-sä'-yäke, *Be thou shot.*
3. Ho-wuh'-yäke, *Let him be shot.*

2. A-che'-yäke, *Be ye shot.*
3. Ho-wen-ne'-yäke, *Let them be shot.*

INFINITIVE MOOD WANTING.

PARTICIPLES WANTING.